CW00554896

SCOTTISH CHURCH HISTORY

Seal of Archbishop David Beaton (actual dimensions 120 by 75 mm). The legend (extending contractions) runs: Sigillum Reverendissimi Patris Domini David Beton, tituli Sancti Stephani in Celio Monte Sancte Romane Ecclesie Presbyteri Cardinalis, Sancti Andree Archiepiscopi, Primatis et Apostolice Sedis de latere Legati.

SCOTTISH CHURCH HISTORY

GORDON DONALDSON

HM HISTORIOGRAPHER IN SCOTLAND

1985

SCOTTISH ACADEMIC PRESS

Published by
Scottish Academic Press Ltd,
33 Montgomery Street
Edinburgh EH7 5JX

SBN 7073 0361 3

British Library Cataloguing in Publication Data

Donaldson, Gordon, *1913-*
Scottish church history.
1. Scotland—Church history
I. Title
274.11   BR782

ISBN 0 7073 0361 3

Printed in Great Britain by
Clark Constable, Edinburgh, London, Melbourne

Contents

Preface

In assembling this selection of writings which have been composed over a period of more than forty years and which have dealt with a wide range of topics, I have tried to attain a measure of cohesion. Nearly all of the material relates to the institutional history of the Scottish Church as a whole. This meant the exclusion of local studies, and it is possible that what I have written on various regions in the period of the Reformation may be brought together in a further volume. The results of my occasional forays into another aspect of church life – the history of worship – have found a place in two chapters of the recently published *Studies in the History of Scottish Worship*.

While there was a certain attraction in the idea of simply reprinting the articles as originally published, I decided to amend them by correction and some expansion. After all, the original versions are still available in print for the enlightenment of the curious, and notes prefixed to some articles indicate in a general way the nature of the revision – sometimes considerable – which they have undergone.

There are four articles which are essentially new. The short one on the appointment of bishops in early medieval times (including some information given in an article on 'The Bishops and Priors of Whithorn' in *TDGNHAS*, xxvii) fits into the context of this volume. The Note and Document on the General Assembly of December 1563 arose from the fortuitous acquisition of a MS relating to that assembly. The article on Sources for Reformation History, while it incorporates material from one of the earliest articles I wrote, ranges widely over historiography and represents a number of thoughts which I had not put into print before. The final paper again represents reflections, even more wide-ranging, dealing with a central theme which runs through all the centuries of church life and looking at some problems to which too little attention is usually given. Some of the thought in this item owes a great deal to the stimulus given by my participation in the discussions which led to the publication in 1966 of *The Anglican-Presbyterian Conversations* (Saint Andrew Press and SPCK), which contained, as Appendix I, the Report of the Group on Church, Community and State.

I have to acknowledge, with warm thanks, the ready consent which the original publishers of various articles gave to their inclusion in this volume: The Scottish Church History Society (1, 6 and 14), The Society of Antiquaries of Scotland (2), The Company of Scottish History (4), The Stair Society (5), *The Innes Review* (8), The Athlone Press (12), The Scottish History Society (11), The Royal Historical Society (13 and 15) and

Cambridge University Press (16). I am deeply indebted for photographs of
Restennet to Mr Gavin Sprott, for photographs of Wharram-le-Street
Church to Mr C. Richmond and Miss H. Gibbs, and for photographs of
Clapham Church, Bedford, to Mr Maurice Leusby (through the good
offices of the Rev. G. G. Cansdale): all of the photographs they provided
enabled me to make comparative studies. Dr Athol Murray, Keeper of the
Records of Scotland, receives a special acknowledgment in the introductory note to chapter 9, but I should like here to express my gratitude to
him and his staff for facilitating the reproduction of Cardinal Beaton's Seal,
affixed to a document in the Morton Papers (GD 150/309).

My old friend Christian Krarup-Hansen, Sognepraest Emeritus of
Lundby, Denmark, was so kind as to send me a copy of *Carlsbergfondet
Årsskrift 1984*, with an article by Thomas Riis, 'Should auld acquaintance be
forgot: Skotsk-danske forbindelser c. 1450–c. 1700'. Had this come into
my hands earlier it would have figured on p. 64, as it gives additional facts
about the commercial relations between the two countries and has several
illustrations, two of them showing (in colour) the handsome monument in
St Peter's Church, Malmö, of David Paterson, who was burgomaster at the
end of the sixteenth century.

G. D.

List of Illustrations

Abbreviations

Aberdeen Reg. – *Registrum Episcopatus Aberdonensis* (Maitland Club)
APS – *Acts of the Parliaments of Scotland*
Baillie – *Letters and Journals of Robert Baillie* (Bannatyne Club)
Bede – *Bede's Ecclesiastical History of the English People*
Boece – Hector Boece, *Historia Gentis Scotorum*, trans. Bellenden (STS)
Brechin Reg. – *Registrum Episcopatus Brechinensis* (Bannatyne Club)
BUK – *Acts and Proceedings of the General Assemblies* (Bannatyne and Maitland Clubs)
Calderwood – David Calderwood, *History of the Kirk of Scotland* (Wodrow Soc.)
Cal. Docs. Scot. – *Calendar of Documents relating to Scotland*
Cal. S.P. Scot. – *Calendar of State Papers relating to Scotland and Mary, Queen of Scots*
CPR – *Calendar of Papal Letters*
Dowden, *Bishops* – John Dowden, *The Bishops of Scotland*
Dowden, *Med. Church* – John Dowden, *The Medieval Church in Scotland*
ER – *The Exchequer Rolls of Scotland*
ES – *Early Sources of Scottish History*, ed. A. O. Anderson
ESC – *Early Scottish Charters*, ed. Archibald Lawrie
Foedera – *Foedera, conventiones, literae* [etc.], ed. Thomas Rymer
Glasgow Reg. – *Registrum Episcopatus Glasguensis* (Bannatyne and Maitland Clubs)
James V Letters – *The Letters of James V*, ed. R. K. Hannay and D. Hay
Keith – Robert Keith, *History of the Affairs of Church and State in Scotland* (Spottiswoode Soc.)
Knox – John Knox, *History of the Reformation*, ed. Dickinson
Knox, Works – John Knox, *Works*, ed. D. Laing (Wodrow Soc.)
M – W. M. Morison, *Dictionary of Decisions*
Melville – James Melville, *Autobiography and Diary* (Wodrow Soc.)
NLS – National Library of Scotland
Patrick, *Statutes* – *The Statutes of the Scottish Church*, ed. David Patrick (SHS)
Picts and Scots – *Chronicles of the Picts, Chronicles of the Scots* [etc.], ed. W. F. Skene
Public Affairs – *Acts of the Lords of Council in Public Affairs*
RMS – *Registrum Magni Sigilli Regum Scotorum*
RPC – *Register of the Privy Council of Scotland*
RPSA – *Registrum Prioratus S. Andree* (Bannatyne Club)
RSS – *Registrum Secreti Sigilli Regum Scotorum*

RSS – Registrum Secreti Sigilli Regum Scotorum (MS)

Reg. K.S. St A. – *Register of the Kirk Session of St Andrews* (SHS)

SA – *Scottish Annals from English Chroniclers*, ed. A. O. Anderson

SCHSR – *Scottish Church History Society Records*

SHR – *Scottish Historical Review*

SHS – Scottish History Society

SRS – Scottish Record Society

STS – Scottish Text Society

St A. Formulare – *St Andrews Formulare* (Stair Soc.)

Spottiswoode – John Spottiswoode, *History of the Church of Scotland* (Spottiswoode Soc.)

Statuta – *Statuta Ecclesiae Scoticanae*, ed. Joseph Robertson (Bannatyne Club)

Theiner – Augustin Theiner, *Vetera monumenta Hibernorum et Scotorum historiam illustrantia*

TB – *Accounts of the Collectors of Thirds of Benefices* (SHS)

TDGNHAS – *Transactions of the Dumfriesshire and Galloway Natural History and Antiquarian Society*

I

Scotland's Earliest Church Buildings[1]

This article, published in the *Records of the Scottish Church History Society*, xviii (1973), 1–9, has been revised in the light of later suggestions by others and reflections by myself.

There is more than a presumption that most of the earliest churches in Scotland were built of wood, and of such churches no remains can be expected to be seen above ground level, but recent discoveries prove that traces of them can still be found by excavation.[2] The earliest reference to a stone church is Bede's well-known account of the erection by Ninian, about the year 400, of 'a church of stone, after a custom strange to the Britons'.[3] The suggestion has been made that foundations to be seen outside the east end of the later cathedral at Whithorn may be the veritable remains of Ninian's *Candida Casa*, but the possibility has also been completely discounted.[4]

After a lapse of 300 years there was another well-known episode. Again the evidence comes from Bede, but this time Bede was recounting something which happened in his own lifetime and his facts are not open to challenge. He relates that about 710 Nechtan, king of the Picts, asked the abbot of Jarrow to send him architects to build 'a church of stone among his people after the manner of the Romans, promising to dedicate it in honour of the Blessed Prince of the Apostles'.[5] We may therefore take it that somewhere in Pictland there was erected, early in the eighth century, a church designed in the style of contemporary Anglo-Saxon buildings and dedicated to St Peter. It is not a novel suggestion that the remains of such a church are to be seen at Restennet, in Angus.[6] At Restennet there are the walls of a medieval priory church which was dedicated to St Peter, and,

---

[1] Information about English buildings is derived mainly from H. M. and Joan Taylor, *Anglo-Saxon Architecture* (paperback, 1980–84), E. A. Fisher, *The Greater Anglo-Saxon Churches* (1962) and *Anglo-Saxon Towers* (1969).

[2] Charles Thomas, *The Early Christian Archaeology of North Britain*, 73.

[3] Bede, III, iv.

[4] Ralegh Radford, 'Excavations at Whithorn', *TDGNHAS*, 3rd ser., xxvii, 118–19; Thomas, op. cit., 14–15.

[5] Bede, V, xxi.

[6] W. Douglas Simpson, 'The Early Romanesque Tower at Restennet', *Antiq. Journal*, xliii (1963), 269 ff.; *Restenneth and Aberlemno* (HMSO), 3; Taylors, ii, 710–11.

incorporated within it but not placed symmetrically, a tower of much greater antiquity. The south doorway of the tower has a semi-circular lintel, cut out of a single massive stone, a feature typical of the earliest Anglo-Saxon churches, those dating from about 700: examples are to be seen in windows at Jarrow and Escomb (Durham), Corbridge (Northumberland) and Ledsham (Yorkshire) and in doorways at Somerford Keynes (Gloucestershire) and Heysham (Lancashire). There are also, at the base of the tower of Restennet, eastern and western arches. The eastern, which would lead into a church, was original, but the western has been pronounced to have been an insertion, which has disturbed the stonework of that wall. Even so, the insertion may have been made not long after the initial building, for the resulting complex at the base of this tower is not unlike that at Monkwearmouth, near Jarrow, and the people who inserted that western arch at Restennet were still copying a current Anglo-Saxon fashion. Such austere semi-circular arches are common in England in that period, but it is hard to find Scottish parallels.

What existed at first at Restennet was only a porch, of one or two storeys, which was subsequently heightened, as happened at Monkwearmouth and Corbridge. The upper part of the tower, though thus later than the base, still shows signs of Anglo-Saxon influence. There are openings of the 'gable-headed' or 'triangular-headed' type, their tops formed by two stones leaning against each other. Such construction is hardly known elsewhere in Scotland at any period, except in the very much later cloister of Oronsay Priory, but it is a common Anglo-Saxon feature: there is an eleventh-century doorway of this construction at Jarrow and windows of the same character at Deerhurst (Gloucestershire), Barnack, Brigstock and Earl's Barton (Northants.), Barton-on-Humber (Lincs.) and Norton (Durham). It may therefore be that the whole of the tower (though not the spire, which could be as late as the fifteenth century) can be placed within the Anglo-Saxon period, unless indeed there was later work which consciously imitated or reproduced an earlier style.

There is, then, at Restennet, in the heart of Pictland, the tower of a church which bore a dedication to St Peter and which has all the signs of imitation of Anglo-Saxon work of dates from about 700 onwards. There can hardly be any doubt that we have here some remains of the building which the Jarrow architects designed for King Nechtan in the early eighth century.

That early phase of Anglian influence in Pictland was displaced, in the ninth century, by Irish influence, after the union of the Picts and Scots under Kenneth mac Alpin. This has left its visible traces in the round towers which were built in Scotland in imitation of the round towers of Ireland. The round tower at Brechin can perhaps be assigned to a point about the end of the tenth century, for we are told that King Kenneth II (971–95) 'consigned the great city of Brechin to the Lord'.[7] Abernethy was almost

[7] *ES*, i, 512.

certainly a more ancient ecclesiastical site than Brechin,[8] and the round tower there seems a more primitive and less sophisticated example, with an undecorated doorway which is a sharp contrast to the highly ornamented doorway at Brechin. It is hard to believe that after the splendour and refinement of Brechin there was a reversion to the simplicity of Abernethy. It has been argued, on the ground of the character of the windows or openings near the top, that the Abernethy tower is later than Brechin, but the stone-work shows clearly that the upper part of the structure represents later rebuilding. The suggestion has been made that at St Andrews one of the towers of the later precinct wall of the priory incorporates the foundations of a third early round tower,[9] and St Andrews is certainly a place where such a tower might well have existed, for it was, like Abernethy, a very early ecclesiastical centre.

Claims are sometimes advanced that yet another round tower of Irish type is to be found on the Orkney island of Egilsay, but it is hard to see any parallels. At Egilsay the walls, instead of tapering gradually, have a slight curvature; the entrance to the tower is within the church and is on ground level, not considerably above it; and the tower is not a free-standing erection, but an integral part of the church. In short, this tower is now *sui generis* in Scotland. But it appears that there were other round towers in the diocese of Orkney: there was one at Stenness in Orkney, the Orkney church of Deerness had twin round-towers, three Shetland churches, at Burra, Bigton and Tingwall, are said to have had round towers, and the Tingwall specimen is authenticated as being still in existence in the eighteenth century.[10] There was thus a northern group of round towers, which might represent Anglo-Saxon influence, for in Anglo-Saxon England, especially Norfolk, there were several round towers attached to churches, for example, Roughton, Haddiscoe, East Lexham and Bessingham; but it is just as likely that the Orkney and Shetland towers represent something brought directly from the continent by the cosmopolitan Norsemen who, after all, brought to Orphir in Orkney a round church, something not found at all on the Scottish mainland in medieval times but found on the continent and in England. Egilsay is certainly later than about 1000, when the Earl of Orkney was converted to Christianity, and it may with some confidence be placed earlier than about 1117, when St Magnus, before being murdered on the island, spent the night in a church; it is impossible that a church of this type could have been erected after that date, as quite different models were by that time familiar.

There may actually be good reasons for assigning Egilsay to a date earlier than another Orkney church, that on the Brough of Birsay, which has been identified with the church built by Earl Thorfinn, about 1060, as a seat for the bishop of his earldom. It was formerly believed that Thorfinn's

---

[8] G. Donaldson, 'Bishops' Sees before the Reign of David I', *infra*.

[9] Douglas Young, *St Andrews: Town and Gown, Royal and Ancient*, 18.

[10] George Low, *A Tour Through Orkney and Scheteland*, 54; George Nelson, *The Story of Tingwall Kirk*, 3–4, 38–9.

church was not on the tidal islet of the Brough but on the adjacent Mainland, where a later church and earl's palace stood, but when the remains on the Brough were revealed it was concluded that they were those of the earl's residence and his church, with domestic quarters for the bishop and perhaps other clergy. Recently the older view has been revived, but difficulties remain. For one thing, it is reckless to believe that the Brough (always subject to erosion) was necessarily a tidal island 900 years ago; it may then have been a promontory of the Mainland, with an isthmus forming bays in which the earl could conveniently beach his ships. Secondly, if the little church on the Brough was not Thorfinn's cathedral, what was it? It was not monastic, for it is not integrated with the nearby buildings to the north in which some have seen a 'cloister', and there is no evidence of any such monastery. From the point of view of structure, the one building on the Scottish mainland which may parallel Birsay is Queen Margaret's addition at Dunfermline to the earlier 'Culdee' church there. If the attribution of the Birsay structure to Thorfinn is correct, then the two buildings come close together in point of time – Birsay 1055–65 and Dunfermline probably 1070–75. Each has a semi-circular apse. This is a feature so rare in the Anglo-Saxon churches with which Margaret had been familiar in England that its appearance at Dunfermline may reflect the incipient Norman influence in the reign of Edward the Confessor. The apse at Birsay, if it was the work of Thorfinn, who had travelled to Rome and through Germany, could have been based directly on a continental model and is quite likely to have followed Scandinavian example: there is a parallel, for instance, in the church of which the remains survive beneath the market-place of Roskilde in Denmark.

If the round towers on the Scottish mainland represented Irish influence, a renewed phase of English influence is demonstrated in a group of five square towers strung out across the country from Dunblane, by Muthill, Dunning and Markinch, to St Andrews. These towers have a good deal in common and, although not all complete as they were originally built, they yet survive in such a condition as to make an adequate assessment possible.

The general character of these towers is sufficiently indicated by their similarity to buildings in England of the Anglo-Saxon period or, at latest, of transitional or very early Norman type; and it must be remembered that Norman influence began in England not later than 1066, indeed earlier, and that was before anything that can be called a Norman period can be said to begin in Scotland. The Scottish towers require examination individually in detail, but it can be said now that the principal features which point to their English affiliations are the two-light windows or openings and the conspicuous external courses which mark off the storeys or stages. In England there are something like 130 surviving Anglo-Saxon towers, and probably two-thirds of them have two-light openings of one design or another. It must always be remembered that these openings are usually towards the top of the tower, and may sometimes represent a later phase of building than the lower stages. Equally conspicuous in the English towers is the series of courses marking off the storeys one from another.

At Dunblane the tower stands in an awkward and irrational relation to the thirteenth-century cathedral, just as the tower at Restennet is awkwardly related to the later priory church. In this instance, the tower walls are neither parallel nor perpendicular to the cathedral walls. The lower stages of the tower, which are conspicuously different from the upper stages, are clearly of earlier date than the cathedral. The main features are three in number, and all have parallels in England. There are two-light openings, consisting of a single archway divided by a column rather than twin arches. Secondly, near the base of the tower is a north doorway, now opening into the cathedral but originally communicating with the open air; this is almost identical with a doorway in the cloister at Jarrow. Thirdly there are the marked string-courses distinguishing the storeys, a feature common to the majority of English towers. There is no certain evidence that there were Culdees at Dunblane, as there were at some of the other places in Scotland possessing early square towers, but the statement made by Bishop Clement in the 1230s that there had been a vacancy in the see of a hundred years or more[11] must relate to a period before the appearance of authenticated bishops in the middle of the twelfth century and indicates a tradition that the place had been an ancient ecclesiastical centre.

The tower at Dunning, now attached to a church of very much later date, closely resembles that at Dunblane both in the construction of its two-light openings and in its type of coursing, though there has been some replacement of stonework in the openings.

Muthill, like Dunning, is situated where a pass through the Ochil Hills comes down into Strathearn. The tower there is again somewhat awkwardly placed in relation to the later medieval church, though less conspicuously so than the towers of Restennet and Dunblane. A string course separates the ground floor from the first floor, but above that the successive stages are marked by a series of offsets. This, though rare in English towers, is not unknown: there is one example at Morland, in Westmorland, dating from the late eleventh century. The two-light openings, though generally similar to those at Dunblane and Dunning, more clearly emphasise the two separate apertures, well recessed within a single archway. The openings at Dunblane, Dunning and Muthill can all be roughly paralleled in English buildings of late eleventh century, sometimes immediately post-Conquest, date: examples are Jarrow, Weaverthorpe (East Riding), Clapham (Bedfordshire), Thorington (Suffolk) and Ledsham (West Riding). The whole character of Muthill is less sophisticated, more primitive, than that of any of the other four towers in this group, and this fact might suggest that it is in part at least of earlier date than the rest. The argument might be advanced to the contrary that it is a late and

[11] Theiner, No. xci.

debased example, but that seems unlikely in view of the fact that in the twelfth and thirteenth centuries, as a great change came over Scottish architecture and highly refined buildings were going up in places far more out of the way than Muthill, a tower of such primitive character would have been quite out of place. Besides, as Muthill was a Culdee seat, there must have been a significant building there before 1100.

Markinch is such a splendid structure that it is hard to believe that it can possibly date back to as early a period as the eleventh or even the twelfth century, but a series of tiny openings, each with its head cut from a single stone, would themselves suggest exceptional antiquity. It owes its deceptively modern appearance partly to the character of its much later spire, which is suited to the relatively modern church with which the tower is harmoniously integrated, and partly to the freshness of the stone-work. Here the historical evidence points to the existence of a church of pre-Norman date. Bishop Malduin of St Andrews (c. 1028–55) granted the church of Markinch to the Culdees of Lochleven.[12] While it might be going too far to see the existing tower as the tower of a church which was standing in the days of Bishop Malduin, it is quite likely that a tower of Anglo-Saxon character was built here during the eleventh century. As the belfry openings here are very similar to those in the tower of St Regulus, the architectural grounds for dating Markinch will emerge in the consideration of the tower of St Regulus. Although Markinch is altogether smaller than St Regulus (16 feet by 17 feet as against 21 feet square), it resembles St Regulus more closely than, for example, Dunning resembles Dunblane, and there is a stronger possibility of two towers designed by the same architect.

The tower at St Andrews is the finest of this group of five, a noble example of an Anglo-Saxon tower at its best. There is no doubt that this tower, like that of Markinch, was designed and completed as a unit, whereas some others may have been erected in successive stages. Attention had often been drawn to the parallel of Wharram-le-Street, east of York, and it is easy to see a close resemblance: the belfry openings at St Andrews, as at Markinch, are genuine twin openings and are not recessed within a single arch, so that they have the same character as those at Wharram-le-Street, which are authoritatively said to be of pure pre-Conquest type.[13] But the tower of St Regulus is more than twice as high as that at Wharram-le-Street. Its great height (108 feet) in relation to the church attached to it and in comparison with Markinch (73 feet) and Muthill (51 feet) at once recalls the description of the early cathedral of Durham, consecrated in 999, which had a western tower 'of wondrous size'.[14] The resemblance to Wharram-le-Street helps, in conjunction with the historical evidence to be considered presently, to date the tower, but the buildings attached to it were altered after it was built. It seems that the western arch is a later

[12] ESC, 6.
[13] E. A. Fisher, *The Greater Anglo-Saxon Churches*, 128.
[14] R. L. G. Ritchie, *The Normans in Scotland*, 39.

insertion and that the building on the west side is an addition, while the chamber to the east of the tower is original, though an extension further to the east was added later. The buttresses strengthening the west side, which are quite out of character, were probably erected to take the thrust of the new opening.

The tower of St Regulus has frequently been attributed to Bishop Robert (1127–44) but this seems untenable. By Bishop Robert's day Norman models of architecture had become the fashion, and Robert himself, whose name shows that he was of Norman origin and who had come to Scotland from Yorkshire, would have followed that fashion. The great Norman cathedral of Durham, which many Scots knew so well, had by this time been building for 50 years; in Scotland itself the Norman work at Holyrood and Dunfermline was starting and the Norman choir of Kirkwall, as well as the earliest Norman parish churches, were being built. It is impossible to believe that in this situation the Bishop of St Andrews, the premier see of Scotland, was putting up anything as outmoded, however splendid, as the tower of St Regulus. Besides, we do know that there was a church at St Andrews before Bishop Robert built anything. Leaving aside the likelihood of a very early church, the result of endowments given by Pictish kings to the monastery of Kilrimont, there are two pieces of evidence for a church at St Andrews shortly before Bishop Robert's day: Ethelred, abbot of Dunkeld, son of Malcolm III and Margaret, was buried in the church of Kilrimont;[15] and there was the picturesque incident in Alexander I's reign, when the king's Arab steed was led up to the high altar of the church of St Andrews in token of the king's gift or confirmation of the lands of the Boar's Chase to the religious establishment there.[16] It is not difficult to see in the church attached to the tower of St Regulus the church in which Abbot Ethelred was buried and the church up to the altar of which Alexander I's Arab steed was led. Bishop Robert may well have been responsible for the enlargement of an existing church rather than the erection of a completely new one.

The tower of St Regulus is the only one of those five Scottish towers which has been studied by historians of the architecture of pre-Conquest England. H. M. and Joan Taylor, in their *Anglo-Saxon Architecture*, Appendix A, have a note on this tower, which they assign to the first half of the eleventh century, though they cautiously add that 'this dating should be regarded as much less reliable than the dating of churches in England'. They take into account the small openings with monolithic heads, which occur here as at Markinch. The illustrations in their book show many examples, in addition to Wharram-le-Street, of the two-light opening with twin arches which we have at Markinch and St Andrews: Kirk Hammerton, Hornby and Appleton-le-Street in Yorkshire and Clee, Glentworth, Rothwell and Waithe in Lincolnshire are just a few of them.

---

[15] *Extracta e Variis Cronicis* (Abbotsford Club), 63; Fordun, *Scotichronicon*, V, xxiv (*Historians of Scotland*, i, 223).

[16] R. L. G. Ritchie, *The Normans in Scotland*, 172, citing Wyntoun.

It may not be true that acceptance of St Regulus as Anglo-Saxon makes all the others also Anglo-Saxon, but if there is more than a probability that St Regulus is pre-Norman it at least greatly strengthens the argument that Scotland had other pre-Norman towers.

It has often been suggested, or perhaps rather assumed, that those five towers were built in the twelfth century and represent survivals of Norman churches of that period. It is true that many of the twelfth-century Norman churches did have western towers. Foundations of them are to be seen at Tyninghame, North Berwick and perhaps elsewhere, while at Dalmeny a twelfth-century tower which collapsed some generations back has been replaced in the twentieth century. At Kirkliston, Uphall and Duddingston the west towers of Norman churches survive, at least in part. Attempts have been made to marry towers like those of Dunblane, Dunning, Markinch and St Andrews to twelfth-century naves and choirs and make composite reconstructions which are attractive in themselves but which it would be difficult to prove represent anything that ever existed.[17] The fact remains that, while we have the towers and we have the Norman churches, in no cases do we find the combination of an unmistakable twelfth-century church with a tower like any of the five we are considering. It should also be kept in mind that in England it is not twelfth-century churches, but pre-Norman, or at any rate very early Norman, churches which have towers of this type. And, finally, some of those towers – Dunblane certainly and Muthill probably – may not originally have had churches attached to them at all. One looks in vain, at least at Dunblane and Muthill, for the kind of arch which at Dalmeny led from the tower into the nave. Markinch had only a modest doorway and the arch at Dunning is an insertion.

One other consideration may help with the dating problem. Besides the five towers which survive in a relatively complete state, there is one other to be taken into account although only its foundations survive. A tower formed part of the early church underlying the Norman nave of Dunfermline Abbey, and this tower is dateable within close limits, or at any rate we have a lower limit for its date. The tower and an eastern chamber attached to it, resembling the original complex of St Regulus, stood at Dunfermline as a Culdee church before Queen Margaret added another chamber and a semi-circular apse. As Margaret's additions cannot have been earlier than 1070, the older building with its tower can be assigned to a point before 1070. If the tower at Dunfermline had survived and had shown features allied to those in the surviving five, the case for assigning them all to the pre-Norman period would be immeasurably strengthened. The dimensions of the Dunfermline tower, to judge from the foundations, would probably be about 12 feet square internally, which puts it in the same class as St Regulus, at 11 feet.

The general supposition has been that southern influence in Scotland did not prevail until after 1100 and that the inhabitants were not capable of

---

[17] E.g., *Trans. Scot. Ecclesiological Society*, i (1903), 29.

noteworthy achievements in architecture until the Normans arrived to teach them. To some extent the trouble has been that in Scotland romanesque has been equated with Norman, whereas in truth, in the wider European scene, romanesque architecture antedated the Normans by centuries and, in particular, nearly all the Anglo-Saxon churches of England are at least partly romanesque.

It is true that the two-light openings on which one necessarily relies in part to date the five towers were not a peculiar Anglo-Saxon feature and that they did not die out with the Norman conquest. They occur in very early Norman work in England, as at St Albans. There they might be taken to be an inheritance from Anglo-Saxon tradition. But they occur in early Norman work in Normandy as well, for instance in the towers of Jumièges. There is no doubt that the origin of the tradition is to be found on the continent, and Normans and Anglo-Saxons alike probably borrowed it from the Rhineland, where there are many examples. On the continent the tradition was one which went on for a long time, and the familiar two-light openings are to be seen in the much later tower of the cathedral of Århus, in Denmark. However, in the Scottish context, and taking into account the absence of two-light openings in buildings identifiably of Norman and later periods, there would seem to be little doubt that the Scottish towers with such openings are not later than 1100.

It remains a mystery why those five towers should be strung across Scotland in a comparatively restricted area. Dunblane, Muthill and Dunning, by themselves, could almost be regarded as a group of Strathearn churches, originating in the generosity of the forerunners of the earls of Strathearn who were later to be so munificent to the church. But Markinch and St Andrews are in Fife, and separated from the 'Strathearn' group. It may seem especially odd that no obviously Anglo-Saxon work is readily visible in Lothian, the part of Scotland most strongly influenced by England. But both there and elsewhere it may be that at least portions of towers of that early type survive in structures which were subsequently modified and have been assigned to later centuries; one obvious candidate is the tower of the church in that ancient ecclesiastical centre, Aberlady.

It may be a waste of time to speculate about the origins of five towers which happen to have survived, while leaving aside others which may have vanished, but if it is worth while examining the question at all the answer is probably to be found not at local or even regional, but at national level. The question is, what evidence is there of the penetration of southern influence into Scotland in the eleventh century? In the main the pattern was quite contrary: Irish influence, based on the expansion of the kingdom of Alba, was pushing south of the Forth and Clyde into Strathclyde and into Lothian. Yet there are certain slight indications of a contrary movement. Duncan I, after all, chose a Northumbrian lady as his queen, and Macbeth, though commonly regarded as a militant opponent of southern influence, employed Norman knights, though not directly from Normandy but from the Normanised court of Edward the Confessor. Besides, the bishopric of St Andrews was held, even before the reign of Duncan I, by a cleric bearing what looks like the unmistakably Anglian name of Alwin. With Malcolm III and the marriage to Margaret, southern influence became much stronger, and must have been exerted in all sorts of ways. It may even be that the many captives whom Malcolm is said to have brought to Scotland from his raids across the Border included some Anglo-Saxon architects.

Yet this diverting speculation could not represent the whole story, for these five towers cannot all be assigned to a single brief period. The belfry openings at St Andrews and Markinch are of pure Anglo-Saxon type and their attribution by the Taylors to the first half of the eleventh century is confirmed by a comparison with English examples which the Taylors date. The western arch of St Andrews, however, so much more ornate than the eastern and with decoration of Norman type, would be the work of Bishop Robert in the twelfth century.[18] Muthill is unique in Scotland and it is hard to find a parallel in England to a two-light opening which has side-piers like those at Markinch and St Andrews and is yet confined within a single enclosing arch. The structure resembles Thorington, Suffolk, which the Taylors call 'Saxo-Norman'. It surely occupies an intermediate place, before the Dunblane and Dunning model in which the side-piers vanish and the design has become that familiar in post-Conquest English churches such as that at Clapham, Bedfordshire.

[18] Cf. *SHR*, xxii, 134.

2

Bishops' Sees Before the Reign of David I

This article, published in *Proceedings of the Society of Antiquaries of Scotland*, lxxxvii (1955), 106–17, has been modified mainly by the inclusion of an account of the origin of the see of Moray.

The attribution to David I of the establishment of most of the Scottish episcopal sees has, if only through repetition, became a convention. Yet, while historians have been in general agreement about David's work, they have differed profoundly as to the details. A recent writer has gone so far as to remark, 'Before David's time St Andrews was the only bishopric in Scotland proper; he added six or more probably eight.'[1] Other modern historians have allowed that two or three sees were founded in the reign of David's predecessor, Alexander I.[2] The older historians and chroniclers were less confident about the extent of David's work. Boece attributed to David the foundation of only four bishoprics, in addition to six previously existing,[3] and he was followed by George Buchanan.[4] John Major says of David, 'Finding four bishoprics in his kingdom, he founded nine more.'[5] (These generous figures would give a total of thirteen bishoprics in the kingdom on David's death, when in truth there were only ten, as Orkney and The Isles were as yet outwith the Scottish realm and Argyll not yet in existence.) Two versions of Wyntoun tell each a different story:

> Bischoprikis he fand bot thre;
> Bot, or he deit, xi left he.

> *Or*

> Bischopis he fande bot foure or thre;
> Bot, or he deit, ix left he.[6]

This confusion might have suggested that the convention requires critical examination.

[1] Mackenzie, W. M., *Scottish Burghs*, 8.
[2] E.g. Dowden, *Bishops*, 47, 98, 144, 294–5; Dunbar, *Scottish Kings*, 51–2; cf. McEwan, *Church History*, i, 164.
[3] Boece, ii, 172, 185.
[4] Buchanan, *Historia* (1582), fo. 77v.
[5] *Historia Majoris Britanniae* (S.H.S.), 141.
[6] *Original Chronicle* (S.T.S.), iv, 384–5.

The source of the convention is undoubtedly the *Scotichronicon*; but the *Scotichronicon* is content to reproduce the statement of David's contemporary, Ailred of Rievaulx,[7] who says something quite different from all later works, with the exception of one of the versions of Wyntoun. He says that in the 'whole kingdom of the Scots' David found three or four bishops – not bishoprics; the other 'churches' were suffering from lack of a pastor – and 'churches' here means episcopal sees, as is apparent from the context and as can be proved by parallel statements in contemporary writings.[8] David, Ailred goes on, restored some old bishoprics and founded some new ones, to make, at his death, a total of nine. This account by Ailred, it will emerge, is altogether more credible than the statements of later writers.

Scotland's first bishop was presumably Ninian, assigned on somewhat slender evidence to Whithorn *c.* 400. Whatever the truth about him, recent opinion is that in the post-Roman period Christianity in southern Scotland was organised on an episcopal, if hardly diocesan, basis, and it has been suggested that there may have been a pattern of bishops' seats; for their location claims have been advanced, with varying degrees of probability, on behalf of Carlisle, Whithorn, Glasgow, Abercorn, Old Melrose, Abernethy, Paisley, Edinburgh, Hoddam and Peebles.[9] This speculation is of little relevance, partly because most of those sees, if they existed, had little if any influence on later development and partly because all of them except Abernethy lay in territory which did not become part of anything recognisable as Scotland until many centuries later.

In the 'Columban' church, as it took shape in the sixth and seventh centuries, jurisdiction pertained to the abbot, who might or might not be a bishop, and there is no reason to dispute Bede's statement that in Scotland (that is, the land north of the Forth and Clyde), the primacy (if we may use the term) belonged to the abbot of Iona, to whom, though he was only a presbyter, the whole province, including the bishops, were subject.[10] Some of the developments in the century after Columba suggest that this scheme might readily undergo modification. When Oswald, king of Northumbria, was introducing the mission from Iona into his realm, it was for a bishop, not an abbot, that he asked,[11] and Aidan and his successors, Finan and Colman, were abbots of Lindisfarne and bishops of the Angles – or, in Irish eyes, 'bishops of the Saxons'.[12] In the same period two Scots, Diuma and Ceollach, became bishops of the Mercians, and Finan consecrated Cedd as bishop of the East Saxons.[13] Thus a kind of tribal, if not regional, episcopate would seem to have been taking shape, under 'Columban' auspices, even before the Synod of Whitby.

[7] *Scotichron.*, v, xlviii; cf. *SA*, 233.

[8] E.g. 'ne diutius [sine] pastore vacillaret ecclesia' (Symeon of Durham [Rolls Series], ii, 204); 'diu ecclesia sine pastore fuit' (Raine, *Historians of the Church of York*, ii, 127).

[9] Charles Thomas, *The Early Christian Archaeology of North Britain*, 16–18.

[10] Bede, iii, 4.

[11] Ibid., iii, 3.

[12] Ibid., iii, 25; *Picts and Scots*, 71, 348.

[13] Bede, iii, 21, 22, 24.

The success of the Roman party at Whitby was very soon followed by changes in ecclesiastical organisation. Archbishop Theodore, regarded as the organiser of the English Church, ruled at Canterbury from 668 to 690, and several of the dioceses of the southern province date their foundation in that period. In the north the same kind of thing seems to have happened, for in 681 bishops were appointed for Hexham and Abercorn, and somewhat later for Whithorn[14] – a development which represents something a little more like diocesan episcopacy. Less significance may attach to the appearance in 660 and 689 of bishops of Kingarth (followed in the next century by abbots of Kingarth).[15] It is true that the Abercorn experiment was shortlived, for Bishop Trumwin, appointed in 681, had to withdraw after Nechtansmere.[16] But Northumbria, though it suffered a military and political defeat, was presently to win an ecclesiastical victory, when early in the eighth century the king of the Picts decided to submit to Rome. About 710 King Nechtan, on the advice of Ceolfrid, abbot of Jarrow, accepted the Roman uses and put his kingdom under the patronage of St Peter.[17] A few years later he expelled the Columban clergy.[18]

In Scotland as in England the success of the Roman party must have been followed by changes in organisation. As Skene observes, 'With the expulsion of the family of Iona terminated the primacy of its monastery over . . . the kingdom of the Picts',[19] and a new organisation had to take the place of the old. It is perhaps to this point that we should assign the alleged bishopric of Abernethy. There is a statement in the *Scotichronicon* that at Abernethy, which was the chief royal and episcopal seat of the Pictish realm, three elections of bishops were made when there was only one bishop in Pictland. Some MSS. read 'Scotland', but that 'Pictland' is correct is apparent from the context.[20] Skene, reading 'Scotland', assigned the Abernethy bishops to the later part of the ninth century; yet, inconsistently, he recognised the existence of an 'old Pictish bishopric of Abernethy', as if it had existed before the union of the Picts and Scots under Kenneth mac Alpin.[21]

As Abernethy was the Pictish capital, and as the church there had been endowed by earlier Pictish kings,[22] nothing would seem more likely than that King Nechtan, after he decided to follow the example of Northumbria in other respects, would follow that example also by planting at Abernethy

---

[14] Ibid., iv, 12; v, 23.

[15] *Picts and Scots*, 71, 73, 76, 349, 351, 359; *Early Sources*, i, 176–7, 198.

[16] Bede, iv, 26.

[17] Ibid., v, 21.

[18] ES, I, 217.

[19] *Celtic Scotland*, ii, 178.

[20] *Scotichron.*, iv, xii. Cf. *Extracta e variis cronicis Scocie*, 44; 'Hiis temporibus fuit sedes illa principalis regalis et pontificalis tocius regni Pictorum; quum fuit solus unus episcopus in regno Pictorum.'

[21] *Celtic Scotland*, ii, 310–11, 397.

[22] ES, i, 121–2.

a tribal or regional bishop.[23] It may be that he would go on to plant bishops elsewhere in his dominions; and there is evidence for the appearance at this point of Curitan, bishop and abbot of Rosemarkie, whom Skene identifies with the legendary Boniface (for whom, according to Wyntoun, Nechtan 'foundit Rosmarkyne').[24] It may be significant of the likelihood that the Romanisers introduced a new concept of the episcopal office, that at this period, when in Iona itself there was a prolonged dispute between the Roman and native parties, a 'bishop of Iona' appears for the first time.[25] Skene assigns likewise to this period St Fergus, a bishop associated with various parts of the country.[26] Whatever the truth about the Pictish bishops of the period in general and about Fergus in particular, it is consonant with the theory that bishops' sees were founded in Pictland on its submission to Rome in the early eighth century, that one Fergustus, or Fergusius, described as a Pictish bishop of Scotland, was present at a council at Rome in 721. He was accompanied by Sedulius, a bishop of Britain of Scottish race, in whom Skene sees a bishop set up by the Strathclyde Britons on their recovery from Anglian domination.[27] Since the see of Whithorn, as already mentioned, came into existence about this time, it looks as if in the early eighth century there may already have been five or six bishops' seats within the bounds of the later kingdom of Scotland.

The position of Abernethy as the chief bishopric of Pictland – if such it had been in the early eighth century – was bound to be affected by the transfer of the devotion of the Pictish kings to St Andrews before the middle of that century. The first known abbot of St Andrews died in 747,[28] though it is much later that we first hear of a bishop at St Andrews. Before we have information about further developments there had occurred the union of the Picts and Scots under Kenneth mac Alpin. How far the apparent domination of the Scottish element in the united kingdom was reflected in the restoration of 'Columban' clergy to central and eastern Scotland it is hard to determine; but on the whole the indications are that communication with Ireland became again closer, and that there was a certain reaction towards the earlier, 'Columban,' tradition, reflected in ecclesiastical organisation to the extent that the development towards a normal diocesan organisation was checked and that there was a reversion to a system based on the monasteries. Presently, too, Scotland was very largely isolated by Norse attacks and settlements, and the process of

---

[23] This suggestion has the support, for what it is worth, of Boece (i, 411).

[24] *Celtic Scotland*, ii, 231; Wyntoun, iv, 122–3.

[25] *Annals of Ulster* (ed. Hennessy and MacCarthy), i, 160; *Picts and Scots*, 73.

[26] *Celtic Scotland*, ii, 232–3.

[27] Labbe, *Sacrosancta concilia*, vi, 1458; *Celtc Scotland*, ii, 220, 232. Fergus is designated 'episcopus Scotiae Pictus', and has been taken to be a Pict who was a bishop in Ireland; but it seems as likely that he was a Pictish bishop (i.e., a bishop in Pictland) of Scottish (or Irish) race, and if the Scots were providing bishops for English sees (p. 12 *supra*) they might well provide one for Pictland. Sedulius was 'episcopus Britanniae de genere Scotorum', and the scribe may have been deliberately varying his diction.

[28] *ES*, i, 238.

assimilation to England and other countries was interrupted for two centuries.

The next recorded development concerns Dunkeld. The church there had been founded *c.* 820 by a Pictish king; and to it Kenneth mac Alpin brought relics of Columba, apparently with a view to its becoming the ecclesiastical centre of the united kingdom, superseding at once Iona on the one hand and Abernethy or St Andrews on the other. The one fact to emerge is that in 865 there died a cleric described in Irish annals as 'abbot of Dunkeld and first bishop of Fortriu'. In printing the Annals of Ulster in his *Chronicles of the Picts and Scots*, Skene reproduced a reading 'primus episcopus' and, contending that this bishop was first in time and not first in rank, was led to regard him as a sole bishop of Pictland and was compelled to relegate the Abernethy bishops to a later date. But the authoritative reading is undoubtedly the Celtic 'primepscop', which in Ireland carried the quite distinct connotation of the chief bishop of a tribe or kingdom, and the element 'prim' normally means 'primary, foremost, chief, principal'.[29] Skene's view of the situation may thus be dismissed as untenable, and it can be accepted that there was at Dunkeld in the middle of the ninth century a chief bishop of Fortriu. Fortriu, while it sometimes had a narrower meaning, is quite consistently used by the Irish annalists to signify the whole of the Pictish kingdom,[30] and it may be so taken here. If there was a chief bishop at Dunkeld, it is a safe assumption that there were other, inferior, bishops elsewhere; that the *primepscop* was an abbot-bishop suggests that the 'Columban' reaction was predominant in central Scotland, but whether the inferior bishops were secular bishops, abbot-bishops or bishops subordinate to abbots cannot be determined.

That is all we hear of abbot-bishops at Dunkeld, and the experiment was evidently not enduring. It may be that a development at St Andrews, begun earlier and interrupted by the intrusion of Dunkeld, was soon resumed. (Boece, who knows nothing of the intervention of Dunkeld, says that the bishop's seat was translated from Abernethy to St Andrews.)[31] It is believed that from 906 until 1093 there was at St Andrews a succession of bishops, bearing such titles as 'episcopus Scotorum', 'epscop Alban' or 'ardepscop Alban', variously rendered as 'head bishop' or 'high bishop' of the Scots or of Scotland.[32] Skene, elaborating this, held that each member of the line was not merely 'high bishop', but sole bishop, and we are further

[29] *Annals of Ulster* (ed. Hennessy and MacCarthy), i, 374; *Picts and Scots*, 361, 405. Professor Kenneth Jackson is my authority for 'primepscop'; cf. L. Gougaud, *Christianity in Celtic Lands*, 219, 221.

[30] E.g., *Picts and Scots*, 72, 76; *Annals of Ulster*, i, 313, 333; cf. Chadwick, *Early Scotland*, 40.

[31] *Scotichron.*, iv, 17, vi, 24; Wyntoun, iv, 182–5, 192–3, 244–7, 318–19, 345; Boece, ii, 53, 122 etc.; *Reg. Prioratus S. Andree*, 113, 116.

[32] Cellach, allegedly the first of the line, is merely 'Bishop Cellach' in *Picts and Scots*, 9; Fothadh, the second, known to the Irish annalists as 'bishop of the islands of Alba', appears simply as 'Bishop Fothach' (*ES*, i, 471; *Celtic Scotland*, ii, 330n; *Picts and Scots*, 10); the third is simply 'Bishop Maelbrigde' (*Picts and Scots*, 10).

asked to believe that after the death of the last of the line, in 1093, Scotland had no bishops whatever for a number of years, until the vacancy at St Andrews was filled by Alexander I and the other sees founded by him or by David.

The alleged St Andrews succession is not of itself wholly convincing. Some of the bishops are known only from Wyntoun and Fordoun, who alone, along with the Register of St Andrews Priory, style them 'bishops of St Andrews'. The fact that they appear in other sources as merely 'Bishop Cellach', 'Bishop Fothach' or 'Bishop Maelbrigde', without territorial designation, is not an argument against their attachment to St Andrews, for the practice of styling bishops in this way went on into the twelfth century: for instance, 'Bishop Fothad' in 1093 and 'Bishop Gregory' and 'Bishop Cormac' twenty or thirty years later. On the other hand, Fothadh, reckoned second of the St Andrews line, is known to the Irish annalists as 'bishop of the islands of Alba' and may belong to the Iona succession mentioned below. Investigation of the credentials of the 'bishops of St Andrews', however, is not relevant to the present argument, which is concerned only to dispute the claim that there was, during these two centuries, only one bishop in Scotland.

It is true that it is not easy to produce the names of other Scottish bishops, besides those in the alleged St Andrews succession, in this period. But this is in no way surprising, in view of the great dearth of information in a period when we know the names of hardly any individuals in Scotland except kings and some of their immediate kinsfolk. And yet the sources do not entirely fail us: we hear of a bishop of Iona in 966, 980 and 986;[33] a bishop from Scotland, Bernelm by name, is said to have attended a council in England in 977 or 978;[34] and in 1055 we hear of a bishop called John, who had been consecrated in Scotland and who was sent to the Orkneys by Adalbert of Bremen.[35] It is perhaps hardly worth while even speculating about 'Gervadius, bischop and prechour of Murraye' and 'Glaciane, ane excellent doctour and bischop',[36] but questions may be raised about 'Dubthach the Scot, chief confessor of Ireland and Scotland' who 'reposed in Armagh' in 1065 and may be the St Duthac of legend, who was chief bishop of Scotland,[37] and about 'John, bishop of Athole', who appears in the *Orkneyinga Saga* in the twelfth century.[38] Such stray names are, however, the least of the evidence that Scotland did not have only one bishop.

The strongest evidence is perhaps the term 'ardepscop Alban' itself. If there was a 'high bishop' or 'head bishop', at St Andrews or elsewhere, there is more than a presumption that there were other bishops, inferior in

---

[33] *ES*, i, 472, 488, 490.
[34] Wharton, *Anglia Sacra*, ii, 220.
[35] *ES*, ii, 8–9.
[36] Boece, ii, 31, 172; cf. *Celtic Scotland*, ii, 369.
[37] *ES*, ii, 10 and n.
[38] Ed. Anderson, 113.

status though not standing in the technical relation of suffragans to a metropolitan. The term 'ardepscop', like the earlier 'primepscop', was in regular use in Ireland, where, indeed, *aird-easpog* is still the term for an archbishop.[39] It would be incorrect to translate the term, when we find it in Ireland or Scotland *c*. 1100, as 'archbishop', since by that time 'archbishop' had come to have the technical sense of a metropolitan who had received the *pallium* from Rome. But there is some evidence of the recognition by contemporaries of the *ardepscop* as, quite simply, a metropolitan without a *pallium*.[40] The title might be rendered into Latin as *summus episcopus*.[41] *Epscop Alban*, again, might be rendered *episcopus Scotorum* – not to imply that the possessor of the title was the sole bishop in Scotland, but to imply that whereas other bishops might be bishops of this see or that see, the head bishop was bishop of the nation, or the bishop *par excellence*, as an early writer puts it.[42] The title *episcopus Scotorum* certainly does not imply a sole bishop, for it remained in use (by the bishops of St Andrews) long after the existence of other sees is well documented. It appears on seals until the end of the thirteenth century.

There are a number of statements in the late eleventh and early twelfth centuries which confirm the view that there was a plurality of bishops' sees in Scotland before the reign of David I. In 1080 we read in an English chronicle that the archbishop of York, in consecrating the bishop of Durham, could not obtain the assistance of the Scottish bishops, who were subject to him.[43] In 1101 Pope Paschal II writes to the suffragans of the archbishopric of York throughout Scotland.[44] In 1108, when Turgot had been appointed to St Andrews after a long vacancy, the bishop of Durham proposed to consecrate him with the assistance of the bishops of Scotland and of the Orkneys;[45] this would suggest that there were at least two bishops on the Scottish mainland at a time when St Andrews was vacant. In 1119 and 1122, when St Andrews was once more vacant, we find the pope addressing 'all the bishops throughout Scotland' and rebuking them for carrying out consecrations without reference to a metropolitan.[46] It would seem a fair comment that, if the Scots were a peculiar people who never had more than one bishop, and sometimes had none, they were remarkably successful in concealing the fact from their neighbours in England and from headquarters at Rome.

The situation in Scotland before the twelfth, perhaps even before the eleventh, century, would merit comparison with the interpretation Dr Wendy Davies has put on the state of the episcopate in Wales, where there

[39] Information from Professor Jackson.
[40] Wharton, *Anglia Sacra*, ii, 234–6; Symeon of Durham (Rolls Series), ii, 204.
[41] Wharton, loc. cit.; *Picts and Scots*, 190.
[42] *Picts and Scots*, 191.
[43] Earle and Plummer, *Two Saxon Chronicles*, i, 289.
[44] Raine, *Historians of the Church of York*, iii, 22.
[45] Eadmer, *Historia* (Rolls Series), 198.
[46] Raine, op. cit., iii, 40–1, 45–6; Robert Somerville, *Scotia Pontificia*, 19–27.

were bishops 'who seem to have occurred in well-defined regions and who
do not appear to have been in any way subject to abbots' and where there
were 'archbishops' who were 'no more than highly honoured or chief
bishops' (*An Early Welsh Microcosm*, 148–9, and *Wales in the Early Middle
Ages*, 160–61). It would appear that in Scotland, at least, some of the 'well-
defined regions' in which bishops operated resembled the dioceses which
emerge into the light of day in the twelfth century. It may therefore be
suggested not only that there was a plurality of bishops, but that they were
established in some of the sees the erection of which has been ascribed to
David I.

When the earliest references to bishops after 1100 occur, they appear in
charters, a source of information then appearing for the first time. It is
somewhat hazardous to argue that, because as soon as charters appear we
find the names of bishops, therefore before there were charters there were
no bishops. And to attribute the 'foundation' of a bishopric to the date at
which there occurs the first casual, isolated mention of the name of a bishop
is wholly unsound. (Yet it is on no stronger evidence that the 'creation' of
various sees has been attributed to Alexander I and David.) It might be
sounder to argue that, because bishops appear when charters appear,
therefore bishops already existed. And this argument receives some
confirmation from the names of the earliest bishops to appear on record. In
most cases the first bishop named is clearly a native – Cormac, Gregory,
Nechtan, Macbeth – and not one of the Anglo-Normans whom the
innovating kings of the twelfth century imported to fill the other high
offices in church and state. 'Gregory', or rather 'Gregorius' (for the
documents are in Latin), was a version of a native name, 'Giric' or 'Grig',
which had been borne by a king in the ninth century and by other members
of the royal house. Each of these manifestly Celtic bishops seems to
represent not the beginning of a new line but the continuation of an old.

The influence of an older regime may be detected in the choice – if
choice indeed there was – of the bishops' seats. It does seem significant
that, while abbeys were planted at sites such as Dunfermline, Scone,
Cambuskenneth and Holyrood, in close proximity to royal castles and
residences, bishops' sees remained at what were evidently old ecclesiastical
sites. If the supposed innovators had not been building on old foundations,
they might have been expected to plant their bishops at the seats of sheriffs,
so that civil and ecclesiastical government should have the same focus; but
cathedral and sheriff's seat coincided only at Aberdeen and Elgin, and in
each of those instances the bishop's seat is known to have been moved.

Ancient survivals are equally apparent in the boundaries of some of the
dioceses. St Andrews straggled up the east coast from the Tweed to the
Dee, including most of Berwickshire, the Lothians and Fife and large tracts
north of the Tay, and extending along the Forth beyond Stirling, up the
Tay to Scone and far into the highlands of Angus. Intermingled with it lay
detached portions of Dunkeld (e.g. Aberlady, Aberdour, Cramond and
Abercorn) and Dunblane (Culross and Abernethy), and the whole of the

scattered diocese of Brechin. By contrast, Glasgow, Galloway and the northern dioceses represent continuous tracts of territory. Once more one feels that if the dioceses had been founded in the twelfth century they would have shown signs of coinciding with, or approximating to, sheriffdoms; but this they never do, except in the one case of Aberdeen, and even it included part of the sheriffdom of Banff. In any event, the contrast between the intermingled boundaries of the central dioceses and the simpler structure of those in the south and north demands some attempt at explanation, however tentative.

The episcopate cannot be considered in detachment, but must be viewed in relation to the remainder of the ecclesiastical structure, of the character of which, at that period, we know far too little. Possibly the maintenance of services and the cure of souls were still, in some parts of the country, dependent on the monasteries, or at least carried on within the framework of an organisation centred on the monastery. Allow that the ancient 'Columban' model had been retained, or had been revived, to the extent that administration pertained to the abbot, who might or might not be a bishop, and that the bishop might still be in a subordinate position in the monastery. What then happened when, as is usually accepted, the office of abbot became secularised? It seems very likely that an abbey would still maintain its bishop for the ordination and supervision of its clergy. If the monasteries were performing spiritual functions at all, the bishop would still be essential; and, while there might be lay abbots, there could not be lay bishops. It may even be that, as the abbots relinquished ecclesiastical functions, these functions would fall increasingly to the bishops, whose importance would grow in consequence. Hence, by a natural process of development, the bishop might emerge from comparative obscurity and become a prominent figure. His sphere of work would, at first, be not a diocese as commonly understood, but the churches dependent on the monastery, which might be scattered over a large area. Such a development would go far to explain the peculiar boundaries of the later dioceses of Dunkeld and Brechin, and perhaps Dunblane. Dunkeld, all else apart, seems to have been the heir of Iona. It included central and western Scotland until a bishopric of Argyll was created c. 1190; thereafter it still retained the parish of Muckairn, and apparently claimed Iona itself.[47]

It is often said that in Dunkeld and Brechin, when the see was 'created' or 'founded' in the twelfth century, the abbot became the first bishop.[48] Such a development is *prima facie* unlikely, for a man already in episcopal orders, although occupying a subordinate position, could more easily be turned into a diocesan bishop than could a lay abbot. But it is, in any event, demonstrably untrue, for at Brechin the line of abbots continued long after bishops began to be mentioned in charters, and we find an abbot of Brechin

---

[47] Hunter, *Diocese and Presbytery of Dunkeld*, i, 75.
[48] Myln, *Lives of the Bishops of Dunkeld* (Bannatyne Club), 4–5; *Celtic Scotland*, ii, 370–1, 400–1.

witnessing a charter by a bishop of Brechin;[49] while at Dunkeld, although
we do not find the name of an abbot so late, the 'abbacy' of Dunkeld is
mentioned *c*. 1150, in a charter to which the bishop of Dunkeld was a
witness.[50] That there was an 'abbacy' but no abbot would be explained on
the assumption that the abbey had fallen to the crown on the death of
Abbot Ethelred, son of Malcolm and Margaret. If a bishop and an abbot
could exist concurrently in the middle of the twelfth century, there is no
reason why they should not have coexisted much earlier.

The monastery, however, is not the whole picture. There were the
culdees, who, whatever they may have been in earlier times, were in their
later days little else than colleges of secular priests. The possibility cannot be
overlooked that in some instances the spiritual functions of abbeys had
wholly lapsed and that those functions were instead performed by culdees.
In any event, the existence of the culdees, bodies of clergy not integrated
into monasteries, might suggest that there were also non-monastic bishops,
who ordained and perhaps superintended them. Moreover, it is difficult to
escape the conclusion that there were, already before 1100, secular priests
serving local churches. When, for instance, a 'church' is 'given' to a body of
culdees,[51] it may be that it had previously been served, and perhaps
continued to be served, by a resident secular priest. If there were such
secular clergy, they were presumably under the jurisdiction of a territorial,
and not a monastic, bishop.

It may be that we can detect, even in central Scotland, the making of
two distinct types of diocese, the monastic and the secular. Dunkeld and
Brechin are clearly monastic; but may it be suggested that St Andrews was
the seat of the bishop who had a sort of residual jurisdiction within the area,
supervising the clergy of the churches served by seculars and not attached
to monasteries? In any event, the dioceses of the south and the north clearly
had a different origin from those of the centre. Glasgow, at any rate, was
the bishopric of the kingdom of Strathclyde, and it had not been affected
by the persistence of the monastic tradition in areas under 'Columban'
influence. To what extent it had been continuously effective is unknown,
but there were appointments in the eleventh century, and the inquest into
its possessions, made *c*. 1120, suggests that its existence as an entity was of
long standing. Galloway, again, whatever its history between *c*. 800 and
c. 1100, emerges in the 1120s as clearly the bishopric of the lordship of
Galloway. The position in the north is more obscure. One can only
speculate as to whether a secular clergy had gained a footing there in the
eighth century and had retained it when the 'Columban' reaction, along
monastic lines, took effect in the centre of the country. But there is another
possible explanation of the northern dioceses. The regions which formed
them were not, in the eleventh century, effectively subject to the Scottish

[49] *Liber de Aberbrothoc*, i, 134, 163.
[50] *ESC*, no. ccix.
[51] E.g., *Reg. Prioratus S. Andree*, 116.

crown. In the far north the earl of Orkney held Caithness and Sutherland and sometimes a good deal more; the ruling house of the province of Moray seems to have been at the height of its power in the eleventh century. Is this situation reflected in the church? The earl of Orkney established a bishopric for his earldom; the king of the Isles established one for his realm; the lords of Galloway established one for their lordship. Is it unlikely that a great mormaer, of Moray or Ross, would establish, or foster, one for his, rather than see his clergy subordinated to the bishop of St Andrews who was associated with the king of Scots? Some such theory would explain the territorial dioceses of the north. In any event, the existence, before 1100, of bishops for areas such as Orkney and the Isles renders it highly improbable that one bishop sufficed for the entire Scottish mainland.

The case of Moray is worth examination. In the 1120s there was a bishop there called Gregorius, at a time when the king had as yet little power in that province, and he must be seen as probably the last of a line of native bishops, appointed by the mormaers. In the 1130s King David suppressed rebellions in Moray and in effect annexed the province to the crown. The burgh of Elgin, described by David as 'my burgh', was in existence by 1136, and Forres and Inverness were burghs before the end of his reign in 1153. By 1160 Malcolm IV could write of the 'province of Elgin', which suggests that Moray, or part of it, was now administered from that town, perhaps by a sheriff, though none is yet mentioned by name. Ecclesiastical organisation went hand in hand with secular: the priory of Urquhart was founded about 1136 and the abbey of Kinloss in 1150 or 1151. It is barely conceivable that those years did not see some reorganisation of the bishopric, but we know nothing until, shortly before David's death in 1153, a second bishop of Moray appears on record, this time with the Norman name of William and obviously selected by the king. Moray revived its separatist tendencies from time to time, but after King William the Lion put down a rebellion in 1187 the province may be said to have been integrated into the kingdom. The king, besides giving lands to the bishopric of Moray, issued several mandates that the bishop and clergy should receive their due revenues and that the people should appear when summoned to the church courts. It is clear that by about 1200 the bishopric was well organised. Its seat was not, however, even now at the sheriff's seat of Elgin. According to Bishop Brice (1203–22), until his day the bishops had not had a fixed seat, but had made use, each according to his own will, of the churches of Birnie, Spynie and Kinneddar. As these places were all within a few miles of Elgin, this makes the avoidance of Elgin the more remarkable, but at the same time it is easy to see facts which confirm the bishop's statement and make the use of those churches intelligible. Birnie still possesses a church with the characteristic Norman architecture of the twelfth century. Spynie likewise had a church of early date, the foundations of which could be seen until two generations ago and which, if its measurements are correctly reported as 74 feet by 35 feet, was of fair size.

Kinneddar was the reputed scene of the labours of St Gerardine (perhaps Boece's 'bischop and prechour of Murraye') in the tenth century, and thus had ancient ecclesiastical significance. Bishop Brice, who professed a regard for the convenience of people who often had to go to the cathedral 'as to a mother', saw that those places were difficult of access because of travelling conditions in bad weather; besides, they were open to the attacks of 'evil doers who are always persecuting the church in those parts' – a remark which suggests that Kinneddar, a mile from the coast, was apt to be pillaged by sea-rovers and that Birnie was equally apt to suffer from the descents of those who would later have been called Highland caterans. The bishop therefore petitioned the pope that Spynie be declared the episcopal see and the pope acceded to the request in 1207. Only in 1224, on the grounds that Spynie was likely to be unsafe on account of war and lacked markets for food and clothing, was the see transferred to Elgin.

Dunblane and Aberdeen also deserve special mention. Dunblane, in its possession of the ancient ecclesiastical sites of Abernethy and Culross as detached parishes, partakes of the character of a monastic bishopric; but on the other hand, in its intimate association with the earldom of Strathearn, whose earls were its patrons, it resembles the territorial dioceses of the north and Galloway in the south. It may be that it had a dual origin: there was within it a monastic bishop, who obtained recognition from the earl as the bishop for the earldom of Strathearn. Aberdeen is to all appearance a purely territorial bishopric, and the choice of Aberdeen as a bishop's seat may well be attributed to a twelfth-century king; but the tradition that the see developed from a monastic bishopric based on Mortlach[52] must not be dismissed merely because it happens to have been incorporated in a spurious charter, and seems rather to represent the strong probability that there were Celtic bishops somewhere in the area, and very likely at Mortlach, before the casual appearance of the equally Celtic Nechtan at Aberdeen in the twelfth century.

Whatever the precise situation before 1100, it is plain that a period of serious dislocation may have intervened before the restorative work of David I. No doubt one reason was the confused political situation following the death of Malcolm III; but another undoubtedly was the question, which was soon to become acute, of the validity of the appointment of bishops without confirmation by a metropolitan. At any rate, St Andrews itself was apparently without a *consecrated* bishop from 1093 to 1109, and again from 1115 to 1127. If St Andrews, the chief see, could be so long vacant, other sees may well have been vacant as long or longer. In Glasgow, we are told, Archbishop Kinsi of York (1055–60) had consecrated Bishops Magsuea and John; thereafter, 'because of hostile invasion and desolation and the barbarity of the land for long the church was without a pastor', or 'almost beyond memory had not had the solace of

---

[52] *Aberdeen Reg.*, i, pp. xvii, 3; ii, 246–7; *Scotichron.*, iv, xlix.

a bishop', until Michael was consecrated between 1109 and 1114.[53] At Dunblane there was a tradition that there had been a vacancy of a century or more.[54] It is not difficult to understand why Ailred should write of 'churches wavering without a pastor'.

Whatever the precise situation before David's reign, it remains true that the changes of the twelfth century were no less than revolutionary. There was, for one thing, a revolution in personnel: no more Celts were appointed to sees. There was also, in some instances, a reallocation of revenues, with the assignation to bishops of funds previously devoted to abbots. Above all, there was the development of a secular clergy and of a complete parochial system and the emergence of a more rigid distinction between the seculars and the regulars, who were now, in the main, confined to the monasteries. The concept of the territorial parish, served by secular priests, almost demanded the institution of territorial dioceses covering the whole country, even although they might be based on old foundations. The principal revolution was not so much a change in the concept of the bishop's office as in the character of the lower levels of the ecclesiastical structure which carried with it a new notion of the nature of the diocese and an extension of the bishop's functions.

Ailred's statement that David found 'three or four' bishops is perhaps not to be taken literally, and it is uncertain whether his account refers to Scotia north of the Forth and Clyde or to the whole of modern Scotland. That David, on his accession, found bishops at Dunkeld, Moray, Ross and Mortlach or Aberdeen is more than likely. St Andrews was without a consecrated bishop, Whithorn had presumably been long without a bishop, and there may have chanced at the time to be no bishop at Brechin, while Dunblane was very likely in a state of decay. Caithness has by far the strongest claim to be regarded as a new foundation by David, but there is an element of mystery about it: presumably Caithness proper, which was part of the earl of Orkney's dominions, originally fell within the bishopric of Orkney, and even when it became a separate diocese its centre seems at first to have been in the north, at Halkirk and Scrabster; the settlement at Dornoch came later. Dunblane possibly underwent such reconstruction in David's reign, if not at his own hands, that it would be regarded as falling in the same category; and if David moved a bishop's seat from Mortlach to Aberdeen, then that see might likewise rank as a new foundation. Glasgow, to which appointments were made when David was earl in Cumbria, would be reckoned as one of his restorations. Some such picture agrees broadly with what Ailred says, and accords better with the facts than does the convention which has dominated most recent writers.

[53] *SA*, 133–4; the development at Glasgow is investigated, with a good deal of scepticism, by Dr Norman F. Shead, 'The Origins of the Medieval Diocese of Glasgow', *SHR*, xlviii, 220–25.

[54] Theiner, no. xci.

Additional Note

The English council of Cealchythe [*Chelsea*], in 816, laid down that no one of Scottish race should be allowed to administer Baptism or Holy Communion in any English diocese, since it was uncertain where and by whom they had been ordained, and stated that it was improper to receive the ministrations of foreigners among whom there was no regular organisation under a metropolitan.[55] It may be that the reference was to Ireland rather than Scotland, but it is hard to see any reason why Scottish orders would not have been covered by the same condemnation. Yet, when we come to the late twelfth century, we find that Queen Margaret, though critical of much else, had evidently no criticism to make of Scottish orders or organisation. The question thus arises whether any change, to regularise the position in Scotland, had occurred during the intervening period, especially as Margaret is unlikely to have taken a less rigid view than the council of Cealchythe. It is possible only to say that there are one or two indications that some such change did in fact take place. There is the *Scotichronicon's* statement that 'Bishop Cellach II of St Andrews', in the late tenth century, was the first bishop of the Scots to go to Rome for confirmation;[56] and there is the claim made by the York historian, Hugh the Chantor, that Bishop Fothad II (d. 1093) was sent by Malcolm and Margaret to make canonical subjection to York as his metropolitan.[57] Some reconstruction may indeed have been done by Malcolm and Margaret. Boece alone, and that in a passage bristling with manifest errors, attributes the restoration and foundation of some bishops' sees to Malcolm III;[58] but it is certainly carrying the evidence from silence altogether too far to say, as McEwan does, 'To the establishment of dioceses they [Malcolm and Margaret] did not in any way contribute.'[59]

[55] Wilkins, *Concilia*, i, 170. The concern here does not seem to have been merely with the activities of *episcopi vagantes*, which the council of Chalons, three years earlier, evidently had in view when it denounced the ordinations carried out by 'certain Scots persons calling themselves bishops' (Labbe, vii, 1281–2). Cf. McEwan, *Church History*, i, 104.

[56] *Scotichron.*, vi, 24.

[57] Raine, *York*, ii, 126, 363.

[58] Boece, ii, 172.

[59] *Church History*, i, 160.

1. Doorway, Dunblane

2. Doorway, Jarrow

3. Restennet Tower

4. Doorway, Jarrow

5. Base of Tower, Monkwearmouth

6. Western arch, Rester

7. Chancel arch, Corbridge

3

The Appointment of Bishops in the Early Middle Ages

The earliest accounts of procedure do not describe in detail how bishops were selected, but the form of words used is explicit that the king, the clergy and the people all had a part. Turgot, the first twelfth-century bishop of St Andrews, was said to have been chosen in 1107 by the king, the clergy and the people; his successor, Eadmer, was said to have been chosen in 1120 by the clergy and people of the land with the king's consent (and the same Eadmer related that in 1120 the bishop of Bangor in Wales was chosen by the 'prince, clergy and people of Wales').[1] In Glasgow in 1174 the bishop was chosen by the clergy and people with the king's consent (*a clero, a populo exigente et rege ipso assentiente*).[2]

These *formulae* were not an expression of a vague sentiment, surviving from primitive times, in favour of a popular voice in the election of bishops, but were in accordance with canon law as it stood at that time. Of course the notion of popular election by clergy and people did represent ancient custom or aspiration: one council at Paris in 557 decreed that the election of a bishop should be left free to the people and clergy and that no one should be intruded into a see by a prince, and another, in 615, declared that election of bishops should have the consent of the clergy and of the people of the city.[3] But this method of selection was also part of the law in the twelfth century. The *Decretum*, codifying canon law down to about 1140, reiterated the need for co-operation between clergy and people: 'It is contrary to reason that any be held a bishop who has not been chosen by the clergy and required [or perhaps demanded – *expetiti*] by the people'; 'The clergy and people are to be concerned in the choice of a bishop and are entitled to elect their own bishop'; 'The consent and desire of the clergy and people are required'; and so on. On the other hand, while no one was to be chosen *regio favore*, the consent (*voluntas, assensus*) of the sovereign was to be desired. The people who wrote accounts of twelfth-century appointments in Scotland were not antiquarians hankering after the good old days of popular election; they were simply stressing that the choice had been

[1] *SA*, 130, 141.
[2] *ES*, ii, 280.
[3] Edward H. Landon, *Manual of Councils of the Holy Catholic Church*, ii, 19, 20.

made in accordance with the existing law and principles of the church. A further indication that this was so is the fact that the author of the twelfth-century *Life of Kentigern* states that he was chosen by the king and clergy of the district of Cumbria[4] – the procedure which the writer regarded as normal in his own time.

The rights of clergy and people soon had a competitor, for as cathedral chapters were organised (in Scotland mainly in the twelfth and early thirteenth centuries) the right to choose the bishop was conferred on them. In 1147 the pope formally gave the election of the bishop of St Andrews to the chapter of canons there.[5] In 1163 the pope took the bishop of Dunkeld under St Peter's protection and provided that no bishop should succeed without election by the canons.[6] And in 1231 Pope Gregory IX, writing to the dean and chapter of Moray, declared that the election of the bishop should be free, and forbade the chapter to carry the pastoral staff and other insignia of the bishop to a secular court from which they would be received by a new incumbent.[7] Canon law was modified to take account of this development, and the Decretals of Gregory IX (1234) imply that election by a chapter was normal practice.

The diocesan clergy did not give up their old right without a struggle and there were contests in which claims were advanced on behalf of them and also, at any rate in name, on behalf of the people. It may be that there was especially strong opposition to the chapter's exclusive rights in sees where there was a chapter of regular clergy – that is, St Andrews, Whithorn and The Isles (at that time based in the Isle of Man). It is certainly in those dioceses that there is most evidence of conflict. In 1239 at St Andrews, on the death of Bishop William, an agreement was made between the prior and canons of the Augustinian house on one part and the archdeacons of St Andrews and Lothian on the other, to the effect that the *communitas* should take part in the election on this occasion, but without prejudice to the right of either party.[8] It may well be that the *communitas* was the body of clergy who had succeeded to the property and title of the Culdees, ousted from the cathedral in favour of the Augustinians and now constituting the staff of the church of St Mary of the Rock. The 'Culdees' certainly figure in the next dispute. In 1253 the Culdees, along with Abel, the archdeacon (representing the diocesan clergy), claimed the right of election when the chapter of canons regular made an election of Robert de Stuteville, dean of Dunkeld. Abel said that the office of archdeacon had existed before the canons regular were introduced and had continued in the church when the Culdees left for St Mary's. The pope provided Abel, acting so he said 'on the advice of those brethren [which must mean the Culdees]' but also 'out of the fulness of apostolic power' – a phrase which

---

[4] *ES*, i, 130–1.

[5] *ES*, ii, 205–6n; Haddan and Stubbs, *Councils*, 225–6.

[6] William Fraser, *Wemyss*, ii, 1–3.

[7] *Register of Moray*, p. 87.

[8] St Andrews University Library, MS DA 890 S 1.

did not concede the rights of any local claimants.[9] The voice of the Culdees was heard again in 1271 and 1297 and, finally, in 1332, on all which occasions they were expressly excluded from a part in the election.[10] These 'Culdees' must not be seen as Celtic nonconformists, for they had been transformed into a corporation of secular priests which provided a rival to the chapter of regulars, and none of those disputes at St Andrews provides clear evidence of any attempt to give weight to the rights of the people of the diocese, to whom the term *communitas* might in itself point.

At Whithorn, the headquarters of the diocese of Galloway, a chapter of Premonstratensian canons regular had been organised in the twelfth century, and their right to elect a bishop was challenged on a broader basis than was the right of the Augustinians at St Andrews. In Galloway the rights elsewhere belonging to the crown pertained to the local lord, and it may be assumed that the earlier bishops were in effect his nominees. In 1235, however, when the see fell vacant by the death of Bishop Walter, the lordship was in dispute and the king stepped in. Gilbert, a Cistercian monk, was 'elected by the clergy and people of the diocese' on 25 February and was approved by the king of Scots in a letter addressed to the archdeacon and clergy on 23 April. The prior and canons, however, 'in the interests of ecclesiastical liberty and their own right' had unanimously elected Odo, one of their own number, on 11 March. They claimed that *their* election had the approval of the king, and petitioned the archbishop of York to consecrate their nominee, but the king showed where his real preference lay by writing to the archbishop on 20 May requiring him not to consecrate Odo. The archbishop appointed a commission to try the dispute, and the decision was in favour of Gilbert, although appeal to the pope was subsequently made in vain on behalf of Odo.[11]

Henry's appointment to Galloway (1253–5), represents something of a tangle, and only a conjecture can be advanced. He was appointed in 1253 by the method followed in the case of Gilbert – formally election by the clergy and people with royal approval, actually nomination by the king. (Henry, who was abbot of Holyrood, does not look like a local candidate, though one cannot be certain.) The appointment so made was opposed by John Baliol as having been 'invalidly made, and to the prejudice of the ancient liberty of his subjects'. Baliol, who had married Devorguilla, heiress of Galloway, was in effect claiming the traditional right of the lords of Galloway to nominate the bishop; the Chronicle of Lanercost says plainly that the dispute was between the king and Baliol over the 'patronage' of the bishopric.[12] The local magnate – Baliol – was able to prevent the king's

---

[9] Theiner, clxii. There is a full account of these proceedings, and an examination of the whole position of the St Andrews 'Culdees', in G. W. S. Barrow, *The Kingdom of the Scots*, 216–32.

[10] Dowden, *Bishops*, 18, 21, 25.

[11] The documents are printed in *SA*, 347–8, and in *Register of Walter Gray* (Surtees Society), pp. 170 *et seq.*

[12] *ES*, ii, 575, 584.

nominee from taking possession, and even in ecclesiastical law Henry was in a weak position, since he had not been elected by the chapter; in 1254 the pope considered the see to be still vacant. The archbishop of York found a means to break the deadlock. On 7 February 1255 he consecrated Henry as bishop, and four days later, to supply any defects in his title, Henry was elected anew, this time by the prior and convent of Whithorn – meeting, however, *in the great church of York*, where they were safe from pressure by Baliol or other mighty layman. The new bishop was confirmed on 24 February following.[13] Henry's subsequent appearance as a witness to the foundation charter of Devorguilla's Sweetheart Abbey (1273) suggests that he ultimately came to terms with the Baliols.

Henry's case had in the long run led to the successful assertion of the propriety of capitular election, and on the occasion of the next appointment, that of Thomas in 1294, there is no trace of any attempt to put forward an alternative method (although there was a dispute between the archdeacon – representing the clergy of the diocese – and the chapter over the jurisdiction during the vacancy). The experience of the chapter had, however, already shown their liability to subjection to lay pressure, and this is evident again in 1294. There were three methods by which a chapter could elect – (1) *per viam Spiritus Sancti*, that is, unanimity; (2) *per viam compromissi* or the delegation of choice to commissioners; (3) *per viam scrutinii* or counting of heads to determine the will of the *major et sanior pars*. The second method was used in the case of Thomas, and it was open to critics to allege that there had been simony, since it was easier to bribe two or three delegates than a whole chapter. John Baliol, king of Scots, objected to the appointment, technically on the ground of suspected simony, but more probably his real reason was that Thomas was chaplain to Robert de Brus and that Bruce was supporting the bishop-elect in opposition to Baliol. Thomas successfully held his ground. The two bishops who came after Thomas – Simon and Michael – were also elected by the chapter.

In the see of The Isles, a chapter was provided by the Cistercian abbey of Furness, in Lancashire, which competed with the rights of the King of Man, the clergy and people. In 1247–8 the chapter elected Laurence, the archdeacon, who set out for Norway to present himself to the king of the Isles and the archbishop of Nidaros (Trondheim) to receive confirmation. A letter came from Man opposing him, and the king refused consent until Laurence should return with him to Man and be elected again in his presence by all the clergy and people.[14] In 1275, by which time Man had passed to Scottish sovereignty, there was a three-cornered dispute involving the convent of Furness, the clergy and people of the diocese and the king of Scots.[15]

In Argyll, where development of a chapter seems to have come late, election by the clergy of the diocese long continued. It is evident that in

[13] No explanation can be offered as to why Henry was styled 'elect' in December 1255.
[14] *ES*, ii, 547.
[15] *SA*, 381–2.

1249 it was difficult, if not impossible, to secure election by a chapter; in 1344 it was alleged that in this see the election pertained to the clergy of the city and diocese together with the chapter; and in 1354 the bishop of Argyll had to explain that there was no chapter seal, because the whole clergy made elections (*non habet commune sigillum, quia totus clerus eligit*). The allegation in 1300 that the dean and chapter had elected a bishop can hardly be taken at face value.[16]

There may well have been instances where an amicable compromise reconciled the rights of the chapter with those of competitors, and this would perhaps be easier where there was a chapter of secular canons. In Aberdeen in 1239 the chapter declared it acted according to custom (*juxta morem*) when it convened along with the clergy of the city of Aberdeen to choose a successor to Bishop Gilbert. The gathering assigned to four of the chapter and three of the city clergy the power to elect – *per viam compromissi* in other words. The king's consent was obtained to the election of Randulph, Abbot of Arbroath, whose appointment was approved by the dean, chapter and city clergy.[17] It was obviously relatively easier to consult the clergy of the city than the entire clergy of the diocese, and much easier to consult clergy than laity. How the last-named expressed an opinion remains obscure, but it rather looks as if the archdeacon was spokesman for them as well as for the clergy.

However, all the procedure which was gone through, and all the *formulae* in which the elections of bishops were expressed, were to some extent a façade. Papal policy in fostering chapters did not succeed in excluding royal influence throughout the twelfth and thirteenth centuries, so that, both before and after the establishment of chapters, the voice of the king was often dominant. Turgot and Eadmer may have been solemnly proclaimed to have been elected by the clergy and people, but everyone knew that they had been appointed by Alexander I and the high-sounding phrases did not obscure the fact. The king was on the whole successful in manipulating capitular election too, and was seldom successfully defied. There was the well-known dispute, beginning in 1178, when William the Lion, ignoring the chapter's election of John 'the Scot' to St Andrews, 'intruded' Hugh, his chaplain, and successfully maintained him in the face of papal authority. The strength of royal influence is indicated by the large number of appointments of royal chancellors, chaplains, chamberlains and clerks and by the fact that elections sometimes took place not in the diocese but at royal residences. Thus bishops of St Andrews were elected at Perth in 1189 and Scone in 1202, a bishop of Glasgow was elected at Perth in 1174 and a bishop of Ross was elected at Dunfermline in 1195.[18] In England Henry II, by the Constitutions of Clarendon (1164), formally insisted that elections should be made in the royal chapel, with consent of the king and his council and by such members of the chapters as he chose to summon to

[16] Theiner, cxxxix, ccclxviii, dlxiv; *APS*, i, 18.
[17] Dowden, *Bishops*, 103–4.
[18] Ibid., 10, 12, 210, 298.

court. The Scots kings did not go so far in form, but in practice the royal licence to elect and approval of the person elected (both almost certainly given in formal documents) were essential.[19] Giraldus Cambrensis wrote of William the Lion: 'He tarnished his whole glory, alas! by one blot, from his earliest days even unto old age. Through the entire breadth of his whole land he permitted no elections to take place at all in any of the cathedral churches, except in tyrannical fashion, at his own bidding; in this too closely following the grievous abuses of Norman tyranny throughout England.'[20] There was in effect, if not quite in form, royal patronage.

There were, however, dioceses where the patron was not the crown but a local magnate to whose family the see owed its origin and endowment – in Orkney the earls of Orkney, in Dunblane the earls of Strathearn and in Galloway the lords of Galloway. The 'patronage' of the bishopric of The Isles, which had at one time belonged to the kings of the The Isles and had apparently passed to the kings of Norway, was formally transferred by the latter to the king of Scots by the treaty of Perth in 1266.

If the intention had been that chapter election would be effective in excluding undue lay influence, it had clearly been frustrated, and further papal action, with the same general intention, took the shape of using the pope's undoubted power to confirm elections as a device to make his own appointments or 'provisions' after quashing elections. Disputed elections were opportunities to intervene, and not infrequently the person provided was one who had been elected, but the practice tended to habituate men to the idea of papal provision. Later, appointments to bishoprics, as to other valuable benefices, were expressly 'reserved' to the pope and this brought pope and king into conflict. This is all a familiar story.[21]

Despite the fact that provision by the pope became normal, the optimism of chapters was irrepressible, and right on until the sixteenth century it was not uncommon for a chapter to elect a candidate although neither pope nor king was likely to pay any heed. Any optimism that may have lingered on the part of the 'clergy and people', in fading recollection of their primitive rights, was even less realistic. The only faint echo of it was perhaps the fact that, right down to the reformation, the bulls issued by the pope when he made an episcopal appointment included one directed to the clergy and another to the people, of the diocese.[22]

[19] Dowden, *Medieval Church*, 48.

[20] *ES*, ii, 401.

[21] Dowden, *Bishops, passim*, citing the documents in Theiner; R. K. Hannay, *The Scottish Crown and the Papacy* (Historical Association of Scotland pamphlet).

[22] R. K. Hannay, 'Papal Bulls in the Hamilton Collection', *SHR*, xxii, 25–41.

4

The Rights of the Crown in Episcopal Vacancies

This article appeared in the William Croft Dickinson Memorial
Number of the *Scottish Historical Review* (xlv, pt. 1) and carried this
note: 'Several years ago, after the publication of E. W. M. Balfour-
Melville's article on "John de Cheam, Bishop of Glasgow" (*SHR*,
xxvii, 176–86), Professor Dickinson asked me to put together my
notes on crown rights *sede vacante* for his information, and he placed
at my disposal such relevant notes as he himself had made. The
purpose was simply our own enlightenment and the clarifying of
our own ideas, and no opportunity or incentive ever arose to cause
me to make a fuller study of the subject, though I have made casual
additions from time to time. It now seems appropriate that the notes
should be published'.

A long chapter in Scottish ecclesiastical history was closed on 24 January
1449/50, when James II, in presence of the three estates, defined the
methods by which disposition should in future be made of the property and
rights pertaining to a bishopric during the interval between the decease of
one bishop and the appointment of his successor. The king's declaration
dealt with the subject under four heads. First to be mentioned were the
movables of deceased bishops, specified as 'all and sundry things, jewels,
gems, goblets, cups, utensils, spoons, vessels of gold, silver or gilt, standing
crops, harvested crops, herds, horses, oxen, cows and other animals, and all
other movable goods whatsoever'. James renounced any right to these
movables and conceded that bishops should have full power to dispose of
them by testament. Secondly it was admitted that the fruits, rents, revenues
and offerings of the churches and benefices pertaining to the *mensa* of the
bishop and all the income belonging to the spirituality should, during the
vacancy, be uplifted by the vicar-general, who was to account for the same
to the successor in the see. Thirdly the temporality of the bishops – ferms of
ecclesiastical lands, whether in victual or money, the issues of courts and the
profits of temporal jurisdiction – should be at the royal disposal. And
fourthly the patronage of benefices in the full gift of the bishop was also
reserved to the crown.[1]

[1] *APS*, ii, 37–8, 61–2; *RMS*, ii, 307.

The history lying behind this document is a history which can be traced, though not indeed in Scotland, as far back as the fourth century, for ever since then church councils had been exercised about the disposal of the property of deceased bishops and had endeavoured to make a distinction between the personal property of a bishop and the property of his see.[2] Certain clear rules are embodied in the twelfth-century *Decretum*: on the death of a bishop neither his own goods nor the goods of his church were to be seized by the clergy or even by the metropolitan, but were to remain in the custody of the clergy of his church until the appointment of his successor; a bishop might make bequest to his heirs of his own goods (*de rebus propriis vel acquisitis*), while the revenues of the see (*sive de agris sive de fructibus sive de oblationibus*) must be preserved for the church.[3]

Such principles could be enunciated by churchmen, but the difficulty of putting them into practice arose from royal claims, almost invariably to temporality, often to other portions of the episcopal property and rights as well. No doubt the kings justified themselves by the parallel of their rights of wardship in lay fiefs, but their claims were sometimes advanced ostensibly on the higher ground that they were the guardians of church property against spoliation – spoliation, that is, by others than themselves. We know little, if anything, about the position in Scotland before the thirteenth century, but the development in England can be traced back to the Conquest, and even to practice in Normandy before the Conquest.[4] Rufus evidently pressed his claims to the utmost, and Henry I's charter of liberties included a renunciation which appears to comprehend the property of the see, as distinct from the personal property of the bishop: 'Sanctam dei ecclesiam ... liberam facio, ita quod nec vendam nec ad firmam ponam, nec mortuo archiepiscopo sive episcopo sive abbate aliquid accipiam de dominio ecclesie vel de hominibus ejus donec successor in eam ingrediatur.'[5] Stephen's second charter sweepingly surrendered the royal claim to a bishop's personal chattels as well, for it explicitly allowed the right of testament to bishops and other ecclesiastics and ordained that in cases of intestacy the bishop's goods were to be distributed, by advice of the church, for the good of his soul; moreover during vacancies in episcopal sees all the possessions thereof (*earum possessiones omnes*) were to be in the hands of worthy men until the appointment of a new pastor.[6] With a strong king on the throne it was very different: Henry II's Constitutions of Clarendon laid down that the revenues (*redditus et exitus*) of vacant bishoprics and abbeys should belong to the king,[7] and in practice this king seized the movables of deceased bishops as well as the temporalities of their sees. So far as movables were concerned, the clerical riposte to the royal

[2] Edward H. Landon, op. cit., i, 24, 35, 147; ii, 250.
[3] Dec. II, ca. xii, quaest. i, cap. xix–xxi and quaest. ii, cap. xliii, xlviii.
[4] Margaret Howell, *Regalian Right in Medieval England* (London, 1962).
[5] W. Stubbs, *Select Charters*, 9th edn. (Oxford, 1948), 117.
[6] Ibid., 144.
[7] Ibid., 166.

claims took the form of papal licences to bishops and other churchmen to make testaments in their lifetimes. Such dispensations were very frequently granted in the thirteenth and fourteenth centuries, as the pages of the *Calendar of Papal Registers* abundantly show.[8] It was because the making of a will by papal licence seemed to offer some protection against spoliation that St Hugh of Lincoln consented to make a will, although he did not approve of a custom whereby bishops might dispose of church goods.[9] It appears that in the course of the thirteenth century the English kings conceded the right of testament and gave up their claim to movables, although they continued to exercise their rights over temporality and patronage.

The course of events in England would undoubtedly be familiar to Scottish churchmen, and it may have been its bearing on crown rights in vacancies which caused Henry I's charter to be engrossed in the Register of Glasgow,[10] though that charter had no relevance to the peculiarly controversial question of movables. Evidence of the contest in Scotland over bishops' movables does not begin until the middle of the thirteenth century, but it is clear that the royal appropriation of such movables continued much longer in Scotland than in England. In 1254 Bishop Abel of St Andrews, who had been a papal nominee, received from the pope a licence to make such disposition of his goods in his last will as should seem best to him for the good of his soul and of his church.[11] Whether this afforded any protection to Abel's goods when he died does not appear, but in view of later events it seems unlikely. The next bishop, Gamelin, though a royal nominee, had to go into exile in 1256 because of differences with the king's councillors, and during his absence on the continent royal officers 'pillaged the goods of the bishopric and consumed it at their pleasure'.[12] There is every reason to believe that seizure of movables was, in fact, the normal practice on a bishop's death. The chronicle of Lanercost records the gossip that in 1275 the bishop of Dunkeld was poisoned so that the king could have his movables, 'because in that kingdom the movables of deceased bishops fall to the king'.[13] We learn, too, that in the year 1274–5 the king 'confiscavit et cepit omnia bona episcopatus' during a vacancy in Ross.[14] If it happened that the patron of a bishopric was not the king but a local magnate, the regalian rights might be exercised by that magnate: thus the earls of Strathearn are said to have appropriated the personal property of deceased bishops of Dunblane,[15] and it seems very likely that the lords of

---

[8] E.g., *CPR*, i, 458, 461, 463, 470, 489, 507, 534–5, 566; ii, 190, 279, 319, 368, 404, 410–11, 486; iii, 69, 168, 225, 252.

[9] There is a sketch of the development in England in F. Pollock and F. W. Maitland, *History of English Law*, 2nd edn. (Cambridge, 1898), i, 518–20.

[10] *Glasgow Reg.*, ii, 591.

[11] *CPR*, i, 298.

[12] *ES*, ii, 586.

[13] *Chron. Lanercost*, 97. The bishop actually died in 1272.

[14] *SHS Misc.*, vi, 49.

[15] Theiner, 157; *CPR*, i, 540.

Galloway would take similar action in their bishopric. Evidence multiplies from about 1290 onwards. Edward I, following what had now become English practice, resigned goods which had come into his hands 'according to Scottish custom' after the death of the bishop of Caithness, and ordered their use for the benefit of the bishop's soul; he also gave special permission to the bishop of Glasgow to make a testament,[16] and in 1296 he conceded to the Scottish bishops generally the right of making testaments disponing their movables, with the same liberty 'as the bishops of the realm of England have'.[17] On the other hand, the guardians of Scotland, where their writ ran, took possession of the *bona et jura* of Moray during a vacancy in that see in 1298.[18] Once the exchequer rolls become available we have details of the *bona* which the king was seizing. During the vacancy at St Andrews following the death of Bishop Lamberton a special account was rendered in the exchequer showing what the king drew from the temporalities of the see;[19] but elsewhere in the accounts we find that the king was drawing wine *de bonis episcopi inventis apud S. Andream*, corn and malt *de blado episcopi S. Andree* and marts and sheep *de bonis episcopi* or *de instauro episcopi S. Andree*.[20] To judge from the terms of the renunciation of 1450 cited at the beginning of this article, wine, corn and cattle may all have been among the bishop's personal movables. In a like way there is a reference in 1329, during a vacancy in the Isles, to *bonis et redditibus* pertaining to the bishop, and the phrase may well cover movables as well as the revenues of the temporality.[21] The normality of the exercise of royal rights in this period is supported by a style in the Ayr MS. whereby the king conceded to the kinsmen of a certain bishop the control, after the bishop's death, of some lands given to him by the king, with the goods thereon.[22]

The full recognition of crown rights was explicit when in 1334 Edward Balliol made over the southern counties to Edward III, for the cession included 'wards and other profits whatsoever which could pertain to us, our heirs and successors, by reason of the vacancies of the bishoprics of the kingdom of Scotland, of the lands, tenements, goods and chattels within the counties and places foresaid pertaining to the same bishoprics'.[23] In 1337 papal nuncios to France and England were to investigate certain 'grievances and oppressions', including 'the receipt and diversion of the property of prelates and churches by the king's officers and the dilapidation of sees and other benefices during vacancy',[24] and there can be no doubt that such an 'oppression' required investigation in Scotland as well. A papal bull of 1372, referring to Scotland, said that under David II 'the movable goods

[16] *Rotuli Scotiae*, i, 6, 7, 10.
[17] *Foedera*, i, 848.
[18] Theiner, 167.
[19] *ER*, i, 109–10.
[20] Ibid., 137–9, 145–8, 224–5.
[21] Ibid., 151.
[22] *Register of Brieves* (Stair Soc.), 51–2.
[23] *Foedera*, ii, 888.
[24] *CPR*, ii, 538.

whatsoever of the bishops of the foresaid kingdom were at the time of their death so applied to royal uses that the bishops were entirely deprived of the privilege of disposing of their goods by testament',[25] and another papal declaration in 1375 was to the effect that the Scottish king's officers and others presumed to seize the movable goods of deceased bishops and appropriate them to the royal treasury or to other uses.[26] In this period there is little evidence of specific instances of the appropriation of movables, but we do find Robert III granting away movables which had fallen to him *jure regio* through the death of Walter, bishop of St Andrews, including a silver cross, an arras, a linen cloth and a large breviary; they were, indeed, granted to the bishop of Aberdeen, apparently for his church rather than for himself personally, but even so the king's right of disposal was being exercised.[27]

Crown action did not, however, go unchallenged. In 1257 the pope excommunicated the 'consumers and invaders' of the bishopric of St Andrews who had made free with its goods during Gamelin's absence,[28] and in 1259 he forbade the king or others to seize 'the movable goods of the foresaid church' in the event of the bishop's death.[29] This was only a specific prohibition, not a general one, though it might have been held to be a denial that the king had any right, either in custom or law, to episcopal property. Papal policy may possibly have vacillated in the thirteenth century, for the inventory of the Scottish records drawn up in 1282 mentions, in addition to the bull of 1259, 'quedam bulla que innuit a contrario sensu quod rex possit habere bona mobilia episcopatuum post mortem episcoporum si hoc habeat a consuetudine'.[30] But there is no question that papal policy was in the main resolutely opposed to spoliation. Scottish bishops, like bishops elsewhere, received licences to bequeath their goods by testament,[31] and James Bennet, bishop of St Andrews from 1328 to 1332, made a testament in which he bequeathed to the pope 2000 florins of gold and a gold ring; most of the bequest reached the pope during the bishop's lifetime, but full discharge was granted to the executors after the bishop's death.[32]

It appears that, in addition to licensing bishops to make testaments, the papacy in the fourteenth century adopted new tactics to counter royal spoliation, by reserving to the Roman church the property of deceased prelates. In 1373 and 1374 two papal mandates were issued on the basis of this reservation. In one of them the archdeacon of St Andrews, as papal nuncio and collector, was instructed to cause to be observed the ordinance

[25] Theiner, 346.
[26] Ibid., 353; *CPR*, iv, 206.
[27] *Aberdeen Reg.*, i, 208.
[28] Theiner, 77; *ES*, ii, 589.
[29] Theiner, 82.
[30] *APS*, i, 108.
[31] E.g., Theiner, 149, 157.
[32] Ibid., 253; *CPR*, ii, 508.

of the present pope in respect of the reservation to the Roman church of the property of deceased prelates and other ecclesiastics. Debts were to be paid, and also the cost of a decent funeral. The reservation was not to extend to books, chalices, crosses, vestments and similar articles belonging to the church of the deceased.[33] In the second mandate, instructions were given to execute the papal reservation of the movables and personal property of the bishops of the Isles and Orkney (not at that time in the Scottish province), the rents and rights of archiepiscopal, episcopal and abbatial *mense* during vacancies and the fruits and rents of all benefices held by archbishops, bishops and abbots at the time of their deaths.[34]

Under papal pressure the kings were brought to issue renunciations. David II formally renounced the right to *bona quecunque mobilia*, papal bulls ratified his renunciation,[35] and Robert II confirmed it[36]; but, as the pope complained in 1375[37] and as the evidence already cited shows, the royal undertakings were not carried out. In the later fourteenth century and the early fifteenth evidence is lacking, but it is reasonable to assume that the seizure of movables continued. At any rate the final renunciation in 1450 – which had been anticipated in 1445 by the formal transuming of the bull of 1375[38] – relates that 'on pretext of a custom confirmed, so it is alleged, by its observance over a very long period' royal officers had applied the movables of deceased bishops to the uses of the royal treasury; it recalls that Kings David and Robert had decreed the abolition of the custom as a hateful abuse; and it gives among the reasons for following their example the spiritual dangers which would be incurred by those defying the apostolic mandates against the 'alleged custom'.

The second head under which the renunciation of 1450 dealt with episcopal property was that of the spirituality – that is, in the main, the teinds of churches annexed to the *mensa* of the bishop, but also probably the episcopal residence and the 'yards' surrounding it (which, like the manse and glebe of a parochial benefice, did not form part of temporality). While the evidence is far from ample, it would appear that in earlier times the comprehensive royal claims during vacancies certainly included the spirituality. There is specific evidence that on the death of the bishop of Ross in 1274 the king seized not only the other *bona* of the see, but also the teinds of the mensal churches of Tarbat and Nigg.[39] And after a vacancy in Galloway in 1294 John Balliol was petitioned to hand over to the official of the diocese the fruits of two churches appropriated to the episcopal *mensa* – Girthon and Inch – which had been uplifted by the crown.[40] Therefore,

---

[33] *CPR*, iv, 108.
[34] Ibid., iv, 152.
[35] Theiner, 353; *RMS*, i, 372; *CPR*, iv, 167.
[36] Theiner, 346.
[37] Ibid., 353.
[38] *Brechin Reg.*, i, 98 ff.
[39] *SHS Misc.*, vi, 49.
[40] *Register of John le Romeyn* (Surtees Soc.), ii, 125.

when in 1322 Robert I made a gift to the priory of Whithorn of the tenths not only of the royal pleas and of wards, reliefs and other casualties, but also of 'the churches of the bishopric pertaining to us by reason of the vacancy of the see', the churches referred to were almost certainly the mensal churches of the bishopric of Galloway.[41] It appears, too, that in 1362, during a vacancy in the see of Moray, the crown uplifted money from the bishop's church of Keith.[42] The renunciation of 1450 provided that the spirituality should, during a vacancy, be administered by the vicar-general – normally the dean – for the benefit of the succeeding bishop. This evidently remained the law: James IV acknowledged that the dean and chapter of Aberdeen had drawn the second teinds of the bishopric during vacancies 'passit memor of mane';[43] and during the vacancy at Dunkeld in 1515, after the earl of Atholl had seized the palace and the episcopal property in anticipation of his own brother's appointment to the see, the dean 'following the common law' claimed that he had the right to conserve the fruits 'for the future bishop'.[44] The law, however, was not always observed – as indeed the Dunkeld case shows – and crown rights were from time to time extended. In 1515 the lords of council allowed the governor, Albany, to uplift the spirituality as well as the temporality of vacant bishoprics.[45] It appears that papal consent was given to the exercise by Albany of exceptional powers over the fruits of 'prelacies' (that is, abbeys and bishoprics) during vacancies, and in 1530 the pope was asked to renew such privileges.[46]

Our third heading, following the sequence of James II's renunciation, is that of the temporality. The disposal of this part of the episcopal property has indeed a long history, but it is not a history of controversy, for the crown's right to uplift temporality was never seriously challenged. The pope explicitly allowed it in 1260,[47] this right was reserved in the renunciations by David II mentioned above, and perhaps the only trace of an infringement of the royal right was the action of John XXII in appointing his nominee to Glasgow in 1323 to have charge of the temporality as well as the spirituality.[48] Normally, of course, the temporality remained with the crown until the new bishop had been consecrated and had taken his oath of fealty, whereupon the temporality was restored to him by a royal gift, latterly under the privy seal.[49] Frequently, however, not least in the generation before the Reformation, consecration was not a necessary preliminary to investiture with the

[41] *RMS*, i, p. 437 n. 21.
[42] *ER*, ii, 165.
[43] *Aberdeen Reg.*, i, 330.
[44] *Rentale Dunkeldense*, 331.
[45] *Public Affairs*, 59.
[46] *James V Letters*, 175.
[47] *Statuta*, lxxiv n.; Theiner, 86–7.
[48] *Statuta*, lxxiv–lxxv n.; Theiner, 226.
[49] *Cal. Docs. Scot.*, ii, 1752; *RSS*, i, 2807, 3286, ii, 2772, 3058, iii, intro p. xl. Several references occur in Dowden, *Bishops*.

temporality, and the crown assumed the power of commanding that its nominees should be put into possession of temporality and spirituality alike.[50]

The fourth and last clause of James II's renunciation reserves to the crown the right to present *sede vacante* to benefices in the patronage of a bishop. The term used in the document is 'collationes', and this has misled some historians[51] into believing that all benefices in the bishop's 'collation' were at issue; but in normal Scottish usage (unlike English) 'collatio' means the act whereby a bishop proceeds to the admission of a presentee of a patron other than himself, so that a bishop gave 'collation' to nearly every benefice in his diocese. The benefices to which the crown should have been entitled were only those of which the bishop himself was the patron, those which were in his full gift. The right of the crown to present to such benefices *sede vacante* was on the whole maintained,[52] though if kings attempted to extend their right to benefices in the patronage of the chapter there were immediate protests.[53] The pope, however, made a serious bid against the royal claims, as part of the general policy of reservation and disregard of the rights of patrons. John XXII in 1323 bestowed a vacant prebend of Glasgow (in the bishop's gift) on his own nominee, and the king had to protest for his own right, as existing beyond the memory of man.[54] In 1337 one of the 'grievances and oppressions' which papal nuncios to France and England were required to expose was 'the king's insistence on his right to appoint to benefices in a diocese during the voidance of the see'[55] (which might suggest that something wider than benefices in the bishop's full gift were in question); and in 1440 the pope spoke of the crown's claim in this particular as a 'pretended custom'.[56] The crown was vigorous in defence of its rights: David II reserved this point when he renounced his claim to episcopal movables, and, as we have seen, it was reserved again by James II in 1450. Not only so, but the provincial council of the Scottish church in 1457 and in 1459 ratified the right as an 'ancient' one and declared that it should stand even against papal reservation.[57] As the Scottish protest against reservation grew stronger, this particular issue figured in parliamentary affirmations of native rights in 1462, 1481, 1482 and 1485,[58] and in 1488 the purchasing at Rome of any benefice pertaining to the king through his right of presentation *sede vacante* was brought under the pains of barratry or unlawful dealings at Rome.[59] It has been shown

[50] G. Donaldson, *The Scottish Reformation*, 38 and n.

[51] Dowden, *Medieval Church*, 199; A. I. Dunlop, *James Kennedy*, 113.

[52] The evidence for later times is very full in *RSS*; for early examples, see *Cal. Docs. Scot.*, ii, no. 927 and pp. 262–3.

[53] *Aberdeen Reg.*, i, 29–30, 74–5.

[54] *Glasgow Reg.*, i, 230, 252; *Statuta*, lxxvi.

[55] *CPR*, ii, 538.

[56] Ibid., ix, 146.

[57] *Statuta*, 79–80.

[58] *APS*, ii, 83–4, 133, 141, 172.

[59] Ibid., 209–10.

that, whatever the strict law on the extent of crown rights in this particular, the crown not infrequently made presentations to dignities, prebends and even parochial benefices which were in the patronage of ecclesiastical institutions (though not, apparently, to benefices in lay patronage).[60]

By 1450, when James II defined the respective rights of the bishops and the crown, the questions of temporality and spirituality had long been settled, but patronage certainly, and movables probably, were still controversial. The king's declaration before the estates had the formal character of an act of redress, made on the supplication of the bishops and at the intercession of the queen. But, although his renunciation of his claim to movables was rightly regarded as a concession to the bishops,[61] there may in truth have been something of a bargain whereby the crown, in surrendering its claim to movables, gained the support of the bishops in its contest with the papacy over its rights of patronage.

[60] Ian B. Cowan, 'Patronage, provision and reservation: pre-reformation appointments to Scottish benefices', in *The Renaissance and Reformation in Scotland* (ed. Ian B. Cowan and Duncan Shaw), 89–92.

[61] It is engrossed in the *Registers* of Glasgow (ii, 370), Brechin (i, 177) and Aberdeen (i, 254).

5

The Church Courts

After this article was published in the Stair Society's *Introduction to Scottish Legal History* (1958) our knowledge of the medieval courts was greatly extended by the researches of Dr Simon Ollivant, whose findings were published by the Stair Society in 1982 as *The Court of the Official in pre-Reformation Scotland*. In revising my article for publication here I have had the benefit of the advice of Dr Ollivant, who made a number of suggestions which have added authority to my account of the pre-Reformation courts.

Before the Reformation

1. *The Ecclesiastical Jurisdiction*. The church's jurisdiction arose primarily from its responsibility for faith and morals. Thus, as matrimony was at once a sacrament and a relationship involving questions of ecclesiastical discipline, the church had competence in all causes concerning marriage and legitimacy, including actions for nullity and questions of dowry. An allied department of ecclesiastical jurisdiction related to moveable succession – the confirmation of testaments and the administration of intestate moveables; heritable property, of course, went to the civil courts. Again, since the observance of an oath concerned the wellbeing of a man's soul, any promise or contract fortified by oath could be brought to an ecclesiastical court for enforcement by excommunication. Yet another branch of the church's jurisdiction derived from the ecclesiastical character of certain parties and property. A clerk or 'spiritual man' might – and often did – appear as a pursuer in a secular court; but as a defender he commonly claimed successfully that the suit should be heard before an ecclesiastical tribunal. Likewise, cases involving benefices and their revenues went normally to a church court. The church's moral responsibility gave it cognisance of cases of slander; it also took care of widows and orphans; and it had the oversight of notaries acting by apostolic authority.

While civil courts were usually checked if they attempted to hear spiritual causes, the church courts on their side tended to draw to themselves causes properly civil, partly because the church courts were staffed with able professional lawyers when the civil courts were not, and partly because the wide range of the ecclesiastical jurisdiction offered ample opportunity for finding reasons or pretexts for bringing actions within its scope. Not least in importance was the development of competence in actions for failure to fulfil obligations; in such cases the sentence of an ecclesiastical court was followed by letters monitorial, disobedience to which incurred excommunication – a process, familiarly known as 'cursing', which provided a 'diligence' for the enforcement of contracts when the civil courts had not yet developed their own procedure of letters of horning for that end. From very early times the civil authority had lent its support to the decisions of the ecclesiastical courts. Later we find parliament in 1449 (*APS*, ii, 35, c. 1), and 1525 (*APS*, ii, 297, c. 6), expressly ordaining that letters should issue from the secular courts to fortify sentences of excommunication; and when, just before the Reformation, ecclesiastical prestige declined and the efficacy of 'cursing' markedly decreased, the need for some such secular procedure seems to have been increasingly felt (*APS*, ii, 342, 357, 482, 485–6, cc. 3, 3, 1, 9, 10).

2. *Officials and Commissaries.* While a vast amount of litigation was conducted before judges delegate appointed *ad hoc* by the pope (see § 5 *infra*) the normal ecclesiastical jurisdiction was vested in the bishop of each diocese, whose judicial functions were in practice mostly delegated to 'officials' and 'commissaries'. The earliest references to officials occur in certain dioceses shortly before 1200. In some dioceses – doubtless because of pressure of business – a commissary general, appointed by either the bishop or the official, might exist alongside the official, the two apparently acting concurrently or the commissary acting as the official's deputy. The three dioceses which were divided into two archdeaconries – St Andrews, Glasgow and Orkney – were divided also into two officialates and elsewhere there were subordinate officialates. The officialate, whether of the whole, or part, of a diocese, might in turn be subdivided, by the appointment of commissaries for smaller areas. In the large diocese of Glasgow there was evidently a well-developed system of subordinate commissariots, though possibly without rigid boundaries and apparently without rigid nomenclature. Again, in Galloway, the commissary for the eastern part of the diocese seems to have taken his style indifferently from Kirkcudbright, Glenken or Desines, while his colleague in the west was known as 'of Wigtown' or 'of Farines and Rhinns'. The diocese of Moray had a commissary at Inverness as well as one at Elgin (e.g., *RMS*, iii, 1469), while in Caithness, where the official and the commissary general would have their seat at Dornoch, there was a commissary substitute with an 'office' in St Peter's Church at Thurso (Mey Papers [Reg. Ho.], nos. 66–8). Besides commissaries in important centres within a diocese, such as Inverness, Thurso or Stirling, there were also commissaries with 'peculiar' jurisdictions at places like Currie and Lesmahagow. The whole picture is less simple than has often been supposed, and the number of judicatures stemming from the bishops' judicial functions was certainly little, if at all,

less than that of the post-Reformation commissariots. Names of the officials and commissaries known to record can be found in D. E. R. Watt, *Fasti Ecclesiae Scoticanae Medii Aevi* (SRS).

Besides the purely judicial delegation by the bishop to officials and commissaries, there was delegation of the bishop's general supervisory functions to one or more archdeacons and, at a lower level, to rural deans, and this carried with it certain judicial duties. The archdeacon was concerned mainly with breaches of discipline by clergy and laity; he held a court to deal with delinquents, and sometimes committed his judicial functions to his own 'official'. The rural dean had a competence in offences against morality not unlike that of the kirk sessions of later times.

REFERENCES: Muirhead, *The Old Minute Book of the Faculty of Procurators in Glasgow*, 11–16; Habakkuk Bisset, *Rolment of Courtis* (STS), ii, 52–3.

3. *The Bishop: Special Commissions.* By appointing officials or commissaries the bishop did not divest himself of his judicial powers, or preclude himself from exercising them either in person or by special (as distinct from general) deputy. The bishops are frequently to be found issuing *ad hoc* commissions for the hearing or termination of particular suits and as late as 1552 it was proposed that matrimonial causes should be reserved to the personal consideration of the bishop.

REFERENCES: *St. A. Formulare, passim*; Patrick, *Statutes*, 138.

4. *Communication between Dioceses.* For the completion of legal proceedings it was often necessary to obtain the evidence of witnesses resident in another diocese, to cite a party resident there, or to require the execution in a second diocese of a sentence passed in the first. Formal communication between dioceses for these purposes was by means of the supplication *vicissitudinis causa*, which takes its name from the stereotyped clause offering reciprocal action when required. The supplication might go in the name of the bishop or in that of his commissary or official. The procedure was not restricted to one province of the church, but was interprovincial or 'international'.

REFERENCES: *St. A. Formulare*, Nos. 219 ff.; 'Justice across frontiers', pp. 53–9 *infra*.

5. *Appeals.* There was not in general any appeal to a judge from a delegate whose jurisdiction was coextensive with his own, as from an official principal or commissary general to the bishop. Where there were two officials, the official principal – e.g., of St Andrews – could hear appeals from the official *foraneus* – i.e., of Lothian. Likewise, appeal lay from subordinate, local commissaries, to the officials. During the brief existence of archbishoprics in Scotland (from 1472 at St Andrews and 1492 at Glasgow), the archbishop or his official principal enjoyed an appellate jurisdiction from any diocesan judge – bishop, official principal or commissary general.

Appeals from bishops (before 1472) and from archbishops (after 1472) could go outwith Scotland for hearing at Rome, but there were repeated complaints about the expensive and protracted nature of this proceeding, and only research in the Roman archives will show how many appeals did go to Rome. Dr Ollivant's opinion is that the ordinary litigant who gave notice of appeal to Rome may really have sought nothing more than delay. However, apart from appeals, application to Rome could bring about the entrusting of a case, in the first instance, to judges delegate, an *ad hoc* tribunal usually of three named persons, two of whom were empowered to act if necessary. The work of such judges had been of major importance in earlier centuries, and they are still found not infrequently in the sixteenth.

The supreme organ of the church in Scotland, more especially before there were archbishops, was the General Council or Provincial Synod; it was not a judicial body, but its president, the 'Conservator', was during the Papal Schism empowered to hear appeals which would otherwise have gone to the Pope. The provincial synod and the diocesan synods were legislative bodies, which might from time to time make regulations affecting the work of the courts; but the law administered in the courts was of course the body of canon law applicable generally throughout western Europe.

REFERENCES: As in Stair Society, i, ch. 11, and also Cooper, *Select Cases*; Muirhead, op. cit.; *Statuta*; Patrick, *Statutes*.

6. *The Courts at Work.* Two sixteenth-century volumes of sentences by officials – one of St Andrews, the other of Lothian – are preserved in the Register House. The only printed selection of entries from them, the *Liber Officialis Sanctiandree* (Abbotsford Club), is misleading in that it concentrates on matrimonial cases. A fairer indication of the scope of the courts may be offered by an analysis of four batches, each of a hundred consecutive cases, taken from the beginning and the end of each of the MS. volumes. While the proportion of cases of each type varies somewhat from one batch to another, a clear general picture does emerge. In the court of the official principal, 25 per cent to 33 per cent of the cases were appeals, mainly from the official of Lothian, but also from the bishops, officials and commissaries general of the suffragan sees of the province of St Andrews. Excluding appeals, the percentages of classified cases are approximately as follows. Executry accounts for the largest proportion of the business – 27 per cent to 41 per cent of the cases; usually the sentence is for a creditor or a legatee against an executor. Matrimonial suits in the widest sense, including 'divorce' or nullity on the grounds of the numerous impediments then recognised (not only consanguinity and affinity but also the spiritual relationship of sponsors at baptism and confirmation), separation *a mensa et thoro*, bigamy, adherence and bastardy, amount to only 4 per cent to 8 per cent. Cases of defamation fluctuate from none to 8 per cent. Sentences for payment of ecclesiastical dues (including teinds and mortuaries) are from 5

per cent to 21 per cent. Up to 6 per cent of the cases deal with disputes over the possession of benefices or revenues. Finally, from 24 per cent to 27 per cent of the sentences are for the rendering of money or goods by one party to another or for the fulfilment of contracts. This last category of cases had arisen from obligations fortified by oath, from agreements in which the jurisdiction of an ecclesiastical court had been expressly accepted, from contracts 'actit' in the books of the officials and from deeds recorded or registered therein. Dr Ollivant has worked out percentages for the Lothian and St Andrews courts separately and they are not strikingly different in their proportions from what is shown by the samples: appeals (in St Andrews only) 28 per cent; executry, 21 per cent and 29 per cent; matrimonial, 6 per cent and 14 per cent; defamation, 7 per cent and 1 per cent; ecclesiastical dues, 11 per cent and 26 per cent; benefices (including the office of parish clerk), less than 1 per cent and 4 per cent; rendering of money, contracts, etc., 27 per cent and 15 per cent.

In addition to the Books of Sentences there are Act Books, for Dunblane, Lothian, Stirling and the Chapel Royal, for various periods in the sixteenth century, all described in Dr Ollivant's work (pp. 8–13). He observes that the Act Book for the court of the official of Lothian shows that this court dealt with between 15 and 50 items a day, as opposed to passing perhaps four or five sentences a month, and concludes: 'Although, of course, a single case resulting in a single sentence might involve a dozen individual Act Book appearances, there was obviously a great deal of business that never resulted in, or was intended to result in, a sentence. The proportion of different categories of business in the Act Book is roughly equivalent to the proportions revealed by the sentences, except in the case of small contract and debt business, which seems to have accounted for about 40% of the court's daily transactions' (private letter 11 December 1983).

REFERENCE: Stair Society, i, ch. 15. More information comes from papers in private muniments, some printed in William Fraser's books and some among the Reg. Ho. Charters (e.g., 76, 112–13).

7. *Confirmation of Testaments.* Already in the thirteenth century testaments had to be given up to the ordinary (i.e., the bishop), who also had power to administer in cases of intestacy. In 1420 it was declared that 'from so far back that there is no memory of man to the contrary, bishops and those holding the jurisdiction of an ordinary have been wont to confirm the testaments of those who die testate in their respective sees and to appoint executors to those who die intestate'. This jurisdiction was jealously safeguarded, partly because the 'quots' paid for confirmation were a useful source of revenue, and parish priests were under obligation to report in writing the names of persons who died in their parishes each year. Minor testaments, up to the value of £40, could be confirmed by rural deans. Our earliest extant records of testaments (now preserved in the

Register House) begin before the Reformation; they were kept by the bishops' officers and record confirmation by the bishops.

REFERENCES: Patrick, *Statutes*, 17, 26, 47, 74–5, 81, 115, 177, 265, 280; *St. A. Formulare*, Nos. 53, 68–72, 166, 177, 259, 422.

The Reformation

8. *The Bishops*. The Reformation brought temporary confusion to the ecclesiastical courts. An Act of Parliament of August 1560 (*APS*, ii, 534, c. 2), which abrogated papal authority in Scotland, laid down that 'no bishop nor other prelate of this realm use any jurisdiction in time to come by the said bishop of Rome's authority'. Quite apart from the constitutional question of the validity of this legislation, it was not at all clear whether the terms of the statute denuded the bishops of their consistorial jurisdiction. In practice, they continued to exercise it, at least intermittently. Archbishop Hamilton of St Andrews issued dispensations for marriage in November 1561 (Morton Papers [Reg. Ho.]), in 1566 (*Lag Charters* [SRS] app. 23) and – in better-known circumstances, for the parties were the Earl of Bothwell and Lady Jane Gordon – in February 1565/6 (Fraser, *Sutherland*, iii, 131–2); in May 1563 his commissioners pronounced a sentence of divorce (Fraser, *Montgomeries*, ii, 163–81); and in April 1564 we find him issuing a monition following on a provision to a parsonage (Fraser, *Haddington*, ii, 265–6). Bishops like Alexander Gordon of Galloway and Adam Bothwell of Orkney, who had accepted the Reformation, and carried on their administrative duties within the reformed church, were possibly in a stronger legal position, for it was plain that they were not acting in virtue of papal authority; at any rate, in 1563 the General Assembly heard appeals from the former's failure to do justice in a wife's suit of adherence and from the latter's sentence in a divorce case (*BUK*, i, 31, 35). Queen Mary thought fit, on 23 December 1566, formally to 'restore' Archbishop Hamilton's consistorial jurisdiction; protestants were indignant, but it is really not at all clear that the judicial powers of the bishops had ever wholly lapsed.

REFERENCE: *Statuta*, clxxiv and clxxviii, notes.

9. *The Reformed Church*. The reformers had their candidates for the consistorial jurisdiction, to some extent in the congregational kirk session, but more especially in the superintendent, who with the session of a chief town of his diocese constituted a regional court. The kirk session of St Andrews began to act in divorce suits in February 1559/60, and, on 18 August following, Archbishop Hamilton remarked to his brother of Glasgow, 'The eldaris callit of every town takis all the causis of our ecclesiasticall jurisdiction and intromettis with our office' (Keith, ii, 5). Presently we find the Lords of Council themselves requesting the kirk session of St Andrews to give sentence of divorce, and expressly granting authority to the superintendent of Lothian, in conjunction with the kirk

session of Haddington, Linlithgow or Stirling, to decide on divorce suits 'quhill the next parliament, that further order be taken' (Warrender Papers [Reg. Ho.], vol. A, fol. 98). There is ample evidence in the next two or three years of a strong tendency for the superintendent's consistory to inherit the jurisdiction of the old episcopal courts and to imitate their procedure and terminology. It is plainly an over-simplification to suggest that the crown at once dismissed the claims of the reformed church to step into the place of the medieval courts. There are two striking illustrations of the conviction of the reformed church that its courts were the heirs of the pre-Reformation courts: the court of the superintendent of Fife, on 5 September 1561, reduced the sentence passed against Sir John Borthwick for heresy by the court of Cardinal Beaton in 1540; and in 1563 the superintendent of Lothian similarly reduced the process of heresy against Sir James Hamilton of Kincavill, also dating from 1540 (Extract Decreet made over in 1912 by the Trustees of Sir William Fraser to the General Assembly's Library in the Tolbooth Church, Edinburgh; cf. *SHR*, x, 156–61).

REFERENCES: *RKS of St. A.*, i, 18–27, 50–9 and *passim*; *Statuta*, loc. cit.; 'The reformers and divorce', in *SHR*, ix, 10–36; Riddell, *Peerage and Consistorial Law*, i, 431, 443; *BUK*, i, 30.

10. *The Court of Session*. The third competitor for the consistorial jurisdiction was the Court of Session. An action of adherence came before it on 19 December 1560 'becaus thair is na consistoreis instant and the office of the spirituale juge quhilkis of befoir wes wont to cognosche in siclike caussis now ceisses'; other consistorial cases were brought to the lords on the ground that 'because the consistorial jurisdiction is abolischeit, the complenaris could get na cursing' or that the 'consistorie sittis not, nor thair is na executionis to be had that way'. Either the facilities offered by bishops, superintendents and kirk sessions were inadequate – which is likely enough; or there was some dubiety about the legality of proceedings before ecclesiastical tribunals. It appears that an Act of Parliament of 1560 – known only from its confirmation in 1581 (*APS*, iii, 221, c. 20) – had permitted actions pending in 'the court of Rome or in the consistories of the samyn' or before judges delegate or subdelegate, to be removed to the civil courts. At any rate, the fact that consistorial cases were coming to the Court of Session implied a claim of civil courts to competence in suits formerly spiritual – a claim not to be ignored when an end was put to the confusion produced by the Reformation.

REFERENCES: *Statuta, supra*, clxxiv–clxxv, notes; Riddell, *supra*, i, 426 ff.; Balfour, 269.

11. *Erection of the Commissary Court of Edinburgh*. The urgent need for a settlement was felt not only by the crown but also by the General Assembly, which in July 1562 petitioned the Privy Council 'that either they give up universally the judgment of divorce to the kirk and their sessions,

or else to establish men of good lives, knowledge and judgment, to take the order thereof'; and in June 1563 petitioned 'for constituting judges in every province, to hear the complaints of parties alleging adultery to be committed by the husband or the wife'. On 28 December 1563 the Privy Council resolved that commissaries should be appointed to exercise the consistorial jurisdiction; letters patent establishing the commissary court of Edinburgh were issued on 8 February following; and on 22 March the commissaries of Edinburgh drew up instructions setting forth the procedure to be observed henceforth in all commissary courts.

The foundation of the new court professedly proceeds on the breakdown of the old system rather than on its abolition – 'the inaction or absence of the jurisdiction of officials and commissaries'. The four commissaries now appointed at Edinburgh had a local jurisdiction in the sheriffdoms or constabularies of Edinburgh, Linlithgow, Haddington, Peebles and part of Stirling, with power to determine actions and causes raised by persons resident there which had been accustomed to be heard in the consistorial courts, including suits concerning teinds, testaments and defamation; they had also a general jurisdiction over actions raised by persons dwelling anywhere in the realm which concerned benefices or matrimony, including cases of divorce and bastardy; they were authorised to accept deeds for registration in their books; and they were to confirm all testaments within the area of their local jurisdiction and testaments from other parts of the realm in which the 'dead's part' exceeded £50.

There were some significant changes in procedure, and indeed in law. Proceedings were now in the vulgar tongue, and there was to be 'mair summar proces and shorter end'. The impediments to matrimony from consanguinity and affinity were much abridged, and the *cognatio spiritualis* arising from sponsorship disappeared. Besides, divorce *a vinculo* had been admitted by the reformed church, and practised even before that church received formal recognition in August 1560.

REFERENCES: *BUK*, i, 19, 34; Riddell, op cit., 431 ff.; Fergusson, *Consistorial Law of Scotland*, ch. ii and appendix xviii; *RPC*, i, 252, xiv, 304–7; *APS*, iii, 240; Bisset, op. cit., 57 ff.

12. *Transition in the local commissariots.* Local jurisdiction throughout the country remained after 1564 with the local commissaries. Those actually holding office (by episcopal appointment) were apparently authorised to continue to act: thus Archibald Menzies was commissary of Dumfries from about 1543 until 1579 and 'usit that charge and office to the gude lyking and contentment of the maist part' of the people of the district; in Glasgow, Archibald Beaton, official general in 1560, was still commissary in 1581; Hugh Craigie was commissary of Moray from 1559 to 1586; and James Duff likewise was commissary of Inverness before and after the Reformation. The manner of filling vacancies was not defined until 1566, when it was laid down that the Lords of Council and Session should present candidates for appointment by the crown. In practice there

were twenty-three local commissariots, their boundaries based on those of the old dioceses and their subdivisions, though the commissariot of Edinburgh absorbed the detached parishes of the diocese of Dunkeld which fell within its bounds.

It appears to have been intended from the outset that appeal should lie from the inferior commissaries to the commissaries of Edinburgh, and thence to the Court of Session.

REFERENCES: *RPC*, iii, 71; Muirhead, op. cit., 16; *APS*, iii, 240; *RSS*, v, Intro. xvi–xvii, vi, Intro. xviii–xix, vii, Intro. xviii, viii, Intro. xvi.

The Commissary Courts

13. *Structure and Organisation.* The developments of 1564–6 were a long way from producing a stable and complete system. We find the General Assembly of July 1569 asking 'that the commissaris may be appointed throuchout the haill realme to cognosce in the caussis of divorcement'; in 1575 all commissaries were charged to produce their commissions and instructions 'quhairby thay use the office of commissary . . . to the effect that sic farther and bettir ordour may be takin anent the using and exerceing of that jurisdictioun'; and in 1578 (*APS*, iii, 105, c. 1) a parliamentary commission was appointed to confer with the Lords of Session 'upoun the confirmatioun of all testamentis within this realme and anent the establishing of commissaris, how mony thair salbe, quhat jurisdictioun thay sall haif, in quhat place thay sall sit'.

The continued instability in a system which still reflected so much of the pre-Reformation structure of the church must be related to the prevailing uncertainty in the matter of ecclesiastical polity itself. The controversy between episcopalian and presbyterian government, which had commenced in 1575 and was to continue until 1690, had an obvious relevance to the question of the appointment, and perhaps even the jurisdiction, of the commissaries. The presbyterian party, in their anxiety to separate the ecclesiastical jurisdiction from the civil, were distrustful of the 'mingled jurisdiction' of the commissaries. It was in the year when the general assembly first drew up a scheme of presbyterian government that royal letters patent ratified the right of the Lords of Session to appoint commissaries as vacancies arose and gave them power to create new commissariots (12 July 1581); and statutory ratification of the jurisdiction of the commissary court of Edinburgh came in 1592 (*APS*, iii, 574, c. 64), when presbyterian government was first recognised by statute.

On the other hand, their right to appoint the commissaries was restored to the bishops by an Act of 1609 (*APS*, iv, 430, c. 8). The pre-Reformation system of appeals to the archiepiscopal courts, however, was not revived. Instead, the four commissaries of Edinburgh (of whom two were now to be nominated by the archbishop of St Andrews and two by the archbishop of Glasgow) retained not only the sole power 'to decyde in all caussis of devorcement', but also the 'power of reductioun of all decreittis pronuncit by ony uther commisseres'. The Act further provided for appeal from the commissaries of Edinburgh to the Court of Session: 'in caise the saidis commisseris [of Edinburgh] performe nocht thair duetie, the lordis of session shall have power to trye, cognosce and determine in the samin . . . and that becaus they ar his majesteis great consistorie. . . . And declairs that it shall be laufull to the saidis lordis of counsaill and sessioun to advocat caussis to thameselffis frome ony of the commissaris upoun just and laufull complentis maid to thame be ony of the subjectis'. The episcopal right of appointment was withdrawn in 1640 (*APS*, v, 278, c. 20), restored in 1662 (*APS*, vii, 373, c. 3), and finally withdrawn in 1690 (*APS*, ix, 133, c. 7).

REFERENCES: *RPC*, ii, 7, 455; *BUK*, ii, 507.

14. *Competence.* The competence of the commissary court of Edinburgh has been indicated in para. 11 above, and it is amply illustrated in *Consistorial Decreets and Processes* and *Lord Hermand's Consistorial Decisions.* Divorce, adherence, legitimacy and defamation evidently accounted for the great majority of the cases, though Hermand does not touch on the last.

The exclusive jurisdiction of the commissaries of Edinburgh in matrimonial causes deprived the local commissaries of one large sphere of work. Executry continued to be one of the principal fields in which they operated, because, although Edinburgh remained a general commissariot, where testaments from all parts of the country could be recorded, yet the distinction proposed in 1564 between major and minor testaments, the latter alone being confirmed locally, was not in practice observed. Possibly local commissaries took cognisance of cases of slander, from which they do not seem to have been excluded, but their records show little evidence of this. A considerable competence in suits following on obligations fortified by oath likewise remained with the commissaries for a long time after the Reformation. In 1622 an oath was sufficient to bring a case within the jurisdiction of the commissary of Glasgow; in the parliament of 1639 (*APS*, v, 603, 606) (significantly enough when episcopal government was abolished), a proposal was approved that '*interpositio fidei* shall not be ane sufficient caus to mak the commissaris judgis in actiones not meirlie consistoriall except conforme to the injunctiones gevin to the commissaris and ratified in parliament 1592', but this did not receive statutory effect and in any case would have been rescinded at the Restoration; and in the third quarter of the seventeenth century recognition was still given to the ancient competence of the commissary courts in such cases. This jurisdiction was, indeed, limited to actions for £40 or less, and even the commissariot of Edinburgh was restricted to cases involving less than £100, yet the commissary courts long continued to hear large numbers of suits for payment of money or victual. The commissaries were, besides, judges in actions by widows, pupils and other 'poor and miserable persons' not exceeding the sum of £20. Each commissariot kept its Register of Deeds until 1809 (Public Records (Scotland) Act), when the right to receive and record deeds was taken away, and the courts were therefore competent in suits arising from deeds recorded in their books.

REFERENCES: Muirhead, op cit., 20–1; *Silvertonhill* v. *His Son*, 1622, M.7553; *Wood* v. *Robertson*, 1672, M.12225; Stair, I, xiv, 3.

15. *Transfer of Functions to Other Courts.* The Act of 1609, which had permitted appeals directly from the inferior commissariots to the Court of Session, ultimately undermined the system of appeal to the intermediate Commissary Court of Edinburgh, and it fell into desuetude in the eighteenth century. The power to review sentences was finally transferred from the Commissary Court of Edinburgh to the Court of Session in 1830, and at the same time jurisdiction in divorce was transferred to the Court of Session (Court of Session Act, 1830). In 1823 (Commissary Courts (Scotland) Act, 1823) the inferior commissariots as hitherto constituted came to an end, each sheriffdom becoming a local commissariot in which the sheriff was to be the judge. The Commissary Court of Edinburgh, with its local jurisdiction now restricted to the three counties of the Lothians, continued as an inferior court until 1836 (6 and 7 Will. IV c. 41). Final abolition was deferred until the Sheriff Court Act of 1876, after which the only survival was the Commissary Clerk of Edinburgh, who continued to confirm testaments of persons dying furth of Scotland.

The Courts of the Reformed Church

16. *Competence.* After the Commissary Courts were established, the competence of the church in marriage and divorce was first disputed and then denied; the decrees which its courts still occasionally gave on such causes were liable to be set aside; and its claim, in 1571, that 'adherents and divorcement ' pertained to its jurisdiction was not admitted. Yet some relics of the old ecclesiastical jurisdiction in matrimonial and slander cases long remained with the kirk sessions and presbyteries. Whether with or without bishops and superintendents, they continued to issue decrees of adherence, as an essential preliminary to an action for divorce on the ground of desertion; on receiving petitions for divorce or nullity, they made inquiries and remitted the suits to the commissaries with a 'recommendation'. They dealt with slander to the extent of ordaining the offending party to make apology and crave forgiveness in public, as the pre-Reformation courts had done. Not only so, but for non-adherence, slander and minor assault they applied the various instruments of correction which were at their command and, often in conjunction with burgh magistrates, imposed fines and imprisonment. With the passage of time, the competence of the church courts was restricted to the internal discipline of the church and to the punishment of offences which were

contrary to morality but did not violate the criminal law, and even the latter branch of their authority has fallen into desuetude in the last century.

It is an accurate interpretation of the post-Reformation development to say that the old church courts and their jurisdiction bifurcated into the secularised commissary courts on the one side and the courts of the reformed church on the other. It is more correct to speak of 'The Reformed Church Courts' than of 'The Presbyterian Church Courts', for some of them originated before the presbyterian system of government was evolved, and continued to operate when the polity of the church was episcopal.

REFERENCES: *St. A. K. S. Reg.*, supra, 257, 268, 361, 381, and see Index; *Statuta*, clxxvi; Riddell, op cit., 431–2; *BUK*, i, 187; Spottiswoode Soc., *Misc.*, ii, 236, 256; *Ecclesiastical Records of Aberdeen* (Spalding Club), 28–9, 48–9, 166–7; *Inverness and Dingwall Presbytery Records* (SHS), xlii ff.; *APS*, iii, 81–2, c.1.

17. *The Kirk Session.* The kirk session made its appearance in the 'privy kirks' of the late 1550s, before there was 'the face of a public kirk' in Scotland, and the records of St Andrews begin in 1559. Yet more than a generation thereafter elapsed before every parish had its session. It seems to have been only in the early seventeenth century and under the direction of the bishops that sessions were at length set up in some of the more remote parishes; and whether the government of the church was presbyterian or episcopalian made little or no difference to the status and powers of the sessions.

18. *The General Assembly.* In the early composition of the General Assembly there can be detected the same Three Estates which at that time composed a Scottish parliament or general council – 'barons' (i.e., nobles and lairds) attending as individuals or as shire commissioners; burgh commissioners, appointed by the town councils; and clergy – superintendents, bishops and ministers. It was only later, and by stages, that the assembly became primarily a gathering of ministers and elders representing presbyteries. No assemblies met between 1618 and 1638 or between 1653 and 1690. The assembly has all along been the legislative organ of the reformed church (though in earlier times its acts often represent aspirations rather than achievements), a court of appeal from the lower courts and a court competent to try ministers, superintendents and bishops and to punish them by deposition; no appeal lies from the assembly to any other court.

19. *The Synod.* According to the original constitution of the reformed church, in the 1560s and 1570s, supervision of clergy and congregations was in the hands of superintendents, commissioners and bishops. These dignitaries presided over synods, which met twice a year and consisted of a minister with an elder or deacon from every parish of the diocese. Later, when the government of the church was episcopal, the bishop presided, but

in presbyterian times the synod became an assembly of ministers and elders without a permanent president. The synod was in earlier times a court of appeal from kirk sessions, and later from presbyteries.

20. *The Presbytery*. The presbytery formed no original part of the Scottish reformed polity, but from 1578 onwards its institution was advocated as one feature of the anti-episcopal programme. A scheme for presbyteries throughout the whole country was drawn up by the general assembly in 1581, but the countenance of the civil power was lacking and little was achieved. Serious development was deferred until the years from 1586 onwards, and statutory recognition was obtained for the first time in 1592. Under the episcopal regimes of the seventeenth century, presbyteries commonly continued to meet, though with diminished powers and apparently with the exclusion of elders. In presbyterian times the presbytery became the effective unit of ecclesiastical organisation, which it still remains.

REFERENCES: As in Stair Society, i, ch. 16; Donaldson, *The Scottish Reformation*.

6

Justice Across Frontiers

This article, as originally published in the *Records of the Scottish Church History Society* (xii, pt. ii) in 1955, bore the forbidding title 'Inter-diocesan and inter-provincial communication before and after the Reformation'. It contained some general information about the competence and procedure of the pre-Reformation courts which is now presented in the preceding paper and it is to some extent an expansion of Section 4 of that paper, but continues the story with some peculiar post-Reformation survivals.

When judicial proceedings in one diocese could not be concluded without reference to another, use was made of the supplication *vicissitudinis causa*, which could be sent either in the name of the bishop or in that of his official or commissary, and directed to either the bishop or the official or the commissary in the other diocese. The style of the supplication, while not invariable, always conformed closely to a single type and contained certain conventional phrases. After the salutation and the narrative describing the events (usually a process) which had made the supplication necessary, the request was introduced by the words *in juris subsidium et vicissitudinis causa requirimus* or some other phrase containing the expression *vicissitudinis causa* or *vicissitudinis gratia*. The request concluded with the phrase *prout nos in similibus seu hiis majoribus onerare volueritis* or some such form of words emphasising the reciprocal nature of the relationship between the suppliant and the person addressed. The style plainly demonstrated that the supplication was a communication between equals who accorded each other mutual recognition, and in simple terms the principle was 'One good turn deserves another'.

Half a dozen styles of such supplications are preserved in John Lauder's *Formulare*, an ecclesiastical style book of the first half of the sixteenth century. In two of them, the archbishop of St Andrews, who sends the supplication, explains to the bishop of another diocese that in a case of divorce in the archbishop's court one of the parties requires evidence from witnesses resident in the other diocese, he sends to the bishop certain articles and requests him to examine the witnesses thereon and transmit their answers. In a third instance, the commissary of the bishop of Dunkeld informs the archbishop of St Andrews that in an executry case the pursuers, who belong to the diocese of St Andrews, require evidence from witnesses in that diocese and, as these witnesses are too aged and infirm to be brought to court, asks the archbishop to make arrangements for their examination. In a fourth instance, the archbishop explains that in a case for the payment of a certain sum of money he has had occasion to excommunicate two persons resident in another bishop's diocese, but without effect, since they have, like Pharaoh, hardened their hearts in contempt of the keys of Holy Church; and the archbishop therefore requests the other bishop to denounce these persons. In a fifth supplication, the archbishop relates that a vicar in his diocese has appointed as his executors two persons resident in another diocese and requests the bishop of that diocese to forbid them to intromit with the vicar's estate until his testament has been confirmed and the quot – the fee for confirmation – duly paid.[1]

Apart from the styles preserved in the *St. Andrews Formulare*, examples are rare of what must have been from its nature a somewhat fugitive writ. A specimen among the Morton Papers in the Register House furnishes an illustration of the procedure. In a suit before the official principal of St Andrews in 1543 between Robert Douglas of Lochleven and Euphemia Wemyss, Mr Andrew Trale, Euphemia's procurator, alleged that witnesses resident in the diocese of Dunblane were necessary. The official therefore supplicated the commissary general of Dunblane to cite these witnesses and examine them on certain articles enclosed with the supplication. The commissary was to send their depositions to the official and at the same time return the writs sent to him.[2]

The procedure was not restricted to one province of the church, but was inter-provincial or 'international'. Thus, turning to the *Formulare* again, we find Archbishop Forman of St Andrews writing to the bishop of Durham. He related that W. R., a notorious Border reiver and disturber of the peace of both kingdoms, had been excommunicated in Scotland on account of his unspeakable misdeeds, but that after he had received a fatal wound his accomplices had caused him to be buried, with due solemnity, near the high altar of a church in Tynedale, in the diocese of Durham, as if he had been a faithful Christian. As this was contrary to canon law and a fearful example to other offenders, supplication is made to the bishop of Durham that the body be exhumed from its resting-place and buried *in loco vili et prophano*.[3] Less picturesque, and probably less unusual, circumstances lay behind another 'international' example – a supplication addressed by Bishop James Chisholm of Dunblane to the bishop of Roskilde, in Denmark, in the early years of the sixteenth century. Katherine Scrymgeour, wife of Robert Sinclair, merchant, had squandered part of her husband's property and carried off more of it when she deserted him and fled to Denmark. The Scottish bishop writes to his Danish brother, making observations on the deceits of women and remarking that it is no

[1] *St. A. Formulare*, i, 257–62.
[2] Morton Papers, 12 July 1543. See also 3 July 1542.
[3] *St. A. Formulare*, i, 257–8.

unworthy task to succour defrauded husbands, and requests him, *vicissitudinis jure*, to cause the 'wicked woman', Katherine, to be brought to judgment and compelled to adhere to her husband or to proceed by some other means to restitution of his goods.[4]

In a somewhat confused situation in the 1560s, such parts of the old consistorial jurisdiction as remained with the reformed church were exercised at 'diocesan' level by the superintendent and his court and at congregational level by the kirk session.[5] The old needs of communication between one unit and another remained, and the *Register of the Kirk Session of St. Andrews* (which incorporates the proceedings of the court of the superintendent of Fife) preserves some of the styles used. Already on 11 March 1559/60 the kirk session of St Andrews requests the kirk sessions of Anstruther and Falkland to cite witnesses to compear in an action for divorce pending at St Andrews. The phraseology is modelled on that of the traditional supplication *vicissitudinis causa*: 'requiring you . . . as perchance it shall happen you in the like case [to] require us . . . that ye summon, warn and charge [*certain named persons*] to compear before us . . . to bear leal and soothfast [witness] in an action and cause of divorce; . . . certifying them, if they compear not . . . we will use all compulsion against them . . . that is, cursing and excommunication. And this ye do, as ye shall in like manner require us in time coming, if it shall happen you to have the like cause before you . . .'.[6] The word *vicissitudo* is not used, but the style is there. That was one kirk session to another, before the erection of the superintendent's court. When the latter did emerge, and had occasion to write to a kirk session, it did not use the *supplicatio*, because it was issuing an instruction to an inferior and not making a request to an equal. Likewise when the kirk session of St Andrews had to ask the magistrates to take action against an offender, a supplication was sent, but again in this case the style of the *vicissitudo*, which indicated a reciprocal relationship between equals, was not used.[7]

The Scottish reformed church recognised as its sisters all those churches which had renounced the Roman supremacy, and it had no doubts about the propriety of relations between them as close as those which had joined one national church to another when all western Europe acknowledged the papal power. In March 1559/60 the kirk session of St Andrews received from one David Goodlad a petition which stated that Margaret Archibald, his spouse, had deserted him as long ago as 1524 and was now in Denmark, where she had bigamously married one Hans Boukle or Buckijliis. David, the petitioner, had shown remarkable patience, but now, after being a grass widower for thirty-six years, was desirous to marry again and had procured the consent of 'ane chaste virgyne past xl yeris of aige'. He therefore sought a divorce from Margaret.

---

[4] NLS, MS. 35.5.9 (B), 89.
[5] *Reg. K. S. St. A.*, i, 22–3.
[6] Ibid., 107–8, cf. 240.
[7] Ibid., 36, 143, 195.

The kirk session drew up an edict (in Latin and in the usual pre-Reformation form), summoning the woman to compear within eighty days. A copy was affixed to the door of the parish church of St Andrews and another was transmitted to the 'minister' of Lund, in Denmark, from whom an acknowledgment was received in August. (His reply, in Danish, was translated by William Christison, minister of Dundee.) In November the kirk session gave its decision that adultery was proved, and sentence of divorce was pronounced, leaving David free to marry again.[8] This case has a bearing on the more important one which was to follow a few years later.

On 29 December 1563 the general assembly received a petition from John Baron, minister of Galston. Baron had probably been in England in Edward VI's reign, he had associated with the English exiles on the continent during Mary's reign and he had married an Englishwoman, Anne Goodacre. His petition stated that his wife, whom he had left at his house in Edinburgh during his absence at Galston, had 'of her own wickedness and evil counsel' gone off to England in June last without his permission and in spite of appeals from him and his brethren that she should remain in Edinburgh until his return. The petition did not request any particular action, but merely 'advice and counsel and direction by what means he might be at liberty from the foresaid wicked woman', whose departure had been 'to his great grief and heart's sorrow'. The assembly ordained letters to be directed in their name by the superintendent of Lothian and the ministers of Edinburgh to the archbishops of Canterbury and York 'requesting them, *vicissitudinis causa*, that they should cause edicts to be proclaimed ... or personal citation to be executed' ordering the woman to compear before the court of the superintendent of Lothian within sixty days after summons.[9] On 10 February 1563/4 a letter was accordingly written by the superintendent of Lothian and the ministers of Edinburgh (that is, John Spottiswoode, John Knox and John Craig) to the English archbishops. It narrated Baron's petition and the ordinance of the assembly (a certified extract of which was enclosed), and proceeded: 'We therefore, in the name of the Eternal God, of his son Jesus Christ, and as ye desire sin to be punished and us your fellow servants in Christ Jesus to serve you or any of you in the like case, most humbly require you to cause your edicts to be published in all such places as you know them to be expedient, charging the said Ann to compear before the session of Edinburgh in the accustomed place of their assembly the 25th day of May next to come to answer by her self and not by her procurator to such crimes as shall be laid to her charge by her said husband and by us for the rebellious departing and other crimes that may be suspected to have ensued thereupon, with certification to her that if she compear not the said day and place we will proceed and minister justice at the said John's instance according to God's word. Further we ... desire you to remit to us ... this our act ... together with your edicts or summonses duly executed and endorsed in authentic

8. Doorway, Abernethy

9. Doorway, Brechin

10. Belfry opening, Wharram-le-Street

11. Belfry opening, St Regulus

12. Belfry opening, Markinch

13. Belfry opening, Muthill

14. Top of Tower, Abernethy, showing rebuilding and recent stonew

15. Western arch, St Regulus

form; which doing ... shall you bind us to the like or greater service
whensoever it shall please you or any pastor within that realm to charge
any of us.' A note was appended to the effect that the 'wicked and rebellious
woman' remained for a season at York.[10]

Matthew Parker, archbishop of Canterbury, recognised the communication as a supplication *vicissitudinis causa*, but considered that it touched
'the state and order of the realm'. Being a dutiful Elizabethan prelate, he
therefore decided to consult the civil authority, and he put the case before
Sir William Cecil, the Secretary, in a letter dated 14 April 1564. Parker
made the following observations: (1) 'This *vicissitudo* is used at the request
of them which agnise [i.e., recognise] one superior governor as subjects of
one realm.' Here the archbishop's law was wrong by pre-Reformation
standards, for the *vicissitudo* had operated between dioceses and provinces
without regard to political frontiers. Yet, as his later remarks will show,
he realised more clearly than his Scottish correspondents that the old
international organisation had been superseded and he was fully conscious
not only of the limits of each national church but of his own dependence
on the national 'supreme governor'. (2) 'It is used where the abode or
continuance of the party to be called is certainly known, in whose territory
the party continueth.' The preliminary detective work, he felt, should be
done by the Scots, and the supplication directed to the bishop of the diocese
where the party was resident. (3) 'Doubtful it is to me by what authority
these requesters do exercise their conference, for they make no mention of
their warrant or commission.' The English Erastian, who a few years before
had written 'God keep us from such a visitation as Knox hath attempted in
Scotland, the people to be orderers of things',[11] may have felt some
uneasiness about dealing with a church which did not enjoy the support of
the civil power. (4) 'I take it that the party is not bound to obey any such
command of the archbishops in England to appear in Scotland'; but clearly
whether the summons should be enforced or not lay with the English
authorities, and the supplication had made it clear that in the event of the
woman's non-compearance decree would be given in her husband's
favour. (5) 'Some doubt may rise whether they go about to practise a
precedent by our assents to divorce the parties and licence the innocent to
marry again.' As the Goodlad case had shown, this 'doubt' was well
founded, and Parker could hardly give his consent to proceedings which
might lead to divorce and re-marriage. (6) The archbishop invoked the Act
of Supremacy on which his church took its stand: 'It may be considered
how it may be taken at the queen's majesty's hands for us to command any
resident within her realm to appear before any foreign power out of her
realm.' Compliance with the general assembly's request might infringe the
law that no foreign prince, person, prelate, state or potentate should enjoy
any power, jurisdiction, superiority, authority, pre-eminence or privilege

---

[10] State Papers, Scotland, Elizabeth (PRO), vol. ix, No. 9 (copy). The original is in
Corpus Christi College (MS. cxiv, No. 209). Cf. *Cal. S. P. Scot.*, ii, No. 54.

[11] State Papers, Domestic, Elizabeth, vol. vii, No. 32, 6 November 1559.

within the realm of England. (7) He hinted at the possibility that compliance would establish a precedent to which 'extreme princes or evil prelates' might appeal for the extradition of fugitives when they desired to 'torment the godly'.

After stating these objections, the archbishop concluded with a constructive proposal: 'If they require justice, it might as well here as there be ministered of us by the queen's laws'; that is, apparently, Baron might raise an action against his spouse in an English court. Parker offered to waive his objections if Cecil thought compliance with the Scottish request to be 'convenient in respect of gratification of such neighbourhood as is now betwixt Scotland and England', and explained that he would await the Secretary's observations before sending an answer to Scotland.[12] No reply, either by Cecil to Parker or by Parker to the Scots, appears to have survived, but the absence of any reference to further developments on the whole suggests that the archbishop's views were allowed to prevail. If so, this incident may be regarded as marking an important stage in the disruption of ecclesiastical unity.

Three minor points of interest emerge from this case: (1) These proceedings of the assembly are not recorded in any extant compilation of assembly acts. (2) While the general assembly styles itself as such, yet John Baron, in his petition, addresses it as 'the maist honorable privie counsell there assembled with the rest of the nobilitie, the superintendents, ministers, commissioners of provinces and kirks' – a reminder that the assembly in its early days was of very different composition from that familiar in later times. (3) The English archbishops were addressed by the Scots as those 'whom God of His providence and mercy hath erected as principals in ecclesiastical jurisdiction within the realm of England', a phrase which demonstrates how much more charitable were the views of the reformers than those of the presbyterians who came after them; because in twenty years' time a Scottish archbishop was censured for giving the English bishops the right hand of fellowship, and by the end of the century 'Anglican' was equated with 'anti-Christian'.

In 1565 we find a faint echo of the terminology of the *vicissitudo*, when three superintendents of the Scottish church, with John Knox, issued a testimonial in favour of Mr Robert Hamilton, afterwards minister of St Andrews, and Robert Campbell of Kinyeancleuch. Writing in name of 'the faithful brethren within the realm of Scotland' to 'the faithful professors of the Lord Jesus in England, France, Germany or elsewhere', they concluded: 'Receive them, therefore, we beseech you, as the servants of God and as our dearest brethren. In doing whereof, as you shall please God, so shall you bind us to the like vicissitude upon the like assurance'.[13] This, however, was a document without legal or judicial significance.

The rapidity with which the supplication *vicissitudinis causa*, as an

[12] Ibid., vol. xxxiii, No. 56 (copy). Original in Corpus Christi College. The papers are printed in *Parker Correspondence* (Parker Society), 205 *et seq.* Cf. Strype, *Parker*, i, 297–8.

[13] Wodrow Soc. *Misc.*, i, 288; Knox, *Works*, vi, 429–30.

effective 'international' instrument in legal proceedings, fell into desuetude, goes some way to justify Archbishop Parker's observations in 1564. In 1574 Jonet Car, an Edinburgh woman, pursued her husband for divorce before the commissaries of the bishop of Durham, instead of raising her action in a Scottish court which would have proceeded by way of supplication to the English diocese;[14] this, it would seem, was the course which Parker had suggested in the Baron-Goodacre case. By this time, of course, the Scottish church courts had lost their jurisdiction in divorce suits, which were handled by the commissary courts. But the proceedings of the courts of the Scottish reformed church in cases of desertion,[15] and their pursuit of delinquents liable to 'discipline', often involved communication between bishops – and, later, presbyteries and synods – within Scotland itself;[16] but beyond two applications by the synod of Argyll, in 1657, one to 'the brethren in Ireland' and the other to 'the presbytery in Ireland',[17] attempts to enlist the assistance of ecclesiastical judicatories furth of Scotland are not conspicuous. Further examination of presbytery records would be necessary before one could generalise, but it would seem that the traditional procedure was superseded. Instead, we find the presbytery of Inverness communicating directly with a delinquent who was fugitive in England,[18] and such a proceeding would seem to have been the inevitable resort after the ancient *vicissitudo* fell out of use.

[14] Maitland Club, *Misc.*, i, 103–4.

[15] The place which decrees of adherence by church courts were to occupy in proceedings for divorce on the ground of desertion was defined in a statute of 1573 (*APS*, iii, 81–2). Provision was made for execution of a charge by a bishop to the minister of the parish where the defender remains, or the minister of the next adjacent parish, but nothing was said of defenders furth of Scotland.

[16] There are numerous instances in the *Minutes of the Synod of Argyll* and the *Presbytery Records of Inverness and Dingwall*.

[17] *Minutes of the Synod of Argyll*, ii, 151, 162.

[18] *Presbytery Records of Inverness and Dingwall*, xxx–xxxii.

7

'The Example of Denmark' in the Scottish Reformation

A note with this title was printed in the *Scottish Historical Review* in 1948 (xxvii, 57–64), but the article which appears below, the outcome of further study which has led to much amendment and expansion, should be regarded as a new piece of work. It owes a great deal to my friend Th. Lyby Christensen of the University of Aarhus, not only because his own writings in the *SHR* have illuminated the whole subject of the relations between Scotland and Denmark in the sixteenth century but because he has unsparingly provided me with guidance and information on the Danish reformation and on the thought and practice of the Danish Church.

Scottish historians, with hardly an exception, have been reluctant to admit that any influence ever reached their country from the north or from the east. The only phase in which they cannot ignore such influence is dismissed, inaccurately and pejoratively, as that of 'viking incursions', to the neglect of the cosmopolitan character of the Norsemen who settled in Scotland and for a time integrated the north of the country into a far-flung culture of a high order. That phase apart, almost everything, from prehistoric times onwards, is seen as having arrived from the south, usually from England or at any rate through England and seldom from any continental country save France – although France is farther from Scotland than Norway is.

Somewhat exceptionally for a country which has on the whole taken a pride in the peculiarity – and superiority – of its institutions, there has long been a general recognition that the ecclesiastical system set up in Scotland after the reformation had no features which cannot be found also in other countries, and the hobby of searching western Europe for parallels has been attended with considerable success. It is nearly sixty years since Janet G. MacGregor, in *The Scottish Presbyterian Polity* (1926), sought far and wide for the 'origins' of that polity and she unearthed in Lutheran churches a number of remarkable parallels, of varying degrees of significance and often without any connection with presbyterianism. In 1932 Louise B. Taylor, on a different tack, did a thesis on 'The Anglican Tendencies in the Scottish reformation'. Anyone who looks at the constitutions of German churches can find in them precedents for such features of the Scottish system as the office of superintendent, the lay diaconate, the endowment of schools and the care of the poor,[1] and it is noticeable that the description of a superintendent in the *De Regno Christi* of the Strassburg reformer Martin Bucer is wholly applicable to the office established in Scotland.[2] Others have looked, not in vain, to the *Forma ac Ratio* of John à Lasco, Francis Lambert's *Reformatio Ecclesiae Hessiae*, the Hesse Church Order of 1537, the Church Order of Ulm of 1531, the Schleswig-Holstein Church Order of 1542 and elsewhere. The most valuable of recent contributions have been those of Professor James K. Cameron in his *First Book of Discipline* (1972) and a series of articles in *SCHSR* (xx, 105–17, xxii, 1–12), the *Journal of Ecclesiastical History* (30, pp. 39–64) and *Reform and Reformation: England and the Continent c. 1500–c. 1750* (ed. D. Baker, 1979), pp. 133–47. He noted several continental parallels and in particular startling similarities between the First Book of Discipline and the *Consultation* prepared under the auspices of Hermann von Wied, Archbishop of Cologne, in 1543.

To discover similarities, even to discover examples of identical arrangements, especially in a period when reformers were peculiarly cosmopolitan and most of the current thought on all ecclesiastical matters was common property throughout western Europe, is no proof that there was direct borrowing or even immediate influence. One can say this without believing, as John Row did, that the Scots 'took not their pattern from any kirk in the world, not fra Geneva itself; but, laying God's Word before them, made reformation according thereunto'[3] – though Row was right enough about Geneva, for there is no element in the Scottish system which is paralleled only in Geneva, and in any event the example of a single town could hardly have been a model for the regional and central administration of a church throughout a whole kingdom. On the whole, writers have been sparing in allegations of conscious imitation. Archbishop Spottiswoode is almost alone in asserting in his *History of the Church of Scotland* (published in 1655 but completed between 1625 and the author's death in 1639) that the Book of Discipline was 'framed by John Knox, partly in imitation of the reformed churches of Germany, partly of what he had seen in Geneva'.[4]

One model, however, had been specifically recommended to the lay notables who led the Scottish revolution, nine months before they commissioned some of their clerical supporters to frame a Book of Discipline. William Cecil wrote to the lords of the congregation on 28 July 1559: 'In our first reformation here, in King Henry the VIII's time . . . if the prelacy had been left in their pomp and wealth, the victory had

---

[1] B. J. Kidd, *Documents illustrative of the continental Reformation* (1911), 230–3; T. M. Lindsay, *History of the Reformation* (1906–7), i, 411; Hermann Dalton, *Johannes à Lasco* (1881), 250–1.

[2] Bucer, *Scripta Anglicana* (1577), 67–8, 69, 73.

[3] Row, *Historie of the Kirk of Scotland* (Wodrow Soc.), 12.

[4] Spottiswoode Soc. edn., i, 371.

been theirs. I like no spoil, but I allow to have good things put to good uses, as to the enriching of the crown, to the help of the youth of the nobility, to the maintenance of ministry in the church, of learning in schools, and to relieve the poor members of Christ. ... Herein I know of no better example in any reformed state than I have heard to be in Denmark.'[5]

What was 'the example of Denmark'? And, first, how did the reformation there come about? Lutheran teaching made considerable headway in the 1520s, especially in the towns, where protestant congregations were organised, sometimes with the countenance of the local authorities; there were some outbreaks of iconoclasm and of attacks on ecclesiastical properties, especially friaries. The king, Christian II, gave a measure of protection to some of the preachers and in 1526 he forbade bishops to seek confirmation in future from the pope, so in effect abrogating Roman supremacy. There followed a phase of some reaction and then a civil war which ended in 1536 with the triumph of Christian III, a friend to reform. King Christian at once initiated his ecclesiastical revolution by an attack on the bishops, who had supported both religious reaction and the political opposition to the new king, and whose wealth might be diverted to an empty royal treasury. The bishops were seized and imprisoned in August 1536. The king ordained that they should lose their temporalities and their political power and that the Word of God should be freely preached. The *Rigsdag*, or assembly of estates, which met in Copenhagen from 15 to 30 October and which may be termed the Danish 'reformation parliament', included representatives of the towns and even of the country districts and it was claimed that there was a record attendance of 1200. It apparently had before it a supplication from the 'preachers and servants of the Word of God from Zealand, Skaane and Jutland', pressing for uniform evangelical worship, a university with instruction in Hebrew and Greek, schools in every city and town, ministers supported by their parishes, a superintendent or visitor in every diocese (to be elected by the preachers but appointed by the state) and the devotion to the sick and the poor of all income from property mortified to them. Proceedings in the *Rigsdag* began with an accusation against the bishops, who were charged with responsibility for the civil war, political intrigues, tyranny and the neglect of their duties. Their temporalities were annexed to the crown for the weal of the realm; their rights of patronage also went to the crown (while the nobles' rights of patronage were reserved). A 'recess', outlining a new constitution for the church, pronounced the bishops deposed and decreed that no others like them were to be advanced to ecclesiastical authority; their places were to be taken by other 'Christianlike' (*kristelige*) bishops and superintendents who could teach, instruct and preach the Holy Gospel and God's Word to the common people and would supervise the parish priests but have no secular authority and no seat in the *Rigsraad* (the aristocratic council of state). While dues which had been oppressive to the

---

[5] Knox, *Works*, vi, 51–5; *Foreign Calendar, Eliz.*, 1558–9, 424; *Cal. S. P. Scot.*, i, 234.

plebs et commune rusticorum were abolished, it was provided that parishioners should continue to pay their tithes (which there had of late been
widespread reluctance to pay); of these, one-third was to continue to go to
the parish priest, one-third to the church fabric and one-third (formerly
destined for the bishop) to the crown. The crown was to maintain the
superintendents, the university professors and the schoolmasters. Freedom
was given to monks to leave the cloisters. Final settlement of the fate of the
monasteries and the chapters and of the details of the distribution of the
revenues was left to the *Rigsraad*; meantime there was to be no alienation
without the consent of the king and the *Rigsraad*. For advice on the further
ordering of ecclesiastical affairs and the inauguration of the first
superintendents, recourse was had to John Bugenhagen, a prominent
Lutheran in Saxony, who came to Denmark in July 1537 and, although
himself only a presbyter, 'consecrated' the first seven superintendents
in September. Meanwhile, in January 1537, eighteen members of the
evangelical party and eight of their opponents had been summoned to a
conference or synod at Odense to draw up an *Ordinatio Ecclesiastica*. After
being approved by Luther and modified in a Lutheran direction by
Bugenhagen it was adopted by the *Rigsraad* and the king and promulgated
in September 1537. As translated into Danish, with some further
amendments, in 1539, it remained the constitution of the Danish church
until the 1680s.[6]

It would be unreasonable to doubt that the Scottish reformers were
well acquainted with the course of events in Denmark and that they would
know precisely what Cecil meant when he recommended such an example.
The Scottish government took a constant interest in Danish affairs. At the
end of 1532 James V wrote to Frederick I recalling how James IV (son of a
Danish princess) had held the Observant Friars in high honour and that
James himself was inclined to love and foster them against Lutheran attacks
but stating that news had come that in Frederick's dominions 'they are
allowed no home'. He therefore urged Frederick, in the strongest terms, to
restore them.[7] Three years later, when James informed the pope that action
had been taken against 'the Lutheran plague', he said that it not only
threatened Scotland 'from Germany, Denmark and neighbouring regions
but was brought across the sea'.[8] Christian III's *coup* in arresting the bishops
in 1536 was sensational, and in 1540 James V, in threatening the Scottish
clergy, alluded to his example.[9] A copy of the *Ordinatio Ecclesiastica* was
presented, apparently by Bugenhagen himself, to Henry VIII, and there is
reason to believe that its liturgical provisions were studied and imitated by

---

[6] The Latin versions of the Recess of the *Rigsdag* and the *Ordinatio* are represented by
extracts in Kidd, op. cit., 325 *et seq.* The Danish translation of the *Ordinatio* (*Den danske
Kirkeordinants af 1539*, ed. Max W. Olsen [Kjøbenhavn, 1936], includes a Danish version of
the recess.

[7] *Letters of James V*, 231–2.

[8] Ibid., 307.

[9] Knox, i, 34.

Archbishop Cranmer,[10] under whom a number of Scots served and whose prayer book was used in Scotland as well as in England. John Macalpine (Machabeus), one-time prior of the Blackfriars at Perth, who had embraced the reformed doctrines and fled from Scotland, made his way to Denmark and was a professor of theology at the university of Copenhagen from 1542 until his death in 1557. He was visited in 1548 by Sir David Lindsay of the Mount and he paid for the publication of one of Lindsay's works. Richard Melville of Baldovy (father of James, the diarist, and brother of the future presbyterian leader), as tutor of James Erskine, apparent of Dun, took his pupil to study under Macalpine at Copenhagen.[11] Miles Coverdale, bishop of Exeter under Edward VI, married a sister of Macalpine's wife and it is curious that there was this relationship between Coverdale, a translator of the Bible into English, and Machabeus, a translator of the Bible into Danish. After being imprisoned by Mary Tudor, Coverdale was released because the king of Denmark, at the instance of Macalpine, interceded for him. He visited Denmark and subsequently preached in Friesland, whence he went to collaborate with Knox at Geneva. John Willock, afterwards superintendent of Glasgow, was at Emden during Mary Tudor's reign and from there paid two visits to Scotland.

There is no need now to labour the importance of the commercial links between Scotland and Denmark, for these have received a fair amount of scholarly exposition within the last few years and articles about them are readily accessible.[12] One of the significant factors to emerge is that in addition to the movement of traders between the two countries there was a substantial amount of Scottish settlement in Denmark, especially in towns on both sides of Öresund, and that it was in such towns – Copenhagen and Malmö in particular – that the growth of Danish protestantism was conspicuous. Scotland supplied two burgomasters of Elsinore – David Thomson and his son-in-law Sander Lyell – three heralds to the Danish college of arms, a professor of medicine, a headmaster of the cathedral school of Roskilde and many more professional men. Fewer Danes went to Scotland, but in 1528 King's College, Aberdeen, had a visit from Hans Bogbinder, a member of a family which played an important part in the agitation for reform in Denmark. Danish books reached Scotland too.[13] Reviewing all the evidence is it possible to doubt that, at least in the east coast burghs of Scotland, for every man who knew what was happening in Geneva a score and more knew what was happening in Denmark? There is one piece of clear evidence that the Danish church settlement was studied

---

[10] J. Wickham Legg, *Cranmer's Liturgical Projects*, xxxiv.

[11] Melville, 14.

[12] Th. Lyby Christensen, 'Scoto-Danish relations in the sixteenth century', *SHR*, xlviii, 80–97, and 'Scots in Denmark in the sixteenth century', *SHR*, xlix, 125–45; James Dow, 'Skotter in sixteenth-century Scania', *SHR*, xliv, 34–51.

[13] Gordon Donaldson, 'Aberdeen University and the Reformation', *Northern Scotland*, i, 133; Cowan and Shaw, *Renaissance and Reformation*, 149.

carefully, probably at an official level: in a collection of papers relating to Scottish ecclesiastical affairs is a document entitled 'De sustentatione et provisione ministrorum verbi in inclyto Danorum et Norvagorum regno', which is a copy in a sixteenth-century hand of certain paragraphs of the portion of the *Ordinatio Ecclesiastica* dealing with church revenues.[14] It is important to note that despite doctrinal and liturgical differences the Scottish church of the reformation and the Danish church accorded each other full recognition. When, in 1560, a citizen of St Andrews complained to the kirk session there that his wife had deserted him and fled to Denmark, the session requested the pastor of the Danish parish where she resided to execute an edict of summons against her; this the Dane did, and his reply to the Scottish kirk session was translated from Danish by William Christison, minister of Dundee,[15] who had spent some time in Norway, where the first reformed bishop of Bergen had been his patron.

The course of events in Scotland during the reformation era had not been wholly dissimilar from that in Denmark. The official countenance given to the reformation for a time by Christian II ten years before the final adoption of a reformed constitution by Christian III in 1536–7 is paralleled by the policy pursued for a time by the Scottish government in 1543 (seventeen years before the 'reformation parliament' met), when the vernacular scriptures were authorised, protestant preachers were commissioned and an alliance drafted with an England which had repudiated the papacy. Equally, the formation of protestant congregations in certain towns, some iconoclasm and damage to ecclesiastical properties, especially friaries, took place in both countries. And in each of them the period between those earlier phases of activity and the final crisis was a tumultuous one, during which the future of the church seemed unpredictable.

The initiative in the events which finally produced an ecclesiastical revolution was taken in Denmark by a king who had just established himself on the throne, but in Scotland by a revolutionary movement which had set up a kind of provisional government under the leadership of the heir presumptive, and power lay in effect with a group of magnates and their supporters. In each country a parliament of unusually wide composition was called, and in each country the parliament had before it a programme prepared by reformers. But the problem was simpler in Denmark than in Scotland: in the former country it was a matter of starting directly to find a substitute for the existing church system, in the knowledge that the government would take the necessary action. In Scotland the situation was shaped, to a greater extent than it was in Denmark, by the spontaneous development of local congregations with their ministers, elders and deacons. This development did not signify any ideological commitment, for the practice was the usual one when the need arose to arrange for reformed worship without the countenance of the civil power: it had been followed by members of the Church of England when

[14] NLS, MS. 29.2.8 (Balcarres Papers, vol. viii), fo. 48.
[15] *Reg. K.S. St. A.*, 44–50 (cf. pp. 55–6 *supra*).

they were persecuted or in exile in Mary Tudor's reign. When the Scottish 'reformation parliament' met, there was, as there had been in Denmark, a denunciation of the bishops, in general terms: 'The bill put in by the barons against the bishops contained rather a general accusation of all living bishops than any special crime'.[16] However, apart from a ban on the exercise of any jurisdiction by papal authority, there was no legislation on polity or endowment so that all that existed, after the parliament as before it, was a system which would now be called congregational, with no organisation at regional level to link congregations together and nothing more at national level than a kind of 'central direction' from the provisional government in one form or another: it was the 'commissioners of burghs, and some of the nobility and barons' who allotted ministers in August 1560 and when the reformed church did first acquire a regional organisation it was in the shape of superintendents appointed by the privy council and acting in its name.[17] True, the Book of Discipline spoke, in wonderfully vague terms, of a 'great council of the church' of undefined composition, but there is no sign that any such body took part in framing a settlement and a body which met in December, commonly thought of as 'the first general assembly', consisted of six ministers and thirty-six 'commissioners of the particular kirks', mostly lairds and burgesses.

A 'Book of Reformation' which was in existence at the time of the parliament may be assumed to have been a stage towards the compilation of the 'Book of Discipline' which was not completed until the following January. There is no evidence that it influenced the deliberations of parliament, but it assuredly represents the settlement which most reformers wanted. The main resemblance between the Danish *Ordinatio* and the Book of Discipline lies less in verbal parallels than in similarity of scope. The table on page 67, in which the contents of the two documents are briefly indicated (in the order of the original in each case) shows how substantial this similarity is.

The closest verbal similarity between the two documents is to be found in the accounts they give of the superintendents and their duties. The *Ordinatio*'s introductory phrase 'superattendentes non vocantur ad canonicale otium sed ad ingentes labores' is paraphrased at the corresponding point in the *Book of Discipline* – 'the superintendents must not be suffered to live as your idle bishops have done heretofore'. Both documents proceed to insist that superintendents must preach not only in their chief cities but throughout their dioceses, the *Book of Discipline* limiting the period during which a superintendent might remain in his capital and the *Ordinatio* laying down the necessity for visiting the whole of the diocese once each year. In both countries the superintendents had to oversee the character, conduct and diligence of the pastors and to supervise the provision made for the poor. Some of the powers of the Danish superintendents, although not mentioned in the *Book of Discipline*, were

[16] S.P. Scot. Eliz., v, no. 16 (*Cal. S.P. Scot.*, i, 471).
[17] Donaldson, *Scottish Reformation*, 137.

Ordinatio Ecclesiastica	*Book of Discipline*
Doctrine	Doctrine
Sacraments	Sacraments
Rites and ceremonies, including those for the sacraments, for preaching, marriage and burial, and (at considerable length) the appointment of ministers.	Abolishing of idolatry Ministers and their lawful election
Schools	Provision for ministers and distri-
The maintenance and provision for ministers and the poor, including:	bution of the rents and patrimony of the kirk:
Rural clergy	Widows of ministers
Tithes; houses and glebes	Stipends (including those of
Deacons	superintendents)
Episcopal revenues	Poor
Urban clergy	Superintendents: their bounds,
Deacons	duties and election
Widows of ministers	
Poor	Schools
Deacons and the poor	Universities
Hospitals	Rents and patrimony:
Superintendents:	Ministers, poor and schools
Duties	Deacons and treasurers
Salaries	Teinds
Election	Other revenues
Other provisions	Burgh stipends
Liturgical matters	Manses and glebes
	Deacons and treasurers
	Ecclesiastical discipline
	Election of elders and deacons
	Services of the church, including preaching, marriage and burial

in fact exercised by the Scottish superintendents – their consistorial jurisdiction, examination of candidates for ordination or institution, inspection of schoolmasters and duties in connection with the payment of stipends. No significant difference can be detected between the Danish office and the Scottish. It is true that in Denmark the title 'superintendent' soon gave way to that of 'bishop', but a leading Scottish reformer remarked, 'I understand a bishop or superintendent to be but one office; and where the one is the other is';[18] and when in 1572 the term bishop was adopted for some of those who had the oversight of the other clergy no objection was raised. The term 'archbishop', thought objectionable as being unscriptural, was dropped in Denmark and regarded with disfavour in Scotland.

The thought which lay behind the arrangements made for *episkope* or supervision in the two countries is not explicit in either the *Ordinatio* or the Book of Discipline, but it is obvious enough. The Danes, in the Lutheran tradition, believed that there was no difference of order between bishop and presbyter but that a distinction in their functions was made purely as a matter of expediency, *jure humano* and not *jure divino*. Such an equation of bishop and priest – *idem est episcopus et presbyter* – was a commonplace at the time, but was no discovery of the reformation, for in medieval times the episcopate had not been one of the seven orders and had been held to differ from the presbyterate only in function.[19] The concept of the 'threefold ministry' of bishop, priest and deacon, which emerged so clearly in the Church of England, was not medieval and was a novelty which had no appeal to the Danes, who had no ministerial deacons, and how far it had an equivalent in the superintendent, minister and reader of the Church of Scotland is debatable. However, in Scotland there were some very strong expressions in support of the divine and scriptural sanction for the office of superintendent or bishop,[20] and these might be hard to reconcile with the view held in Denmark that the superiority of the superintendent was only a matter of human expediency. The Copenhagen Articles of 1530, in line with Lutheran thought generally, declared that 'Christian bishops and priests (which are the same) are nothing other than preachers and ministers of the pure Word of God', with no worldly greatness, no participation in warfare.[21] In both Scotland and Denmark the new superintendents were drawn from lower social classes than their medieval predecessors and did not belong to powerful noble families. It was understood in Denmark that bishops should have no civil power and should not take part in politics by sitting in parliament or council or in any other way, and this was more or less in accord with the reluctance of the Scottish reformers to allow ministers or bishops to act as judges in civil courts and their rejection of places in parliament for superintendents *qua* superintendents, though some

[18] Calderwood, iii, 162.
[19] Donaldson, *Scottish Reformation*, 102–11.
[20] Pp. 95–6 *infra*.
[21] Olsen, op. cit., 42.

superintendents took seats in other capacities and the church had not yet set its face against representation in parliament. It seems clear that in some respects Danish institutions and Danish ideas were more radical than those of the Scots.

When we take into account the dignity enjoyed by the Scottish superintendents – 'My lord superintendent', *Dominus Superintendens*, 'Father', 'Venerable Father', *Episcopus* and so on – as well as a lavish life-style provided not only by their own ample salaries but by the abundant hospitality they received on their visitations, we may reflect that they were more like 'proud prelates' than the Danish bishops were, and we certainly could not fall into the error of alleging that they received no more honour than ordinary ministers; and if we read the censures for slackness so mercilessly heaped on them by general assemblies (and ignore other evidence) we might be tempted to conclude that they had not ceased to 'live as your idle bishops have done heretofore'.

The Scottish superintendents were initially appointed by the civil power, but the intention was that they were later to be chosen by the clergy of the diocese; in Denmark they were to be chosen by the clergy, subject to crown confirmation. Somewhat similarly, provision was made in both countries for the voice of the congregation in the appointment of ministers. In Scotland the intention of the reformers was straightforward election of ministers by congregations, but in practice patronage survived, though it seems to have been tempered by consultation with the people in some instances. In Denmark, equally, the intention was election by 'the best men of the congregation' but this was qualified by recognition of the rights of patrons in some cases, and a kind of compromise operated. In both countries the minister, however he was selected, was examined and admitted by the superintendent or his deputy: in Denmark this duty fell to the *provst* (equivalent to a rural dean) but in Scotland a superintendent, if he did not act in person, apparently gave an *ad hoc* commission to 'learned men'. The book used in conducting services, containing liturgy, psalms and hymns, was a *Salmebog* in Denmark and a Psalm Book in Scotland.

Cecil's recommendation of the example of Denmark had been on the ground of the Danish treatment of the ecclesiastical property. There are indications that that example may have been in the minds of the Scots both when they compiled the *Book of Discipline* and when they arrived at the compromise which was necessary after that book proved impracticable. The claimants to shares in the church revenues were the same in both countries, broadly as mentioned by Cecil – the crown, the nobles, the reformed clergy, the schools and the poor. In both countries consideration was also shown to those whom the Danes called *plebs et commune rusticorum* and the Scots 'the poor labourers of the ground', oppressed as they had been by some of the clerical exactions. In Denmark the crown's needs were ultimately met by the annexation to it of the episcopal revenues, but it was also decided that the crown should uplift the third of the tithes which had previously been the bishops' share, in order to devote them to ecclesiastical purposes. In Scotland, the *Book of Discipline* made no provision for crown requirements but, when it was abandoned, one-third of all ecclesiastical revenues was collected by the crown partly to augment the royal revenues and partly to pay stipends to the reformed church. Curiously enough, redistribution of ecclesiastical revenues based on a division into thirds had a precedent also in Sweden, where in 1526 the king demanded two-thirds of the entire income of the clergy for one year. The principle laid down in both the *Ordinatio* and the *Book of Discipline* for the maintenance of the reformed clergy was that they should be supported by the tithes of their parishes – though in towns these might have to be supplemented by other ecclesiastical dues. In Denmark the principle was modified because the *Ordinatio* provided that the annexation of parochial tithes to bishoprics, canonries and abbeys should stand: in Scotland the *Book of Discipline* implied the separation from bishoprics and abbeys of those parish churches which had been annexed to them and the use of all teinds for parochial purposes; but this barely practicable suggestion was superseded by the 'assumption of thirds' already mentioned. The Scottish superintendents and university professors were, according to the *Book of Discipline*, to be maintained directly from the episcopal temporalities; in Denmark they received their salaries from the crown to which those temporalities had been annexed. In both Denmark and Scotland friaries were at once suppressed, but monasteries more tenderly treated. In neither country was there any 'dissolution of the monasteries'. Danish monks were allowed to leave the cloister or to remain until they died, and in Scotland events took a similar course. No provision was made in Scotland, as was made in Denmark, for the corporate life of those monks who chose to remain in a monastery, but in practice the remaining monks, in gradually diminishing number, formed a chapter for legal purposes until their deaths.

It has already been mentioned that the Danes did not have ministerial deacons, and the Scots, of course, had lay deacons. According to the *Book of Discipline* the latter were to receive the revenues of the church and distribute them to ministers, teachers and hospitals, but in practice they can at first have done little more than look after the poor fund. In Denmark there were, continuing from the medieval system, *kirkevaerge*, who should probably be equated with the English churchwardens and the Scottish 'kirkmaisters' (who also continued from pre-Reformation times, with responsibility primarily for the fabric of a parish church). In the Danish version of the *Ordinatio* they are styled *kirkevaerge eller diakoner* and in the Latin version *aediles sive diaconi*, and their functions appear to have been enlarged: there were to be two in every parish for the administration of tithes, two in every city and town, two or more to supervise the allocation of their dues to the poor. Possibly they were called *diaconi* or *diakoner* simply to put their office into a scriptural context. The Scottish deacons administered the kirk-rents, the Danish the *kirkerenten*. It is not quite clear that the two offices should be precisely equated, but no one has worked out the relationship between the Scottish deacon and the 'kirkmaister'.

8

The Parish Clergy and the Reformation

Reprinted from *Innes Review*, x, 5-20.

The service of the Scottish parishes in the pre-reformation church was in the hands of priests whose status and emoluments varied widely, because the parish ministry was only one part of a highly complex structure. In the vast majority of parishes a very large proportion of the revenues was diverted to the endowment of a cathedral chapter, a bishopric, a religious house, a collegiate church or a university foundation, leaving usually only a small residue to provide a stipend for a vicar in the parish. In only some 14 per cent of the parishes did the entire revenues remain in the hands of a parson properly so called.[1] (The Latin term was *rector*, but 'rector' was unknown in the Scottish vernacular in this sense, and the correct idiomatic translation of *rector* is 'parson'.) There were indeed the many cathedral canons who held parsonage revenues as their endowment and who were known as 'parsons' of this parish or that, but they must not be mistaken for resident parish priests, because they did not as a rule take any part in the service of the parish from which their title derived, but left parochial duties to the vicar. In general, therefore, it was a vicar who was parish priest. Not infrequently, however, the vicar was himself inactive in the parish: he might be a pluralist, he might be engaged in some secular occupation, he might be unable or unwilling for one reason or another to minister in person; and when this was so, the work of the parish might be in the hands of an assistant priest or curate.(The *curatus* was properly the man who had the cure of souls in the parish, whether he was parson, vicar or assistant, but there are undoubted instances of the use of *curatus* and 'curate' in sixteenth-century Scotland to mean a priest deputising for, or assisting, the parson or vicar.) There were also, of course, very large numbers of chaplains, serving altars in private chapels, parish churches, collegiate churches and cathedrals, and while they were not, strictly speaking, parish clergy, some of them were in effect attached to the parochial system.

The priests serving the parishes, whatever their status and titles, were in the main secular clergy, but there were exceptions. When a parish was appropriated to a house of canons regular (Augustinians or Premon-stratensians) it was a common practice for a canon of the house to be appointed as vicar of the parish, and it would appear that such canon-vicars

---

[1] Ian B. Cowan, *The Parishes of Medieval Scotland* (SRS), p. v.

very often served their parishes in person. Monks of other orders were not as a rule associated with parochial ministrations except to the extent that the nave of an abbey church was itself not infrequently used as a parish church for the district in which the house was situated, though in some houses – certainly Dunfermline and Melrose and very likely others – one monk was specifically detailed to serve as parish priest and could even be styled 'vicar'. Friars, it need hardly be said, performed no parochial work, although they carried on a very active ministry of an extra-parochial kind.

Ideally, the foundation for a study of the attitude of the parish clergy to the reformation would be the compilation of biographies of several hundred individuals – the parsons, vicars, curates, canons regular and monks who were concerned in the service of the thousand or so Scottish parishes in 1560. The material is not inadequate, but, while the careers of a proportion of the clergy can be sufficiently traced simply by the use of a limited number of official records,[2] there are a good many cases where the requisite evidence can be found only as a result of prolonged and laborious searches in a variety of other sources, printed and manuscript, so that the systematic compilation of a complete survey is possibly beyond the power of any individual scholar. (Dr Charles Haws, who did succeed in producing a nationwide survey by his own industry,[3] concurred: 'the subject is perhaps beyond the scope of any individual scholar'.) The essay which is now offered is a mere introduction, based only on a general acquaintance with the record evidence and on special investigations, of greater or less thoroughness, of three areas – the dioceses of Orkney[4] and Galloway[5] and the sheriffdom of Perth – and it must be understood that the conclusions tentatively put forward are based on such limited research. It would be useful to have additional regional studies, each of which would be worth while in itself besides yielding its contribution to the general picture (though the regional approach has its snares, if only because it can hardly hope to deal adequately with the numerous pluralists and the many clergy who moved from one part of the country to another).

A realistic approach to the subject must involve a readiness to acknowledge that the motives which shaped the attitude of the clergy were diverse. Many would argue that there was less altruism and disinterested-ness in those days than in our own, and few would be found to contend that there was more, but judgment on such an issue is not possible. If little is said in the following pages about the effects of individual conscience and intellectual conviction, the reason is not that such effects are discounted, but because they are not merely imponderable but incalculable. The historian must confine himself to discussion of those motives which can be calculated from the evidence at his disposal, and among such motives were com-

---

[2] For an account of those records, see 'Sources for Scottish Church History 1560–1600', *infra*.

[3] Charles H. Haws, *Scottish Parish Clergy at the Reformation* (SRS), p. v.

[4] Cf. 'Bishop Adam Bothwell and the reformation in Orkney', *SCHSR*, xiii.

[5] Cf. 'The Galloway clergy at the reformation', in *DGNHAS*, 3rd ser., xxx.

pliance with the law of the land, financial considerations and leadership or pressure from superiors.

The legal situation was shaped by events extending over several years before and after 1560, for the Scottish reformation was somewhat less precipitate, as well as in some respects less radical, than is popularly believed. Ever since 1543, when the administration of the Governor Arran had made its brief experiment in official support for a reformation, to the extent at least of authorising the scriptures in the vernacular and entering into an alliance with Henry VIII, there had been recurrent phases when ecclesiastical properties, especially the friaries and monastic houses in or near burghs, were threatened with violence. Then, during the late 1550s, not only did separatist reformed congregations develop in a number of towns, but some of the clergy in possession themselves began to use unauthorised forms of service.[6] The events of 1559–60 were therefore no sudden and unforeseen shock. This meant, for one thing, that many ecclesiastics had the opportunity to secure their financial position by feuing their property and thereby raising capital sums in anticipation of the deluge; it meant also that, among the regulars, certainly some of the more zealous reformers, and possibly also some of the more timorous conservatives, had already left their communities before 1560.

When the storm came, it was violent enough. There was a phase, in 1559 and 1560, when many clergy, especially of higher rank, were forcibly dispossessed and when ecclesiastical property generally was regarded as being at the disposal of anyone who cared to resort to force. But the violence did not last, for those proceedings did not receive the sanction of law, and the situation was one in which neither the hopes of the reformers nor the fears of the conservatives were fully realised. It is true that the parliament of 1560 adopted a new Confession of Faith; but there was no compulsion on anyone, cleric or lay, to subscribe it – unless, of course, he actually held office in the reformed church or taught in a school. It is true, too, that the same parliament passed an act forbidding the use of the Latin rite, and it is true that there were in succeeding years some prosecutions of 'mass-mongers'; but there was no penalty for a negative refusal to join in the work of the reformed church. Not only so, but the parliament did not legislate on ecclesiastical polity except to the extent of abrogating papal authority, nor did it legislate on endowments; and the consequence was that, while the reformed church received recognition in things spiritual, the entire structure of the old regime remained intact as a financial system, still upheld by the law.[7] It followed that the great majority of the clergy were guaranteed the continued enjoyment of a substantial part of their revenues.

The one group of clergy who appear to have suffered expropriation were the possessors of certain chaplainries and prebends founded on revenues within burghs, for those revenues were assigned by act of council

---

[6] G. Donaldson, *The Making of the Scottish Prayer Book of 1637*.
[7] *RSS*, v, Intro.

to 'hospitals, schools and other godly uses'[8] (though, at least in some cases, it was not until 1567, when the queen gave the burghs formal gifts of those revenues,[9] that this proposal took effect, and it seems likely that the holders kept their liferents). The position of the remaining holders of benefices was governed by the 'assumption of thirds', likewise in terms of an act of council.[10] The intention was that while the 'old possessors' retained two-thirds of their income, the thirds should be uplifted by the crown, partly for its own purposes and partly to pay stipends to the clergy of the reformed church. The scheme itself was not unstatesmanlike, designed as it was to avoid needless dislocation and to satisfy the competing claims of the government, the existing clergy and the reformed ministry. Not only was it not revolutionary, it was not wholly novel, because there were several precedents for heavy financial exactions from the church, and at one earlier stage, when the 'three tenths' and the 'Great Tax' were being exacted by James V in the 1530s, the prelates had learned what it meant to be mulcted of not much less than a third of their revenues. Further, the assumption of thirds was in many ways even less unfavourable to the existing clergy than it threatened to be. For one thing, while the majority of the holders of benefices obeyed the law which required them to produce rentals showing their revenues, and while such figures as can be tested suggest that most of the rentals were probably reasonably accurate, a good many men did not give up rentals at all and others gave up rentals from which some of the fruits had been negligently or fraudulently omitted; and the machinery for the detection of such defaulters seems to have been so inadequate that in the 1570s particulars were still being elicited of revenues which had been concealed in 1561 and which the old possessors had been enjoying all those years.[11] Moreover, thirds were regularly 'remitted' not only to certain classes of benefice-holders – university teachers, senators of the college of justice and the dignitaries and canons of the chapel royal – but also to individuals, sometimes on grounds of hardship, sometimes apparently for no other reason than that they had influence at court. And finally, although failure to pay the third was followed by the process of 'putting to the horn', this had become a mere formality with no serious consequence, so that many 'hornaris' went for years with their thirds unpaid,[12] only rarely does 'horning' seem to have been followed by escheat of moveable goods, and not until 1573 did it result in the loss of the liferent of the benefice.[13] The operation of the assumption of thirds was much criticised for its unfairness to the reformed church,[14] but it can hardly be regarded as other than tender to the rights of the old possessors. Not only did the old possessors retain

[8] *RPC*, i, 202.
[9] *RSS*, v, p. xiv.
[10] *TB*, x *et seq.*
[11] There is much evidence in *RSS*; cf. 'The "new enterit benefices", 1573–1586', in *SHR*, xxxii, 93–8.
[12] The evidence is in *TB*.
[13] *APS*, iii, 74 c. 8; the occasional escheats are in *RSS*.
[14] *TB*, xxi, xxv–xxvi.

their livings, but until 1566 it was not the law that clergy of the reformed church should even succeed them as they died. In the intervening years, the entire machinery for appointments to benefices went on very much as before, and the queen, the bishops and lay patrons disposed of benefices at their will, very often to laymen, whose rights thus formed a new set of vested interests, identical legally and financially with those of the old possessors. It is quite a mistake to believe that the law with regard to benefices and their fruits was on the side of the reformed church before 1566.[15]

It should perhaps be added that the last word on the financial position cannot be said until a thorough examination has been made of the scores of volumes of Acts and Decreets of the Court of Session which relate to this period and record the lawsuits relating to ecclesiastical revenues. However, the general impression one forms is that the old possessors had no more difficulty in collecting their revenues after 1560 than they had had before 1560, and no more difficulty than the reformed ministers had in collecting their stipends, for in every period – and certainly not least in the generation before 1560 – a vast amount of litigation has arisen from the reluctance of a proportion of the laity to render to the clergy what has been due to them. It is also worthy of note that with the retention of the two-thirds of the revenues there went, of course, the retention of the title, so that everyone who had held office in the church in 1560 continued for the rest of his life to be designated as he had been before 1560 – parson of X, vicar of Y, and so forth. It is an elementary, but not uncommon, error to believe that there was any religious significance in the use of such titles: they were nothing more than designations, denoting the enjoyment of certain revenues, to which the individuals bearing them were by law and custom entitled, irrespective of whether those individuals were old priests, new ministers or lay titulars. The retention of old styles was as true of regulars as of seculars: John Henderson was officially designated 'ane of the bruther conventuall of Dunfermeling' when he was appointed reader at Cleish in 1575.[16]

Another source which requires examination from this point of view is the Record of Testaments, which can be relied on to yield conclusive evidence of the financial position of the clergy. Inspection of a number of entries, taken at random, confirms the impression conveyed by other records. Some of the clergy (such as William Ainslie, vicar of Maxton, who kept three servants, and David Barchane, vicar of Suddy and Kilmure, who had 16 oxen, 4 cows and 68 sheep) were very comfortably off in the years after 1560. Many more had a fair competence, and if some of them were poor and the payments due to them in arrears, they were in no worse case than some of the clergy of the reformed church. Thus, William Abercromby, prior of Scone, had 'chamber gear and clothing' worth only £20 and debts due to him amounted to £264; but Robert Blinseill, minister of Wigtown, had 'books, chamber gear and clothing' worth only

---

[15] *RSS*, v, Intro.
[16] *RSS*, vii, 171.

£13 and the debts due to him (including part of his stipend over a period of ten years) amounted to £286. Examples could be multiplied.

The situation may be summed up as follows. A priest's conscience *might* dictate that he must celebrate mass in the old way, and he *might* be unlucky enough to be caught during one of the very occasional phases of prosecution. Again, he *might* have scruples about paying his third (though if he wanted to quiet his conscience he could remind himself, with perfect truth, that the third was a tax collected by the crown, and partly to supply the financial needs of the government); he *might* decline to pay and he *might* incur legal proceedings on that account, but even so the consequences were unlikely to be serious. On the whole, therefore, the old possessor had a good chance of living without interference and with a guaranteed income, whether or not he accepted the reformed faith, though in certain areas and at certain times he would have to be circumspect. It can be said in general that for a dozen years or so after 1560 no legal disabilities and only limited financial disabilities were attached to refusal to take part in the work of the reformed church and even to refusal to accept its doctrines.

The financial considerations with a bearing on the question of active participation in the reformed ministry were complex. In general it may be said that there was only a limited financial inducement to the beneficed clergy to conform to the new regime and serve as ministers, exhorters or readers. The cathedral or diocesan dignitary, the parson or the vicar, did, indeed, usually lose his third; he lost his right to offerings, the levying of which ceased in 1560 or 1561;[17] and, from 1563, in terms of one of Queen Mary's acts, he also lost his right to a parish manse – or at least his exclusive right to the manse, for the act envisaged the possibility that the manse might be shared between the possessor of the benefice and the minister or reader now serving the parish. That such sharing might take place is suggested by other examples of peaceful coexistence, such as the bequest of a gown by the minister of Tranent to the non-conforming vicar of the parish.[18] On the other hand, the beneficed man who did not conform was still assured of two-thirds of his stipend for life, in effect by way of retirement pension or redundancy money, and if he undertook service in the reformed church, his only reward, as a rule, was permission to retain the other third of his stipend and the exclusive possession of his manse. Such a proposition can hardly have had more than limited attractions except to men who were either sincerely interested in the reformation or subjected to some manner of pressure or persuasion. It can at least be said that the prospect of a 50 per cent addition to a man's stipend, and the enjoyment of a free house, were considerations to be weighed in the balance against the contrast between a life of leisure and the strenuous labours of a parish minister. If the balance in material considerations was about even, then conviction or influence would easily turn a man one way or the other.

[17] *TB*, xiv.
[18] Ian B. Cowan, *Blast and Counterblast*, 31.

In practice, a very considerable number of the beneficed clergy of all ranks took part in the work of the reformed church, and the parish clergy who did so generally continued to minister in their own parish churches and to their own parishioners. Such men are for the most part easily identifiable and traced. The clearest cases are those in which a parson or vicar who was in office in 1560 is subsequently recorded[19] as having his third 'allowed' to him in consideration of his service as a minister or a reader, but even when we find merely that the vicar in office before the reformation and the minister or reader in office after the reformation were men of the same name the identification hardly admits of dispute. When a parish priest served after the reformation in a new parish, it is sometimes less easy to be sure of his identity, and there were instances of quite surprising mobility. One would not, for example, expect the vicar of Terregles and Twynholm, in the south-west, to appear as minister of Perth, and, but for the fact that he happens to be the well-known John Row, the identification might have escaped notice.[20] Even more unexpected is the identification of Matthew Litstar, who became reader in two Shetland parishes, first Delting and later Fetlar; he has no known antecedents in Shetland, and would never have been identified with Matthew Paterson, who appears as curate in Kirkcaldy from 1553 until 1557, but for a solitary reference to him under the style 'Pauterson alias Litstar' in a Kirkcaldy protocol book,[21] combined with the knowledge that there were numerous links, through commerce, between Shetland and Kirkcaldy.[22] Such an example shakes one's confidence in any facile assertion that any particular cleric of the reformed church had not been one of the pre-reformation clergy, and there may be many cases where there was a change of parish (not to mention a change of name, in an age when surnames were not yet wholly stabilised) and where conclusive evidence of identity is not forthcoming. 'Curates' attached to parishes but unbeneficed are much more obscure figures than the parsons and vicars, many of them probably not on record at all, and in the few instances where the post-reformation reader can be identified with the pre-reformation curate, even of the same parish, the evidence is quite fortuitous: e.g., but for an unusual entry in the Books of the Assumption of Thirds, referring to 'Thomas Manderstoun, quha wes curat and now reidar' we should not know that the curate in the parish of Tyninghame became reader there after 1560;[23] and only an incidental reference in a

---

[19] In the Accounts of the Collectors of Thirds of Benefices or in the Registers of Stipends.

[20] *DGNHAS*, loc. cit., 44, 58.

[21] Dysart Burgh Records: David Alexander's Protocol Book (in Register House), 1065, 1071, 1077, 1091, 1099, 2000. For these references and other particulars of Litstar I was indebted to the late Rev. L. Nowosilski, who devoted to the clergy of that part of Fife an industry probably unparalleled in this field.

[22] Cf. G. Donaldson, *Shetland Life under Earl Patrick*, 70; *Court Book of Shetland* (SRS), 105; Barbara Crawford, *Essays in Shetland History*, 143–60.

[23] Books of Assumption, i, 75. Another entry on the same page refers to the unnamed curate of another parish 'quha is now reidar'.

criminal trial discloses that John Allan was curate and minister at Mennar.[24]
Other known examples of curates who became readers are John Thomson,
at Kinkell in Aberdeenshire, and John White, at Tullycheddill.[25] This is
probably the field in which there is most need for further investigation and
in which additional research may make serious revision necessary of any
figures which can at present be put forward. This is strikingly illustrated by
one example. Dr John R. Todd, in his Ph.D. thesis on 'The Reformation
in the Diocese of Dunblane', searched the Dunblane Testaments and
Consistorial Act Book to unearth the names of pre-reformation curates,
and as a result he drastically modifies the picture which Dr Haws presents:
according to the latter, seven Dunblane parish priests, three of them
curates, served in the reformed church, whereas Dr Todd has discovered
that fourteen parish priests, ten of them curates, did so. If the margin of
error is as wide as this, then any figures or percentages put forward must be
regarded as very provisional.

However, in the present state of our knowledge it seems likely that over
the whole country the proportion of those priests who conformed and
continued to minister in their existing spheres of duty under the new
regime was at least a quarter. This is the figure suggested by a rough check
in the *Thirds of Benefices*, but there are two qualifications, which may cancel
each other out: first, some of the holders of benefices so counted were men
appointed after 1560, and, second, there were (as work on individuals
demonstrates) many conformers who were not shown in the *Thirds of
Benefices*. The ranks of the conformers were headed by four bishops. Two
of them – Robert Stewart of Caithness and James Hamilton of Argyll –
were not consecrated, but the doubts which have occasionally been thrown
on the consecrations of Adam Bothwell of Orkney and Alexander Gordon
of Galloway are not justified: Bothwell's charters usually give the year of
his consecration and Gordon was consecrated for the archbishopric of
Glasgow in 1550 (and, having been so consecrated, was made titular
archbishop of Athens). All four committed themselves without qualification to the reformed cause and three of them continued to act in the
oversight of their dioceses after 1560. Of the dignitaries, the treasurers of
Dunkeld, Brechin and Ross and the archdeacon of Shetland were already
in 1561 numbered among the ministers of the reformed church,[26] and
others followed their example later. The 'parsons' who took the same
course – whether genuine parsons or cathedral canons – are too numerous
to specify, and it is somewhat remarkable that the earliest official list of
beneficed men who were recognised as ministers – a list certainly
incomplete but giving a rough and ready indication of the proportions of
the ranks of conforming clergy – names ten parsons and includes only
twenty-two vicars, while in a second official list – again incomplete – there

[24] Pitcairn, *Criminal trials*, I, i, 422.
[25] *RMS*, iv, 948, 2062; *TB*, 224, 254.
[26] *TB*, 91–3.

are seventeen parsons and thirty-seven vicars.[27] These figures might suggest that parsons, who were in the main of higher educational attainments than the vicars as well as of better ecclesiastical standing, showed more independence and initiative in making a decision; and certainly as the years passed and the number of conforming clergy in general increased, the proportion of vicars among them rose considerably.

But if some such picture, however sketchy, represents the situation for the whole body of clergy, it also emerges very plainly that the situation was by no means uniform over the entire country. In Galloway, out of about thirty-six vicars who can be traced, twelve continued to serve in their own parishes under the new regime, four more probably did likewise, and a further three seem to have served in other parishes. In Orkney, out of thirty-four clergy who are certainly known, or who may be strongly presumed, to have been in office in 1560, fourteen continued to serve the parishes attached to their benefices, four or five others may have done so and four more served in the reformed church in other spheres. In Perthshire, by contrast, out of about a hundred clergy who held parochial benefices at the reformation, only seven can be shown unquestionably to have continued to serve their parishes; in another ten instances the evidence is inconclusive, while two served as ministers but not in their old parishes.[28] Thus the percentage of those who may be called active conformers can be put at about fifteen for Perthshire, at nearly fifty for Galloway and at over sixty for Orkney. One possible explanation of these quite remarkable figures may be this: Galloway and Orkney had bishops who supported the reformation and presumably influenced their clergy to come over with them, whereas the bishops among whose dioceses the Perthshire parishes were distributed were Robert Crichton of Dunkeld, William Chisholm of Dunblane and John Hamilton of St Andrews, all of whom took a conservative line. Other examples, however, make it clear that leadership from the bishop was not the only influential factor. It would probably emerge on examination that a higher proportion of clergy conformed in Fife, the heart of the diocese of St Andrews, than in Perthshire, but if so this could reflect the strength of reforming opinions among the burgesses and lairds there as well as the probability that Archbishop Hamilton made less strenuous efforts against the reformation than did Crichton of Dunkeld; on the other hand, in the twenty-five parishes of East Lothian (also in St Andrews diocese), only four parsons and vicars and one or two curates joined the reformed ministry, although in that area also there were lairds zealous for reform.[29] A series of detailed investigations would certainly be necessary to determine the influence, varying from district to district, of the

[27] Ibid., 91–3, 149–51.
[28] The survey of Perthshire has been less thorough than those of Orkney and Galloway.
[29] Dr John Durkan has suggested to me that the influence of St Andrews Priory (see p. 83 *infra*) may partly explain the situation in Fife, and Dr Cowan has suggested that the number of conformers may have been higher in districts where vicarages were mostly very poor and lower in districts where two-thirds of a vicarage might provide a competence.

local lairds who were sometimes the patrons of the parish priests and were often partly responsible for paying stipends. One demonstrable example of what may have happened quite often is the case of Colin Campbell of Glenorchy, who established William Ramsay, formerly his chaplain at Finlarig Castle and curate of Killin, as minister of Kenmore, in the heart of Perthshire, and contracted to pay him a stipend.[30] Between priest and patron there might, however, be influence either way, for the opinions of a convinced reformer in a parish church might affect the attitude of the local people of all classes. Yet another possibility to be kept in mind is that the bishops and superintendents who were organising the reformed ministry may not have pursued a uniform policy towards the old clergy. The official attitude of the reformers in 1560 was, if not to discourage the acceptance of priests as ministers or readers, at any rate to do nothing to facilitate it,[31] and some superintendents may have tried to follow this policy; bishops like Bothwell and Gordon, however, were almost bound to take a different view, and this might partly explain the high proportion of conformers in their dioceses. Whatever the precise nature of the pattern, the explanation of it is not a simple or a single one.

Monks and canons regular were in a different financial position from the secular clergy. Their portions, or pensions in lieu thereof, continued to be payable to them, without deduction of a third, after the reformation as before it, and those emoluments were valuable: the monks of Glenluce had quantities of meal, bear, butter, cheese and peats, in addition to cash, and the whole 'portion' was worth about £60 in the Scots money of the time;[32] the monks of Dunfermline received, in satisfaction of their portions, £50 each with £1 for coals;[33] and the figures for other houses are comparable.[34] In addition, the monks were still entitled to their 'chambers' and 'yards' in the abbey precincts.[35] Altogether, therefore, a monk enjoyed a fair competence, far greater than the average stipend of a vicar, and was not likely to feel any financial compulsion to supplement his income by working for the reformed church; on the other hand, however, should he become minister, he retained his monastic income and received a full stipend in addition. Such at least was the position where the law was observed and the machinery of monastic finance worked smoothly. But neither the observance of the law nor the smooth working of financial machinery was characteristic of sixteenth-century Scotland, and monks did not, any more than seculars, always receive what was due to them. There were many instances where a monk had to resort to litigation to extract

---

[30] William A. Gillies, *In famed Breadalbane*, 261–3.

[31] Knox, i, 337, ii, 269; *BUK*, i, 5.

[32] Acts and Decreets, xxxiv, 141, 352.

[33] Ibid., xxxvii, 30; *RSS*, v, 3037.

[34] E.g., Acts and Decreets, xxxiv, 114; *RSS*, vii, 1580; *Charters of Inchaffray* (SHS), xcix–c; *Public Affairs*, lvi.

[35] Acts and Decreets, xxxiv, 141; *RSS*, vii, 1888; cf. Hay Fleming, *Reformation in Scotland*, 613.

his portion from the commendator,[36] and, while it would be hard to determine whether this kind of thing was a novelty for regulars any more than it was for seculars, or whether monks were in fact any more irregularly paid after 1560 than they had been before 1560, that does not alter the fact that the monk was in some sense at the mercy of the head of the house, who could clearly put pressure on men who were not of the same mind as himself: an example of sorts had been set by Mary of Guise in 1559, when she 'stopped the portions' of the canons of Cambuskenneth who had 'forsaken papistry';[37] and where the abbot or commendator went over to the reforming side, then it might of course be the turn of the conservatives to suffer. At the same time, hasty generalisation may be curbed by consideration of the action raised by John Philp, a monk of Kinloss, against his abbot, for his portion for no less than ten years,[38] because the abbot was on the reforming side and Philp, who had become a minister, had actually received financial help from the abbot when his ministerial stipend failed in 1565. Again, of three canons of Scone who had to sue for their portions, one was a minister and one a reader, the third not a member of the reformed ministry.[39] It is plain that disagreement on principles between abbot and monk did not lie behind every instance of litigation over portions.

The identification of the monks who passed into the ranks of the reformed clergy tends to be more difficult than the identification of the seculars who did so. There is no record evidence comparable to that of the 'allowance' of thirds to parsons and vicars, and we do not even have the assistance of continued location in a parish as evidence, except in a few cases where a monk is of the same name as the post-reformation minister of the parish in which the monk's house was situated. It can hardly be doubted, for instance, that John Watson and Thomas Haliwell, monks of Melrose, were identical with the John Watson and Thomas Haliwell who appear as minister and reader at Melrose; other examples are Patrick Cowill, monk of New Abbey and reader there; Walter Miller, monk of Culross and reader at Clackmannan, Tulliallan and Culross; William Kirkpatrick, monk and minister at Kilwinning; and John Sanderson, monk of Glenluce and reader there. Again, when a minister or reader in a parish lying near a monastery, or in a parish appropriated to that monastery, has the same name as one of the monks, we can be reasonably confident that they are one and the same: for example, John Hutchison, monk of Culross, was minister at Crombie, a parish formerly appropriated to his abbey; John Mason, monk of Lindores, was reader at Auchtermuchty, a parish formerly appropriated to his abbey; Thomas Turnet, monk of Kelso, was reader at Yetholm, a parish formerly appropriated to his abbey; and William Hood,

---

[36] Acts and Decreets, xxxiv, 114, 141, 352; Reg. of Deeds, vii, 175; RSS, vi, 134, 171, vii, 1580.

[37] Knox, i, 213.

[38] RPC, i, 680–1.

[39] RSS, vii, 272.

monk of Coldingham, was reader at Stitchill, a parish formerly appropriated to his priory. But when the only evidence is identity of name,
without any association in place, it is better to reserve judgment, though
much depends on how common the name is, and a fair degree of certainty
is sometimes attained when it emerges that, years later, a minister and a
monk of the same name died about the same time. (The approximate date
of the death of a monk may often be found from the Register of
Presentations and Register of the Privy Seal, which record the gifts of
monks' portions made as the monks died off.)

The positive evidence is thus far from complete, though there is a good
deal of negative evidence, for there are very many monks with names
which are not to be found among those of the reformed clergy. The general
picture which emerges is that the monks were not a conspicuous element in
the ranks of the new ministry. It is possible to say with some confidence that
among the Cistercians only two monks from Melrose and one from
Glenluce became readers, although each of those communities had about
fifteen members in 1560. These were houses which had maintained a
reasonable number of inmates, unlike some others where numbers had
declined sharply.[40] But, whatever the total strength, the number of monks
who entered the reformed ministry was rarely more than two or three.
Possibly the determining factor was often simply this: accustomed to a
fairly secluded life in the shelter of the community, a monk generally
preferred to enjoy his portion, which was adequate to support him,
without undertaking ministerial labours, and to continue a life of
comparative ease and comfort which did not differ materially from the life
he had lived before 1560. It would require a certain effort to uproot himself
and enter on a life which involved constant dealing with the public, and it is
significant that at Glenluce, for example, the solitary monk who entered
the reformed ministry was the member of the house who had already been
responsible for its parochial work before 1560; to him the exertions of a
parish minister represented a less radical change in his way of life. Nor is it
hard to understand the preference of a monk, if he was going to serve in the
reformed church at all, for service in a parish close to his monastery, for
only thus could he make much use of the 'chamber' and 'yard' to which he
was entitled.

When we turn to the canons regular, who so often held vicarages, the
task of identification becomes much easier, because the same evidence is
available for them as for secular vicars. Their record is demonstrably
different from that of the monks, and it is not surprising that men already
accustomed to parochial ministration took quite readily to work in the
reformed church. In the Premonstratensian houses of Whithorn and
Tongland the canons were peculiarly subject to the influence of their
reforming bishop, Alexander Gordon, because the canons of Whithorn
were the chapter of the bishopric of Galloway and the bishop was com-

---

[40] Mark Dilworth, *SCHSR*, xxi, 236–7.

mendator of Tongland. In Whithorn there was, indeed, the contrary influence of the prior, Malcolm Fleming, who was a rigid conservative, but his views evidently did not command much following among the monks. At any rate, out of eleven canons of Whithorn who survived the reformation, two clearly did not take part in the work of the reformed church, but seven certainly became readers and one or two more may have done so. At Tongland, eight canons survived the reformation, and of them five appear as readers. With hardly an exception the churches in which the canons of Whithorn and Tongland served as readers were churches which had been annexed to their houses before the reformation. The Perthshire Augustinian houses of Scone and Inchaffray likewise made an important contribution to the ministry: it is unlikely that in 1560 the two communities together numbered as many as thirty canons, of whom some would be beyond the age for active service; yet nine canons from those two houses appear as ministers, exhorters or readers. The commendator of Inchaffray was Alexander Gordon, the reforming bishop of Galloway, and the commendator of Scone was Patrick Hepburn, bishop of Moray, who, while he may have done little to aid the reformed church, did nothing to hinder it.[41] At the Augustinian priory of St Andrews, where the office of commendator was held first by the Lord James Stewart, one of the leaders of the reforming party, and then by Robert Stewart, the reforming bishop of Caithness, and where the subprior was John Winram, who became a superintendent, there was every encouragement to the canons to enter the reformed ministry, and no less than twelve canons who had taken service in the reformed church were still alive in 1572.[42] Augustinian Holyrood and Cambuskenneth, too, made their contributions, with at least four ministers and four readers respectively, and the small Premonstratensian houses of Holywood and Soulseat each produced at least two readers. From Augustinian Jedburgh, where there may have been only four or five canons, William Moscrop went to become minister at St Mary's Isle, where there was an Augustinian cell. Premonstratensian Dryburgh, with a strength of about a dozen canons, provided three readers, all serving in parishes which had been appropriated to the house – Lessudden, Gullane and Mertoun. The prior of the small Augustinian house of Blantyre, William Chirnside, became a minister, but he seems to have been a secular, holding the priory *in commendam*.

Although the friars did not form part of the pre-reformation parish ministry, something should be said of their work in the reformed church. They were entitled to pensions, or 'wages', but only at the modest figure of £16 per annum, and, unlike the monks, they no longer had free quarters, so that the financial attraction of a minister's or reader's stipend may well have been considerable. Yet it is certainly clear, negatively, that a good many friars, although recorded as receiving their 'wages' in Scotland after 1560, did not serve in the reformed church, for no men bearing their names

[41] Cf. p. 86 *infra*.
[42] *BUK*, i, 222.

appear on the roll of its ministry. On the other hand, to determine positively how many friars did become ministers or readers would be a task of peculiar difficulty, because identification is nearly always hazardous. Friars are on the whole more poorly documented than secular priests, monks and canons regular, and they were not associated with benefices or parishes, so that evidence of location is of little help. Occasionally, indeed, the evidence from proximity may be convincing: e.g., it can hardly be doubted that Alexander Young, prior of the Carmelites of Tullilum, near Perth, became minister of Methven; William Smith, prior of the Carmelites of Banff, may well be identical with the man of that name who appears as vicar and reader at Banff in the 1560s; Charles Hume, friar of Dumfries, is probably to be identified with the reader at Kirkbean and Troqueer, especially as Charles was at that time a rather uncommon Christian name; John Auchinleck, warden of the Greyfriars of Haddington, may be presumed to have become reader at Athelstaneford and John Black, a Perth friar, may have become reader at Dunning. But proximity is not enough: even although Smith was a much less common name in Scotland then than it is now, who can say whether John Smith, friar in Dundee, is to be identified with the John Smith who became reader at Inchture, eight miles from Dundee? Sometimes there are complications: James Ramsay was a friar at Inverness or Elgin; but James Ramsay was the name of a monk of Melrose; there was a reader called James Ramsay at Alloway in Ayrshire and another of the same name at Fearn in Angus – have we here two, three or four individuals? Friars were in any event probably more mobile than most other priests, and too often, without any evidence from location or proximity to help us, there is nothing except identity of name, which is far from sufficient. An excellent illustration of the kind of work which is necessary to investigate the biographies of friars but which in the end may lead only to possibilities and probabilities is a note by Rev. Ian A. Muirhead which demonstrates the likelihood that out of ten friars of Inverness and Elgin who are known to have survived the reformation, five became ministers or readers.[43] Elizeus MacCulloch and Henry Smith, Dominicans of Ayr, may be identical with the readers at Balmaclellan and Glasserton, and James Dodds, prior of the Dominicans of Wigtown, may have become minister at Dalry in Galloway.[44] Others who deserve investigation are Robert Fisher, reader at Dalyell, James Fotheringham, reader at Covington, James Carruthers, reader at Eastwood and Parton, and John Paton, reader at Dunnottar, all of whom bear the names of friars.

Contemporaries were well aware of the number of clergy who conformed and carried on their work in their parishes. It was to them that Ninian Winyet was alluding when he wrote: 'At Pasche and certane Soundays efter, thai techeit with grete appering zele, and ministrate the sacramentis till us on the Catholic manere; and be Witsonday thai change

[43] *SHR*, xxviii, 89–90.
[44] I am indebted to Dr John Durkan for these suggestions.

thair standart in our plane contrare'.[45] But he also points to the numbers of monks (including, of course, canons regular) who entered the reformed church: 'Quhy admit ye to be your prechouris . . . [men] of na experience, nor yit haifand praeeminence by utheris of godly leving, except ye call that godly to covet a fair wyfe and ane fatt pensioun, by the lawis of the monastik lyfe, quhilk sindry of thame hes professit?'[46] Another observer, the Jesuit de Gouda, also speaks of the monks who had turned ministers, but remarks as well on the acceptance of men with no previous clerical experience: 'The ministers, as they call them, are either apostate monks, or laymen of low rank, and are quite unlearned, being tailors, shoemakers, tanners or the like'.[47] The historian who surveys the ministry of the reformed church and, after listing those who had previously been secular priests, monks, canons regular and friars, notes how many of them are apparently without antecedents among the pre-reformation clergy, is at first inclined to agree with de Gouda. But a little reflection suggests that such a view may be ill-considered. For one thing, the reformed church drew not only on parsons, vicars, and regulars, but also on chaplains and on unbeneficed clergy: e.g. Walter Pyle, exhorter at Southdean, had been a chaplain in Jedburgh; Thomas Skirling, reader at Crail, had been chaplain of St Nicholas in the collegiate church of Crail; Alexander Ramsay, reader at Aberdour (diocese of Aberdeen), had been 'chaiplane of Oure Lady Pietie in the yle of the parroche kirk of Abirdoure'; and John Sinclair, reader at Dumfries, was presumably the sir John Sinclair who had been the possessor of an altarage in Dumfries church. Further investigation would probably reveal many similar cases, and there were in addition men who had not held benefices but to whose former priestly status the appellation 'sir' is a safe guide: for instance, Michael Boncle, minister at Innerwick in 1567, must be identical with sir Michael Boncle, the natural son of a burgess of Dunbar, legitimated in 1558.[48] It would in any event be worthy of note that, while a very high proportion of the ex-priests and ex-monks were fit only to be readers, a good number of the men found capable of the full ministry of word and sacraments in the reformed church were men previously unknown to record, and if they had indeed been tailors, shoemakers or tanners they must have been reasonably well educated, albeit possibly self-educated, men. Further, on looking through the lists of priests who were prosecuted for saying mass in 1563 one observes that a good many of them, too, have no known career in the pre-reformation church, and this makes one cautious about stressing the non-priestly element in the post-reformation ministry.[49]

---

[45] Winyet, *Works* (STS), i, 53.   [46] Ibid., 101.

[47] Pollen, *Papal negotiations with Queen Mary*, 135.

[48] *RMS*, iv, 1304.

[49] The dangers arising from incomplete records, or incomplete examination of records, hardly need stressing: e.g., Gilbert Foulsie, who became Archdeacon of Orkney in 1561, had evidently been a member of a religious order (*RSS*, v, 3308), and Francis Bothwell, who became treasurer of Orkney about the same time, had been a friar, but I have not found either of them recorded as a member of a Scottish community.

The record of service in the reformed church, while it is the easiest evidence to come by, is not the only evidence which shows the attitude of the clergy to the reformation. There must have been many who accepted the reformed faith but did not undertake work as ministers, and proof of this may occasionally be found. There are, for example, some lists of priests who formally renounced their former doctrines, but by no means all of the men named appear among the reformed clergy.[50] There is, again, the case of the dignitaries and prebendaries of the chapel royal. They were in a specially privileged position, because, as thirds were not exacted from them, they were therefore in possession of their full pre-reformation revenues. It is perhaps hardly surprising that few of them served in the reformed church, though one conspicuous exception was John Carswell, the chancellor of the chapel royal, who became superintendent of Argyll.[51] Yet it must not be concluded that the other prebendaries were out of sympathy with the reformed cause, because the testament of George Clapperton, the subdean, shows that he died in the reformed faith.[52] No doubt examination of the testaments of other clergy would yield similar information, for in his will a man often made a kind of profession of faith. Again, some light is thrown on the opinions of the bishop and canons of Moray by their agreeing, in 1569, to contribute to the repair of their cathedral so that it could be used for reformed worship,[53] and on the attitude of Henry Sinclair, bishop of Ross, by the fact that he did not scruple to furnish bread and wine for the communion service of the reformed church.[54] There is a dearth of memoirs and private letters for that period, but the *Correspondence of Sir Patrick Waus*[55] shows how easily a parson accepted the change in 1560. Andrew Blythman, one of the Charterhouse monks, seems to have become an elder in the parish church of Perth.

Another kind of evidence which may be used to throw light on the attitude of individual clergy to the reformed church is proof of their entering into matrimony. It is easy to find examples of men whose names do not appear among the reformed clergy but who married in or after 1560: Robert Douglas, provost of Lincluden, scandalised his prebendaries early in 1560 by intimating his intention to marry;[56] Magnus Halcro, chantor of Orkney, married in 1563;[57] after Malcolm Reid, vicar of Reay, died in 1567, we hear of his widow;[58] Alexander Dunbar, dean of Moray,

[50] *St. A. K.S. Reg.*, i, 11–18.

[51] John Stoddart, who had been presented to a prebend in the chapel royal in 1559, became parson and minister of Campsie, and Henry Yair, another prebendary, is said to have become an exhorter.

[52] Edinburgh Testaments, 21 September 1574.

[53] *RPC*, i, 677.

[54] Ibid., 492.

[55] Ed. Robert Vans Agnew.

[56] *Protocol Book of Mark Carruthers* (SRS), 190.

[57] *Protocol Book of Gilbert Grote* (SRS), 229.

[58] *TB*, 211.

was another dignitary who married.[59] The Dunfermline parish register discloses that Andrew Law, 'sometime a popish priest' but otherwise unknown, married in 1562.[60] Marriage need not, however, in every case prove that there had been a change of conviction. There were only too many priests who before 1560 had been married in all but name, and they did not all react in the same way to the change of custom – for there was no change in law, in the sense of a specific enactment – which came at the reformation. Some of them had no doubt already adopted the reformers' opinion that compulsory celibacy was wrong, and those who had done so would presumably hasten in 1560 to make their mistresses 'honest women' by marrying them. But others, in spite of their manner of life, may yet have upheld clerical celibacy in theory, and may still have adhered to that view after 1560 – only to find, however, that it was no longer permissible for them to live in sin and that the courts of the reformed church did not acknowledge that their priestly character was any excuse for abstaining from matrimony. Sometimes, therefore, the marriage of former clergy took place under constraint and does not indicate any change of opinion;[61] but John Anderson, vicar of Cleish, after being compelled by the kirk session of St Andrews to marry Eufame Pattoun in 1564, subsequently carried his acceptance of the new ways a stage further and became reader in his parish.[62]

It must not be thought, even when it is recorded of a priest that he accepted office in the reformed church, that he had necessarily undergone a profound change in his convictions. There were vicars of Bray at the Scottish reformation as at other ecclesiastical revolutions, those who conformed to what seemed for the time to be the fashion, the prevailing opinion, but who were equally ready to change again. For instance, William Telfer, canon of Whithorn and vicar of Cruggleton in Galloway, appears as reader there in 1562 and so continues for twenty years; yet in 1563 'sir William Telfer' was convicted for saying mass at 'Crugiltoun', so it appears that this vicar-reader was quite prepared to do a little 'mass-mongering' when he thought that the mass was coming into fashion again.[63] John Colville, vicar of Cathcart, was reader there in 1563 and 1568, but he also was prosecuted for saying mass in 1563.[64] And John Morison, who after his 'recantatioun' had been 'admittit reader in Mithyll (Methil)', was subsequently summoned for administering baptism and marriage 'efter the papistical fasson.'[65]

The periodical changes in the government's policy, and not least the vacillations of Queen Mary herself, were such as to tax the agility of even the most determined vicar of Bray. Anyone who hoped that the queen's

[59] *RSS*, vi, 2494.
[60] *Dunfermline Parish Register (SRS)*, p. 9.
[61] *St. A. K.S. Reg.*, i, xiv.
[62] Ibid.
[63] Pitcairn, *Criminal trials*, I, ii, 428 ('Congiltoun' is a mis-reading).
[64] Ibid.
[65] *St. A. K.S. Reg.*, i, 226–7.

return in 1561 would lead to the nullifying of the reformers' achievements of the previous year would be disappointed by Mary's proclamation forbidding any alteration in the state of religion which she found on her arrival in her kingdom;[66] those who looked to the influence of the conservative north-east to bring about a reaction against the reformation found their hopes blighted by the queen's campaign against Huntly in 1562; again, if the 'mass-mongers' of 1563 expected official countenance, they found instead that the law would take its course in terms of the queen's own proclamation, and indeed the year 1563, with its act about the manses and its prosecutions of 'mass mongers', represented a high-water mark for the time being of crown favour towards the reformed church. From 1564 to 1566, official policy was much less favourable to the reformers, and the expansion of their ministry was seriously hampered by lack of funds, for very little of the income from the thirds was allotted to stipends.[67] Towards the end of 1566, however, Queen Mary's attitude changed radically. She ordained that benefices worth less than 300 merks should, as they fell vacant, go to ministers; she gave a very substantial assignation for stipends from the thirds – £10,000 in money, and victual worth perhaps nearly as much; she made several gifts to burghs of the ecclesiastical revenues within their bounds.[68] On top of all this, in April 1567 she formally took the reformed church under her protection and undertook to defend it against any interference from overseas.[69] After Mary was deposed, the government of the new reign did not at first go any further than she had gone, for proposals made at the parliament of December 1567 to dispossess the 'old posessors' of benefices were not accepted, and instead their titles were confirmed.[70] Meantime, however, the attitude of the reformed church towards the beneficed clergy had changed. In 1560, so far from being given any specific encouragement to serve in the reforming ministry, they had not received any recognition in virtue of their existing status; but in 1566 an invitation was issued to all beneficed men to support the reformed church,[71] and from that time onwards the whole drift of the reformers' policy was towards imitation of the policy pursued in England, whereby the reformed church would take over the existing benefices and their holders. It was a logical development of this policy that in 1573 a statute was passed[72] whereby every beneficed clerk was to take an oath to the king, to acknowledge a bishop or superintendent of the reformed church as his ordinary and formally to give his assent to the Confession of Faith, on pain of deprivation. This measure represented a challenge to men who had hitherto been under no compulsion to admit their refusal to comply with the new regime. There are indications that the threat of deprivation may

[66] RPC, i, 266–7.
[67] TB, xxvi–xxvii.
[68] RPC, i, 487 et seq., 494; RSS, v, Intro. xiv.
[69] APS, ii, 548.
[70] Ibid., iii, 37 cc. 2, 5, 31 c. 26, 33 c. 36.
[71] BUK, i, 92.
[72] APS, iii, 72 c. 3.

have stimulated some priests to a belated decision to become active conformers and to undertake work as readers, but there was no obligation on them to do so. The number of deprivations does not appear to have been very large, for the records of crown presentations contained in the Register of the Privy Seal reveal only some twenty between the date of the statute and the end of 1574 and only another four between that date and the middle of 1577. It must, of course, be borne in mind that these records are only of benefices to which the crown had the right to appoint, and, while the number of such benefices was certainly very large in that period, what proportion of the whole it represented has not been worked out; and it must also be taken into account that by this time probably about a third of the men who had been in office in 1560 were dead. Yet, with all qualifications, the figures are not very impressive, and suggest that the amount of determined and persistent recusancy was limited. Certainly, if particulars are to be sought of priests who carried their resolution to adhere to their old beliefs to the extent of incurring financial loss, they are to be found in those records of deprivations.

9

Sources for Scottish Church History 1560–1600

An article on 'Sources for Scottish ecclesiastical organisation and personnel 1560–1600' appeared in the *Bulletin of the Institute of Historical Research*, xix (1944), 188–203. What follows below deals with a more extensive field and contains some critical evaluation of narrative sources as well as reflections on the general historiography of the period. The paragraphs dealing with administrative records have greatly benefited by being vetted by Dr Athol Murray, Keeper of the Records of Scotland, who has injected the results of his own expert study of the relevant volumes and has supplied the modern office references – without which, students are warned, it can now be inordinately difficult to gain access to some of those records.

Until recently accounts of the Scottish reformation and its aftermath were based almost wholly on material available in print and especially on printed narratives, while the masses of records which remained in manuscript were largely ignored. There were two honourable exceptions: Bishop Robert Keith, in the eighteenth century, toiled among the national archives while they still lay untended in the forbidding vaults of the Laich Parliament House, and pioneered the use of privy council records and the financial records relating to the church; and Thomas McCrie, a Secession minister, though he came on the scene after the records had found a worthier home in the Register House, had no indexes to guide him to the many registers in the use of which he in his turn was a pioneer. Keith did not much like the reformers, but his history did not continue down to the appearance of the presbyterians, whom he would have liked even less: McCrie on his side applauded reformers and presbyterians alike although he was too well informed to identify the two. But in neither case did bias detract from the value of the record material which those writers presented, and McCrie's *Andrew Melville* shows a range of scholarship which has not yet been surpassed in this field.

The narratives had a long innings almost free from competition, and they created a conventional picture which record evidence proves to be inadequate, but too few of the narratives have even now been subjected to critical examination. Knox's great *History of the Reformation* was examined in the edition by Professor Dickinson and came out of the test very well. While Knox had his bias, both personal and ecclesiastical, he wrote before the classical controversies of later times emerged and he was free from the prejudices of writers who interpreted past history in terms of 'establishment' and 'voluntaryism', 'prelacy' and 'erastianism'. Accounts of the years of crisis in the 1560s by Knox's contemporary, George Buchanan, have been criticised by William Gatherer in *The Tyrannous Reign of Mary Stewart* and by myself in *The First Trial of Mary, Queen of Scots*. Buchanan emerges with little credit. He had no hesitation in saying things which he knew to be false, which his contemporaries knew to be false and which he knew his contemporaries knew to be false. It would be reckless in the extreme to accept anything on the uncorroborated evidence of a man who was not trying to write history as we understand it; he was writing literature, in the way painting is done by an artist who spurns the representational approach. The criticism to which Buchanan has been subjected was indeed directed at him as a writer of primarily political history who – although he once took the moderatorial chair at a general assembly – was so uninterested in the religious movement that he did not even mention Knox's name until he introduced him on the occasion of James VI's coronation in 1567. Another narrative, Sir James Melville's *Memoirs*, has had some critical examination,[1] but that work also is one which shows so little interest in the religious movement that it never mentions by name either Knox or any other protestant minister. Various narratives received some incidental criticism in the voluminous notes to Hay Fleming's *Mary, Queen of Scots*, but again it was mainly political history that was at issue. Those narratives which deal primarily with ecclesiastical affairs have so far escaped exposure to systematic examination.

Perhaps the most influential of the narratives is that by David Calderwood, who, as he was not born until 1575, had no personal knowledge of either the reformation or the rise of presbyterianism. Much of his material came from records and documents which he quoted *in extenso*, but one of his narrative sources was the *Memorials of Transactions in Scotland* by Richard Bannatyne, who, as he was Knox's secretary, had first-hand information about the later years of the reformer and the critical events of the early 1570s. Calderwood follows Bannatyne very closely, though he draws on at least one other narrative, the *Autobiography and Diary* of James Melville, who was only a boy in the years of which Bannatyne was able to write with first-hand knowledge. A trivial indication of Calderwood's use of Melville rather than Bannatyne relates to a comment on the retention of other offices by John Douglas, rector of St Andrews University, when he became archbishop of St Andrews in 1571. Bannatyne has it that the complaint was against putting 'more upon the back of an old unable man than *ten* persons are able to bear', but Melville's version is 'to lay upon an old weak man's back that which *twenty* of the best gifts could not bear' and Calderwood's is 'that so many offices were laid

[1] Ed. Donaldson for the Folio Society, 1969.

upon the back of an old man which *twenty* men of the best gifts could not bear'.[2] Another variation occurs in accounts of what happened when Archbishop Douglas turned up at parliament. Bannatyne writes that 'the superintendent of Fife inhibited the rector of St. Andrews to vote *as one of the kirk* till he should be admitted by the kirk', but Calderwood has 'the superintendent of Fife inhibited the rector of St. Andrews to vote *at this parliament* till he be admitted by the kirk'; it could be argued that Calderwood makes the superintendent's censure more sweeping, for Douglas might have voted without claiming to represent the kirk.[3] Calderwood shows tendentiousness by throwing in his own comments. Thus, when Douglas was inaugurated as archbishop, he was, according to Bannatyne, asked 'if any simoniacal paction was made or yet to be made with any' and answered 'that none was nor should be made': Calderwood has it that when Douglas was asked 'if any simoniacal paction was made or was to be made' he answered 'None', and then adds, 'But it was not true'.[4] In reproducing the important letter in which Erskine of Dun put before the Regent Mar the claim that episcopal government was of divine institution, Calderwood includes a particularly emphatic phrase to the effect that to take away the office of a bishop 'were to alter and abolish the order which God hath appointed in his kirk'. Now, this phrase appears in the Bannatyne Club edition of Bannatyne, but it is omitted in the edition of 1806.[5] This is a lesson in the danger of relying on a possibly imperfect edition or even of relying on a printed version at all.

Calderwood may not often be open to the charge of deliberately manipulating evidence, but attention has been drawn to one instance of this. When arrangements were made in 1572 that ministers should be admitted to the titles of bishops and some of the episcopal revenues in return for carrying out the duties of superintendents, Knox's words, as given by Bannatyne, were that 'the Church of Scotland should not be subject to that order which then was used, considering the lords of Scotland had subscribed, and also confirmed in parliament, the order already and long ago appointed, in the Book of Discipline'.[6] I more than once criticised recent writers, such as Professor A. M. Renwick, for closing the quotation with the word 'order', so representing Knox as objecting that the Church of Scotland should not be subject to 'that order' (*sc.* episcopacy); Renwick goes so far as to repeat '*subject to that order*' in italics as 'sufficient to show that Knox objected to diocesan episcopacy'.[7] However, this particular distortion or misrepresentation, far from being of recent origin, goes back to Calderwood and his contemporary William Scot in his *Apologetical*

[2] Richard Bannatyne, *Memorials of Transactions in Scotland* (Bannatyne Club), 228; Melville, 31; Calderwood, iii, 211.

[3] Bannatyne 183; Calderwood, iii, 138.

[4] Bannatyne 224; Calderwood, iii, 207.

[5] Calderwood, iii, 158; Bannatyne 199; *Journal of the Transactions in Scotland . . . by Richard Bannatyne* (1806), 281.

[6] Bannatyne, 257.

[7] A. M. Renwick, *The Story of the Scottish Reformation* (1960), 164.

Narration, and they were followed a few years later by Alexander Petrie, whose *History of the Catholick Church* was published in 1662.[8] Professor Hannay used to say that a lot of historical error had arisen because people had failed to read to the end of a sentence, but in this instance it is hard to believe that the fault was originally due to mere carelessness rather than deliberate suppression, though the many who have delighted in repeating the error in later generations may have been guilty of nothing worse than carelessness in not going back to the earliest source. This particular variety of suppression is an error difficult to bring home to a perpetrator, for after all, to the extent that the words he prints reproduce correctly those of his source, he is telling the truth; but he is not telling the whole truth, and a partial truth may be no better than falsehood. Recourse has been had to this device by a recent writer who wanted to exaggerate the extent of the divergence between the English and Scottish reformers. He had before him a contemporary report, as follows (in modern spelling):

> I have talked of late with them all, to search their opinions how a uniformity might be had in religion in both these realms. They seem willing that it so were, many commodities are alleged that might ensue thereof. Howbeit *I find them so severe in that that they profess and so loth to remit any thing of that that they have received, that I see little hope thereof.* With other I have dealt more liberally than with them. They find it so expedient that there shall lack no goodwill in them thereunto.

By printing only the words I have italicised, the false impression was given that all the ministers were opposed to 'uniformity'.[9]

It is a short step from the omission of a phrase to the judicious – or dishonest – alteration of a word or two to impose a false meaning. The compilers of the *Book of Discipline*, in a well-known passage, explained carefully why they thought the office of superintendent was '*most* expedient for *this* time' (my italics), but this passage has often been distorted. Petrie again was an early offender here, when he wrote, 'a thing *expedient at this time*'[10] (Petrie's italics). Hasty reading could convert the passage into an assertion that the office of superintendent was no more than 'an expedient for a time' or even 'avowedly a temporary expedient'.[11] Possibly no amount of evidence can prevail against disingenuousness, but some statements by narrative writers may be readily corrected by a simple reference to records. For example, Petrie has it that 'howbeit some of the popish bishops had embraced the reformation, yet had they not any power but according to commission',[12] and other writers have been more specific

[8] Calderwood, iii, 207; Scot (Wodrow Soc., 1846), 26; Petrie, 375.
[9] James Kirk, *SHR*, lix, 27, *Second Book of Discipline*, 9.
[10] Petrie, 218.
[11] J. M. Reid, *Scotland Past and Present*, 76.
[12] Petrie, 386–7.

that such bishops acted only 'as commissioners of the assembly'.[13] But what we know of the assembly's proceedings is to the effect that these bishops did not receive any commission until 1563, while the record evidence is that for each of the financial years 1561 and 1562 the bishop of Orkney was paid 'for his visitation, oversight and labours taken upon the kirks of Orkney and Shetland in place of a superintendent' and that in 1562 the bishop of Galloway received a stipend as 'overseer there'.[14] That is a clear case, but evidence even like this will not overcome the myopia of a writer who remarks in adjacent sentences that the conforming bishops acted as 'commissioners' and that the statutory recognition given in 1567 to superintendents and 'commissioners' was 'withheld' from those bishops.[15]

The offending Petrie had a certain militancy which is not so discernible in his predecessors. The reason, presumably, was that the presbyterian interpretation by Calderwood had been challenged by Archbishop Spottiswoode, whose *History* was published in 1655. Petrie, whose work appeared seven years later, criticised Spottiswoode for omitting relevant information about the superintendents by failing to disclose all the *Book of Discipline* had said about them, and other writers have censured Spottiswoode's version of the *Book* as less complete than that given by Knox. Calderwood, however, might be more open to censure, for he almost ignores the *Book of Discipline* and instead cites the *Book of Common Order*, which, conveniently for him, does not so much as mention superintendents.[16] Spottiswoode, who did insert the *Book of Discipline*, however imperfectly, wrote admiringly of Knox, whom he was ready to defend against 'some malicious and wicked spirits who have studied by many forged lies to deprave his fame, only out of hatred of true religion, whereof he was a zealous promover'.[17] But Spottiswoode could not extend his admiration to Andrew Melville, 'who was lately come from Geneva, a man learned (chiefly in the tongues) but hot and eager upon any thing he went about, labouring with a burning desire to bring into this church the presbyterial discipline of Geneva'.[18] Spottiswoode echoes the opinion of those who knew Melville. The Regent Morton accused him and his followers of disturbing the peace of the church 'by their conceits and oversea dreams, imitation of Geneva discipline and laws';[19] Andrew's own nephew, James, acknowledged that before his uncle's arrival 'many knew not yet the corruption and unlawfulness of that invention of man [episcopacy]' and that several ministers were 'informed more thoroughly by Mr Andrew of the unlawfulness of bishops and the right manner of governing of the kirk by presbyteries';[20] and Lord Glamis noted as a

[13] Kirk, *Second Book of Discipline*, 143.
[14] *TB*, 150, 152.
[15] Ian B. Cowan and Duncan Shaw, *The Renaissance and Reformation in Scotland*, 105.
[16] Calderwood, ii, 51–120 (cf. iii, 163n).
[17] Spottiswoode, ii, 180.
[18] Ibid., 200.
[19] Melville, 168.
[20] Ibid., 32, 48, 52.

novelty that 'it is asked whether it be necessary in the church to have the office of bishops . . . or whether all ministers, enjoying equal power and not subject to the authority of any bishop or superintendent, ought . . . to choose men suitable in religion, to discipline them and to remove them from office'.[21] William Scot, writing about the same time as Spottiswoode, had already claimed that Melville 'had no power to command the meanest minister, let be to overrule assemblies',[22] and Petrie, writing after Spottiswoode, was more emphatic: 'If we compare what was done before in the assemblies, this question concerning the bishops was not a new motion made by Andrew Melvin come lately from Geneva: he had not power to command the meanest minister, and far less to overrule the assembly'.[23] The nineteenth-century scholar Thomas McCrie, however, preferred something more like the Spottiswoode (and contemporary) interpretation: Melville had brought about 'a change of sentiment' among his fellow-countrymen on this issue.[24]

That Melville was indeed an innovator in condemning the office of superintendent or bishop and advocating the transfer of power to presbyteries is demonstrated by the following catena of quotations (in modern spelling):

1561. 'Without the care of superintendents, neither can the kirks be suddenly erected, neither can they be retained in discipline and unity of doctrine; . . . of Christ Jesus and of his apostles we have command and example to appoint men to such charges'. (*Reg. K.S. St. A.*, i, 75)

1564. John Spottiswoode, superintendent of Lothian, John Knox and John Craig, ministers, address the archbishops of Canterbury and York as those 'whom God of his providence and mercy has erected as principals in ecclesiastical jurisdiction within the realm of England'. (P. 58 *supra*)

c. 1567. 'There is no article in the whole body of the law which has been handed down with greater care, approval and exposition than that which deals with the duties of bishops. . . . We should notice very carefully what power Paul attributed to bishops, whose functions he praised in remarkable, yet fitting, terms, for they are in a sense the equivalent of kings so far as the nature of their respective offices permits'. (George Buchanan, *The Art and Science of Government among the Scots* [ed. D. H. McNeill, 1964], 44–5, 57)

1571. 'We have expressed plainly by scriptures that to the office of a bishop pertaineth examination and admission to spiritual cure and office, and also to oversee them who are admitted. . . . To take this power from the bishop or superintendent is to take away the office of a bishop, that no bishop be in the kirk; which were to alter and

[21] pp. 128–9 *infra*.
[22] Scot, 34.
[23] Petrie, 386.
[24] McCrie, *Andrew Melville* (1899), 64.

abolish the order which God has appointed in his kirk'. (Erskine of
Dun, in Calderwod, iii, 157–8)

1572. Knox recommends 'That all bishoprics vacant may be
presented, and qualified persons nominated thereunto'. (Calderwood,
iii, 766)

1572. 'We think good that they that had the names of archbishops
heretofore, that hereafter, in these things concerning the function of
the kirk, they shall use the name of bishop, and not archbishop'. (The
General Assembly, in Calderwood, iii, 221)

1575. 'Anent the question proposed by certain brethren . . . whether
if bishops, as they are now in the Church of Scotland, have their
function of the Word of God or not, . . . they think it not expedient to
answer directly'. (BUK, i, 340, 342–3)

1578. James Boyd, Archbishop of Glasgow: 'I understand the name,
office and modest reverence borne to a bishop to be lawful and
allowable by the scriptures of God; and, being elected by the kirk and
king to be bishop of Glasgow, I esteem my calling and office lawful.
. . . I am content . . . to be examined by the canon left by the Apostle
to Timothy, I Ep. cap. iii; seeing that place was appointed to me at
my receiving, I understand therefrom the duties of a bishop'.
(Calderwood, iii, 429)

1583. 'The government of the kirk does consist in the authority and
power of the bishops, to whom are committed the dioceses and
provinces in government. The office of bishop is of the apostolic
institution, and most agreeable to the primitive purity of the kirk of
God. The ordination and ordinary judgment of pastors belongeth to
the bishop, without whose authority whosoever does presume to the
pastoral care enters not at the door but over the dyke'. (Archbishop
Adamson, in Calderwood, iv, 53–4)

1586. 'I offer me to prove that the office of a bishop, as it is in my
person, in all points is according to God's word'. (Archbishop
Adamson, in Calderwood, iv, 500)

These extracts put it beyond doubt that it was the bishops, and not Andrew
Melville, who maintained the convictions of the reformers.

The first of those passages must have caused considerable discomfiture
to the first scholar who transcribed it. David Hay Fleming (1849–1931)
combined loyalty to his strict Secession sect with meticulous scholarship
and enthusiasm for investigation of records. I have sometimes remarked, 'If
you think you've found out something new about the Scottish
reformation, go and look at Hay Fleming'. And while he made his own
views plain enough, it would be hard to detect him in any manipulation of
evidence or suppression of facts, however disagreeable the facts were. (It
was Hay Fleming who, after examining the statement that Calvin played

bowls on Sunday and – to his own satisfaction at least – disproving it, concluded triumphantly, 'Thus is history falsified and good men slandered'.) It must have been a shock to find that the St Andrews Kirk Session Register contained a firm declaration that the office of superintendent had dominical and apostolic warrant. Fleming could not expunge it or even make his own comment upon it, but he inserted in a footnote a quotation from David Laing to the effect that the superintendents' office 'conferred no degree of superiority over their brethren and that it had no great pecuniary advantage'.[25] This was a typical piece of falsehood about the superintendents, paralleled by statements that 'the office conferred on them no precedence or superiority over their brethren'[26] or that they 'had no special honour accorded to them'.[27] Hay Fleming knew that Laing's statement was untrue, for the volume he was editing showed how a superintendent was styled 'my lord' and exercised many functions not performed by ministers, and the note which immediately precedes that quotation from Laing gives an indication of the 'pecuniary advantages' which superintendents enjoyed, but he shuffled on to David Laing the responsibility for misleading the reader. Such subtle deviousness is almost enviable.

As controversy intensified with the passage of time, so misinterpretation of history increased. The later Covenanters and the Cameronians, in their anxiety to demonstrate the right of the church to 'independence', made much of what they called its 'intrinsic power', a phrase which remained potent until the days of the Disruption, and they attributed their own beliefs to the reformers, who, they alleged, 'assembled in their first national synod in the year 1560, by virtue of that intrinsic power granted by the Lord to His Church; nor did they so much as petition for the indulgence of the then authority'.[28] In truth, of course, the reformers repeatedly petitioned the civil power and their Book of Discipline was itself a petition to the 'authority'. Equally, McCrie, who, with all his scholarship, was something of a pamphleteer (on a generous scale) on behalf of anti-establishment opinion, lapsed into remarking that the superintendents 'derived the special powers with which they were invested from the general assemblies',[29] whereas in truth they were appointed by, and acted in name of, the lords of council.[30] Keith, who, as a non-juring episcopalian, believed firmly in the right of the sovereign to nominate bishops, scored a good debating point when he wrote that if the 'lords of the secret council' could nominate a superintendent, 'there might be little ground to complain of the same power when lodged in a lawful king'.[31]

---

[25] Reg. K.S. St. A., i, 73n.
[26] Wodrow Soc. Misc., i, 322.
[27] J. L. Ainslie, Ministerial Order in the Reformed Churches, 110.
[28] Alexander Shiels, A Hind let loose (1744), 42.
[29] McCrie, Andrew Melville, 45.
[30] Donaldson, Scottish Reformation, 226–8.
[31] Keith, i, 311.

So much for the perils of relying on narratives, especially until their texts are critically evaluated, and ignoring records. The earlier essays in printing records concentrated on legislation, whether of parliament, general assembly or privy council, while administrative and financial records in general remained in manuscript, and reading of the legislation not only did little to correct the narratives but sometimes compounded their errors and introduced fresh misconceptions as to what really happened. It must be recognised that records of legislation are evidence that the legislation was passed, but not that it was ever carried out. This is true of records of legislation even at their best, but it happens that records of legislation relating to the Scottish reformation are gravely defective. In the *Acts of the Parliament of Scotland* there appear only three pieces of legislation assigned to the 'reformation parliament' of 1560 – authorising the Confession of Faith, abolishing papal authority and forbidding the Latin rite – but there was certainly a fourth act, known only from its confirmation in 1581,[32] permitting the transfer of litigation from the Roman courts to the Court of Session, and a number of other acts, of which only the 'heads' are extant, were at least considered if not passed into law.[33] As to the General Assembly, the original registers were destroyed by fire in 1834 and we are dependent on selections which were made by various hands at different times. *The Acts and Proceedings of the General Assemblies* (Maitland and Bannatyne Clubs, 1839–45) brought together most of these selections in a convenient way but it lacks authority, it is demonstrably incomplete, it cannot be relied on to produce the precise words of the original record and it sometimes prints the comments of collectors as if they were part of the register.[34] Proposals for a better edition, gathering together all the scattered material which survives, have not so far gained enough support. The weakness of the *Register of the Privy Council* is that it has a gap from January 1554 to September 1561 and other gaps later.

It is also important to remember that the Assembly records, even as far as they go, in the main represent programmes and proposals not capable of immediate realisation because the assembly lacked either executive power or the government support which would have been necessary to implement its resolutions. The peril of relying solely on the records of the assemblies is exemplified in 1580 and 1581, when the assembly denounced the inclusion in the church of bishops and of readers and commanded them to demit office. William Scot concluded roundly, 'both bishops and readers were thrust out'[35] at this point, and many later writers have said much the same. But the office of bishop was not abolished at any date before 1638, and there is ample evidence that the style and office of reader were retained

[32] p. 46 *supra*.
[33] Keith, i, 324–6.
[34] Donaldson, *Scottish Reformation*, 140; cf. pp. 58 *supra* and 113 *infra*.
[35] Scot, 39.

well through the seventeenth century and that the style, at least, survived until the eighteenth or even the nineteenth.[36] Confirmation must always be sought from other sources before it is concluded that acts of assemblies, and even acts of parliament and council, were carried completely into effect.

This is where the administrative records come in to show what really did happen. Many of the most important of them owe their existence to the crown's interest in and management of the ecclesiastical revenues. From 1561 onwards, persons who held benefices, whatever their attitude to the reformed church, in general retained two-thirds of their revenues, while a third was collected to augment the revenues of the crown and make a payment to the clergy of the reformed church.[37] The 'assumption of thirds' involved a survey of all benefices in Scotland (except those in the dioceses of Argyll and the Isles and a number which were negligently or fraudulently concealed), the compilation of an estimate of the financial requirements of the reformed clergy and the creation of a new financial office, 'the collectory'.[38] The administration of the scheme had a chequered career for a dozen years, but in 1573 there was a reorganisation, including among other changes a fresh survey which elicited particulars of many revenues previously concealed.[39] Besides administering the 'thirds', the crown had the disposal of benefices for which no return had been made in the original survey and of revenues 'omitted' from the statements given there. Alongside these novel arrangements, the crown's rights of patronage survived and the reformation rendered possible the assumption by the crown of powers of provision and confirmation formerly exercised by the court of Rome.[40] Far and away the greater part of the property of the church was subject to control by the crown in one way or another.

The Books of Assumption in which the survey of the benefices was recorded have not survived in a complete form. A volume containing the original record for Fife, Lothian, the Borders and Dumfriesshire, with considerable imperfections, is in the Register House (E.48/1/2), and the original record for the east and north-east – Perthshire, Angus, Kincardine, Aberdeen, Banffshire and Moray – is in the National Library (MS 31.3.12), apparently complete. A copy, made in 1605, of those two original records, also in the Register House (E.48/1/1) and running to 417 folios, is what I have always regarded as 'the principal volume' because it brings so much together within two covers, and it is indexed. In Edinburgh University Library (MS Dc.4.32) there is a copy made in 1624 of the record for the west and north, from Kirkcudbright to Inverness, Ross, Caithness and

---

[36] E.g., *Reg. K.S. St. A.*, ii, 529, 704n, 742; *South Leith Records* (ed. D. Robertson, 1911), 5, 7, 9, 19, 22, 24–5, 34, 44, 110, 119, 128, 129, 144; *Stirling Presbytery Records* (SHS), passim; W. A. Gillies, *In Famed Breadalbane* (1938), 309, 326, 328; *Diary of Rev. John Mill* (SHS), lxii; W. Stephen, *Inverkeithing and Rosyth*, 273.

[37] *RPC*, i, 192–202.

[38] *T.B.*, Intro.

[39] 'The new enterit benefices', *SHR*, xxxii, 93–8.

[40] This development is explained in the introductions to *RSS* v–viii, which contain most of the evidence.

Orkney. Two MSS in the National Library (31.3.13 and 31.3.16) contain abridgments. These Books of Assumption are compilations of rentals, some of them made *ad hoc* in or about 1562 but a number belonging to dates before 1560. As the nearest thing to a Scottish equivalent of the *Valor Ecclesiasticus*, they deserve far more attention than they have had; what I have called 'the principal volume' was not even foliated until it was decided to make an index to it in the 1940s.

The principal record of the Collectory, the Accounts of the Collectors of Thirds of Benefices, were printed, mostly in an abridged form, for 1561–72, by the Scottish History Society in 1949; the series (E.45) continues to 1597, but the account for 1574 is a mere fragment and accounts for 1575, 1587 and 1591–4 are not extant. An account formerly attributed to 1597 is only a duplicate of the 1595 account but there is in addition a fragmentary account (E.45/25) for crop and year 1597. Each account follows much the same plan, and the record is consequently easy to use. First is set forth the 'charge' or income in the form of lists of thirds (or, where appropriate, entire benefices), arranged topographically, beginning with the 'charge' of money and proceeding to the 'charge' of wheat and the various other crops, each in turn. The statement of the quantities of grain etc. is followed by the 'defeasance' of the portion of the crop which was disposed of without conversion into cash and then by a statement of the sums of money realised by the sale of what remained 'undefeased'. After each of the fruits has been dealt with in this way, a total is given of the thirds which were collected in cash and of the money realised by the sale of 'undefeased' fruits. The latter part of the account is the 'discharge' of this total of money. It gives lists of thirds remitted to holders of benefices, the sums paid to superintendents, commissioners, ministers, exhorters and readers, payments to students, pensions and other disbursements made according to royal precepts, thirds in arrear and the salaries and expenses of the officials of the Collectory. In 1561 and 1562 and from 1573 onwards all the information for each year is to be found in a single account, the Compt of the Collector General, but from 1563 to 1566 the accounts of the collector general deal only with the receipt and expenditure of the balance of money remaining after the deputy collectors (who accounted directly to the auditors) had disbursed the greater part of the thirds which they collected, and from 1567 to 1572 there are no accounts of collectors general.[41] From 1563 to 1572, therefore, details must be sought in the Compts of the Sub-Collectors[42] of Thirds (E.46), which existed, during these years only'[43] for the eleven districts into

---

[41] The account for 1564 is bound with that for 1563. Both are badly mutilated. The 'Compt of the Collector General 1567–8' does not form part of the series, but arose from the transference in 1567 of the duties of collection to the collectors appointed by the church.

[42] The contemporary title was usually 'chamberlain' or 'collector depute' until 1566 and 'collector' from 1567 to 1572.

[43] The accounts formerly titled '1573' are duplicates of accounts for earlier years. The conclusion of each complete 1572 account shows that the affairs of the sub-collectors were wound up with those accounts.

which the country was divided for the purposes of collection and distribution. There are now numerous gaps in the sub-collectors' accounts[44] and some of the volumes are imperfect, but as most of the items were unchanged in two or more successive years the value of the series is not seriously impaired. The extant volumes supply information which is not given in any of the accounts of collectors general, for in the latter we learn only the total sum assigned for stipend in each district, whereas in the former (except in 1566) the reformed clergy are usually named and their several stipends stated separately.

We are thus provided with a substitute for the earliest Register of Stipends or Book of Modification of Stipends which, although in use from 1561 (as references in the Collectors' Accounts prove), has not survived. For 1567 there is a Register of Ministers, Exhorters and Readers, stating the payments made to each individual, and this volume (E.48/2), which was kept up to date by additions and corrections until 1573, was printed by the Maitland Club in 1830. A similar volume for 1574, now in the National Library (MS 17.1.4) and printed in abridged form in *Wodrow Society Miscellany*, i, 319–96, was probably removed at some date from the Register House and is really the first of the series of the Register of Assignations and Modifications of Stipends, extant for 1576, 1578–80, 1585–6, 1588–91, 1593–7, 1599, 1601, 1607–8 and 1614–5 (E.47). This Register is valuable for information about the staffing of the parishes and it gives particulars about how each stipend was composed. For 1594, 1603 and 1605–9 there are Books of Assignations and Superplus of Thirds, bound together in one volume (E.48/3) titled 'Superplus of Thirds'. They give an account of the whole fruits of vacant benefices, the thirds of benefices not held by ministers, and the stipends of vacant ministerial charges: the major part of these revenues was assigned to ministers, the 'superplus' remaining after this deduction. There is an account of the Register of Assignations of Stipends and Books of Superplus in Acts of Sederunt of the Court of Session, 2 December 1785, 4 December 1793 and 11 March 1795, quoted in Connell, *Tithes*, iii, 25.

The office of Treasurer of the New Augmentation, combined with that of Collector General, was created to deal with the revenue accruing from the temporalities of bishoprics annexed to the crown in 1587, consisting mainly of dues and payments received from feudal vassals. There are a number of accounts and rentals of dates 1592–1600 (E.49). The scope of this work was reduced when their temporalities were restored to the bishops in 1606. From 1611 the joint account for the Collectory and Temporality was engrossed in the same volume as the Comptroller's Account (E.24).

---

[44] A table in *TB*, xli, showing which accounts are extant, did not include accounts for Fife, 1565 (E.46/3/6) and Linlithgow etc., 1566 (fragment, E.46/6/3). Copies of some accounts may be found outside the national archives: e.g., a copy of the 'charge' for Orkney and Shetland, 1565, in the archives of the city of Edinburgh, and an extract from the Account of the Collector General for 1562, in an Orkney charter chest, are printed in J. B. Craven, *History of the Church in Orkney 1558–1662*, 11, 50.

Grants of the ecclesiastical revenues which the crown controlled took the form of presentations to and gifts of the many benefices which were in the royal patronage, pensions from thirds or from benefices, tacks of teinds and other fruits, and confirmations of presentations, pensions and tacks made by other granters. In general gifts were made of benefices without cure of souls and presentations to benefices with cure, but the distinction was not rigidly observed, especially before 1567. In the reformation era various factors extended royal patronage, so that the crown had the gift or presentation of nearly all dignities of cathedrals, a great many dignities of collegiate churches, and at least one-third of the parochial benefices. Gifts of abbacies and some of the writs used in promotions to bishoprics passed the great seal, the remainder were under the privy seal. The Registers of the Great Seal, Privy Seal, Presentations to Benefices and Signatures in the Office of the Comptroller, in which those grants under the seals could be entered, constitute a record of the distribution of the church property which is independent of and complementary to the accounts arising from the work of the Collectory. The Register of the Great Seal is printed for this period and the Register of the Privy Seal is now printed to 1584, but it must be remembered that not all the grants issued under the seals were recorded in the registers.

The Register of Presentations (CH.4) which exists for the years 1567 to 1587 and 1595 to 1663, is of much wider scope than its name suggests, for in the first and second volumes, extending to 1587, true presentations amount to not more than half the entries, and a contemporary title 'Register of beneficial matters'[45] (i.e. matters relating to benefices) is more appropriate. This register is technically a register of 'signatures' or royal warrants for the issue of letters under the seals, and not of those letters themselves. It is tempting to relate it to the Register of Signatures in the Office of the Comptroller (E.2, a register of warrants for crown gifts of all kinds), which appears to contain no presentations and very few entries relating to tacks or pensions from ecclesiastical revenues except in the years from 1587 to 1591, a period for which no register of presentations is extant.[46] The feature which is at once most puzzling to the archivist and most important for the historian is that in practice the Registrum Secreti Sigilli and the Register of Presentations supplemented each other. The registers do not give *verbatim* transcripts of presentations, but their entries contain all the essentials,

---

[45] Register of presentations, i, 71. A contemporary title of vol. ii was 'Registrum S.D.N. regis beneficiorum, pensionum, confirmationum earundem, monachorum et canonicorum portionum'.

[46] Register of Signatures vols. 14 and 15 relate exclusively to ecclesiastical revenues, 1587–91. They supplement the Registrum Secreti Sigilli for those years, but do not contain all the information given there. Register of Presentations vol. iii seems at first sight to begin in the middle of an entry, but fo. 9 (misplaced) has the commencement of the entry. It seems that a gap in this Register of seven or eight years before 1595 existed in the eighteenth century (Ridpath, *Diary* [SHS], 147). Dr Murray has investigated these registers and informs me that 'There were separate registers [of signatures] for the comptroller, treasury and temporality (treasury of new augmentation). "Register of signatures in the office of the

including the cause of the vacancy, the name of the previous holder, and the title of the official responsible for giving admission to the benefice. The acts of caution by which presentees found surety for the avoidance of dilapidation were from 1585 to 1587 recorded in the Register of Presentations, from 1592 to 1625 in an independent register, and from 1625 once more in the Register of Presentations. The names of cautioners are appended to a number of the presentations recorded in the Register of Signatures. The association of the act of caution with the records of presentations suggested that the Register of Presentations was connected with crown finance and was related to the Register of Signatures in the Office of the Comptroller. The act of caution is generally of the same date as the presentation and adds little to our knowledge, but the Register of Acts of Caution may record a very few presentations not entered in any other registers, especially between 1592 and 1595. The Register of Presentations is indexed from 1567 to 1587 and there is an index of supplementary 'beneficial matters' in the Register of the Privy Seal for those years. The printed volumes of the Privy Seal Register, as far as they go, include supplementary information from the Register of Presentations. From 1587 to 1600 a single index of 'beneficial matters' includes all entries in the Registers of the Privy Seal, Presentations, Signatures and Acts of Caution.

There are many indications that the administration of the ecclesiastical revenues was not conducted without a vast amount of litigation. The complaints of the ministers that they had often to resort to legal process in order to obtain payment of their stipends are confirmed by the Collectors' Accounts, which record the payment of fees to the procurators, solicitors and advocates who were maintained by the reformed church and by the Collectory and which contain long lists of 'restis dependand' (i.e. arrears about which litigation was proceeding) and 'restis be horning' (i.e. arrears for the recovery of which a process had been completed). The majority of the cases which came before the courts arose from action by the holder of a benefice to exact payment of teinds from parishioners; the pursuer was usually a parson or vicar recently instituted, but was occasionally a pre-reformation holder. Many processes resulted from the claims of ministers against holders of benefices, parishioners, or tenants, for thirds assigned in stipend, and some followed on action by the collector for payment of thirds. A number of cases dealt with the rights of ministers and readers to the manses and glebes to which they were entitled by acts of parliament.

---

comptroller" is a misleading title as most of the volumes relate to the treasury (17 out of 21 up to 1600).' Pointing out that the volumes formerly numbered 12 and 13 are now 14 and 15, he goes on: 'These are temporality registers, for the kirklands annexed to the crown in 1587, and therefore have no direct connection with the register of presentations. The main purpose of all the registers of signatures seems to have been to serve as a record of compositions for charters and other grants and each was kept by an official concerned with revenue *collection*'.

This litigation is well represented in the Acts and Decreets (of the Court of Session) (CS.5) which thus forms a most valuable quarry for the ecclesiastical historian.[47] Similar matter is to be found in the Particular Registers of Hornings, which are, however, very incomplete for this period,[48] and also in the *Register of the Privy Council*. Documents concerning actions not recorded in the registers survive in isolation among family papers and elsewhere.[49]

The archives which have been described can be used primarily to show the distribution of the ecclesiastical property among laymen (including the crown) beneficed men who took no part in the work of the reformed church, and the reformed clergy. Facile estimates, beginning with that of Knox, who saw 'two parts freely given to the devil' while 'the third must be divided between God and the devil', have underestimated the proportion enjoyed by the reformed church, because they have ignored the position of holders of benefices who acted as ministers and who, besides continuing to draw two-thirds of their revenues, were usually allowed to retain their third also.[50] It is to be observed that even the registers of stipends do not take account of the two-thirds of benefices to which ministers had been provided 'of old' (i.e. before 1567). In such cases the third alone was technically stipend and was set down in the registers, which make no reference to the fact that the incumbent was drawing his two-thirds as well. The entire fruits of 'new provided benefices since our sovereign lord's coronation' (1567) appear in the registers as stipend. A careful survey of personnel is plainly an essential preliminary to an understanding of the allocation of the revenues. It should be noted, further, that a few bishops and commendators had their thirds remitted on condition that they sustained ministers at the churches annexed to their bishoprics or abbeys, that there were remissions and gifts to towns for the support of their ministers, and that there were substantial assignations of thirds to education and the poor. None of those revenues can properly be reckoned among the 'devil's' share. In order to obtain accurate statistics it is necessary to consult not only the 'discharge' in the collectors' accounts, for that is a discharge of money only. The discharge of a substantial part, very often the major part or even the whole, of the thirds which consisted of crops and other products must be sought in the 'charge' under the sub-headings of 'defeasance' or 'defalcation' (occasionally 'discharge'), and a large part of this 'defeasance' went to the reformed clergy either in the form of remissions (to beneficed

---

[47] The volumes covering the period 1560–1600 number some 160, and there is no index. Vol. 55 is devoted entirely to cases concerning benefice fruits, 1574–90, but is far from including all such cases in those years. The remarks made in the text are based on an examination of a number of volumes, chosen at random, all of which were found to contain several decreets of ecclesiastical interest.

[48] For details, see M. Livingstone, *Guide to the Public Records of Scotland*, 144–50.

[49] E.g., Reg. Ho., misc. eccl. documents (CH.8), nos. 13–14; Mey papers (GD.96), nos. 158, 242b.

[50] Although the 'allowance' of the third in such cases was not statutory until 1567 (*APS*, iii, 37, c. 7; cf. *RPC*, ii, 495), it had been usual since 1561.

men who acted as ministers) or as stipends. A minor *caveat* is that in the years 1563 to 1566, when nearly all the payments to ministers are to be found in the sub-collectors' accounts, a few have strayed into the accounts of the collector general, where they jostle such items as a sum given to the queen 'to play at the cards' and the expenses incurred in the pursuit of the earl of Bothwell when he fled to the north in 1567.[51]

It should be the aim of students of these records not only to estimate the financial position of the reformed church in the period 1561–7 but also to trace the various developments which led to the amelioration of that position in later years. A larger share of the thirds was enjoyed by the reformed church as a result of the restriction of the crown's claim to the 'superplus', and inefficiency in the distribution of stipends, which had been the subject of frequent complaint, should have become less serious as a result of the cessation of the civil war and the reorganisation of the Collectory in 1573. According to the legislation of 1567, all benefices which fell vacant were to go to men who would serve in the reformed church. An analysis of crown presentations is required to show how far this rule was observed and how the proportion of 'unqualified' presentees diminished in the course of years. The hold of the reformed church on the benefices was greatly strengthened after 1573 by deprivation of holders who would not accept the reformers' confession of faith, and at a later date by sequestration of the livings of persons who, presented after 1567, did not make residence at their churches. The right of the reformed clergy to succeed to the bishoprics was established in 1572. Thereafter vacant sees were almost invariably given to ministers, and the *formulae* used in their promotion (nomination, licence to elect, mandate to consecrate, and restitution of temporality) are to be found in the Registrum Secreti Sigilli and Register of Presentations. The attempt to find a place for the monastic houses, as entities, in the framework of a reformed ecclesiastical constitution[52] enjoyed less success; their fortunes, like those of the bishoprics, can be readily followed in the *Register of the Privy Seal.* However, there were two ways in which the reformed church obtained some profit from the monastic revenues. The regular clergy were allowed to enjoy their 'portions' for life, and as they died these portions became available for distribution by the crown, which might occasionally give them to ministers or students.[53] The 'dissolution of the prelacies', which meant the distribution of the spirituality of the monasteries and the bishoprics among the parish churches from the teinds of which it was derived, had been demanded in Mary's reign,[54] and there is evidence that it was partially achieved in the early 1590s by the separation of some paro-chial benefices from the abbeys and bishoprics to which they had been

---

[51] *TB*, 187, 191, 193.
[52] *BUK*, i, 210, cf. *RSS*, vi, Intro. p. xvi. That these provisions were not wholly a dead letter is shown by *RSS*, vi, 1801.
[53] Gifts of monks' and nuns' portions are recorded in *RSS* and Reg. Pres.
[54] *BUK*, i, 59–60.

annexed.[55] All the modifications which affected the relations of the reformed church with the benefices are of more than financial significance, for they can be regarded as different aspects of a single process in the evolution of church organisation. We start in 1560 with two distinct structures – on one side the organisation of the reformed congregations and on the other the fabric of the church, still endowed and not yet truly disestablished – linked only by the beneficed clergy who acted as ministers in their own parishes. In succeeding years we can trace the tendency of these two structures to merge or coalesce.

In the record which the Collectors' Accounts give of the allocation of that portion of the ecclesiastical revenues which was enjoyed by the reformed clergy we have in effect a statement of the salaries of the staff of the church, and a thorough examination of this record would illuminate many features of ecclesiastical organisation, such as the position of the bishops who accepted the reformed faith and continued to exercise some of their episcopal functions and the periods during which superintendents and commissioners served and the territory for which each was responsible. The work of all such overseers is illustrated in the Acts and Decreets, where processes dealing with manses and glebes usually give the name or title of the official who had designed the boundaries of the glebe and sometimes state the date of the visitation on which he did so. Research on the administration of the Collectory would contribute to our knowledge of the duties which the superintendents performed in connection with the collection of thirds and assignation of stipends. Statistics for the numbers and disposition of the parochial clergy, especially in the 1560s, would indicate the efficiency of the overseers who had the power of 'planting kirks' and admitting ministers to charges. The territorial distribution of the clergy itself requires special study. As the Register of Ministers, Exhorters and Readers and the Register of Assignations and Modifications of Stipends cover a period during which one minister often had charge of two or more parishes, with readers assisting him, the compilation of lists of pastors for separate parishes presents certain difficulties. Entries in the *Fasti Ecclesiae Scoticanae* sometimes stated that a minister was translated from one parish to another when in fact he had charge of both concurrently. Even when such lists are accurately compiled they tend to mislead the student of organisation; it is more satisfactory to approach the subject from the biographical angle than the territorial, but possibly no means of reproduction (except a facsimile) can convey a correct impression of the state of affairs revealed by the registers themselves. It is important to exclude from lists purporting to show the strength of the reformed clergy many titulars who, although laymen, enjoyed the style of 'parson' or 'vicar' and have sometimes been mistaken for ministers. Investigation is required of the payments (recorded in the collectors' accounts) to the legal and clerical officers of the church – the solicitors, procurators, and agents, the

[55] E.g., *RSS*, lxii, 137, 146, 147, 155; Book of Assignations and Superplus of Thirds, 1594, fos. 17, 37; *RMS*, v, 2070.

clerks of the general assembly, and the first recorded clerk of a presbytery. One prime field for investigation is the machinery for making appointments to benefices and the place in it of those responsible for giving formal admission, because here lies the key to the seat of administrative authority in the church. The successive changes, as the ecclesiastical constitution was more than once modified and the political position of the church more than once changed, have been explained in my introductions to the volumes of the *Register of the Privy Seal* down to 1584, and the development thereafter has been sketched in my *Scottish Reformation* (pp. 217–18, 220–1). There was on the whole far less dislocation than might be suggested by the superficial idea that the church was swinging violently from episcopacy to presbytery and back again, and even the statutory authorisation of presbyteries in 1592 did not produce uniformity. The series of crown presentations, continuous from 1567, can be supplemented from other sources. Presentations by patrons other than the crown, of dates both before and after 1567, must exist among family papers.[56] The collation is from its nature a somewhat fugitive writ and only a few specimens can have survived in private charter chests;[57] two or three are extant in collections now preserved among the national records, and one of these collections includes a 'progress' of presentation, collation (by a superintendent), and institution, of date 1570.[58] The deed of institution, being a notarial instrument, had more chance than a collation of attaining permanence, and copies of many are to be found in notarial protocol books.[59] The evidence of the collations and institutions which have survived can be reinforced by the many references, in crown gifts and confirmations, to presentations by other patrons, collations and provisions by bishops, the examination of presentees' qualifications, and institutions or admissions. There are similar references in the Acts and Decreets, where processes often state the date of presentation, the name of the previous holder, the cause of the vacancy, and particulars of collation and admission.

The value of presentations extends far beyond the information which they give about the method of admission to benefices. In cases of vacancy by deprivation the presentation of the new holder frequently states by whom his predecessor had been deprived and so reveals in whose hands lay disciplinary authority over the clergy. Probably no beneficed clergy were deprived before 1573 (except in cases where a process in the civil courts had led to forfeiture), but in that year, when the reformed church had at last

---

[56] E.g., Reg. Ho. Charters (RH.6), 1896; Misc. Eccles. Documents (CH.8), 39–40; *Calendar of Laing Charters* (ed. John Anderson), 727; *Calendar of Writs of Munro of Foulis* (SRS), 84.

[57] Erroll Charters (Inventory in Reg. Ho.), 753; *Laing Charters*, 1019; J. B. Craven, op. cit., 10; *Calendar of Yester Writs* (SRS), 741.

[58] Reg. Ho. Charters, 2205, 2207–8, cf. 2153, 2523. Among the Breadalbane Papers (GD.112) are two collations to the vicarage of Clachan Dysart, 1576 and 1583.

[59] E.g., Reg. Ho. Protocol Books (NP.1), Duncan Gray (NP.1/16), 25, 41, 83, James Colville (NP.1/11), 46; John Cunynghame (B.20/1/1), 116, Kingorne (NP.1/186), 1580–97, fo. 5. For a list of Protocol Books, see *Sources and Literature of Scots Law* (Stair Soc.), 289–90.

attained the full status of establishment, a statute required all holders of benefices to accept the reformed confession of faith, on pain of deprivation.[60] Thereafter there were numerous deprivations for failing to appear before a bishop, superintendent, or commissioner, to give subscription to the confession of faith, the oath accepting the royal supremacy, and the oath of obedience to the ordinary. Presentations following on such deprivations seldom state explicitly by whom the deprivation had been carried out, but they sometimes give the name or title of the bishop, superintendent or commissioner before whom the recusant should have taken his oaths, and it may be presumed that this official was responsible for carrying out the deprivation. Deprivations for non-residence or immorality required a process before the ordinary, and in the presentations which followed the judge who had passed sentence is usually named. Down to 1584 most of the evidence is at hand in the printed *Register of the Privy Seal* and is discussed in the editorial introductions. After 1584 recourse must still be had to the original MS record.[61] Once again, as in the study of collations, it is noticeable that the presbyteries were of little importance until about 1590. A statute of June 1592, recognising the powers of presbyteries, synods, and general assemblies, to deprive,[62] may show that their authority in this respect had not previously rested on a strong foundation.

The evidence which can be collected from presentations and other sources about the disciplinary and administrative functions of bishops, superintendents, commissioners, synods, and presbyteries, is especially important in view of the paucity of records of church courts for the period before 1600. Those registers of kirk sessions, presbyteries, and synods, which survive[63] require to be examined as judicial and administrative records instead of being dismissed as *registra enormium delictorum*[64] which are of value to the social historian only. Of outstanding importance among the extant registers is the *Register of the Kirk Session of St. Andrews*. This includes the proceedings of the consistorial court of the superintendent of Fife from 1561 to 1572, and the specimens of summonses, sentences, edicts, testimonials, and processes, which it contains should be compared with pre-reformation *formulae*[65] to show how far the reformed church adopted the judicial styles of the old episcopal courts. The register reveals the functions of the superintendent not only in the correction of moral offences, but in examining, admitting, suspending, and depriving ministers and readers. The St Andrews Register is the earliest extant record of a kirk session, and now we have in print to accompany it the earliest surviving

[60] *APS*, iii, 72.

[61] RSS, lvii, 139, 172, lix, 20, lxii, 26, 35, lxiii, 258, 262; Reg. Pres., ii, 174.

[62] *APS*, iii, 542–3.

[63] Thomas Burns, *Church Property* (Benefice Lectures, 1905); *Sources and Literature of Scots Law*, 154–62; extensive Register House holdings listed in Repertory CH2.

[64] *Reg. K.S. St. A.*, 1.

[65] Preserved, for example, in the court books of the officials (cf. 'The Church Courts', *supra*) and in *St. Andrews Formulare* (Stair Soc.).

records of a presbytery – Stirling, beginning in 1581 – and the earliest extant records of a synod – Lothian and Tweeddale, beginning in 1589 – both edited by Dr James Kirk, the former for the Scottish History Society and the latter for the Stair Society. These and other registers which are extant for periods before 1600 all yield valuable evidence on the working of ecclesiastical organisation, and they can be supplemented by papers recording isolated acts of church courts which survive in various collections.[66] It is most important, for the history of administration and procedure, to have not selections but complete texts, or at any rate texts which give the full forms and styles – and also the sederunts, so that the courts can be viewed realistically in human terms and not as mere abstractions and so that church organisation can be related to society.

For the study of personnel, either in groups or as individuals, we have no records which give complete lists of the clergy at the reformation. The Books of Assumption yield the names of many holders of benefices, but not of all. The 'charge' of thirds in the Collectors' Accounts (except in the case of the sub-collectors for Moray) gives the names of benefices only, but these accounts supply many names of clergy in the lists of thirds remitted or 'given free' and of thirds in arrear. Supplementary information must be obtained from presentations, where previous holders are named, and from the general biographical sources. The lists in the Collectors' Accounts of 'allowed benefices' down to 1572 give us the names of the men who conformed and continued to 'serve at their own kirks and cures', but do not include all clergy who conformed, since those who had held benefices elsewhere than in the parishes where they served as ministers, those who had been members of regular orders, and those who had been only chaplains, vicars pensionary, or curates without benefices, must be traced individually. Comprehensive lists of the reformed clergy can be compiled from the Collectors' Accounts for the period before 1567, and thereafter from the other registers already described. How far the diverse information is adequate for a survey which would show how much continuity there was in personnel can be judged from the earlier article in this volume on 'The Parish Clergy at the Reformation'. For the period between 1567 and 1600 the significant study would be one showing the gradual increase in the proportion of benefices held by ministers. Not all the pre-reformation clergy who failed to take part in the work of the reformed church were deprived, and the legislation of 1567, making it illegal to present 'unqualified' men to benefices, was not at first rigidly observed. Information about the education and parentage of many who became ministers in the 1570s and later can be obtained from the records of presentations and the Collectors' Accounts, as it was the practice from 1568 to make payments out of the thirds to students and schoolboys and from 1572[67] to equip them with chaplainries and prebends of collegiate churches.

---

[66] E.g., Mey Papers, 188 (act of synodal assembly of Caithness, 1580); Balcarres Papers (NLS), vi, 88 (act of the 'exercise' of Edinburgh in 1578); J. B. Craven, op cit., p. 77.
[67] BUK, i, 214.

The relevant entries in the Collectors' Accounts have been printed for the period to 1578.[68] The abundant biographical material existing in the Collectors' Accounts and the records of presentations was not used consistently or exhaustively in the compilation of the *Fasti ecclesiae Scoticanae*, though additional information, derived from the sources which have been described, was incorporated in a supplementary volume (viii).

The archives which had their origin in the administration of the ecclesiastical property were almost entirely neglected in the study of the development of ecclesiastical organisation. With the records of the church courts they ought to be regarded not as illustrative matter which could confirm or amend the accounts given by narratives but as the primary source for a reconstruction of the constitutional and administrative history of the church. 'The reconstruction', I wrote in 1944, 'might well be based on a foundation of regional studies, since most of the significant problems concern local historians and are indeed problems relating to territorial units – the diocese, presbytery, and parish.' When I made that plea for regional studies I noted that some authors of local histories, led by Dr William Stephen (who collected the supplementary material for *Fasti* vol. viii) had made good use of this record material. Subsequently, between 1947 and 1960, I published studies of the Reformation in the dioceses of Galloway and Orkney, and in the 1970s one of my Ph.D. students, Dr John Todd, wrote a thesis on The Reformation in the Diocese of Dunblane. Yet a writer in 1983, who surely suffers not merely from shortsightedness but from blindness, remarked that 'local reformation studies have scarcely begun in Scotland' and 'the first step in this direction was taken by I. B. Cowan' in 1978.[69]

The study in greater depth, even a 'reconstruction', of 'the constitutional and administrative history of the church' may not produce extensive revision of the broad outlines as they have been understood by historians. The trouble has been that all the labours of historians have had little effect on a kind of folk-memory which preserves a grave distortion of the facts. This emerged very clearly in some of the comments made when my *Scottish Reformation* appeared in 1960. A good many reviewers seemed to think that I had advanced quite novel views: one said that I had given the Scottish Reformation 'a new look', another comment was that the book was 'revolutionary'. But, as so often happens, the reviews revealed more about the reviewers than about the contents of the book and in this instance revealed how ignorant the reviewers were of previous writings on the subject. I suppose the points where I was believed to be injecting some novelty were in my emphasis that the reformers did not believe in the inviolable parity of ministers and consequently were not opposed to a reformed episcopate or the exercise of supervision by individuals and that the reformers did not propose to exclude the laity from control over the church and make it a kind of clerical preserve.

[68] In an appendix to *Early records of the university of St. Andrews* (SHS).
[69] Norman MacDougall (ed.), *Church, Politics and Society in Scotland 1408–1929*, 66, 80.

But those points were far from novel and had all been made many times before. Hill Burton, a century ago, wrote that 'Knox did not direct his denunciations at the principle of prelacy' and he criticised those who saw in Knox 'an enemy to an Episcopalian hierarchy' (v, 75, 79). At the very end of last century, in *A Manual of Church Doctrine*, H. J. Wotherspoon and J. M. Kirkpatrick stated firmly, 'We do not find at the Reformation, or for some time afterwards, any hostility to Episcopacy as a form of government' (p. 90); and this sentence was retained when the work was revised in 1960 by Professor Torrance and Dr Selby Wright, who added a note that 'the office of Superintendent was not designed as a temporary office in the Kirk, as is often averred' (p. 9n). Hume Brown, in his *John Knox* (1895), stated that 'Knox raises no objection to the office of bishop in itself. Its existence, indeed, he takes for granted', and that Andrew Melville 'was driven to the very opposite pole from the position of his great predecessor' (i, 356, ii, 279). Sheriff Macphail made a very quotable remark in *SHR*, xxii, 19 (1925): 'His experiences in the French galleys may not indeed have filled John Knox with a spirit of sweet reasonableness, but, except as regards the Mass, he was sanity itself compared with those who came after him. The rot started as early as 1574 when Mr Andrew Melville unfortunately returned to Scotland with his Swiss-made theology and fantastic political theories.' Sir Robert Rait was more temperate. In his admirable little *History of Scotland* (revised 1930), p. 141, he has 'Knox had never regarded the administrative office of a bishop as unscriptural', whereas Melville 'held that Episcopacy is not only not expedient but not lawful in any form'; and in the volume *Scotland*, where he collaborated with G. S. Pryde, Rait wrote of the reformed church as 'not yet presbyterian' (53) until Melville 'taught the essential "parity" of all ministers and denounced the episcopal office as unscriptural' (57). R. L. Mackie, in his *Short History of Scotland* (1930) put it neatly that Knox had 'dreams of a Church not unlike the Anglican Church, with bishops – only he would call them superintendents – and with a prayer book – the English Book of Common Prayer would serve till he framed a simpler one' (240). Professor Hannay, in his lectures, declared that there was no evidence that the office of superintendent was meant to be temporary. More recently, Dr Stewart Mechie, in a modest little pamphlet which did not receive the attention it deserved but which summarised the history of *Episcopacy in the post-Reformation Scottish Church* (Porch Library, St Andrew Press, n.d.), stated: 'There is no passage in Knox's writings which, fairly interpreted in its context, can be regarded as a condemnation of episcopacy in itself'. Principal Burleigh, in his *Church History of Scotland* (1960) declared, 'It is true, of course, . . . that Knox was not a Presbyterian, since he did not insist on ministerial "parity"', but the Principal considered it was 'pointless' to say so, surely because he was well aware that no one outside scholarly circles was going to believe it. However, the latest in the long line of historians of the Scottish Reformation, Professor I. B. Cowan, did not consider it pointless to give his judgment: 'Knox himself does not appear to have objected to the office [of bishop] as such . . . and it was not until the acceptance of the Second Book of Discipline that the office of bishop was condemned'.[70] Of course all of those writers may have been mistaken, and it would have been quite in order for reviewers of *The Scottish Reformation* to say (if they could prove it) that I was mistaken, but they were not entitled to accuse me of eccentricity or originality.

[70] I. B. Cowan, *Blast and Counterblast* (1960), 40.

10

The General Assembly of December 1563

Reference is made in the previous chapter, 'Sources for Scottish Church History 1560–1600', to the imperfect state of our knowledge of the proceedings of the early general assemblies, owing to the loss of the original records, and in *The Scottish Reformation* (p. 140) I remarked specifically that 'the material which preserves the proceedings of the sixteenth-century general assemblies, consisting as it does of abridgments and selected extracts, seldom discloses the composition of the meetings'. The point of those observations has been reinforced by an examination of a MS. narrating part of the proceedings of the general assembly of December 1563. The fragment, which came into my hands recently, consists of four pages containing:

(1) the latter part of the sederunt, in the shape of a list of 'commissionaris of kirks and cuntreis';
(2) part of the early proceedings of session 1, finishing, at the foot of a page, in mid-sentence;
(3) part of the later proceedings of session 3; and
(4) the beginning of the proceedings of session 4.

The early part of the sederunt, preceding the part now printed, would contain the names of nobles, officials, superintendents, bishops and ministers. Sources already printed, especially Calderwood, disclose, either in summary lists of the membership or in the course of the proceedings which are narrated, the presence of the following: The Duke of Châtelherault, the Earls of Argyll, Moray, Morton, Rothes, Glencairn and Marischal, Lords Lindsay, Ruthven and Erskine; the Secretary, Comptroller, Justice-Clerk, Clerk Register and two Lords of Session – Henry Balnaves and Gavin Hamilton, Commendator of Kilwinning; the superintendents of Angus, Fife, Lothian and the West and the Bishops of Galloway and Orkney; the lairds of Kelwood, Abbotshall and Cunninghamhead; and only seventeen ministers, two of them 'commissioners' who carried out the duties of superintendents on a temporary basis. Thus the list of commissioners of kirks and countries is the most valuable part of the new material and it suggests that Calderwood's 'barons, burgesses and gentlemen' is his gloss on 'commissioners'. No indication is given of the method used to select this rather heterogeneous body of commissioners. We know from burgh records that the town councils selected burgh commissioners, and in this instance the appointment of Little, Marjoribanks and Barron duly appears in *Extracts from the Records of the Burgh of Edinburgh 1557–71* (p. 175). That this was standard procedure is evident from *The Buik of the Kirk of the Canagait* (Scottish Record Society, p. 74), where a routine 'style' for such an appointment is to be found. But it is hard to think of how nominations were made for the three divisions of Ayrshire or for 'Selkirk and South'.

The names of the commissioners are in accord with what we should expect. The geographical distribution seems to be shaped partly by the ease or difficulty of access to Edinburgh in a winter month and perhaps partly by the extent to which enthusiasm for the reformation could cause men to make light of difficulties of travel: commissioners were drawn predominantly from east coast areas from the Mearns to East Lothian and from the south-western districts from Glasgow to Wigtown. With no representation from Aberdeen and beyond, none from the west north of Glasgow and a ratio between east and west of 2 : 1, this assembly already showed the pattern which was to persist for a long time except when James VI took steps to redress the balance in favour of the northern parts of his realm.

Eighteen of the twenty lairds (including one peer, Lord Glamis) can be certainly identified, and each one's presence at an assembly is consonant with other evidence of his ecclesiastical alignment. Eight of them are known to have been active in the reforming cause before 1560; all of them, except possibly one, had been associated with the revolution of 1560 in such ways as attending the 'reformation parliament', signing the first Book of Discipline or attending the 'first general assembly' of December 1560; five of them are known to have attended other general assemblies, and if the records were more complete would very likely be seen to have been regular attenders; four of them signed the Ayrshire Protestant Bond of 1562; ten of them were to be active in the party which supported the revolution of 1567 and the deposition of Mary (though the issues between the two parties at that point were political, and men of all religious persuasions were to be found on both sides).

There were twenty-five other commissioners in addition to those who were clearly present as lairds, most of them obviously burgesses but one or two of them undesignated. Many of them can, like the lairds, be readily identified. First among Edinburgh's representatives was that distinguished lawyer Clement Little, whose involvement in burghal factions had not been conspicuous but who had from time to time shown his alignment with the protestant party and who is best known for a bequest of books to the ministers of Edinburgh which formed the nucleus of the library of the University. The second Edinburgh representative, John Marjoribanks, had taken the same line as Little in divisions on religious issues. The third name, that of John Barron, is surely an error for James. There was indeed a John Barron in Edinburgh, but he is hardly known, whereas James, the dean of gild, had been a protestant in the 1550s and something of a leader of that faction until his death in 1569; he was to represent the burgh again at the assembly of December 1566. The representatives of the adjoining burgh, Canongate – John Acheson, John Hart and presumably John Macneil, although the scribe has not distinctly bracketed his name with the other two – all appear as elders in the local kirk session when its records begin in 1564–5 and may well have been elders earlier. St Andrews sent the prestigious John Douglas, rector of the university and future archbishop, and William Cook, who was also a graduate and was a bailie of the burgh; both were among the first elders chosen when the kirk session was constituted in 1559. Whether the town of Dundee was deemed to be entitled to seven representatives (one of them a peer and three of them lairds) because of its pre-eminent reputation for 'godliness' cannot be determined, and one suspects that the scribe carelessly bracketed the representatives of the sheriffdom of Angus with those of the burgh; but in James Haliburton Dundee had a commissioner who was perhaps the outstanding figure among the burgesses present in this assembly. In view of his very close and prominent involvement in the revolution of 1559–60 he might easily be taken as the most significant of all the burgesses who supported the reformation, but it must be remembered that he was more than a burgess. He was a member of the lairdly family of Pitcur, he was a graduate, he was provost of Dundee for thirty-three years, and is perhaps the closest approximation to that better known man John Erskine of Dun, who played the three parts of laird, provost of Montrose and superintend-ent of Angus. Patrick Vaus, a commissioner for 'Wigtown' (whether burgh or shire) also had more than one role. He was laird of Barnbarroch and had been parson of Wigtown since 1545 and parson of Douglas since 1560, but he did not act as a minister. The first of the representatives named for Perth, Patrick Murray, may well have been Patrick Murray of Tibbermuir, who had been prominent among the lords of the con-gregation. The burghs of Dunbar, Tranent, Selkirk, Kirkcaldy and Kinghorn were apparently represented by local lairds and not by resident burgesses, but it may be that some of those individuals represented 'cuntreis' rather than merely burghs. Glasgow's representative, James Fleming, may be the man of that name who is known for his acquisitions of ecclesiastical property. Renfrew's choice was an unusual one, for Mr Andrew Hay was a cleric of both the unreformed and the reformed church; parson of Renfrew since 1552, he accepted the reformation to become minister there in 1561 and he later acted as 'commissioner' (that is, in effect, superintendent) of part of the diocese of Glasgow. Further investigations at local level might well yield information about the other burgesses who came to the assembly, but the general impression one forms is that the burghal representatives were a fairly prestigious lot and that what might be called the rank and file of ordinary burgesses were at best not conspicuous.

The MS is almost certainly not a fragment of official record. It contains errors and corrections which are more likely to appear in a copy than in an original: examples are the omission of 'kirk' after 'haill' in the first paragraph of the text; the substitution in the same paragraph of (apparently) 'fornication' for 'the reformation' – perhaps by a scribe who was accustomed to kirk session minutes; the impossible 'theretablie' in the third paragraph on page 3; the substitution of 'Kingorne' for 'Kyrkcaldy' in the list of commissioners; the deletion of 'glorie of his God' before 'edificatioun' at the end of the text; the appearance in the margin of 'M. Robert Lokart' twice over on p. 4, although only one paragraph relates to that individual. It is perhaps worth noting also that according to other sources this assembly was the first one at which a moderator was appointed, and this item might have been expected to come at the opening of the proceedings, but it does not appear at all in this MS.

It would on the whole seem most likely that the MS is a contemporary copy, made by a scribe who was not over-careful and whose attention was apt to wander. It seems less likely to be a draft: perhaps the one feature which might suggest this is the rather casual way in which untidy brackets are used to group together the names of the commissioners for various places.

The bulk of the proceedings related here can be found, either at length or in abridgement, in other sources, and the material not so found is relatively unimportant, like the decision about hours of convening and the entry about Robert Lockhart. At the same time, it is useful to have what look like the *ipsissima verba* of the assembly's proceedings in trying superintendents and the decisions about teinds and stipends. One realises afresh that the phrase which was firmly in the assembly's mind in 1563 – that tenants should have 'their own teinds upon reasonable composition' – was the phrase which lay behind Charles I's proceedings more than sixty years later. A transcript of the MS follows.

Commissionaris of Kirkis and Cuntreis

M Clement Litle
M Johnne Marjorybankis }for Edinburgh
Johnne Barroun
The laird of Braid [Robert Fairlie] for Sanct Cuthbertis Kirk
The lard of Spott [George Home] for Dunbar
Walter Cant and }for Leith
Johnne Broun
The laird of Prestoun [David Hamilton] for Tranent
Thomas Scot of Hanyng for Selkirk and South
M Johnne Douglas }for Sanctandrois
M William Cok
Thomas Scot of Abbotishall for Kirkcaldy
The laird of Grange [William Kirkcaldy] for [Kyrkcaldy *del.*] Kinghorn
The laird of Balvaird [Andrew Murray]
Patrik Murray and }for Sanct Johnestoun
Patrik Bursone

Johne Hairt ⎱
Johne Achesoun ⎰ for the Cannogait
Johne Makneill
M James Halyburtoun provest ⎤
Rychart Blyth ⎟
Robert Kyd ⎟
The Lord Glammys ⎟ for Dunde
The lard of Grange [William Durham] ⎟
The laird of Powry [Thomas Fothringham] ⎟
The laird of Brigtoun [? Alexander Strachan] ⎦
M Walter Lyon for Montrose
The lardis of Glenbervie elder and younger ⎤
   [Archibald and William Douglas] ⎟
The laird of Fethircarne [? Alexander Ogston] ⎬ for the Mernis
Alexander Wischeart ⎦
Robert Campbell of Kingincleuch for Cyle
The lard of Bar younger [John Lockhart] for the Galstoun
Charlis Campbell for Air
The laird of Bergany younger [Thomas Kennedy] ⎱
The laird of Kelwod [George Corrie] ⎰ for Carrik
The laird of Cunynghameheid [William Cunningham] for Cunynghame
M Andro Hay for Renfrew
James Flemyng for Glasgow
The laird of Garless [Alexander Stewart] ⎱
M. Alexander Menzeis (?) ⎰ for Nethisdale
[p. 2]
M Patrik Vauss ⎤
Gavin Dunbar ⎟
David Murray ⎬ for Wigtoun
Alexander Mur ⎦

Anent the questioun movit be Johnne Knox, minister of Edinburgh, to the haill assembley, quhidder he ressavit charge of the haill [kirk] than convenit in Edinburgh eftir the begynnyng of fornicatioun [*sic: rectius* the reformatioun] to advertice the brethering to convene at quhat tyme ony nowmer of the kirk suld chance to be trublit and that for thair counsale to be had.

   [*Margin*: Questioun be M Knox. Declaratioun.] To the quhilk the Lord Lindesay, the lardis of Kelwod and Abottishall [and] Cunynghameheid, the superintendentis of Anguse, Fyffe, Lothiane, West and Galloway, Maister Johne Row, William Chrystesoun, M Robert Hammiltoun, M Christofer Guidman, ministeris, within the maist part of the haill assembley maid thair declaratioun that thai remembrytt werray weill that the said Knox wald haif had himself exonerit of the forsaidis charge and that the kirk than present wald nawayis suffer him to refuise the sam but at he suld continew as befoir at advertice from tyme to tyme as actions suld be gevin.

[*Margin*: Houris of convenyng.] And becaus na uther caussis occurrit the houris of convening to be at aucht in the mornyng and tua efter none and the fyrst day eftir this of convenyng to be on Monunday nixtocum and for that purpoise that the exercise be continewit quhill eftir the end of this assembley.

[*Margin*: Eftir none. Tryale of the superintendent of Lothian.] The said day the kirk convenand eftir none according to the ordour tane and observit anent the tryell of superintendentis ministeris and utheris of the kirk, accusatioun is to be laid to thair charges tuiching thair doctrine maneris conversatioun and executioun of thair offices.

First was removit out of the assembley M Johne Spottiswod, superintendent of Lothiane, and libertie was gevin to all men to accuse and nane complenand upoun him he was commandit to returne agane in the assembley, the comp[l]aint of the kirk of Calder alwayis reservit to the end of the assembley: nochttheles requeistit the kyrk to gif him libertie to returne to his formair air [*sic*. ? *rectius* cure] because he was abill to discharge

[p. 3]

[*Margin*: Anent assignatioun of stipendis.] Also ordanis supplicatioun to be gevin in to the secreit counsale that [upoun *del*.] provisioun may be tane that every minister have his stipend assignit to him in the rowme quhair he laubouris and travallis.

[*Margin*: Act anent glebis and manssis.] And that the act of parliament anent manssis and glebis be mair specialie condiscendit on and that this be eikit to the supplicatioun with the formair anent the stipendis assignatioun.

Anent the lamentabill complent of the puir lauboraris of the ground within this realme and unmercifull exactioun of thair teindis be the erllis, lordis, baronis and utheris takkismen of the same.

[*Margin*: Anent the supplicatioun for teyndis for the tenentis.] It was theretablie [*sic*] requirit at the nobilitie thair present and utheris haifing interes that the puir laubouraris suld have the teyndis of that ground quhilk thai lauborit for ane ressonable compositioun ouder [*sic*] of money or vittale to be payt to the erlis, lordis, baronis or utheris forsaidis.

Bot becaus this requeist culd nocht be fullie answerit to nor satesfiet be this nummer of the nobilitie heir present in respect it tuicheit the haill nobilitie and utheris quha for the maist parte war absent, nochttheles my lord Duikis grace, the Erlis of Ergile, Murray, Marschell, Glencarne and Rothes, the Lordis Ruthven, Lindesay and Comptrollar, thair present in the assembley, consentit to the requeist abonementionet for thair awin partis.

[*Margin*: Teyndis.] And forder ordanit the superintendentis in thair boundis to travell with the erlis, lordis, baronis and utheris that leydis teindis that thai wilbe content to suffer the puir tennentis within thair boundis respective to leid thair awin teyndis upoun ressonable compositioun of money or vittalis as said is, quhairby the saidis teindis may evidentlie resave sum eise and releiffe, and that the saidis superintendentis report the answer of every man particularie tuiching the premissis to the nixt assembley.

Attour the hail assembley heir present hes forther concludit and fully consentit that for thair awin partis the tennentis and occupyaris of the ground sall have thair awin teyndis upon compositioun as said is.

[p.4]

The four sessioun of the assembley haldin in Edinburgh the xxix day of December 1563

[*Margin*: Anent the buik of disciplin and ourseing thairof.] The same day it was thocht neidfull for fordir affirmatioun of the buik of disciplin that the Erle Marschell, Lord Ruthven, the Lord Secretare, the Commendatare of Kilwinning, the Bischop of Orknay, Clerk of Register, Justice Clerk, M Henry Balnavis, David Forres and Maister George Buchquhannane, ony four or thre of thaim, ourse the said buik and diligentlie considder the contentis thairof, noting thair jugementis in wrytting and report the same to the nixt assembley generall of the kirk and gif ane parliament chance to be in the menetyme that they report thair saidis jugementis to the lordis of the articlis that sall chance to be chosin befoir the said parliament.

[*Margin*: M Robert Lokartt.] And that the saidis lordis befoir depute sall begin to ourse the said buik incontinent eftir the dissolvying of this assembley or at the leist at the sext day of Januare nixtocum and thaireftir to continew quhill the said buke be halely oursene, the quhilk to do the haill kirk presentlie assemblit gevis to thame power.

[*Margin*: M Robert Lokart.] Anent the supplicatioun gevin in be M Robert Lokart making narratioun anent his being in court of lang tyme and his laubouris thairin and in speciale for help of civile unitie and concord of this realme etc. and how the same he allegit to be weill and sufficientlie knawin to the brether heir assemblit and in speciale unto sic as remane in court and namelie to thame of the quenis majesteis prive counsale and becaus of the evill allegeances and sayingis of evill toungis and of men jugeing wrang of him, quhom he desyrit God to forgeve he had socht the jugement of the haill kirk begynnyng about thre yeiris bipast thairto to be the defence of his guid fame and name and the glorye of his God and seing his guid name and fame doith appertein thairto and to the [glorie of his God *del.*] edificatioun and weill [*torn*] it was the command of God that he suld sa do and that in the [*torn*]

II

Lord Chancellor Glamis and Theodore Beza

Reprinted from *Scottish History Society Miscellany*, viii (1951), 89–113.

INTRODUCTION

The regency of James, earl of Morton (1572–8) was a critical period in the history of the Scottish reformed church. It had not yet been possible to establish a system of church government which would at once meet the needs of ecclesiastical organisation and also solve problems affecting the civil constitution and the church endowments. Until 1567 the reformers had lacked crown support, and after that date there had been years of disturbance, resulting in a long delay in dispossessing holders of benefices who had not accepted the reformed faith. Morton himself saw clearly that the lack of a 'settled polity' had been 'partly through want of the allowance of the authority at the first reformation, and partly because the benefices of cure were of long time suffered to be possessed by persons repugnant to the [reformed] religion'.[1] The regent's own policy, not unaptly summed up by his critics as 'conformity with England',[2] was what may be called the 'Anglican' policy, whereby the reformed church was to take over the old system of government with all its titles, dignities and benefices. In 1567 the reformers had secured the succession to the parochial benefices as they fell vacant; in 1572 they similarly secured the succession to the bishoprics; and a statute of 1573[3] at last made it possible to deprive beneficed men who would not conform and to appoint ministers in their places. These developments offered the reformed church the prospect of inheriting the entire ecclesiastical structure. Before the process could be completed it was interrupted through the arrival in Scotland (in 1574) of Andrew Melville, bringing with him what Morton called his 'conceits and oversea dreams, imitation of Geneva discipline and laws'.[4] From 1575 controversy over the lawfulness of episcopacy and the inviolable parity of ministers became acute. There was also raised the issue of ecclesiastical independence, centred

[1] *Wodrow Soc. Miscellany*, i, 289–90; cf. *APS*, iii, 89.
[2] Melville, 45, 60; Calderwood, iii, 394.
[3] *APS*, iii, 72.
[4] Melville, 68 (cf. 54).

16. Dunblane Tower

17. Dunning Tower

18. Muthill Tow[er]

19. Tower at Clapham, Bedford

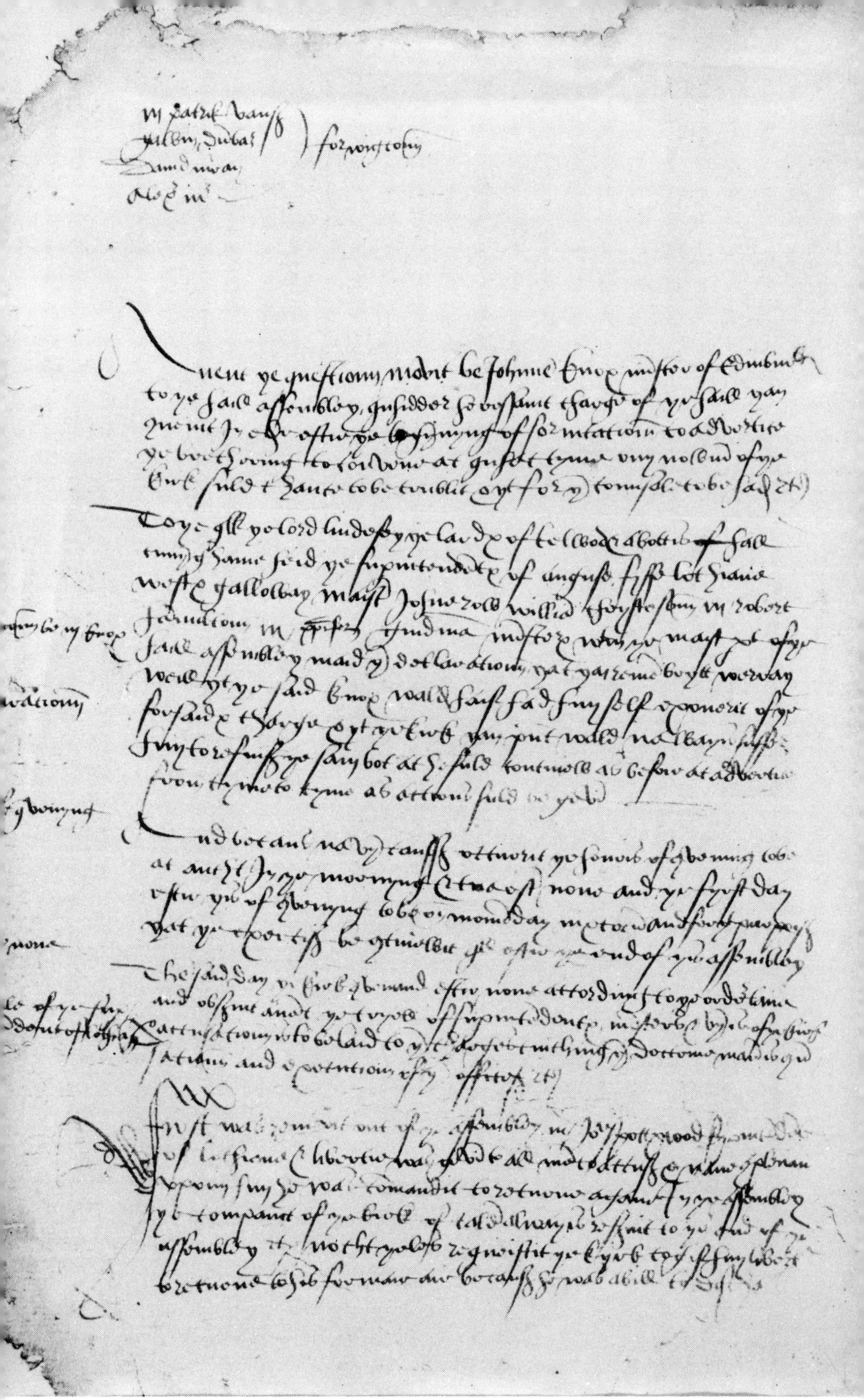

20. Page of proceedings of General Assembly, December 1563

21. Flyleaf and title-page of Bishop
Jewel's *Apologia*, 1562

The inscription on the flyleaf shows that
this copy was presented by Thomas
Randolph to Lord James Stewart, later
earl of Moray and regent. The title-page
bears a stamp (*inset*) showing that it
was subsequently in the possession of
Clement Little, an Edinburgh lawyer,
and that it passed, with many other volumes from his collection, to the library
of Edinburgh University.

To the right honorable the Lorde
James Stewarde from Tho Randolphe

Virtus pro amicitys

Apologia Ec
clesiæ Angli
canæ.

ROMAI.

Non enim me pudet Euangelii CHRISTI, Pô-
tentia siquidem est Dei ad salutem omni credenti
ti. &c.

LONDINI
Anno Domini
M. D. LXII.

IAM GEVIN TO EDINBVRGH & KIRK OF
GOD BE MAISTER CLEMENT LITIL
THAIR TO REMAN. 1580

largely round the position of the General Assembly. The Assembly had established its practice of regular meetings under a sovereign unsympathetic to the Reformation, and it was open to question whether it was proper that these meetings should continue, independently of the royal will, under a 'godly prince'. The functions of Assemblies, and of church courts generally, were also in dispute, and various attempts were made to define ecclesiastical jurisdiction.

John, eighth Lord Glamis, had been closely associated with the Earl of Moray during his regency and was a regular attender at meetings of the privy council from December 1567. He was an extraordinary lord of session from 1570 until 1573, when he became chancellor. In that office he worked very closely with the Regent Morton, who was his first cousin once removed, but he was also on good terms with the General Assembly, which lamented his death, and even with Andrew Melville, who wrote an 'epigram'.[5] He evidently earned widespread respect for wise and moderate statemanship. About 1577 an English observer described him as 'a good protestant, and a favourer of the king; he is holden very wise and discreet, wealthy, but of no party or favour'.[6] He was killed at Stirling in 1578 in a scuffle between his retainers and those of the Earl of Crawford.

Apart from his position as chancellor and leading supporter of Morton, Glamis had special reasons for concerning himself with the current ecclesiastical controversies, for he was a member of commissions on ecclesiastical polity in March 1575 and October 1576.[7] As a statesman, he saw clearly enough the implications, for the civil as well as the ecclesiastical constitution, of Melville's insistence on the parity of ministers and the independence of the General Assembly, and realised that difficulties would arise if the existing polity in the church should be hastily overthrown. At the same time he probably learned that the arguments from expediency which alone he could advance would carry no weight with the doctrinaire Melvillians, who took their stand on the divine right of 'parity' and the unlawfulness of episcopal government. Apparently in genuine doubt, Glamis decided to consult Theodore Beza, the Swiss theologian from whom Melville claimed to have derived his views and for whom, as Calvin's successor, Scottish protestants of all opinions had great regard, and to ask him for a clear ruling on some of the points at issue. The letter of Glamis is apparently extant only in a copy in the British Museum, from which it is now printed.[8]

Perhaps because some thought it inconceivable that a sixteenth-century Scottish peer could write good Latin, there has sometimes been speculation whether a letter which went in the name of Glamis and expressed the questionings in his mind was actually composed by him. Professor Hannay wondered if Melville himself could have penned it, but it seems unlikely

---

[5] *BUK*, ii, 405; Melville, 60; Calderwood, iii, 397.
[6] *Cal. S.P. Scot.*, v, 253.
[7] *APS*, iii, 89; *BUK*, i, 365; cf. Spottiswoode, ii, 221.
[8] Additional MSS., 28, 571, fols. 110–11.

that anyone as firmly committed as Melville was could have formulated the doubts which the letter put forward. Another possible candidate might have been Scotland's prime Latinist, George Buchanan, one of the king's tutors, or Buchanan's colleague Peter Young, though the term *tutor*, as used in the letter, is probably a synonym for 'regent' – *tutor et dominus prorex* – in line with the use of 'tutor' familiar in Scottish private law for a guardian of a minor or rather 'pupil'. I consulted Dr Donald Abbott, a classical scholar and Buchanan expert on the staff of the Scottish Record Office, and he wrote that 'the style struck me as being slightly "official", as if written by someone more familiar with legal and ecclesiastical Latin than by someone like Buchanan with a more literary outlook', and concluded that as Glamis was 'an educated man of the time . . . there seems little reason to doubt that he would be capable of writing it himself'. The chancellor may well, however, have consulted others on the style of the epistle, just as he clearly conferred with others on its matter.

No copy of the original Latin version of Beza's reply is known to survive. In 1580, however, it was translated and published in English as *The judgement of a most reverend and learned man from beyond the seas, concerning a threefold order of bishops: with a declaration of certaine other waightie points, concerning the discipline and governement of the church*. The translator was John Field, who acted as a sort of secretary to the English presbyterian party led by Thomas Cartwright.[9] Field was in very close touch with Melville's followers in Scotland, and could easily have obtained a manuscript copy of Beza's reply to Glamis. Beza's work distinguishes three categories of bishops – of God, of man and of the devil – and was commonly referred to as his treatise *De triplici episcopatu*. The bishop of God, he argues, is simply the pastor or minister. The bishop of man is a pastor to whom is given certain power over his fellows (with safeguards against tyranny). Such an office, he was at pains to show, had no scriptural warrant, but was 'brought in of man, by little and little . . . a privy custom'. The bishop of the devil, again, 'sprouted forth of the corruption of the bishop brought in by man', arrogated to himself sole authority over the clergy, invaded temporal dominion and wasted the patrimony of the church. Such bishops are the image of the beast and their hierarchy an anti-Christian primacy. After this general statement on episcopal government, Beza turns to the questions sent by Glamis. His answers are now printed following on the translation of each question.[10]

Beza's 'treatise' achieved notoriety. John Whitgift, archbishop of Canterbury and strongest opponent of Cartwright, rebuked the writer because his 'book of a threefold episcopacy, sent to this island and not long

---

[9] The Latin version may never have been printed. The British Museum catalogue classified Field's book as a translation of an unidentified work by Beza. Richard Bancroft stated that Beza wrote 'the discourse of his three kinds of bishops . . . and sent it unto a man of great state in that country [Scotland]' (*A survay of the pretended holy discipline* [1593], 50). It is perhaps significant that the 'treatise' is referred to by contemporaries under various titles.

[10] Field's spelling and punctuation have been modernised.

after translated into the English tongue, flying through the hands of many, set a new torch to the flame that was before almost quenched'.[11] James Melville testifies that when the work appeared in Scotland it 'did mikle guid'.[12] Dr John Bridges, in *A defence of the government established in the Church of England* (1587), devotes nearly a hundred pages to answering Beza's work. Hadrian Saravia, another defender of the Anglican establishment, wrote an *Examen tractatus de episcopatuum triplici genere*. In his dedication, he states his view that 'Dominus Glamius' had sought from Beza not his advice (*consilium*) but rather his support (*suffragium*), and indicates that he had seen a copy of the letter of Glamis as well as of Beza's reply (*epistolarum autem ipsorum nactus exemplaria*). Elsewhere, Saravia wrote: 'I pass over what I have myself written . . . in my book *De diversis ministrorum gradibus* and in my defence against the answer of Mr Beza, and more largely in my confutation of his book *De triplici genere episcoporum*. I cannot wonder enough at the Scotchmen, who could be persuaded to abolish and reject the state of bishops, by reasons so ill grounded, partly false, partly of no moment at all, and altogether unworthy a man of such fame. If the Scots had not more sought after the temporal means of bishops than after true reformation, never had Mr Beza's book persuaded them to do what they have done.'[13]

To facilitate the preparation of the texts for publication, the Bodleian Library copy of *The judgement of a most reverend and learned man* was temporarily deposited in the National Library of Scotland, and while it was in Edinburgh negative photostats were made for preservation in the University Library. I have to thank Bodley's Librarian for his ready consent to lend the book and the staffs of the National Library and the University Library for their help in arranging the loan and making the photostats.

Additional Note

Ten years after this was published, I received additional information, thanks to Robert M. Kingdon in Geneva. He sent me an offprint of his note 'Concerning Theodore Beza' in *Bibliothèque d'humanisme et renaissance, Travaux et Documents*, tome xxiii, which states that M. Dufour (who collaborated on the *Bibliographie* of Beza's works), after being doubtful about the attribution of the *De triplici episcopatu* to Beza, was convinced that the tract was indeed Beza's when he discovered a letter from Andrew Melville to Beza which can be dated 26 August 1584 and which attributes the tract to Beza. A footnote explains: 'This is the proof text: "Scriptum de triplici episcopatu tuum omnino nunc edendum est: quod utrique regno futurum valde opportunum". It is a postscript to a letter from Melville to Beza, preserved in the Archives Tronchin, 5, fol. 255, now part of the collection of the Musée historique de la Reformation in Geneva. The letter

[11] Strype, *Whitgift* (1822), ii, 166.
[12] *Diary*, 55; cf. David Calderwood, *Altare Damascenum* (1708), 83.
[13] Saravia, *De ministrorum gradibus* (1840), xxiii–xxiv; Hooker, *Works* (1883), i, 75 n.

is dated "Londini, 26 Augusti". The year of its writing can be fixed by the dates of Melville's visit to London [pp. 182–4 *infra*] and by the fact that it mentions an earlier letter, from the pastors of Scotland to those of Geneva and Zurich, one original of which is preserved in the Geneva Bibliothèque publique et universitaire, MS. fr. 410, fols. 26–7, and which is dated London, 1 July 1584. A translation of this latter letter, in the more complete version sent to Zurich, is published in [Calderwood, iv, 158–67] but without exact date. ... Gordon Donaldson, in his "Lord Chancellor Glamis and Theodore Beza", published and commented on the text of the letter from Glamis to Beza which provoked the writing of the *De triplici episcopatu*.'

In a letter dated 17 May 1961 Mr Kingdon adds: 'As far as we know, no printed Latin version of Beza's reply to Glamis has yet been discovered. Professor Meylan has called to my attention a manuscript here, however, which may be a contemporary minute of the reply. We have not as yet studied it carefully enough to be sure. It is a piece listed as "Six questions et réponses sur l'épiscopat. En ˙ Latin. N.s.; s.l.n.d. Avec corrections et additions de la main de Pierre Martyr et de Th. de Bèze" in Fréd. Gardy's published *Catalogue de la partie des Archives Tronchin acquise par la Societé du Musée historique de la Réformation* (Geneva, 1946), p. 150 (vol. 78, no. 11, Archives Tronchin, this part now housed in the Bibliothèque publique et universitaire de Genève).'

LETTER OF GLAMIS TO BEZA

Clarissimo viro D. Theodoro Bezae.

Cupieram iam pridem ad te vir clarissime scribere teque variis de rebus quae apud nos in quaestionem vocantur consulere, partim ecclesiae vestrae Genevensis in religione et doctrina consensione motus, praecipue autem nominis ac eruditionis tuae quam opera tua pie et erudite summa cum ecclesiae utilitate in lucem aedita abunde testantur fama et celebritate impulsus, verum quod maxime volui hactenus propter locorum intervalla et turbulentum nostrae regionis et ecclesiae statum facere non potui; nunc illud exequendi occasionem eamque commodissimam mihi iam tandem oblatam esse plurimum gaudeo. Venit enim ad nos et optimus et eruditus meo iudicio Claudius Colladonius[14] Genevensis, tibi (ut ex Johanne Scringero[15] satis intellexi) bene notus et familiaris, quem de statu vestrarum ecclesiarum diligenter consului quantum quidem per temporis brevitatem quo apud nos vixit et occupationes meas quibus interea distinebar licuit. Ecclesias autem vestras tam bene pieque constitutas esse in

---

[14] Claude Colladon was a member of a well-known Genevan family. Son of the more famous Germain (1509–94), he was a member of the council of the two hundred in 1579, councillor and secretary of the Prince de Condé in 1583 and councillor of Henry IV in 1595 (*Historisch-Biographisches Lexikon der Schweiz*).

[15] 'Scringer' is likely to be a version of Scrymgeour. I have not traced the John here mentioned. Henry Scrymgeour (d. 1572), professor of Civil Law at Geneva, left no son; his sister married Andrew Melville's elder brother and was the mother of James, the diarist.

ipis persecutionum fluctibus et evangelium Christi libere et sine pharisaico fermento praedicari vobiscum ex animo laetamur, simulque hanc faelicitatem ut solida et constans sit Deum optimum maximum ecclesiae suae custodem et vindicem oramus. Doctrinam quidem de filio Dei vobiscum eandem retinemus et profitemur adeo ut tametsi caeterae regiones et ecclesiae in hac extrema mundi senecta opinionum quasi monstris turbentur, nos tamen singulari dei optimi maximi beneficio in doctrina adeo consentimus ut nulli inveniantur qui eam oppugnare vel velint vel audeant. At in disciplina et politia, in qua viri alioqui pii et de universis religionis capitibus recte sentientes nonnunquam dissentire deprehenduntur, nondum satis inter nos convenit. Nam una cum papistica superstitione disciplina aliquandiu a maioribus nostris usurpata ante annos aliquot sublata est. In eius autem locum nulla commoda honestaque ecclesiae regendae ratio adhuc subrogari potuit, praesertim cum principes nostri vel a vera religione fuerint alieni vel cum recte de praecipuis Christianae fidei articulis sentire caeperunt bellis tamen civilibus impediti eam in rem prout voluerunt incumbere non potuerint. Nunc autem ab omnibus prioribus illis impedimentis liberi, et pacem et talem regem nacti (cuius egregia indoles et in vera religione educatio tantum nobis promittunt quantum a quopiam in ea aetate expectari possit), de disciplina aliqua ecclesiastica constituenda laboramus. Maxime vero cum illius tutor et dominus prorex universaque nobilitas et regni (ut vocant) ordines eam in partem diligenter incumbant verum quum de singulis disciplinae capitibus paulo diligentius inquirimus evenit ut multa nobis obiiciantur de quibus nonnihil dubitamus, etsi bene sperem mihique ipse persuadeam nos in ea re non minus quam in religione consensuros. Sed quum intelligam ex librorum tuorum [sic], quos summa cum voluptate lego et admiror, et eruditorum ac piorum literis et sermone singularem tuam pietatem summa cum eruditione et humanitate coniunctam praetermittere non potui quin hoc praesertim tempore hisce de rebus ad te scriberem. Quamvis autem multa sint de quibus tuam mentem et sententiam requirerem, quaedam tamen eaque praecipua tibi referam, ne nimia longitudine aut orationis prolixitate tibi variis ecclesiae negotiis occupatissimo esse vedear molestus.

   1. Quum in singulis ecclesiis singuli pastores ac ministri constituti fuerint quumque par et aequalis omnium in ecclesia Christi ministrorum potestas videatur, quaeritur sitne episcoporum munus in ecclesia necessarium, qui ministros quum res postulabit ad comitia vocari, ad ministerium admitti et iustis de causis ab officio removeri curabunt; an potius omnes ministri aequali potestate fungentes nulliusque superioris episcopi imperio obnoxii viros idoneos in doctrina cum consensu patroni ius patronatus habentis et ipsius populi eligere, corrigere, et ab officio removere debeant. Ut autem retineantur eiusmodi episcopi movere nos duo possunt: unum populi ipsius mores et contumacia qui vix ac ne vix quidem in officio contineri potest nisi eiusmodi episcoporum qui universas ecclesias percurrant[16] et invisant authoritate coerceatur; alterum leges regni longo

---

[16] MS. reads procurrant. Field's translation has 'run through'.

usu et inveterata consuetudine receptae ut quoties de rebus ad reipublicae salutem pertinentibus ex publicis regni comitiis agitur nihil sine episcopis constitui potest, quum ipsi tertium ordinem et regni statum efficiant, quem aut mutare aut prorsus tollere reipublicae admodum esset periculosum.

2. Post reformatam religionem consuetudine receptum est ut episcopi et ex ministris pastoribus senioribus tot quot iidem episcopi iusserint unum in locum conveniant cum praecipuis baronibus et nobilibus religionem veram profitentibus et de doctrina et de moribus inquisituri. Nunc vero, quum princeps verae religionis studiosus sit, quaeritur an eiusmodi conventus cogi possint sine iussu vel consensu principis, an solis ministris convenire liceat quoties voluerint, an denique nobilibus aliisque pietatis studiosis et senioribus qui apud nos quotannis ex populo atque adeo ex ipsa nobilitate eliguntur sine mandato regis ad eiusmodi comitia venire liceat et expediat. Quandoquidem nobilium et laicorum conventus aliis videtur sub principe pio non necessarius, quum sola consuetudine nulla vero certa lege sub principe religionem impugnante paucos ante annos receptus fuerit, quo plus authoritatis eiusmodi comitia haberent; quum praeterea periculosum videatur ne si nobiles tam frequentes et frequenter sine consensu regis conveniant aliis de rebus quam ad religionem pertinentibus aliquando deliberent. Alii vero nullo modo reiiciendos arbitrantur quin potius valde necessarius videtur hic conventus ut nimirum nobiles religionem omni studio et conatu promoventes in comitiis tanquam παραστάται et adiutores ministris adsint ac de ipsorum vita moribus populi et id genus aliis testimonium perhibeant. Alioquin futurum si princeps parum pius postea regnaverit ut neque ministri tuto convenire neque decreta sua executioni mandare sine nobilium consensu et auxilio possint.

3. A quo, hoc est a rege an ab episcopis, eiusmodi comitia ecclesiastica cogi et quum coguntur quibus de rebus leges ferre possunt?

4. Debeantne excommunicari papistae eodem modo quo apostatae an vero leviori paena puniendi sint?

5. Quibus de causis aliquem excommunicare liceat? Verbi gratia: si quis homicidium patrarit asserens se id vel necessitate vel vim vi repellendo fecisse (eaque de re paratus est iudicium subire neque adhuc a rege aut occisi proximo quovis accusatur) licetne ecclesiae de homicidio inquirere, sitne dolo malo an casu vel necessitate factum, et homicidam cogere ut secundum delicti qualitatem publicam in ecclesia paenitentiam in sacco et cinere agat aut recusantem excommunicatione faeriat eique aqua et igni interdicat?

6. Quum superiori saeculo magnae facultates eleemosinae nomine[17] a principibus aliisque multis concessae sive episcopis monasteriis et huiusmodi quumque tantae opes videantur potius obesse quam prodesse episcopis et monasteria in republica et ecclesia sint inutilia; quaeritur quid de eiusmodi bonis, quae semel ecclesiae consecratae fuerunt, fieri debeat. Nam quum episcopi et ministri ex decimis satis habeant unde commode et

---

[17] MS. reads nomina.

honeste vivere possint, an princeps potest cum consensu statuum regni reliquam partem inferre ut vel in suos vel in publicos usus convertere illi liberum sit, praesertim cum eiusmodi bona non tam in decimis quam in praediis rusticis aut urbanis consistant. Quaequidem quaestio quum potius civilis quam ecclesiastica esse videatur, constitueram tibi hac in re non esse molestus, sed quia complures pii ac eruditi apud nos existimant has res quae semel piis usibus destinatae fuerunt non posse in profanos usus etiam publicos conferri, non potui hoc quoque argumentum silentio apud te praeterire.

Haec sunt, vir clarissime, quae hoc tempore mihi in mentem venerunt et de quibus te in huiusmodi disputationibus optime exercitatum consulere volui. Etsi autem sum tibi vel ipso fortassis nomine ignotus, tamen quum eiusdem corporis sumus membra nosque eadem religio in Christo coniungat, me rem neque ab hominis Christiani officio alienam neque tibi viro humanissimo ingratam facturam [sic] existimavi si de ecclesiarum nostrarum statu constituendo et de nonnullis capitibus quae apud nos controvertuntur paucis ad te scriberem. Quod si audacius apud te, virum alioquin maxime occupatum, fecisse videar, id totum humanitati tuae et purae religionis propagandae studio utrique nostrum divinitus concesso acceptum feries. Si autem hasce meas primitias lubenter susceperis mihique quum per occupationes licet responderis, te rem ecclesiis nostris summe necessariam et longe mihi gratissimam facturam [sic] intelliges. Caetera ex Colladonio, cuius ingenium et mores quum nobis omnibus valde placuerint tibi commendarem nisi vobis quam optime notum esse intelligerem. Dominus Jesus te suo spiritu fortitudinis et constantiae adversus omnium hostium insultus et impiorum malitiam muniat, et nobis ac ecclesiis quam diutissime incolumem conservat. 13 Calend. Maii. 1578.[18]

Tuo obsequio paratissimus,
GLAMIUS.

TRANSLATION, WITH BEZA'S ANSWERS

To the most illustrious D.[19] Theodore Beza.

I had already been long desirous, most illustrious sir, to write to you and to ask your advice on various matters which are called in question among us, partly prompted by the agreement of your church of Geneva with ours in faith and doctrine but especially impelled by the credit and renown of your reputation for that scholarship which is abundantly attested by your works, published with godliness and learning to the utmost profit of the church; yet I have not hitherto been able to fulfil my great desire, because of the long distance between us and the

---

[18] The date, as given in the MS., must be wrong. Lord Glamis, the Chancellor, to whom contemporaries unanimously attribute the letter, died on 17 March 1577/8 and was succeeded by an infant son. Internal evidence shows that the letter was written during Morton's regency, which ended on 12 March 1577/8. James Melville (*Diary*, 55) attributes the letter to April 1576, which seems a likely date. There are some obvious scribal errors in the MS., and the final figure of the year may be wrong.

[19] 'D.' represents 'Dominus', any translation of which would be misleading.

disturbed condition of our country and our church. Now I greatly rejoice that a most convenient opportunity of carrying out my intention has at last been offered to me. For we have had a visit from Claude Colladon, a Genevan in my judgment worthy and learned, well known to you personally (as I was fully assured by John Scringer); from him I made careful enquiry about the condition of your churches, so far at least as was possible considering the shortness of his stay among us and the affairs which meantime preoccupied me. We rejoice from our hearts that your churches are established so firmly and soundly in the very midst of persecution and that the gospel of Christ is preached among you freely and without the leaven of hypocrisy; and at the same time we implore Almighty God, the keeper and champion of His church, that this happy state of affairs may be stable and enduring. We do indeed hold and profess with you the same doctrine concerning the Son of God, so that, although other countries and churches are, in these latter days, troubled by almost unnatural opinions, yet we, by the special grace of Almighty God, so agree in doctrine that none may be found who would wish or dare to attack it. On the other hand, adequate agreement has not yet been reached among us on matters of government and constitution, on which men otherwise devout and right-minded on all points of religion are sometimes found to differ. For the form of government which for some time was practised by our ancestors was overthrown some years ago along with the popish superstition and in its place it has not hitherto been possible to substitute a convenient and fitting form of church government, particularly because our sovereigns either were hostile to the true faith or, after they had begun to accept the chief points of Christian doctrine, were yet hindered by internal strife from being able to pay attention to the matter as they wished. Now, however, we are free from all those earlier hindrances; we have secured peace and enjoy the rule of a king whose outstanding ability and upbringing in the true faith promise us as much as could be looked for from anyone of his age; and we are striving to establish some ecclesiastical constitution. Actually the king's tutor and regent, with the whole nobility and the estates of the realm (as they are styled) are giving their careful attention to the matter, but when we make somewhat more careful enquiry with regard to each point of government it happens that many matters come before us on which there is considerable uncertainty, athough I had high hopes, and even have conviction, that we shall agree in that matter not less than in our doctrine. As I learn from what you have written in your books, which I read with the utmost pleasure and admiration, and from the letters and conversation of learned and devout men, of your extraordinary godliness, joined with learning and generosity, I could not fail, especially at this time, to write to you on these matters. Although there be many points on which I should ask for your views and judgment, I shall refer to you only the most important, lest by excessive length or tediousness of words I seem troublesome to you, fully occupied as you are with diverse church affairs.

1. Since a pastor and minister is appointed in each congregation, and since the power of all ministers in the church of Christ seems to be equal and identical, it is asked whether it be necessary in the church to have the office of bishops, who will be responsible for summoning the ministers to synods when circumstances demand it, for admitting to the ministry and for removing from office for just causes; or whether all ministers, enjoying equal power and not subject to the authority of any bishop as superior, ought, with the consent of the patron (having the right of presentation) and of the people themselves, to choose men suitable in

religion, to discipline them and to remove them from office. Two considerations can move us to the retention of bishops: one is the character and unruliness of the people, who can only with difficulty, if indeed at all, be retained in their duty unless constrained by the authority of bishops, who visit and inspect all the churches; the other is the laws of the realm, accepted by long established use and lasting custom, which provide that whenever there is deliberation in the public assemblies of the kingdom about matters concerning the safety of the state nothing can be settled without the bishops, since they form one of the three orders and estates of the realm, to alter or wholly uproot which would be most perilous to the commonwealth.

Answer

Whereas Satan's bishop hath been the overthrow of the church and all Christian kingdoms whose head is the Roman Antichrist, it is to be looked unto of all hands, especially of all godly princes, that they at once abolish it, if they mind the reformation of the church and their own safety. As for the bishop ordained by man, and brought into the church by little and little, whereby Satan made him a way for greater things, it had been tolerable, so that with all the ancient good laws providing for the resisting of the governing by some few had been in their former force again. But, besides that the state of the world being quite changed, experience of so many ages doth teach us too well that, unless this root also be plucked up, it will come to pass that the same fruit will sprout and bud forth again. Finally, seeing the Lord hath so often decided this controversy of superiority among his own disciples, that he shut it clean out, seeing the rule both for doctrine and good order of the church is to be sought for out of the very writings of the apostles: and it is manifested the churches then prospered, when all this authority of one man over the rest yet was not; but as that grew up, so all things fell to decay. Finally, seeing where the remnants of this government by a few are not clean taken away the work of the Lord is openly hindered, our judgment is that after the chasing away of this device of man the churches shall be well provided for if they may be repaired according to the writings of the apostles.

And the reformation, as it seemeth to us, consisteth herein, that first the whole kingdom is to be divided into regions. Again, the regions into parishes, either of cities or country towns: that in places most fit, and of greatest assembly, be placed pastors, being lawfully propounded by the company of their own elders to the king's Christian majesty, or the deputies thereof, and allowed of all. Lastly, being received of their own people, over whom they are to be set, they be placed, promulgation having gone before; and that in every parish the pastor may have with him fit men to assist him, who also may, being watchful, salve up the offences not so weighty, leaving the other of greater importance to the whole eldership. Also, that eldership, made of the pastors of parishes, both of city and country, and a sufficient number of men approved for their godliness and wisdom, lawfully also chosen as is aforesaid, be placed in most fit places, who, assembling at a certain time and place, may determine of the church affairs of their own government, according to the prescript laws first set down in a general council and afterwards confirmed by the authority of the sovereign majesty.

In this company let there be chosen by common voices one first in order – not superior in authority – who shall be thought most fit, and that without making choice of any certain place, and but for a certain time. After the expiring whereof, either let another be chosen or else the same man is to be established again for another time by a new consent; whose office is to make report of the common affairs to the company, to demand their judgments and to give sentence by the judgment of the eldership, having no authority given him over his fellows, to whom rather he is most subject. In this assembly let nothing be debated of besides matters of conscience, and that by the word of God and the laws of church discipline established, drawn out of the word of God, not one whit meddling with the authority of the civil magistrate. And let the sovereign majesty and the lawful magistrate thereby appointed be keepers of this order and the punisher[s] of those that seditiously rage against it.

But if any shall imagine that this sudden abolishing of both these bishops will minister occasion of new stirs (although we see not with what conscience the bishops may so challenge to themselves the goods of the church, or else call themselves bishops, and live like princes of this world), yet for to keep the common peace the sovereign majesty may leave unto them which are now bishops their revenues whole for their life time, so they trouble not the well-made order of the church, with providing there be none chosen into their place when they be dead. As for the frowardness of the people, it may be kept down better a great deal by other reins than by the authority of a false named bishop; as by preaching of the word of God, by censures of the church and the authority of the magistrate of the country, against the open trouble[r]s of the public state, either ecclesiastical or civil. The churches may very well be visited at set times, without any great cost and bishoplike pride, by them whom every eldership hath chosen under the king's majesty's authority – which will not be always necessary, if the elders do rightly execute their office.

This sitting of the bishops with the authority of the voice in the public estates of the kingdom came in with a manifest abuse, contrary to the Word, and therefore in our mind is to be utterly abolished; for the bishop hath nothing to do in ordering of mere civil affairs. Yet forasmuch as in such assemblies especially some things many times happen belonging to the establishing of the estate and order of the churches – the keepers whereof the godly magistrates ought to be, and not the over-turners, as we are taught by the example of holy kings – it is very necessary that as often as the meetings of the land are proclaimed intelligence thereof be given to the chief elders, who may be present in the behalf of their seignories; yet not sitting as judges, but dealing about matters of the church only with the estates of the land, as their elderships have given them in charge – except the states think good, upon extraordinary occasion, that they ask counsel of God about some other affairs also. If also the king's majesty think good to admit into counsel, amongst the pastors or elders, one who shall be thought to be wise and experienced in things, he may admit him, though not as a pastor or elder, yet as a citizen. And it were injurious to remove from their office in the church, the pastors, and much less the elders and deacons, otherwise laymen from that degree which they hold as citizens, either in the commonwealth, or in the assemblies. But the king's majesty, and all the princes and lords, are to be exceeding wary that they make not courtlike governors of their pastors, to the great endamaging of the church, as we have a fair example in Eusebius of Nicomedia in the court of Constantine. As for the right of the patronage, lest some man should say that it was gotten for himself, our judgment is that it may be concealed [*sc.* conceded], but not without some conditions: namely, that he which shall be chosen by the free voices of the eldership should be offered by the patrons to the king's majesty, being also to set upon his charge after the consenting of his flock.

2. After the Reformation it became the accepted custom that the overseers[20] and as many of the ministers, pastors and elders as the overseers commanded should assemble in one place with the notable barons and nobles professing the true religion, to investigate matters of both faith and morals. Now, however, when the sovereign is careful of the true religion, it is asked whether assemblies of this kind can be summoned without his order or consent, or whether it is permissible for the ministers alone to assemble as often as they wish, or, finally, whether it is lawful and expedient for nobles and others given to devotion, and the elders who are chosen among us yearly from the people and also from the nobility, to come to such assemblies without the king's command. A gathering of nobles and laity seems to some to be unnecessary under a godly prince, because it was accepted a few years ago, by custom alone and not by any particular law, under a sovereign hostile to the faith, whereby such assemblies might have more authority; and, moreover, there may seem a danger that the nobles, gathering so often and in such large numbers without the king's consent, should sometimes deliberate on matters other than those concerning religion. Others again think that they should not be rejected, but rather that this assembly seems decidedly necessary to wit that the nobles, advancing the faith with all zeal and effort, may be present in assemblies as assisters and helpers to the ministers and bear witness to others with regard to their own life, the morals of the people, and so on. Otherwise it will come about, if a prince not attached to the faith should ascend the throne in the future, that the ministers may not be able to assemble in safety or have their decisions enforced without the consent and help of the nobles.

Answer

Councils are necessary in the church for many causes, both to the retaining of agreement and also to the seeking of remedies by common advice for the dangers which fall out; and, last of all, to take order for those that rest not in the judgment of particular seignories, if they think they have any injury

---

[20] 'Episcopi' clearly covers superintendents, conforming bishops and the 'commissioners' who acted where there was neither a superintendent nor a bishop.

done them. And these councils are either of a whole nation, or of some one region or province (or diocese, as they have begun to speak, after the description of the provinces of Rome), divided into many seignories.

It is necessary that the councils of the provinces be divided for many causes, and, except there be other urgent causes, they would be appointed rather every half year than quarterly, lest in the discoursing of matters they spend the time in vain. And it will be best for the avoiding of ambition that the council be not always assembled in the same place of every province: but as soon as one half year's synod is discussed it may be determined by common consent where shall be the place of the next following. It will be very well that two of every seignory of the province, chosen by common voices, and sent with some commission, be present at these councils: one a pastor and the other an elder or a deacon. Neither would we have any strife about sitting, who should sit first or last, but every one to sit as it shall fall out, without any contention, and the judgment to be given as any one shall sit.

Now, he that shall govern the whole action, who was chosen for this one thing by common consent of voice, the chief pastor of the place being in the beginning president, which office shall end when the council shall be ended. There are no matters in question to be propounded to these councils to take knowledge of, but such as are more spiritual and belong to that province, where they are to be decided without appeal by the word of God and the rules there set down, without any brabling or disturbance of the company. Yet if any great private controversy shall fall out in the provincial synod, where some may think that he hath cause to complain of injury done unto him, he may put up his complaint to be decided in a general council, when it shall be thought good to assemble it.

Furthermore it is chiefly required that if all the laws of the church be established of the king's Christian majesty, it followeth that the councils are to be assembled by his commandment and direction and not otherwise. Neither yet is there a new commission every time to be sought for of the king for that purpose, seeing his majesty hath once established a law touching the set times of ordinary synods. But yet if there arise just cause of suspicion of handling in these meetings other matters besides mere ecclesiastical, it shall be safe for the king's majesty to send one of his subjects, whom he will, to disgrace [sic] by his presence the meeting of the synods; where yet he is not to be as a judge, except some thing fall out where it is necessary that the authority of the civil magistrate be put between [i.e., interponed].

A general council of the land is not to be assembled but upon great causes, which seeing they agree not with set times it followeth that they are not to be standing neither; but as often as some thing shall seem to fall out of so great weight, either in doctrine or in government of the church, as cannot well be decided but in a general meeting, that province is to be careful to put other provinces in mind concerning that matter, in these half year's synods; that with the consent of all, or the greater part, they go unto the king's majesty, who (as being a Christian prince, is to desire nothing more than the peace of the churches) ought without any stay or doubting, at the suit of the churches, to appoint a place and time for a general meeting, as the need of the churches shall require. And the same order may seem to be kept in the general councils which is in the provincial, whether before the king's majesty himself, as in some general councils the emperors of Rome have been present, or before the honourable lords of the king's majesty. And last of all, whatsoever shall be allowed by the common consent of the synod shall be confirmed by the king's majesty's express authority, after the example of the godly emperors.

3. By whom, that is by the kings or the overseers, can such church assemblies be summoned and, when they are summoned, on what matters can they legislate?

Answer

We have answered the first part of this question already. To the second we answer: First, it is not lawful, no not for the angels themselves, to make any laws for the conscience, but the church is to be upholden by those which the Lord hath enacted, seeing we are now to look for no new revelation, the whole counsel of God touching our salvation being fully and perfectly made manifest. Our judgment also is that the discipline or good order is to be sought for out of the word of God and to be kept inviolable, as the second part of Christian doctrine. Yet there remaineth two things, whereof there may, yea and there ought, to be laws set down in the church. For, first of all, whereas everything is not expressly and in so many words set down in the writings of the prophets and apostles, therefore in controversies both concerning doctrine and the substance of church discipline the council ought to comprehend the deciding of them in unfallible and plain heads, as by certain rules, like as it was done profitably in those right approved councils both oecumenie [*sic*] and particulars, against the blasphemy of the heretics and the malapertness of the disordered. And whereas there come many questions in the seignories, especially when there is dealing about marriages, though there cannot be certain rules set down touching them out of the word of God, yet, so near as may be, rules drawn out of the comparing of the scriptures are to be set down, after which they may be decided, yet is neither anything taken from the word of God by the putting to of this, so it be rightly done. But this is rather an interpretation of the word of God, and a declaring how one followeth upon another. Again, where the substance both of doctrine and ecclesiastical discipline abideth whole and unchangeable, yet must the outward circumstances of the order need be changed, for the same reason of the person and places abideth not always. For we see the apostles' love feasts taken away, and the decrees touching blood and that which was strangled. The governors of the church are to provide also that all may have intelligence at what time and place it is expedient for anything to be done in the church: yet so as the doctrine itself, under which we also comprehend the ordaining of the sacraments, abide whole as God hath set it down. Further, that in setting down the laws of this order there be set down nothing foolish or unprofitable, much less any of the old customs retained which either is already stained with superstition or which may easily make a way to superstition. Lastly, that in all these there be a great regard of simplicity, and that the church be not loaded with a multitude of rules.

And for avoiding of the diversity of rites it is necessary that these canons, as in old time they called them, be set down in their general councils, that anything in the same land may be changed according to the time. But whatsoever shall be set down in those councils is to be established by the authority of the king's Christian majesty, as, next after God, the keeper and defender of the churches.

4. Ought papists to be excommunicated in the same way as apostates, or are they to be punished with a lighter penalty?

Answer

We see not what sword of excommunication may be drawn out against those men who, though they were set into the church by no vain baptism, yet never entered into the fellowship of the pure church. Yea, the doors are always to stand open that they may come to hear the word of God, and they are carefully to be allured thither, if at any time (as the apostle saith) they may repent and get out of the snare of the devil, of whom they are holden captive. But if any shall be thought to sin in an open contempt, our judgment is that it ought wholly to be put over to the Christian magistrate. We think that it beseemeth a Christian magistrate to deal much by lenity in the matter of religion towards his subjects, not being troublesome sectaries and such as of knowledge blaspheme.

5. For what causes may it be permissible to excommunicate anyone? For instance, if anyone has committed murder, alleging that he had done it by necessity or in self-defence (being ready to undergo trial on the matter and not being already accused by the king or by any neighbour of the deceased), is it permissible for the church to investigate the murder – whether it has been by evil guile, chance or necessity – and to summon the murderer so that he may do public penance in church in sackcloth and ashes according to the degree of the offence or, on his refusal, strike him with excommunication and forbid him fire and water?

Answer

No man earnestly repenting is to be excommunicate, but after repentance rather ought to be received. And the cause of excommunication ought to be most weighty and a public offence, seeing that only the extremity of the diseases must have extreme remedies. Yet may such men, after the thing be known, be suspended from receiving the Lord's Supper (they were wont to call such men restrained), for whom this is thought to be a necessary remedy, that for the greatness of their offence they may be an example to others, or that their repentance doth stand in need of trial. As for the present question: If the magistrate, put in mind of his duty, do wink at such faults, and yet it be probable that none is rashly accused, we think that the eldership may call him forth, and there, as the matter shall require, to exhort him to the acknowledging of the offence; which if ye shall deny, he is to be left to the judgment of God, neither are the elders to proceed any further in the hearing of witnesses.

6. Since in earlier times great riches, under the name of alms, have been granted by the kings and many others to bishops, monasteries and such like, and since such wealth seems rather a hindrance than an advantage to bishops, while monasteries are useless in the state and in the church, it is asked what should be done with such goods, which once were dedicated to the church. For, as bishops and ministers have enough from the teinds on which to live comfortably and honourably, it is asked whether the sovereign, with consent of the estates of the realm, can appropriate the remainder so that he be free to convert it into his own or the public use, especially as such goods do not consist only of teinds but also of lands in the country or the towns. This question may seem to be rather a civil than an ecclesiastical one, and I had decided not to trouble you with it, but as many godly and learned men among us think that goods once allotted to pious uses cannot be granted to secular uses, even those of the nation, I have been unable to pass over this question in silence in consulting you.

Answer

Concerning the goods of the church: First of all we suppose great heed ought to be taken that none do stain himself with handling the church goods. For if God hath taken revenge of such sacrileges even amongst the very idolators, what trow we will his judgment be against them which have spoiled his churches and have profaned the things which were set apart for his true worship?

Moreover, it is evident that this turneth greatly to the reproach of the name of God and of his holy gospel, as though, forsooth, papistry hath been abandoned not for the love of the truth but to rob the church of her goods, and as though new thieves have entered in the room of the old. Now, even as abundance doth overwhelm the church, so it is to be feared lest she be brought into great straits by want, whilst many nowadays are no less sparing and niggardly in upholding the true ministry than heretofore kings and princes themselves have been overlavishing: we think it needful to keep a mean in this point, which so we take will be the best, if first a view be taken of the daily expenses which are necessary to be made, than if somewhat be laid up for so many things extraordinary, whereas no just reckoning can be made, and both of these be accounted not sparingly or slenderly, but bountifully and liberally, seeing that the church by the goodness of God hath plenty. Therefore that number is to be made of parishes and pastors which may very well suffice the people, and every one is to have an honest living allowed. Order also is to be taken for the elders, who are to assist the pastors that they may conveniently discharge their duty. It would be also unjurious that the widows and children of the pastors which are dead should be brought to beggary, who, in a care of their calling, were constrained to lay aside the care of providing for their family. Schools also and universities, seeing they are the seminary of the church, are not the least part of the care thereof. Care also is to be had of alms houses and hospitals, and of churches, that they be kept in reparations and new builded if need require. Last of all (as I say before), seeing the churches have plenty, order must be taken what shall be brought into the church treasury yearly, from whence may be fetched that which may suffice in time of war or famine, lest then it be to seek when it should be in a readiness. When all these things shall faithfully and frankly be brought by supputation into one sum still yearly, good and sufficient men are to take order for their collecting such a way as shall be without trouble or strife. That which shall be found to be overplus is not to be lavished out with other public revenues, but to be laid up by itself (for these are of another nature, though not always gotten after the honestest sort by the covetous priests), and we think that it may be taken and bestowed for the service of the kingdom, when the public necessity thereof require it, especially if the people be so much the more eased.

These, most illustrious sir, are the matters which have come into my mind at this time and about which I wished to consult you, who are most practised in arguments of this kind. Although I am not known to you, perhaps even by name, yet we are members of the same body and are joined in Christ by one faith and I considered that I would be doing a thing not foreign to the duty of a Christian or displeasing to you, a most courteous man, if I wrote to you briefly about the settlement of our church affairs and about certain topics in dispute among us. If I should seem to have acted rashly in approaching you, who are otherwise much occupied, you may attribute it all to your generosity and to the zeal for the advancement of the pure faith which God has granted to each of us. If, however, you receive this essay gladly and reply to me when your other business allows, you know that you will be doing something most needful for our churches and most pleasing to me. The rest you will learn from Colladon, whose intelligence and character, since they were most acceptable to all of us here, I should commend to you were I not certain that he is already very well known in Geneva. The Lord Jesus defend you by his spirit of strength and perseverance against the attacks of all enemies and the malice of the wicked, and preserve you safe to us and the churches as long as possible. 19 April 1578.

Most ready for your service,

GLAMIS.

12

Foundations of Anglo-Scottish Union

This article, reprinted from *Elizabethan Government and Society: Essays presented to Sir John Neale* (ed. S. T. Bindoff *et al.*, 1961) is the only one in this volume which is not concerned purely with church history. But it seemed important to include it because it does bring out the central importance of religious and ecclesiastical attitudes in laying foundations for Anglo-Scottish union. The point is made that initially and for a considerable period the primary consideration was the consciousness of a protestantism which the two countries shared but also that after unity and agreement were disrupted and in each country rival parties or factions developed within the church, each of the factions, on both sides, had very close links with a corresponding faction on the other side. Some elaboration of the point thus made is presented in the two articles which immediately follow, the first of them dealing with the association between episcopalians in the two countries and the other dealing with the relations between presbyterians in the two countries.

The important phase of Anglo-Scottish collaboration in the 1540s has recently received further attention in my *All the Queen's Men*, which in turn owes a great deal to Dr Marcus Merriman's article on 'The Assured Scots' in *SHR*, xlvii, 10–34.

The treaty in which it was finally agreed that 'the two kingdoms of England and Scotland' should on 1 May 1707 'and for ever after, be united into one kingdom by the name of Great Britain' had been preceded, a century earlier, by the union of the two monarchies. But constitutional instrument and dynastic accident, while they could unite two states, could not in themselves unite two peoples. Nor was it inevitable that a union of those two kingdoms which had for so long existed in one small island would be enduring, for continental history presents us with plenty of examples of the disruption of similar unions – the Scandinavian kingdoms, Holland and Belgium, Spain and Portugal; in each of those instances, although union was for a time achieved, the ultimate solution was separation. The path to a lasting union of England and Scotland was neither straight nor smooth, and it would not have come about without the assistance of non-political factors.

A sixteenth-century Scot was not far wrong when he observed that since the Norman Conquest 'there had not been an English king who had not seriously aimed to unite the two kingdoms'. Nor were all the attempts at union by way of conquest: while there were phases of attempts at conquest, by 'the more warlike and ambitious' English kings, 'the wiser . . . sought to unite the two dynasties by marriage, with the view and intent that an heir should be born to succeed naturally to both realms'.[1] But if there were thus phases when statesmen strove for union by peaceful means – not excluding guile – there were also long periods when there was only the persistent, but often unobtrusive, penetration into Scotland of English culture and English institutions, quietly working to bring about the assimilation of the two peoples. And a good deal of Scottish history has been nothing else than the story of a conflict, or at least a tension, between two opposing tendencies – the tension between native and external influences, between independence and domination from the south.

When anglicisation was first seriously attempted in Scotland, in the eleventh century, it had produced sharp enough reaction: on the death of Macolm III and his English queen, Margaret, in 1093, the Scots 'drove out all the English who were with King Malcolm before', and accepted Duncan II as king only on condition that he dismissed his English and French followers.[2] But the reaction was neither lasting nor effective. Anglicisation progressed so far in the twelfth and thirteenth centuries that Edward I's marriage scheme was welcomed by the Scots, and there can be little doubt that had it matured there would long ago have been a union closer than that achieved in 1707 and closer than that existing today. Scottish institutions would not have been differentiated from those of England, Scottish nationality would never have developed. But the three centuries of war (1296–1560) which followed the two centuries of peaceful penetration conditioned the two peoples to enmity. A traveller in Scotland in 1435 had remarked that 'nothing pleases the Scots more than abuse of the English',[3] an act forbidding any Englishman to 'have benefice, secular or religious' in Scotland was passed by the Scottish parliament in 1466,[4] in the early years of a king who was ultimately overthrown by subjects who accused him of 'inbringing of Englishmen',[5] the records of seaport burghs contain frequent entries about guarding the secrets of the town from English sailors;[6] and so late as 1566, when men were still unaware that Anglo-Scottish relations had been permanently altered by the Reformation, the Scottish government, on the ground that Englishmen

[1] Thomas Craig, *De unione regnorum Britanniae* (SHS), 242.
[2] *SA*, 118.
[3] P. Hume Brown, *Early travellers in Scotland*, 27.
[4] *APS*, ii, 86 c. 9.   [5] Ibid., ii, 210.
[6] I owe this information to Professor W. Croft Dickinson who read a draft of this paper and made many valuable suggestions.

were 'searching out of secrets and taking of inspection of sundry strengths and other sure places', appointed a 'searcher of all Englishmen resorting and repairing within the realm of Scotland'.[7] In England, so late as the first year of Elizabeth, parliament revived an act of Henry VIII making it a felony to sell, exchange or deliver a horse to a Scotsman;[8] a statute of Richard II forbidding the sending of arms or victual into Scotland without licence had never been repealed;[9] and when the English taught their children archery they encouraged them to take good aim – so at least a Scot believed – by saying, 'There's a Scot! Shoot him!'[10]

Thus, when Henry VIII brought forward a marriage scheme identical with that of Edward I, the task confronting him was far more difficult. Even in the promising early months of 1543, when there seemed to be no obstacle in the way of the betrothal of the infant Queen Mary to Prince Edward, the English envoy in Edinburgh reported that if the Scots were threatened with subjection to England 'there is not so little a boy but he will hurl stones against it, and the wives will handle their distaffs, and the commons universally will rather die';[11] and by September, when the situation had taken a turn for the worse, he was complaining that 'never was so noble a prince's servant so evil entreated as he is among those rude unreasonable people, and never had to do with so inconstant and beastly a nation'.[12] Henry handled a delicate situation with singular ineptitude, and in succeeding years Hertford's devastating invasions, the battle of Pinkie and the English occupation of south-eastern Scotland further alienated the Scots, who had to appeal for French help to drive out the English and who sent their queen to France to be betrothed to the heir to the French throne. The campaigns of the 1540s represented the last active phase of the three hundred years of war, which thus ended in failure for England.

But England, which had lost the war, was to win the peace. Ever since Flodden thoughtful Scots had been reflecting that continued hostility to England and the continued use of their country as a tool of France were likely to lead to further disasters and that there might be a better future in collaboration than in antagonism. When the Regent Albany proposed to invade England in 1523 he met with opposition from those who said:

> For the love of France the realm of Scotland suffers great pain as daily appears, for our nobles are slain or taken, our commonalty murdered, our lands overrun, our houses and fortresses burned and razed; we lose the profits of our lands; which mischief we need not have had, but for the love of France and what helps France . . . If we would keep amity with the realm of England we were out of all these dangers.[13]

---

[7] *RSS*, v, 2921.
[8] 23 Hen. VIII c. 16; 1 Eliz. c. 7.
[9] 7 Ric. II c. 16.
[10] Craig, op. cit., 393.
[11] Sadler, *State Papers*, i, 70; cf. *L. & P. Hen. VIII*, xviii (1), 184–5.
[12] *L. & P. Hen. VIII*, xviii (2), 90; cf. 81.
[13] Hall, *Chronicle* (1809 edn.), 665.

Other Scottish rulers were to find, like Albany, that while the Scottish nobles would defend their own soil they would no longer cross the Border in the interests of France. Such opinions were reinforced in the 1550s by the fear of French domination. It proved to be altogether too much for the Scots to have their country ruled in the French interest by a Frenchwoman, Mary of Guise, French troops garrisoning Scottish fortresses and Frenchmen thrust into offices in Scotland, and there soon had to be a statute against those speaking evil of the queen and the French.[14] The fear grew that Scotland was going to share the fate of Brittany and, through marriage, be absorbed as a province into France. The earl of Argyll was heard to remark in 1559 that 'the France ar cumin in and sutin down in this realm to occupy it and to put furtht the inhabitantis tharoff, and siclik to occupy all uther menis rowmes pece and pece, and to put away the blud of the nobilitie'; and, it was added, he 'makis the exampill of Brytanny'.[15]

But another cause was operating in favour of Anglo-Scottish amity, and that was the progress of the Reformation. Already in the 1530s England was at once an example and a refuge for Scots who had adopted reforming opinions; then, in 1543, the policy of an Anglo-Scottish alliance accompanied by the authorisation of the vernacular Bible in Scotland had been adopted for a brief space; and in the years following, when English military policy did so much to alienate Scotland, sympathy with the Reformation was sufficiently strong to ensure that England still retained allies among the Scots. Only the existence of some motive stronger than patriotism can account for the very considerable countenance which the English received from Scotsmen between about 1545 and 1548, and neither the compulsion which armies could exert on the inhabitants of occupied territory nor the existence of financial inducements can explain the number of collaborators whom the English found in Scotland.[16] The attraction exerted on the Scots by a country which had broken with Rome was not seriously interrupted by changes in the political and military situation: it was in February 1543, when the prospects of an Anglo-Scottish treaty were most promising, that Sadler reported that if a cartload of Bibles, Primers and Psalters were sent to Scotland 'they wolde be bought every one';[17] but on 1 November 1547, less than two months after Pinkie, the governor of the English garrison in Broughty Castle reported that there was much desire in Angus and Fife to have Bibles and Testaments and 'other good English books of Tyndale's and Frith's translations'.[18] In June 1548 Lord Methven, puzzled to find an explanation of 'the caus that Inglis men is fawvorit and the authorite nocht obeyit nor servit', found four 'prynsipall thingis quhilkis is the caussis': three of the four were material considerations – the desire for security, profit and stable government – but first, before

[14] *APS*, ii, 499–500.
[15] *Scottish correspondence of Mary of Lorraine* (SHS), 427.
[16] For observations on the record evidence in *RSS*, iv, see *SHR*, xxxiii, 42–3.
[17] *Hamilton Papers*, i, 445.
[18] *Cal. S.P. Scot.*, i, 35.

those other three, he put the fact that 'part of the legis has tayn new apoynzionis [opinions] of the scriptour and has don agan the law and ordinance of haly kirk'.[19] When John Knox remarked to Cecil in June 1559 that the perpetual concord between the two realms, for which he had long looked, would be effected by the preaching of Jesus Christ crucified,[20] he was proposing to build on a well-laid foundation.

In the whole period down to 1603, religion probably did more than anything else to foster the consciousness of common aims and a common destiny. The later picture of Anglo-Scottish ecclesiastical relations, one of antagonism or at least diversity, has done much to obscure the unity which was uppermost in men's minds in the early years of Elizabeth's reign. This is not the place to recount the substantial approximation of the two Churches in that period, in respect of doctrine, polity and worship,[21] but some illustrations may be given of the cordial friendship and complete understanding between the Church defined by the Elizabethan settlement of 1559 and the Church which emerged from the Scottish revolution of the following year. The Scottish reformers thought of England as 'of the same religion' as themselves, and as having 'enterprised like reformation of religion' with them, while English churchmen noted with satisfaction that English intervention contributed to the success of the Scottish revolt in 1560 and regarded that achievement as the culmination of their own triumph a few months earlier.[22] Archbishop Parker's apprehension about 'such a visitation as Knox hath attempted in Scotland, the people to be orderers of things',[23] belonged to a phase when the Scottish reformers were only rebels, with neither English countenance nor a constitutional position in their own country, and his oft-quoted comment, far from being typical, is an isolated jarring note.

In that early stage, a common Protestantism was no doubt the primary consideration, and in later years the political situation was sometimes such as to make men ready to emphasise the harmony between the two Churches, as in 1571, when the king's party in Scotland besought Elizabeth to 'take upon her the maintenance and protection of the true religion preached and established by law in both the realms';[24] and again in 1585, when the articles for a treaty between England and Scotland began with a reference to 'the better maintenance of the true, ancient, Christian religion which they now profess'.[25] But it is also true that the insular and unique character imposed upon the Church of England by the state was not much reflected in the thought and writings of the earlier Elizabethan churchmen, and was no obstacle to the recognition of other reformed churches,

[19] *Scottish correspondence of Mary of Lorraine*, 241.
[20] *Cal. S.P. Scot.*, i, 218.
[21] G. Donaldson, *The making of the Scottish prayer book of 1637*, 7–22, and *The Scottish Reformation*, chs. iv–vii.
[22] Knox, *Works*, i, 382; vi, 44; *Zurich Letters* (Parker Soc.), i, 88, 109, 113, 116, 124, 140.
[23] PRO, S.P. 12/7/32; *Parker Correspondence* (Parker Soc.), 105.
[24] *Warrender Papers* (SHS), i, 105.
[25] Ibid., i, 192.

including that of Scotland, while the Scots on their side acknowledged the archbishops of Canterbury and York to be 'those whom God, of his providence and mercy, hath erected as principals in ecclesiastical jurisdiction in England'.[26]

Next to religion, it was language that was uppermost in men's minds as a link between the two peoples. In a letter which the English privy council proposed to send to the Lords of the Congregation in July 1559, the hope was expressed that 'this famous isle may be conjoined in heart as in continent, with uniformity of language, manners and conditions'.[27] John Maitland of Thirlestane, who, as chancellor of Scotland from 1587 to 1595, 'held the king on two grounds sure, neither to cast out with the kirk nor with England',[28] thought of 'this isle' as 'naturally joined by situation, language and most happily by religion'.[29] And the king whom he advised likewise thought of the two countries as 'joined in unity of religion and language'.[30]

The history of an English dialect in Scotland goes back to the sixth and seventh centuries, when Anglian penetration made parts of southern Scotland racially and linguistically little else than an extension of northern England; and from the eleventh century, when those areas were incorporated in the Scottish kingdom, south-eastern Scotland, the most English part of Scotland, played a steadily increasing part in the development of the country.[31] Almost the entire eastern seaboard of Scotland and all the more fertile, productive parts of the country were by the sixteenth century Anglo-Saxon, in language if not in race, and the Gaelic-speaking Celts were confined to the barren mountains of the centre and west. The Scottish state – the Scotland which counted politically and economically – was consciously Anglo-Saxon, and would have indignantly repudiated the suggestion that it was anything else.[32] The linguistic triumph of the Anglian element in Scotland meant in itself that Scotland, viewed from the standpoint of English policy, presented a picture quite different from either Wales or Ireland.

The Gaelic-speaking area was all the time shrinking. Of course in the central and west highlands the old tongue was still an important element. When a new parish clerk was elected in the parish of Duthil, on upper Speyside, in 1537, he addressed the parishioners *in eorum ydiomate*,[33] and John Carswell, superintendent of Argyll and bishop of the Isles in the 1560s,

---

[26] p. 58 *supra*.

[27] *Cal. S.P. Scot.*, i, 234–5.

[28] Melville, 271.

[29] *Cal. S.P. Scot.*, x, 377–8; *Warrender Papers*, i, 196; cf. ii, 82, 141.

[30] *Basilikon doron* (STS), ii, 302.

[31] Already by 1200, it seems, the people of Perthshire, unlike those of Argyll, were acquainted with English: *Scotichronicon*, vi, 40.

[32] The Lowlander's contempt for the Highlander and his 'Irish' tongue appears in William Dunbar, *Works* (STS), ii, 121.

[33] William Fraser, *Chiefs of Grant*, iii, 269. I am indebted to Mr D. A. McKay for this reference.

found it advisable to provide a Gaelic translation of the Book of Common Order for congregations where the humbler folk, at any rate, knew no English. Sir Thomas Craig was probably going too far when he remarked at the opening of the seventeenth century that 'there is not a single chieftain in the highlands and islands who does not either speak, or at least understand, English',[34] for one of the provisions of the statutes of Iona in 1609 was that men possessed of goods worth 60 cows should send at least their eldest son or daughter to be educated in the lowlands until they could speak, read and write English,[35] and one of the reasons advanced for an education act in 1616 was the desirability of the suppression of 'the Irish language'.[36] At the same time, most men of substance in the highlands were probably already bilingual, and the paucity of deeds and records in Gaelic is so striking[37] as to suggest that there was no difficulty about the use of English for legal purposes. Apart from the central and west highlands, Lowland Scots had hardly a rival. In the reign of James IV an Ayrshire man who believed that Gaelic 'suld be all trew Scottish mennis lede [speech]' had yet to refer to that tongue as a thing of the past – 'It was the gud langage of this land'.[38] And in Galloway, where in the later fifteenth century a priest had been considered disqualified for the service of a parish because he did not understand and could not speak intelligibly the language (*ydioma*) of the place,[39] there is no indication of any language difficulty at the Reformation.[40] In the three most northerly Scottish counties, again, the Norn tongue was extinct in Caithness and on the way to extinction in Orkney, and even in Shetland, where the latest deed in the old language belongs to 1607, there is a good deal of evidence that the majority of the inhabitants were now at least bilingual.[41]

Lowland Scots itself, a branch of northern English, had by the sixteenth century no doubt diverged widely from the English of England,[42] but those who used it were all but unanimous that the language which they wrote and spoke was 'English'. John Barbour (d. 1396), recounting a Scottish struggle for independence, in *The Bruce*, claimed to write 'Ynglis',[43] and the chronicler Wyntoun (d. *c*. 1420) professed to be translating from Latin

---

[34] Craig, op. cit., 288.

[35] *RPC*, ix, 28–9.

[36] Ibid., x, 671–2.

[37] Donald Mackinnon, *Catalogue of Gaelic MSS.*, 295–6. There are no Gaelic documents among the very ample muniments at Dunvegan Castle: I. F. Grant, *The MacLeods*, 242n.

[38] William Dunbar, *Works* (STS), ii, 22.

[39] *CPR*, xiv, 192–3. I am indebted to Professor I. B. Cowan for this reference.

[40] W. L. Lorimer, 'The persistence of Gaelic in Galloway and Carrick', *Scottish Gaelic Studies*, vi, vii, shows how little credence is to be attached to statements that Gaelic survived in the south-west through the seventeenth century.

[41] Per Thorsen, 'The third Norn dialect – that of Caithness', *The Viking Congress*, 232–4; Hugh Marwick, *The Orkney Norn*, xxiv; G. Donaldson, *Shetland life under Earl Patrick*, 78–80.

[42] A Spanish visitor said that James IV's speech differed as much from English as Aragonese from Castilian: Hume Brown, *Early Travellers in Scotland*, 39.

[43] *The Bruce* (STS), i, 91.

into 'Inglis'.[44] Even Blind Harry, who in the late fifteenth century narrated the deeds of William Wallace in a work marked by bitter hatred of the English, had no doubt that the Scots shared the language of their enemies, for in describing a Frenchmen he wrote:

> Lykly he was, manlik of contenance,
> Lik to the Scottis be mekill governance,
> Saiff of his tong, for Inglis had he nane.[45]

William Dunbar, who flourished at the beginning of the sixteenth century, wrote many of his poems at a time when the marriage of James IV to Margaret Tudor and the accompanying 'treaty of perpetual peace' promised to transform Anglo-Scottish relations, but he was not merely expressing his Anglophile leanings when he spoke of his language as 'oure Inglisch' or when he crudely expressed the superiority of the English spoken in Lothian over that which prevailed in Ayrshire:

> I tak on me ane pair of Lowthiane hippis,
> Sall fairar Inglis mak, and mair perfyte,
> Than thow can blabber with thy Carrik lippis.[46]

There were, indeed, one or two dissentient voices, but their claims that Scotland had a distinctive language lacked confidence. Thus, the Anglophobe who wrote *The complaynt of Scotlande* (1549), protested that he wrote in 'domestic Scottis langage' but elsewhere spoke of English and Scots as 'of ane langage';[47] and although the provincial council of the Scottish Church decreed in 1552 that a catechism should be set forth 'in our vulgar Scottish tongue',[48] when the Catechism appeared it contained a translation of the Lord's Prayer into 'Inglis'.[49] A little earlier, Gavin Douglas, who translated the Aeneid 'furth of Latyn in our Scottis Langage' or 'in the langage of Scottis natioun', had endeavoured to purge his diction of Anglicisms and had found the design not wholly practicable:

> Kepand na sudron bot our awyn langage . . .
> Nor yit sa cleyn all sudron I refuse,
> Bot sum word I pronunce as nyghtbouris doys:
> Lyke as in Latyn beyn Grew [Greek] termys sum,
> So me behufyt quhilum (or than be dum)
> Sum bastard Latyn, French or Inglys oyse [use]
> Quhar scant was Scottis – I had nane other choys.[50]

---

[44] *Original Chronicle* (STS), ii, 4–5.

[45] *Schir William Wallace* (STS), 245.

[46] Dunbar, *Poems* (STS), ii, 10, 15.

[47] *Complaynt* (EETS), 16, 106.

[48] Patrick, *Statutes of the Scottish church* (SHS), 144.

[49] *Catechism of John Hamilton*, ed. T. G. Law, 249. A similar uncertainty is reflected in an act and proclamation relating to the vernacular scriptures in 1543, for the act reads 'Inglis or Scots', while in the proclamation 'Inglis' is deleted and 'vulgare' substituted: *APS*, ii, 415, 425.

[50] *Aeneid* (STS), ii, 1, 6.

But Douglas did not convince his readers, and his protest went unheeded, for Sir David Lindsay, a few years later, described Douglas as the rose of 'Inglis rethorick'.[51] Lindsay's view, like that of almost all his fellow-countrymen, was that English was the common speech of Scotland,[52] and John Major had remarked that the chief tongue of the island of Britain was 'English, which is spoken by the English and by the civilized Scots'.[53]

King James V (d. 1542) was said to have been such an enthusiast for the vernacular that he, 'hering ane of his subjectis knap suddrone [affect southern speech], declarit him ane traiteur',[54] but if there had ever been the slightest possibility that he, or Gavin Douglas, or any other staunch defender of Scottish linguistic peculiarities, could succeed, that possibility vanished with the Reformation. Religion and language were not merely the principal links between the two peoples; they were closely related. It is one of the most important facts in their history that the Scottish people never had a printed Bible in their own tongue. There has indeed survived, from a date so early that it belongs rather to the last phase of Scottish Lollardy than to the beginnings of the sixteenth-century Reformation, a Scottish version of the New Testament;[55] but it was not printed until the nineteenth century, and it is at the best not a fresh translation but a version of Purvey's revision of Wyclif's New Testament – a version in which the word-forms have been altered but which is not genuinely Scots in either vocabulary or grammar. Any possibility that a Scottish version of the scriptures might have prevailed disappeared when copies of Tyndale's New Testament, in print, arrived in Scotland about 1527; it was succeeded in Scottish use by Coverdale's version and then by the 'Geneva' Bible, which was the first to be printed in Scotland (1579). Not only was the Bible heard by everyone in church, and no doubt read in many homes, but it was and long continued to be the essential reading-book in schools; in any event so little Scottish vernacular prose may have been in print that the choice of reading matter would lie between Latin and English. It is when we turn to verses in which passages of scripture were paraphrased in a vigorous and picturesque vernacular[56] and to the occasional pieces of translation in Archbishop Hamilton's Catechism that we appreciate what Scotland lost, and how her national identity suffered, through the failure to use the vernacular in the service of the reformed Church.

Nor was the Bible the only vehicle of English influence in the Church. The first service-book of the Scottish reformers was the English Book of Common Prayer, and when that book was largely superseded by a less conservative liturgy, the one adopted was no less English, for it was the

[51] Lindsay, *Works* (STS), i, 57.
[52] Ibid., ii, 319.
[53] Major, *Greater Britain* (SHS), 18.
[54] *Catholic tractates of the sixteenth century*, ed. T. G. Law (STS), 105.
[55] *New Testament in Scots* (STS); T. M. A. Macnab, 'The New Testament in Scots' (*SCHSR.*, xi), 82–103.
[56] See *Devotional pieces in verse and prose* (ed. Bennett, STS) and *The gude and godlie ballates* (ed. D. Laing, 1868).

book which had been used by a congregation of Englishmen exiled at Geneva in Mary Tudor's reign – the book known after its adoption in Scotland as the Book of Common Order. No attempt was made to turn into the vernacular even that most popular part of public worship, the metrical psalter, and English versions were always used (though in some editions with Scottish orthography). Even the official formularies of the Church – its Book of Discipline and its Confession of Faith – were composed in a language which, if not quite English, is a very emasculated Scots.[57]

It might be inferred that the vernacular was felt to be a folk-dialect lacking in the dignity suitable for solemn use, but such an inference would leave out of account the important personal associations of some of the Scottish reformers with England. Like many of his fellows, Knox had had a career south of the Border and among English exiles before he took part in the organisation of a reformed church in his own land, and he acquired such a marked English diction that his ablest critic reproached him with forgetting 'our auld plane Scottis', and added: 'I am nocht acquyntit with your Southroun'.[58] But whatever the reason for the predominance of English in the Scottish Church, that predominance was so marked that Scottish ministers must have turned more readily to English than to Scots when they put pen to paper. The compilers of the Negative Confession, in 1581, again, like Knox, drew on themselves the derision of their theological opponents because they 'knapped suddrone' or affected English speech.[59] The Negative Confession was of course a formal document, for which Scots may have been considered unsuitable, and in the more intimate *Autobiography and diary* of the Rev. James Melville we find a language still Scots, though already modified by English influences. Within half a century, however, the anglicising work of the Reformation had completed its effects on Scottish divines, and Robert Baillie, who was born in 1599, grew up to write pure English.

Already before 1603 the Scottish vernacular was in a fair way to being displaced as a literary language. English seems to have been favoured for verse before it was generally adopted for prose: James VI wrote his *Essays of a prentise* in almost pure English, his *Reulis and cautelis*, in the same volume, in pure Scots, and William Fowler likewise wrote Scots prose and English verse. The prevalence of English was complete in the poets William Alexander and William Drummond. The preference of poets for English was not the result simply of slavish imitation of English models, for Scottish poets used the 'Spenserian' form of sonnet years before Spenser, and it is the more striking that English was so readily adopted for verse, in that there was a long tradition of Scottish vernacular poetry. With prose there was no

---

[57] We have the Book of Discipline only in the histories of Knox and Spottiswoode, either of whom could have anglicised its language, but the Confession of Faith is in the Acts of the Parliaments of Scotland.

[58] Ninian Winzet, *Certane Tractatis* (Maitland Club), 118.

[59] *Catholic tractates of the sixteenth century*, 105.

such tradition; it may be said that Scots prose was extinguished before it had a chance fully to develop and, while official records like the acts of parliament and privy council show how effective and vigorous it was, it was never adapted for use in the loftier subjects like theology and philosophy. In prose works generally there was a change direct from Latin to English, without an intermediate phase of Scots. King James VI's most important prose work, his *Basilikon doron*, has been pronounced to be 'practically the last serious piece of prose writing of which we can certainly say that it was conceived and written down in Scots while that was still a national literary language'; but, while the MS. was in Scots, the printed versions, even that produced for very private circulation in 1599, were in English.[60] One later work, Habakkuk Bisset's *Rolment of courtes*, written in the reign of Charles I, was said by the author to be in 'my awin maternal Scottish langaige', and has been claimed as 'perhaps the latest specimen of literary Middle Scotch existing',[61] but it has little of Scots about it save the spelling. It is plain that about the period of the union of the crowns Scots, as a literary language, passes into a tunnel from which it was to emerge – and then merely for restricted use in verse – only in the eighteenth century; and this could not have happened had the domination of English not been assured by developments before 1603.

The lowering, and finally the disappearance, of the language barrier between the countries would of itself, even had there never been political union, have resulted in the dissemination of English literature in Scotland. Already, in and before the reign of Elizabeth Tudor, the two nations had come to share a common literary heritage. Chaucer of course inspired many Scottish poets and was hailed by William Dunbar as 'reverend Chaucere, rose of rethoris all' and as 'all the lycht' of 'oure Inglisch'.[62] To Scottish poets he was 'our Chaucer'. But it was not only poets to whom he was known. Among the 'tales' mentioned in *The complaynt of Scotlande* 'the taylis of Cantirberrye' have first place,[63] and among the proverbs recorded by a Scottish minister in the early seventeenth century is this: 'Ye are lyk Chaucers cuke, ye seime busier nor ye are'[64] – though the allusion should have been to the serjeant of law. Sir David Lindsay refers to 'Chawceir, Goweir and Lidgate laureate', whose 'sweit sentence through Albione bene song', and mentions that 'Chauceir wrait of Troilus, how that he luiffit Cressida'.[65] Robert Maxwell, bishop of Orkney from 1526 to 1541, had 'ane Inglis buke of Goweir' and David Panter, bishop of Ross from 1547 to 1558, had copies of the works of both Gower and Chaucer.[66]

[60] *Basilikon doron* (STS), ii, 105, 117. The same practice had been followed in the composition and printing of William Fowler's account of the baptism of Prince Henry in 1594: Fowler's *Works* (STS), iii, pp. xxvii–xxviii.
[61] *Complaynt of Scotlande* (EETS), p. xxvii.
[62] Dunbar, *Poems* (STS), ii, 10.
[63] *Complaynt*, 63.
[64] M. Anderson, *Proverbs in Scots*, no. 1731.
[65] Lindsay, *Works*, i, 56, 147.
[66] *Innes Review*, ix, 7.

The existence of a common language, or at least the ability of educated Scots to read English, may well have militated against the development of a Scottish printing press. The first experiment in printing in Scotland belongs to the earliest years of the sixteenth century, but until the middle of the century activity was intermittent and, so far as can be judged from the books which have survived, the total production down to 1600 was still very small. Copies survive of no more than thirty books which were printed in Scotland before 1560, and only some 380 items are known to have appeared by 1600.[67] (Besides, two printers who were temporary migrants from south of the Border – Vautrollier and Waldegrave – were responsible for 120 or so out of this small total.) There was necessarily a large import trade, and, while Latin works for scholars seem to have come mainly from the continent,[68] books from England were in a tongue readily enough understood by Scottish readers with less pretension to scholarship. Some imported volumes were not welcome to the authorities: in October 1555 it cost the burgh of Edinburgh 18d. 'for hadder [heather] to burn Inglische buiks on the mercat croce';[69] but as the entry is the first in a series dealing with church expenditure no doubt these volumes were heretical. It is hardly likely that John Norton, an English bookseller, would have set up a business in Edinburgh, as he did about 1588, had there not been a market in Scotland for English books, though he proceeded to import directly from Germany so that continental books might be as cheap in Scotland as in England.[70] Whether Scottish works were sometimes printed in England because of the lack of presses at home may perhaps be doubted: it is true that three editions of the Negative Confession were printed in London[71] and that the first edition of Knox's *History of the Reformation* came from Vautrollier's press there, but these issues may have been designed for the English puritan market.

At a time when the vehicle of advanced instruction was so often still Latin, linguistic approximation did nothing of itself to make England an educational centre for Scots. Yet, in the eyes of the discerning, English universities already offered certain advantages. It may have been in-doctrination with protestant theology rather than the dissemination of southern culture that was in the mind of the duke of Norfolk in April 1560, when he suggested to Cecil that the Scottish hostages for the treaty of Berwick should be placed at Cambridge or Oxford,[72] but the suggestion was in any event consonant with the wishes of some Scots, for Lord Ruthven, father of one of the hostages, asked specifically that his son should

[67] Aldis, *Books printed in Scotland before 1700* (annotated copy in NLS).

[68] *Innes Review*, ix, 15. The library of Clement Little, preserved in Edinburgh University, shows an overwhelming preponderance of books of continental origin, and the items published at London were mainly theological – the works of Calvin, Peter Martyr and Bishop Jewel.

[69] *Extracts from records of burgh of Edinburgh*, ii, 363.

[70] *RPC*, iv, 459; Calderwood, v, 77.

[71] *STC*, 22020–2.

[72] *Cal. S.P. Scot.*, i, 344.

be sent to Cambridge 'to be brought up in fear of his Lord God'.[73] It appears further that native education, whatever standards it may have achieved later, was not at that time highly thought of by the more cosmopolitan or far-seeing among the Scots. It is true that as early as 1496 there had been an act of the Scottish parliament ordaining that barons and freeholders of substance should send their eldest sons not only to grammar schools but also for three years to 'the sculis of art and jure',[74] whereas it was not until 1559 that a comparable measure was even proposed in England;[75] but Scottish performance lagged far behind legislative intention. John Major remarked, early in the sixteenth century, that it was a reproach to the gentry of Scotland that they educated their children neither in letters nor in morals,[76] and while Major's views were coloured by his own affectionate memories of his studies at Cambridge it is only right to say that he was so fair-minded as to admit that Cambridge was 'somewhat inferior to Oxford'[77] – a proposition which became more doubtful at and after the Reformation, when most of the intellectual activity was at Cambridge.

In the appreciation of the merits of an English education, as in so much else that contributed to Anglo-Scottish amity, one of the pioneers was John Knox, who insisted that both his sons should have a sound Anglican upbringing, and sent them to school in England; subsequently they both graduated at Cambridge and the elder was beneficed in the Church of England.[78] Adam Bothwell, who, as bishop of Orkney, introduced the Reformation to that diocese and was himself a student of theology, Hebrew and science, recommended that his nephew, John Napier – later famed as the inventor of logarithms – should be sent 'to the schools' abroad, 'for he can learn no good at home'.[79] Another of Scotland's reforming bishops, Alexander Gordon of Galloway, seems to have agreed with his brother of Orkney about the poor quality of Scottish education: at any rate, he followed John Knox's example of sending his sons abroad, for John Gordon, after studying at Paris and Orleans and spending many years in France, ultimately settled in England as dean of Salisbury,[80] and his brother, Laurence, spent some time at Cambridge.[81] While some Scots clung to the tradition of completing their education on the continent, the Reformation had created difficulties which explain a petition of the general assembly in 1579 that the sending of children to continental universities should be prohibited, because through foreign education 'the youth of this realme is corrupted by pestilent popery'.[82] Some may have thought that Scottish

[73] Ibid., 325.
[74] APS, ii, 238.
[75] Hist. MSS. Com. Salisbury, i, 163.
[76] Greater Britain, 48.
[77] Ibid., 25–6.
[78] Knox, Works, vi, pp. lxiii–lxv; McCrie, Knox (1874), 416; DNB s.v. Knox, John.
[79] Mark Napier, Memoir of John Napier of Merchiston, 67.
[80] DNB.
[81] Cal. S.P. Scot., iii, 530; iv, 504.
[82] Calderwood, iii, 446.

education was sound intellectually as well as safe theologically: it was said of Glasgow under the principalship of Andrew Melville that 'ther was na place in Europe comparable for guid letters, for a plentifull and guid chepe mercat of all kynd of langages, arts and sciences',[83] but this was merely the opinion of the principal's admiring nephew, and Melville's own successor, Thomas Smeton, took a different view. Smeton, who had been a schoolmaster at Colchester before becoming principal at Glasgow in 1580, began to send students to England for advanced studies – Hugh Fullerton, who had graduated at Glasgow in 1578 and who later became minister at Dumfries and Kilmarnock; William Lynne, who had graduated at Glasgow in 1583 and was later admitted to Emmanuel College, Cambridge;[84] John Gibson, who graduated at Glasgow in 1583, then matriculated at St John's, Cambridge, and was ordained in England;[85] and possibly Archibald Anderson, who matriculated at Cambridge in 1585.[86] But Glasgow students were not alone in pursuing this course: Alexander Hume, after graduating at St Andrews, proceeded to Oxford in 1580;[87] Thomas Maxwell studied at Trinity College, Cambridge, before being ordained in London in 1578;[88] Thomas Richardson, a native of Leith, graduated B.A. at Oxford in 1575;[89] Patrick Simpson, after graduating at St Andrews in 1574, completed his education in England and then returned to the ministry of the Church of Scotland;[90] Thomas Davidson, from St Andrews, was a 'bursar' at Cambridge in 1587;[91] and Richard Murray, who graduated at Edinburgh in 1597, went on to Cambridge for a B.D.[92] When, in 1595, the twelve-year-old earl of Moray proposed to go to 'the schools' in England, he had no difficulty in obtaining his tutor's approval.[93]

There was not as yet a two-way traffic in education in the sense that Englishmen attended Scottish universities. When Andrew Boorde wrote in 1536 from Glasgow 'wher I study and practyce physyk',[94] he did not mean that he was a medical student, and even an internationally famed Scottish scholar like George Buchanan obtained an English pupil only because the English ambassador in Edinburgh sent his son to him.[95] Nor were Scots yet receiving teaching appointments in English universities, though many of them attained distinction as professors on the continent. But Scots were already taking part in the education of Englishmen by teaching in schools in

[83] Melville, 50.
[84] Cal. S.P. Scot., vi, 635–6; Munim. Univ. Glasguen., iii, 3, 4; Venn, Alumni Cantab., iii, 122; Hist. MSS. Com. Salisbury, viii, 192.
[85] Register of Presentations, ii, 113, 115; Venn, ii, 211; Hist. MSS. Com. loc. cit.
[86] Venn, i, 28.
[87] McCrie, Melville, note FFF.
[88] Venn, iii, 166.
[89] Alumni Oxon.; Brasenose Coll. Reg.; Hist. MSS. Com. Salisbury, v, 207.
[90] Fasti Ecclesiae Scoticanae, iv, 318.
[91] Register of Presentations, ii, 4, 33, 72, 75, 167, 169.
[92] Scots peerage, i, 226–7; Venn, iii, 229.
[93] Cal. S.P. Scot., xi, 530.
[94] DNB.
[95] Cal. S.P. Scot., v, 565.

England: David Black was a schoolmaster in England for about seventeen years before he became minister at St Andrews in 1590;[96] a Scot called Guthrie had an 'academy' at Hoddesdon, Hertfordshire, in 1584,[97] and between 1584 and 1586 one of his masters was William Cowper, afterwards bishop of Galloway;[98] Alexander Hume taught in an English school for some time before becoming rector of the High School of Edinburgh in 1596;[99] Andrew Oliphant had to be 'inhibited to meddle with the teaching of a school at Bridlington without licence' in 1564;[100] Thomas Smeton, as already mentioned, was a schoolmaster at Colchester for some years before he joined the staff of Glasgow university;[101] and in 1563 the town council of Edinburgh was very diffident about inviting James White, 'Scottisman in Londone', to become master of their High School, because they understood that he 'hes greit proffit be his scole in Londone, and that he is ane man of excellent lernyng bayth in Lating and Greik tongue'.[102]

When we turn from academic education to other kinds of culture, there is less detailed evidence of Anglo-Scottish contacts. There is some reason to believe that there was a good deal of English influence on Scottish music, perhaps dating from the reign of James III, who patronised an English musician. According to John Major, the English were in their musical accomplishment 'first in all Europe. For though in France or in Scotland you may meet with some musicians of such absolute accomplishments as in England, yet 'tis not in such numbers.'[103] Allowance must, however, be made for Major's habit of upholding the superiority of England over Scotland – he professed even to love the peals of English bells,[104] which so many Scots have been temperamentally incapable of appreciating – and his testimony would not in itself prove that Scotsmen regarded England as a model. It is more significant that Robert Richardson, a Scottish commentator on the rule of St Augustine, twice brackets England and Scotland together as the only countries where there prevailed certain forms of music which he detested, and from this it may be fairly inferred that the two countries shared a tradition in church music.[105] It seems that Scottish organists had learned from English masters,[106] and there is other evidence that English and Scottish music had the same characteristics.[107] The Scots did not look exclusively to England as a model, for in 1553 a prebendary of

[96] *Cal. S.P. Scot.*, xii, 352; *Fasti Eccl. Scot.*, v, 420.
[97] Melville, p. xxxvii.
[98] *Fasti Eccl. Scot.*, vii, 345; *DNB.*
[99] McCrie, *Melville*, note FFF.
[100] Purvis, *Tudor parish documents*, 108.
[101] *Fasti Eccl. Scot.*, iii, 410; *DNB.*
[102] *Extracts from records of burgh of Edinburgh*, iii, 157.
[103] *Greater Britain*, 27.
[104] Ibid., 110.
[105] Robert Richardson, *Commentary on the rule of St. Augustine* (SHS), 80, 142.
[106] John McQuaid, 'Musicians of the Scottish reformation' (Edinburgh Univ. Ph.D. thesis, 1949), 9–10.
[107] H. G. Farmer, *History of music in Scotland*, 86–7, 112–13.

Edinburgh was permitted to leave for France as well as England, 'thair to remane for the space of ane yeir . . . to the effect that he may have and get better eruditioun in musik and playing nor he hes', [108] besides, James V patronised Italian musicians[109] and Queen Mary no doubt introduced French musicians. But the music of the court and chapel of King James VI was very largely provided by the Hudson family, five Englishmen who enjoyed continuous royal patronage until the end of the century.[110] They represented a link between English and Scottish music even before they came to Scotland, for one of them had been acquainted with the Scottish priest-composer, Robert Johnson, after he had been exiled to England for heresy.[111] Two of the Hudsons contributed also to the poetry, as well as the music, of the Scottish court.[112] The family appears to have been introduced to Scotland by James's father, Lord Darnley, along with his other English servants,[113] and recalls the important link between England and Scotland which was provided by the family of Lennox, which, owing at first to its place in the royal succession after the Hamiltons and later to the marriage of Darnley to Mary and the accession to the throne of a king who was the heir of Lennox, played a part in affairs out of all proportion to its members' ability and gifts of leadership. Matthew, the fourth earl, Darnley's father, had taken Henry VIII's side against the French interest (and the rival family of Hamilton) in 1544 and, on his forfeiture, was an exile in England for twenty years. His wife, the daughter of Margaret Tudor by the earl of Angus, seems to have been essentially an Englishwoman in outlook and preferences; his brother, Robert, bishop of Caithness, shared in the family's exile and was appointed to a prebend of Canterbury, but returned to Scotland to work for the reformed church in his diocese. English musicians were only one part of the Lennox heritage – an English heritage – on which James VI entered as the heir of his father and his paternal grandfather.

In drama there is less evidence at our disposal than there is in music, though it is well known that English players were finding their way to Scotland, for they appeared in Edinburgh more than once in the 1590s and reached Dundee and Aberdeen in 1601.[114] But much more revealing is the evidence of English influence on what may be called folk drama, shown by the introduction to Scotland of the cult of Robin Hood. As a supposedly historical figure he was already well known in Scotland in the fifteenth century,[115] but his association with popular festivities seems to have been a development of the early sixteenth century. John Major said 'the feats of

---

[108] *Extracts from records of burgh of Edinburgh*, ii, 176.
[109] *Letters of James V* (HMSO), 169–70.
[110] McQuaid, op. cit., 29, 32 sqq.
[111] Farmer, op. cit., 110.
[112] *Works of William Fowler* (STS), iii, pp. xix, xx.
[113] R. H. Mahon, *Tragedy of Kirk o' Field*, 117, 137–8 and n; cf. *Cal. S.P. Scot.*, ii, 215.
[114] A. J. Mill, *Medieval plays in Scotland*, 299–306; Arthur Melville Clark, *Murder under Trust*, c. 8.
[115] Ibid., 23 and n, 25.

this Robert are told in song all over Britain';[116] *Robene Hude and Litil Jhone* is one of the very first works known to have been printed in Scotland, and it was one of the 'tales' mentioned in the *Complaynt of Scotlande*; and Robin's archery was proverbial – 'Manie speiks of Robein Hude that never schot in his bow'.[117] It is certainly somewhat remarkable that in Edinburgh the festivities traditionally associated with 'the abbot of unreason' or 'the abbot of narent' were transferred to Robin Hood sometime between 1493 and 1518[118] and that in Aberdeen a similar change was made, because by 1508 Robin Hood and Little John had for the time being superseded the 'abbot and prior of Bonaccord'.[119] The celebrations were sometimes so boisterous that there was an act of parliament against them in 1555, but it was not successful in suppressing them.[120] One of the most curious illustrations of the increasing anglicisation of Scotland in our own day has been the addition to the Scottish Kalendar of the alien figure of Guy Fawkes, the anniversary of whose attempt to blow up the English parliament (even though with a Scottish king) passed unnoticed in Scotland until less than a generation ago. It may be that the popularity of Robin Hood indicates a similar stage in anglicisation in the early sixteenth century.

The Scottish educational system may, even then, have tended to produce more men with professional qualifications than could hope to find lucrative employment in their own poor country. It was not literally true, as was said, that Scottish universities were turning out more divines than could be absorbed at home,[121] for right down to the end of the century there were many Scottish parishes without ministers, but it was true that the level of stipends was at that time so low that the ambitious may well have felt that their noblest prospect was the highroad to England. A contemporary remarked that if richer livings were available in Scotland many 'clerks' would return from abroad:

> Our countrie clerkis beyond the seyis
> Wald draw thame hame from all countries,
> Of Ingland, France and uther partis,
> Quhair thay ar scatterit in all airtis,
> Becaus at hame thay will not give
> Sufficient quhairon thay may live:
> Quhais number as I understand
> Is greiter nor is in this land
> Of ministeris.[122]

---

[116] *Greater Britain*, 156.
[117] M. Anderson, op. cit., no 1128.
[118] *Extracts from records of burgh of Edinburgh*, i, 66, 176.
[119] *Aberdeen burgh records* (Spalding Club), i, 439–40.
[120] *APS*, ii, 500; *Extracts from records of burgh of Edinburgh*, iii, 107–8; *Diurnal of occurrents* (Maitland Club), 263.
[121] *Cal. S.P. Scot.*, vi, 635–6.
[122] John Davidson, *Dialog betwix a clerk and ane courteour* (1573–4), sig. A. vi. b.

Sir Thomas Craig, writing at the very beginning of the seventeenth century, made some pertinent observations. 'In England', he said, 'there are many wealthy benefices, and the Church has ample revenues; whereas in Scotland the Church is so lean and impoverished that its dignitaries can barely subsist on their stipends'. Craig does, indeed, qualify this statement elsewhere, but he also mentions, in more general terms, that all professional men were apt to feel straitened in Scotland: 'Nowadays in Scotland rewards for learning are few and far between, and they alone keep learning alive (for learning thrives ill on an empty stomach).'[123]

The material attractions of life in the south were considerable, and already in the sixteenth century Scottish clerics had learned – a thing they have never since forgotten – that there were good livings to be had south of the Border. To determine how many Scots were pushing their fortunes in the English Church would require prolonged searches in diverse sources, many of them unprinted, and all that can be done here is to mention the results of some sample investigations and to give a few illustrations. Naturalisation in England was technically a requirement before a Scot could be appointed to a benefice, and many Scottish clerks appear in records of naturalisation,[124] but it is by no means always possible to show that they subsequently obtained the preferment they sought. Nor is it always easy to trace the further careers of men whom Scottish records show to have emigrated, like John Hoggart, a prebendary of the collegiate church of Restalrig, who went to England in the 1560s.[125] But English diocesan records readily yield the names of Scots who held benefices, and state papers refer to others. In the diocese of Durham ten or more Scots were serving parishes in the 1570s;[126] in the diocese of Lincoln there were at least four;[127] there were a few in London;[128] and others are to be found in York, Chester and Devon. [129] Already in the sixteenth century, therefore, we can discern the beginnings of that traffic which was to reach its full fruition in the late nineteenth and early twentieth centuries, when, out of five successive archbishops of Canterbury, three were Scots. The English

[123] Craig, op. cit., 329, 332–3, 381, 455.

[124] *Letters of denization and acts of naturalisation* (Hug. Soc.), i; cf. *Scottish Antiquary*, viii, 9–14, 58–61.

[125] Books of Assumption, i, 151*v*.

[126] *Injunctions and other ecclesiastical proceedings of Richard Barnes* (Surtees Soc.), 29, 31, 35–8, 55, 74, 76–7. The inhabitants of Durham and Northumberland complained in 1565 that many churches 'have no priests unless they be vagabond Scots, who dare not abide in their country' (G. Baskerville, *English Monks and the Suppression of the Monasteries*, 284–5).

[127] *Lincoln Episcopal records in the time of Thomas Cooper* (Linc. Rec. Soc.), 6, 196, 203, 210, 212, 229. They were John Davidson (Saperton), George Frude (Braceborough), Thomas Maxwell (Scrafield) and John Menzies (Swayfield).

[128] Duncan Anderson, 'minister at Aldersgait' (*Cal. S.P. Scot.*, ix, 280); James Coldwell (*Scottish Antiquary*, viii, 11; *Returns of aliens* (Hug. Soc.), ii, 50; *Cal. S.P. Scot.*, iii, 541; iv, 38); John Douglas (Newcourt, *Repertorium*, ii, 542, 544); David Inglis (ibid., i, 741, 918–19; Hist. MSS. Com. *Salisbury*, vii, 353–4).

[129] Purvis, *Tudor parish documents*, 140; *Cal. S.P. Scot.*, x, 20; Hist MSS. Com. *Salisbury*, ix, 287.

house of commons really showed remarkable prescience when it recommended in 1607 that Scotsmen should not hold in England an ecclesiastical office entitling them to a seat in the house of lords, the headship of a university college or more than one tenth of the inferior church benefices.[130]

In so far as the motive of the migrants was nothing more than pecuniary advantage, the most appropriate comment on the traffic was made by Bishop John Skinner more than a century ago: the Scottish Church, he said, 'ought to have none for its ministers but those who expect their reward in a better country than England, and from a Master whose kingdom is not of this world'.[131] But it would be less than fair to believe that finance has been the only motive. Major, early in the sixteenth century, had been in no doubt that the standards of church life in England were far superior to those in Scotland – the parish churches were more numerous, they were more richly adorned, the churchmen were of 'an honest walk and conversation' and in general 'the ecclesiastical polity of Scotland is not worthy of comparison with that of England'.[132] As the century proceeded, a comparison between one 'ecclesiastical polity' and another came to have meanings which Major had never dreamed of, but at every stage there were those in Scotland who would have subscribed his statement. In the later years of Henry VIII, and in Edward VI's reign, England received as refugees Scots of reforming views who were as yet obtaining no countenance at home. Many of them returned to Scotland after a Reformed Church was set up there in 1560,[133] but others remained, to serve in the Elizabethan establishment – John Mackbrair, for example, a Cistercian monk of Glenluce, who was imprisoned for 'heresy' in 1550 but escaped to England, where he became vicar of St Leonard's, Shoreditch (1552–3), vicar of Billingham (1565) and vicar of Newcastle (1568),[134] and Robert Richardson, naturalised in 1540, who was presented in 1559 to the living of St Matthew's, Friday Street, which he held until his death.[135] Such traffic was not entirely one-way, for the successive changes in the ecclesiastical polity of England had more than once sent refugees from England to Scotland, and Christopher Goodman, after associating with Knox at Geneva, became minister first of Ayr and then of St Andrews.

The 'commodities' which 'might ensue' from 'a uniformity in religion in both these realms' had been perceived as early as 1560,[136] and such 'commodities' were increasingly appreciated as the years passed and a

---

[130] John Bruce, *Report on the . . . union . . . of England and Scotland* (1799), ii, pp. cxxxiv–cxxxv, cxxxix–cxl.

[131] F. Goldie, *Short History of the Episcopal Church in Scotland*, 72.

[132] *Greater Britain*, 27–8, 129.

[133] G. Donaldson, *The making of the Scottish prayer book of 1637*, 4.

[134] *TDGNHAS*, 3rd ser. ix, 158 sqq; Newcourt, i, 687; *Injunctions of Richard Barnes*, 42, 55, 57, 75, 85.

[135] *Naturalisations*, i, 206; *Returns of aliens* (Hug. Soc.), ii, 11; *Sede vacante institutions*, 76; Hennessy, 435.

[136] *Cal. S.P. Scot.*, i, 471.

growing number of men in the two countries looked forward to the union of the two crowns, for contemporaries found it hard to conceive of unity without uniformity. The Scottish Reformed Church turned out to be essentially imitative, alike in its theology, its polity and its liturgy. The spark of originality which can be detected at the outset in the Confession of Faith of 1560 and the first Book of Discipline was soon extinguished, and when the initial agreement among Scottish reformed churchmen was disrupted Scottish ecclesiastical affairs were dominated by two factions, each of which was in agreement with a corresponding party in England. Scottish presbyterians maintained the closest relations with the English movement led by Thomas Cartwright and Walter Travers (who were invited to chairs at St Andrews university in 1580), and the vision of a British presbyterian church, which was to inspire the Westminster Assembly in the 1640s, was present in many minds as early as the 1570s. The Scottish presbyterians received a great deal of encouragement from ultra-protestant diplomats like Walsingham and William Davison, in whose hands the conduct of Anglo-Scottish political relations lay for so many years. In 1590 Queen Elizabeth, in her capacity as self-appointed governess to the Scottish king, wrote to him: 'Let me warne you that ther is risen, bothe in your realme and myne, a secte of perilous consequence, such as wold have no kings but a presbitrye';[137] but a more superfluous and impudent piece of advice has seldom been given: the peril was one of which James had been aware from almost his earliest awakening to political consciousness, it was a peril against which he had legislated six years earlier, and it was a peril which would never have reached the proportions it did but for the policy of Elizabeth's own servants. Scottish episcopalians, on their side, looked with no less fidelity to Anglo-Scottish uniformity, but they received no encouragement from Queen Elizabeth, who evidently did not regard Anglicanism as a commodity for export, and until the 1590s they received no appreciable encouragement even from English bishops.[138] Yet they could not but regard England with friendly eyes, and when reaction against presbyterianism went so far that it produced views on church order attaching to the 'apostolic succcession' an importance which the first reformers had not done, Scots had the additional reason for seeking office in the Church of England that it was now thought to confer orders superior in validity to those conferred in Scotland. It was not until 1610 that Scottish bishops received consecration at the hands of English bishops, but David Lindsay, who was to be one of the bishops consecrated after the succession was thus restored to Scotland, had already in January 1604 sent one of his sons to be ordained by the bishop of London.[139]

It is only right to add that while some Scottish clerks passed into the English ministry because they were reformers, others crossed the Border

[137] *Cal. S.P. Scot.*, x, 350; *Letters of Elizabeth and James VI* (Camden Soc. xlvi), 63–4.
[138] 'The attitude of Whitgift and Bancroft to the Scottish Church', *infra*.
[139] Ordinations register, Bishop of London, 1578–1628 (London Guildhall Lib. MS. 9535/2) f. 112a.

because they were themselves in need of reform. The most conspicuous example is Paul Methven, who had been educated in England under Bishop Coverdale and had married an Englishwoman, before becoming minister of Jedburgh in 1560. In 1562 he was deposed for adultery and took refuge in England, where he seems to have been commended by Coverdale and Grindal to Parkhurst, bishop of Norwich, who welcomed him as 'an excellent preacher' and 'a good and learned man'. The Scottish general assembly was indignant that such a man should intrude himself into 'the ministry of England', but in 1570 Methven obtained naturalisation and was subsequently instituted to four benefices in the south-west of England. The peerage writers, ignoring his earlier career, know him only as the respectable prebendary of Wells who was the ancestor of the noble family of Methuen.[140] Another Scottish delinquent was David Wood, minister of Kinghorn, who was deprived at the beginning of 1563 because he had defamed a reader, and disappeared from Scotland. At the end of 1571, 'Davie Woode, Scotte, denyzen and preacher', was said to have been in England for ten years. He seems to have retained the hot temper which had occasioned his expulsion from Scotland, for in 1567 Bishop Grindal described 'Wood the Scotsman' as 'a factious fellow', and his connection with two benefices which he held in the diocese of Lincoln seems to have been none too happy, ending in deprivation in one case and resignation in the other. Apparently, too, Wood's Scottish orders were called in question, but not until 1581, when 'David Wood, a Scottishman pretending himself a minister in the church' was 'by some vehemently suspected to have no calling in that function'.[141] More fortunate was John Morrison. Minister of Whitekirk, he was deprived 'for certain offences' in 1580; but in 1582, in a document which has attained some fame among those interested in the English attitude to non-episcopalian orders, he was licensed by Archbishop Grindal, and became curate of St Botolph's, Aldersgate.[142]

The attraction of a more opulent country lay, in one way or another, behind many of the intellectual and ecclesiastical connections between England and Scotland, and some Scots were candid enough in their admissions of the impression made on them by the wealth of the south. What they thought of London, for instance, is clear enough from the verses, with the refrain 'London, thou art the flower of cities all', in which the English capital was praised by William Dunbar, a poet who was satirical enough about the dirt and untidiness of Edinburgh.[143] Dunbar's admiration for London was shared by Major, though Major, with his

---

[140] *Cal. S.P. Scot.*, i, 680; *Fasti Eccl. Scot.*, ii, 124; *Zurich Letters* (Parker Soc.), i, 131, 167; *Naturalisations*, i, 169; *Register of Matthew Parker*, i, 320; F. W. Weaver, *Somerset incumbents*, 115, 128, 474; Hist. MSS. Com. *Salisbury*, ii, 514; Burke, *Peerage*.

[141] *Reg. K.S. St. A.* (SHS), i, 176–7; Grindal, *Remains* (Parker Soc.), 291; *Lincs. Episc. Records*, 15, 20, 140, 203, 293, 314n; *Returns of aliens*, ii, 65; *Acts of P.C.* 1581–82, 71.

[142] Register of presentations (Register House), ii, 46; *Returns of aliens*, ii, 284; Newcourt, i, 916; Strype, *Grindal*, 596.

[143] Dunbar, *Poems* (STS), ii, 261–3, 276–8.

wider experience of cities, was less extravagant with his superlatives, and said only that London was 'the largest and fairest in its situation' of all the cities of Britain.[144] Such remarks show plainly enough that the Scottish inferiority complex was not the product of political union, and Dunbar and Major point forward to those denationalised Scots who are the greatest detractors of their own country. But to what extent the wealth of England affected the Scottish economy it is not so easy to determine. According to an observer in 1598, England came fourth in importance among the countries with which the Scots traded – after the Low Countries, France and the Baltic[145] – and, while there are no contemporary statistics to support his estimate, the impression one forms is that trade with the Low Countries and the Baltic, at least, played a greater part in the Scottish economy than did the English trade.

Yet trade with England was not negligible, and often prospered in spite of political hostility. It was so tenacious that in 1550, 1551 and 1552, after Scotland had been drawn completely into the sphere of French political influence, there was a stream of requests for safe-conducts permitting Scots to trade with England.[146] It may well be, too, that the proximity of England would always have nullified Scottish attempts, by legislation,[147] to keep their raw materials at home and encourage native manufactures; certainly Scottish wool was always welcome in England and English cloth welcome in Scotland, whatever the political situation might be and whatever acts of parliament and council might say – and an act of parliament condemned English cloth not only because its import drained coin from the realm but also because it had 'onlie for the maist parte ane outward shaw, wantand the substance and strenth quhilk oftymes it appeiris to have'.[148] In 1546, when the two countries were at war, a correspondent of Cardinal Beaton wrote from Edinburgh: 'as to my lorde Borthuik, he hes sauld his woll to men that hes put it in Ingland, like as all the merchandices and vittales on this syde of the watter [i.e., south of Forth] passis thair'.[149] And in 1555 William Mudy, whose interests were in Orkney and Caithness and who dealt in the produce of the seas, complained to the queen regent, Mary of Guise, that although he had received nearly 1,000 merks for his 'schipe and fysche', he would have received £1,000 from 'the Inglis men' had he been licensed to contravene the statute forbidding the export of victual, fish or salt.[150] Not only was it recognised that England was an attractive market, but the complaints sometimes heard in our own day that the best Scottish produce is diverted to England were anticipated in the sixteenth century. In 1542, in spite of acts of parliament,

---

[144] *Greater Britain*, 21.
[145] Hume Brown, *Early travellers in Scotland*, 87.
[146] *Cal. S.P. Scot.*, i, 183–90.
[147] *APS*, ii, 290, 347, 495.
[148] *APS*, iv, 119.
[149] *Scottish correspondence of Mary of Lorraine* (SHS), 162.
[150] Ibid., 398.

Englishmen were buying white fish and herring on 'the north cost in Anstruthir, Crail, Sanct Monanys and in all utheris the townis of the cost side . . . and thairby makis exhorbitant derth of the fysche, sua that na freman of burgh can get ane pennyworth tharof'.[151] And in 1551 the Scottish privy council considered that the reason for 'the greit and exhorbitant derth . . . of all kynd of victuallis and viveris' was 'throw the having of the samyn furth of this realme to the partis of Ingland and uthairis', but perhaps overstated its case by going on to protest that English cattle were devouring the good Scots grass: 'the Inglis gudis of Ingland, sik as nolt, scheip and horse and uthairis, ar sufferit to gang and pasture within the boundis of Scotland'.[152] In 1566 there was again a complaint that 'Inglischemen dailie resoirtis and repairis within this . . . realme . . . and . . . frequentis marcattis, fairis and uthiris commoun places, and thair byis in grete quantitie sindrie marchandice guidis, coirnis, bestiall, armoure, wapinis and all uthir geir quhilk thai think necessare for thame',[153] and in 1576 and 1580 we find prosecutions for transporting horses, cattle, sheep, wool and other goods to England.[154]

It hardly modifies the general picture of England as a market for Scottish goods that Burghley was told in 1590 that horse dealers in the north of England could get higher prices in Scotland than their own country, especially as his informant was concerned to emphasise the fellowship among the Borderers and 'their accordance of manners' – not, he added, 'that the Skottes take of us, but we of them, as the evill is ever more infectyve than the good'.[155] Concern over the fraternising of Borderers was nothing new: the *Complaynt of Scotlande* lamented 'the grit familiarite that Inglis men and Scottis hes had on baitht the boirdours, . . . in marchandeis, in selling and bying hors and nolt and scheip, . . . the quhilk familiarite is expres contrar the lawis and consuetudis baytht of Ingland and Scotland',[156] and a Scottish statute of 1587, alluding to 'the mariage of the kingis majesties subjectis upoun the dochteris of the brokin men and thevis of Ingland', forbade Scots to marry 'ony Englishe woman dwelling in the opposite marchis' without express permission.[157] It was more important that no one could fail to see how adventurous Englishmen were to be found in every part of Scotland where commercial profit was to be reaped: they turn up on the farthest fringes of the land – in Shetland, in Mull and in Loch Carron.[158] Some proposals made in 1548, to the effect that England should provide ships to exploit the Scottish fisheries, and that under English auspices harbours should be built and craftsmen imported to give

[151] *Public Affairs*, 513.
[152] *RPC*, i, 114–15. For similar complaints, see *Public Affairs*, 69, 361, 367, 369.
[153] *RSS*, v, 2921.
[154] *RSS*, vii, 764, 2310A.
[155] *Cal. S.P. Scot.*, x, 388.
[156] *Complaynt*, 106.
[157] *APS*, iii, 464–5.
[158] *RPC*, ii, 654–5; xiv, 332 sqq.; *Cal. S.P. Scot.*, v, 668; x, 503; G. Donaldson, *Shetland life under Earl Patrick*, 53, 70–1; *RSS*, ii. 1665.

instruction in mining, the working of wool, skins and hides and other trades,[159] anticipate some of the eighteenth-century developments, when, after political union, English capital and English technical skill were applied to the exploitation of Scotland's natural resources. In the sixteenth century, however, little was achieved along such lines, though Bevis Bulmer, an English mining engineer, is heard of in Scotland in 1566,[160] in 1585 Englishmen were in partnership in working Scottish mines,[161] and in 1598 an Englishman called Gavin Smith was associated with James Aitchison, James VI's goldsmith, in the invention of an 'artificial pomp' for raising water out of mines.[162] All such activities, however contrary some of them were to the economic thought of the time, brought Englishmen and Scotsmen into contact with each other. There is nothing to suggest that their relations were as a rule other than amicable, and they must have fitted quite well into the pattern of an association between two races conscious of their common religion, common language and common political destiny.

The Franco-Scottish alliance had at one stage been so close that it anticipated Winston Churchill's famous offer of 1940, because French and Scots enjoyed common nationality, in virtue of a concession made by Louis XII and confirmed by later sovereigns down to Louis XIV and in virtue of a reciprocal concession by the Scottish parliament in 1558.[163] The Anglo-Scottish amity never went so far. The articles discussed in July and September 1585 included one to the effect that Englishmen and Scotsmen should be naturalised in each others' country,[164] but this was not incorporated in the treaty as finally agreed. It is however, something of a curiosity that Elizabethan lawyers sometimes seriously contended that Scots were not aliens in England. The evidence is reviewed in part by Sir Thomas Craig in his *De unione regnorum Britanniae* (1605). He observed that, negatively, there was no English statute depriving Scotsmen of the power to enjoy the same rights and privileges as the English or debarring them from possession of property in England,[165] and went on to cite evidence positively favourable to his claim, beginning with a spurious law of pre-Conquest times whereby Scotsmen, in reward for their services against the Danes, were granted co-citizenship with the English,[166] but proceeding with opinions given in the courts during the sixteenth century. He relates that a Scotsman on trial in the court of king's bench on a charge of rape 'demanded as a foreigner the customary privilege of *dimidietas linguae* ... that half of the jury should be of his own tongue[167] ... After consultation the judges of both courts [i.e. both benches] disallowed the

[159] *Cal. S.P. Scot.*, i, 144–5.
[160] A. L. Rowse, *The England of Elizabeth*, 131, and reference there.
[161] *RPC*, iv, 22–3.
[162] *APS*, iv, 176.
[163] *APS*, ii, 507, 515.
[164] *Warrender Papers*, i, 194, 201.
[165] *De unione*, 335, 339.
[166] Ibid., 341.
[167] In terms of 28 Edw. III c. 12 and 8 Hen. VI c. 29.

Scotsman's claim, and on the ground that a Scotsman had always been held an Englishman and not an alien or foreigner in England, and that the Scottish tongue was not a foreign language'.[168] The same judgment is alluded to by Peter Wentworth in his *A pithie exhortation to her majestie for establishing her successor* (1598): 'There was a judgment in the King's Bench in Michaelmas term, 13/14 Elizabeth, that a Scot was not to be accounted in England for a stranger, but rather a subject, and also that the language of the Scots is not a strange language, but mere English'.[169] Craig also recounts that 'the question whether Scotland is within the realm of England, or, as the expression is, within the four seas, was keenly argued by John Stowell against George Lord Zouch in the Michaelmas term of the 4–5th year of Queen Elizabeth, as Plowden reports in his *Commentaries*'.[170] The argument in this case was founded on the supposed dependence of Scotland on the Crown of England, but it might have been relevant to cite the phraseology of 25 Edward III stat. 1, which was concerned with the rights of inheritance of children born 'beyond the sea, out of the ligeance of England', and which was possibly ambiguous in its relevance to Scotland.

Whether this evidence supports Craig's conclusion that 'Scotsmen are indisputably English citizens in the eye of the law'[171] is more than doubtful, especially in view of the abundant evidence that Scots did apply for naturalisation – not to mention the statute 7 Henry VII c. 6, whereby all Scots not made denizens were to depart the realm. Yet the possession of a common language, which so impressed judges of the English courts, must have made it hard for Englishmen to regard Scots as foreigners, just as it is hard for us today to regard Americans as foreigners. If Englishmen were prepared to acknowledge the dialect of the Scots to be 'English', strangers from the continent must have seen even less to differentiate one people from the other, and the similarity was such that it enabled Queen Elizabeth to expect the Spanish ambassador to believe her when she laid on the Scots the responsibility for unfortunate incidents: many of the pirates of whom he complained in 1565 were, so she said, Scotsmen (though she added, a little oddly, that they spoke English to avoid being known),[172] and when he complained about the extent of puritan nonconformity in 1566, 'she said that those who disobeyed were certain ministers, not natives of the country, but Scotsmen'.[173] Any tendency there was to accept the Scots as in practice English citizens would be encouraged by the adaptability of the Scots who settled in England. The author of *The complaynt of Scotlande* looked with a jaundiced eye on the capacity of the Scots for merging their identity in that of the English: 'quhoubeit that there be abufe thre thousand Scottis men, and there wyfis and childir, that hes duellit in Ingland thir

---

[168] *De unione*, 347; Sir James Dyer, *Reports* (1714), iii, 303–4.
[169] *A pithie exhortation*, part ii, 11.
[170] *De unione*, 348; Edmund Plowden, *Commentaries* (1816), i, 368, 376.
[171] *De unione*, 347.
[172] *Cal. S.P. Spanish*, 1558–67, 440.
[173] Ibid., 553.

fyftye yeir by past, and hes conquest be there industre batht heretage and guidis, yit nocht ane of them dar grant that thai ar Scottis men, bot rather thai man deny and refuse there cuntre'.[174] But Peter Wentworth puts it more objectively: 'The meanest Scottishmen that are setled in England are content to forget their countrie, kindred and parents, and to frame and apply themselves unto us, that they may freelie enjoy their poor condition or calling.'[175] Two examples may be given of Scots of humble rank who settled in England: Isobel Barton, sister of James Barton, of Leith, was married in Newcastle about 1564 to Peter Richardson, 'ex genere nautarum quos *killmen* vocant', and had two sons, one of whom had to obtain naturalisation in Scotland in order to inherit the property of his maternal kinsmen; and John Kene, of Alnwick, had similarly to obtain a licence to succeed his uncle, also called John Kene, in property in Selkirk.[176] The history of such self-effacing and adaptable Scots is not easy to trace; but the kind of contribution they could make to the life of England is shown by the careers of Edmund Anderson, one of Queen Elizabeth's chief justices, and William Davison, one of her secretaries, who were both of Scottish descent.

From the marriage of Margaret Tudor to James IV in 1503 a union of the crowns was never a remote contingency, for through the whole century, except during the twenty years between the birth of Elizabeth and the death of Edward VI, there was never more than one life between the Scottish line and the English throne, and more often than not the heir presumptive was north of the Border. And in the course of the twenty years when the Scottish succession did seem more remote there was the proposal for another marriage – of Prince Edward to Mary, queen of Scots – which was meant to hasten union. That project was accompanied in its later stages by an attempt at propaganda on the part of the English government and by discussion of the material advantages which would accrue from union,[177] and there were serious plans for the amalgamation of the two kingdoms into one kingdom of 'Great Britain'. That term already had a long pedigree, and this was not the first time that the negotiators of a marriage had used it, for in 1474, when a marriage between Cecilia, daughter of Edward IV, and James, son of James III, was proposed, the commissioners had declared their purpose to be the advancement of the peace and prosperity of 'this Nobill Isle, callit Gret Britanee'.[178] Besides, John Major had written his *Historia Majoris Britanniae* (1521) and his use was

---

[174] *Complaynt*, 104.

[175] *A pithie exhortation*, part ii, 76–7.

[176] *RSS*, 292, 339. Thomas Short, of Holy Island, was heir of Thomas Short, armourer in Edinburgh, in 1546 (*RSS*, iii, 1438, 1461).

[177] *An exhortacion to the Scottes to conforme themselfes to the . . . union betweene the two realmes*, by 'James Harryson, Scottisheman' (1547); *An epistle or exhortacion . . . from the Lorde Protectour . . . to the . . . inhabitantes of the realme of Scotland* (1548); *Cal. S.P. Scot.*, i, 140–1, 180–1.

[178] Denys Hay, 'The term "Great Britain" in the Middle Ages' (*Proc. Soc. Antiq. Scot.*, lxxxix), 61.

only one of many instances in the humanistic Latin of the period.[179] The name was in such general currency in the second half of the century that it was the obvious choice when James VI sought a name to designate the united realm after 1603.[180]

The currency of a single name for the island may itself have fostered the concept of a united Britain as a political unit. And it is also significant that there developed a new fashion in historiography which thought in terms of Britain. Major, on the Scottish side, dealt with English and Scottish history in alternate chapters of his *History of Greater Britain*. Polydore Vergil, though professing to write only an *Anglica Historia*, made a serious effort to trace Scottish material and did incorporate a good deal of information about Scottish affairs, not exclusively in so far as they impinged on English history.[181] Hall has a certain amount of Scottish material, though only in connection with Anglo-Scottish relations, but Holinshed, probably stimulated by the great likelihood of the accession of a Scottish king, produced a complete history of Scotland, detached from his English chronicles. Meantime Matthew Parker's church history had been *De antiquitate Britannicae ecclesiae*. By the time Camden wrote a description of Scotland for his *Britannia* it was not difficult to be prophetic, but he derived much satisfaction in his later editions from the 'divine and heavenly opportunity now fallen into our laps . . . that Britain . . . should . . . by a blessed union be conjoyned.'.[182]

The union of the two peoples who formed that united Britain had been in the making for generations, indeed for centuries, before political union was achieved, and the events of 1603 and of 1707 were only two incidents in the long process of creating a united nation. That process is one of which we have not yet seen the end: it is one of which it would not be easy to determine the beginning; but the process was carried a long way forward in the sixteenth century by many factors which contributed to the anglicisation of Scotland, and the beginnings of most of the developments which have brought the two nations closer together during their political partnership can be discerned in the period before the union of the crowns.

[179] Ibid., 62.
[180] S. T. Bindoff, 'The Stuarts and their style' (*EHR*, lx), 199, 201.
[181] Ed. Denys Hay (Camd. Soc. 3rd ser. lxxiv), pp. xix, 40, 238–42.
[182] Camden, *Britain* (trans. Holland, 1610), 'Scotland', p. 3.

13

The Attitude of Whitgift and Bancroft to the Scottish Church

Reprinted from *Transactions of the Royal Historical Society*, 4th series, xxiv (1942).

The friendship and understanding which had joined the reformed churches of England and Scotland in the early years of Elizabeth's reign were not menaced until shortly after Whitgift's accession to the see of Canterbury in 1583. The new primate had to deal with problems which had been quite unknown to his predecessors – problems arising from the success of the Scottish presbyterians and the efforts of their English imitators. The constitution of the Scottish reformed church, after developing in the direction of 'conformity with England', had not attained stability before being undermined by the emergence of intransigent presbyterianism. In 1581 the general assembly had approved the full presbyterian programme, and in August 1582 a *coup d'état*, the 'Ruthven raid', by the ultra-protestant party among the Scottish nobles had produced a government favourable to the first brief presbyterian experiment. In England also the struggle between presbyterianism and episcopacy had begun, and Whitgift himself had been the protagonist of the episcopalian cause. The English crown was immune from such *coups d'état* as made possible three changes in the constitution of the Scottish church within five years; but the English presbyterians had powerful friends among the radical politicians and diplomats. Already there were signs of co-operation between the ecclesiastical rebels in the two British kingdoms, and the incipient alliance soon had political repercussions, for the conduct of Anglo-Scottish relations was during several years in the hands of Francis Walsingham and William Davison, two diplomats who, as secretary and ambassador, consistently used their influence on behalf of the Scottish presbyterians, whom they alleged to be the only sincere supporters in Scotland of the cause of 'amity with England'.

King James escaped from the 'Ruthven raiders' at the end of June 1583. Whitgift was nominated to Canterbury in August, and the initiation by him of a policy of severe repression of presbyterianism in England coincided with the opportunity presented to Archbishop Adamson of St

Andrews by a new Scottish government – the 'anti-presbyterian dictatorship' of Captain James Stewart, Earl of Arran. The character of Partick Adamson suffered severely at the hands of his presbyterian opponents in his own day, and few attempts have been made in subsequent generations to ascertain the truth about him; but even his enemies paid tribute to his ability, particularly in letters and oratory, and rated him as a highly dangerous, although treacherous and dishonest, adversary.[1] His portrait seems to show an intelligent, strong and capable nature which might have fitted a lawyer, or even a man of action, better than a cleric. A search for weapons against the presbyterians, who claimed a divine right for their system, led Adamson to assert the scriptural and apostolic origin of episcopacy; and, from the moment of his appointment as archbishop (1576), he had made it clear that he would not be subordinate to the general assembly.[2] With these convictions there apparently went the idea – present in the minds of some other moderate men among his contemporaries – that episcopal government in the Scottish church would contribute to Anglo-Scottish friendship and smooth the way for the Scottish king's accession to the English throne.[3] It was not only in government, but in worship also, that Adamson sought conformity with England. A commission given to him when he was at the height of his power referred to 'a uniform order in form of common prayer'. The phrase meant more than insistence on the use of the Book of Common Order, for it is known that Adamson used 'the English ceremonies' in celebrating a marriage, and that his enemies accused him of 'filthily adulterating the state of public prayer with the simplicity of rites in ministration of the sacraments'.[4]

On the initiative of Adamson, there was co-operation between the English and Scottish primates. The narrative of the Scottish archbishop's mission to England in the winter of 1583–4, described briefly by sixteenth- and seventeenth-century historians, can be reconstructed more fully from the original sources, including the correspondence which passed between the two archbishops.[5] Adamson had numerous motives for making a journey to England. There seems no reason to doubt that he wished to leave

[1] Melville, 53, 293; John Row, *History of the kirk of Scotland* (Wodrow Soc., 1842), 115; *Historie and life of king James the sext* (Bannatyne Club, 1825), 205; Brit. Mus., Cotton MSS., Calig. C. ix, fo. 161.

[2] Calderwood, iii, 371–2; iv, 500.

[3] Cf. *Cal. S.P. Scot.*, ii, 439; vi, 705; viii, 56.

[4] Calderwood, iv, 145, 163; Wodrow Soc., *Miscellany*, i, 417.

[5] There are accounts of Adamson's mission in Melville (p. 141), Calderwood (iii, 763; iv, 49, 55, 431–2), Calderwood's *Vindiciae contra calumnias Johannis Spotsuodi* (edn. 1623, p. 54) and Brit. Mus. Add. MSS. 32,092, fos. 42–5. The Whitgift-Adamson correspondence, which is used throughout this and the succeeding paragraphs, is as follows: (*a*) Adamson to Whitgift (copy, undated, but either late December 1583 or early January 1583/4), Brit. Mus., Add. MSS. 32,092, fo. 75*v*; (*b*) Whitgift to Adamson (copy, dated 4 January 1583/4), ibid., fo. 76*r*; (*c*) Adamson to Whitgift (copy, undated, probably late April 1584), ibid., fo. 76*v*; (*d*) Adamson to Whitgift, 16 June 1584, Harl. MSS. 7004, fo. 3 (copy in Add. MSS., 32,092, fo. 79*v*), printed (except the endorsement) in Thomas McCrie, *Life of Andrew Melville*, appendix iv.

Scotland and visit the continent for the sake of his health. At any rate, the English ambassador in Edinburgh accepted this without question, King James's letter of credit and his licence to leave the kingdom are explicit about it, and even after the excuse, if excuse it had been, was no longer necessary, Adamson persisted in it.[6] It was alleged that he was glad to escape from impending excommunication by the general assembly; and it is possible that the Scottish government considered that the pursuit of its ecclesiastical policy through a critical stage would be easier in the absence of one against whom the full fury of the presbyterians was directed. There was, in any case, important diplomatic business which necessitated that Adamson should have audience of the queen of England, but it was realised from the first that the journey had significance for ecclesiastical affairs, and the rumour was current that the archbishop would go to Geneva and other places overseas to obtain from the continental reformed churches condemnation of the Scottish ministers and their opinions.[7]

The mission was arranged by 29 October 1583; but three weeks elapsed before Adamson left Scotland, travelling south on the *equi gradarii* ('ambling nags') suitable for a sick man. His arrival in London on 30 November was immediately noted by one of Walsingham's agents, who reported to his master that the archbishop 'keeps himself quiet as yet'.[8] Adamson proceeded with diplomatic work, but also communicated with Whitgift, sending him 'articles' which contained a statement of the views of the Scottish presbyterians – *propositiones ministrorum Scotiae serenissimo regi oblatae* – with a refutation of them, and asking for an interview.[9] Whitgift, although personally willing to accede to this request, decided not to act without reference to the government, and he therefore sent a copy of Adamson's 'articles' to Burghley, whose advice he asked. Perhaps acting on Burghley's recommendation, he sent his chaplain to Adamson to explain to him that the queen's permission must be obtained before the two archbishops could meet. Meanwhile, Adamson had learned, to his great distress, that a copy of the 'articles' had fallen into the hands of Walsingham, of whose enmity he was well aware, and he foresaw their use by the English secretary and his friends in Scotland to discredit the Scottish government and Adamson himself. Whitgift, when he wrote to Adamson on 4 January 1583/4, declared that the leakage was unaccountable, as he had retained the original of the 'articles', and Burghley, he believed, had retained the copy sent to him. The inference must be that a copy had been abstracted from Burghley's office by an agent of Walsingham. The English primate reiterated that Adamson must take the initiative in asking for the royal consent before Whitgift could hold any discussion with him, but

---

[6] S.P. Scot. Eliz., xxxiii, 71, 74, 94 (*Cal.*, vi, 681, 684, 707); *RSS*, viii, 1569.

[7] *Cal. S.P. Scot.*, vi, 691, 696, 703, 706; *Border Papers*, i, 188.

[8] Ibid.; *Cal. S.P. Scot.*, vi, 702; *RSS*, loc. cit.

[9] *Cal. S.P. Scot.*, vi, 705, 706; Adamson's 'articles', of which there is a copy in Latin in Add. MSS. 32,092, fos. 73–5, are printed (in translation) in Melville, 148–53, and Calderwood, iv, 50–5.

promised to give him his opinion of the 'articles'. It was, of course, through Mr Secretary Walsingham that Adamson had to apply for the queen's permission to live for a time at Oxford or Cambridge and to confer with Whitgift or any other learned men whom Elizabeth might think it fit that he should consult. The necessity for sending such an application was, he felt, hardly consistent with his dignity; but he wrote a courteous letter to the secretary and offered to make him a present of a 'Galloway nag'.[10]

Adamson succeeded in part of his mission. He visited Lambeth Palace and had a conversation with Whitgift, receiving a copy of one of the English primate's books against the presbyterian Cartwright and promising that in return he would give Whitgift copies of some of his own writings. Moreover, he was entertained by the archbishop of York at his house, and met the bishop of London, who lent him money which Adamson 'dishonoured his country'[11] by failing to repay. He also despatched copies of his 'articles' to the French church in London and to Geneva and Zurich, and spent part of his time in preparing some books for the press. The difficulties which he encountered were, however, more notable than his successes. Copies of his 'articles' found their way not only to Scotland but also into the hands of the English presbyterians, who thought that they contained matter suitable for discussion at their conferences.[12] The enemies of the archbishops put obstacles in the way of further conversations between them and spread a rumour that they were conspiring for the restoration of Romanism, with the result that Adamson had to expound his protestant faith in four or five public sermons. His son-in-law and biographer, Florence Wilson, tells us that in these sermons Adamson gave such high praise to King James that Elizabeth commanded him to desist, and that he continued in private to advocate the right of the Scottish king to the English crown.[13] A number of influential Englishmen – *nobiles quidam* is Adamson's phrase – who desired the overthrow of episcopacy approached the Scottish archbishop with a suggestion that he should engineer the abolition of bishops in Scotland in order to set an example to England. But it was more to the archbishop's mind to defend episcopacy and to warn England against presbytery; and this he did.[14]

The English presbyterians showed their interest in Adamson's mission

[10] Adamson's application to Walsingham, which is undated (like most of his letters), has been attributed to December 1583, but was probably written after Whitgift's letter of 4 January 1583/4. S.P.Scot. Eliz., xxxiii, 94 (*Cal.*, vi, 707).

[11] Sir James Melville, *Memoirs* (Bannatyne Club, 1827), p. 315.

[12] Hist. MSS. Comm., *Report*, xii, pt. ix, 149–50. The MS. collection which includes the minute book of the Dedham *classis* contains a copy of *Propositiones ministrorum Scotiae serenissimo regi oblatae* among writings which were 'inserted . . . because they were conferred of in our meetings'. The leakage of Adamson's 'articles' into the hands of the English and Scottish presbyterians may have taken place through Jean Castel, minister of the French church in London (cf. Cotton MSS., Calig. C. ix, fo. 161), or through Walsingham and William Davison.

[13] P. Adamson, *Poemata sacra* (1619), sig. A. 3 *verso*.

[14] P. Adamson, *Opera* (1619), sig. T. 2 *verso*.

and their appreciation of the danger from it, not only by accusing the archbishops of Romish tendencies and by urging Adamson to change his policy, but also by criticising Whitgift for negotiating with the Scottish primate. Their spokesman was Robert Beale, who was a member of Walsingham's group of left-wing and pro-puritan politicians and whose interest in Scottish ecclesiastical affairs is proved by the existence of his collection of manuscripts relating to the Scottish church.[15] On 7 May 1584, shortly after Adamson had left England, Beale wrote to Whitgift, alleging that it was 'vehemently suspected that the archbishop of St Andrews is lately departed hence with such an approbation of our rites here as carryeth with it a condemnation of the form used there; whereon it is not unlike but at the first some hold will be taken to the great disadvantage of the church'. Whitgift sent the letter to Burghley, and with it a refutation of the charges against him: 'It may be that I have spoken in the mislike of the churches in Scotland, but not of late nor upon any conference with the bishop of St Andrews, for whatsoever my opinion is of that platform, yet I have learned not to be curious *in aliena republica*. All the conference that ever I had with the bishop of St Andrews I made known to your lordship, since which time I have not seen him; neither hath he my hand to anything.'[16] Whitgift, although clear in his own mind as to the character of Scottish presbyterianism, had been discreet. His discretion saved him from censure by the civil authorities, and it was of service to the English government, which avoided serious friction with the English puritan party or with the Scottish presbyterians, who might at any time regain power. But it did not guard him from the suspicion of the Scottish ministers, among whom distrust of the English bishops was now for the first time sown, and it impeded Adamson's efforts to secure a united front against presbyterianism. The letter written to Whitgift by the Scottish primate shortly before he left England is in a tone of disappointment. Adamson's sense of failure at the rather meagre results of his mission was aggravated by other difficulties. On his arrival in England he had given away as presents the horses which had brought him south (his enemies called him a spendthrift), and he now found himself without mounts for the return journey. His health had not recovered sufficiently for him to use a swift horse, and he asked Whitgift to give him a sturdy beast to carry him home, promising to let the English primate have a better one in return before Whitsunday.

It was at the end of April or the beginning of May 1584 that Adamson went back to Scotland, boasting of his intention to abolish presbyteries and restrict the power of the ministers,[17] and shortly after his return the Scottish parliament passed the 'Black acts' which overthrew the presbyterian system and established the most effective episcopacy which Scotland had known since before the Reformation. The Scottish presbyterians were in

[15] Hist. MSS. Comm., *Report*, ii, 45. For Beale's character and views see Fuller, *Church History*, ix, v, 9.
[16] Strype, *Whitgift* (1822), i, 295, iii, 97; Hist. MSS. Comm., *Bath MSS. at Longleat*, ii, 23. [17] *Cal. S.P. Scot.*, vii, 138.

despair, and the irreconcilables among them crossed the border into England, where they were befriended by Walsingham and welcomed by the English puritans. The English government's attitude towards the refugees remained one of indifference, in spite of pressure on one side from Walsingham and other puritan politicians, who wanted support for the Scottish malcontents in order to bring about the fall of the pro-episcopal Arran government, and on the other from the Scottish government itself, which, after an attempt at conciliation, urged the English government to banish the exiled ministers or at least to restrict their activities.[18] Adamson, flushed with his success at home, had an exaggerated idea of his influence on the English notables whom he had met,[19] and attempted to persuade Whitgift to advise hostility towards the exiles. On 16 June 1584 he wrote to the English archbishop explaining the Scottish government's policy. Presbyterianism had been overthrown, he said, not only because it was repugnant to the scriptures and to the practice of antiquity, but because the democratic assemblies had shown themselves to be instruments of sedition. The ministers who had gone to England had not been banished, but had fled before violence had even been threatened, and they ought not to be allowed to remain in England, or, if they did remain, to preach. He had not yet had an opportunity to send 'your grace's Galloway nag'. Whitgift, with his usual consideration for the civil power, notified to the queen the receipt of this letter, and presumably informed her of its contents.[20] The primate's scrupulous subservience to the government made it impossible for him to do more, although his antagonists, the radical politicians, had no such scruples and allowed their ecclesiastical preferences to influence their politics. There is no evidence that Whitgift continued to correspond with Adamson; but in January 1584/5 he received from Scotland a letter from an unnamed Scotsman which indicates that he continued to be interested in developments north of the border.[21]

On the downfall of the Arran government in November 1585 the episcopacy which the 'Black acts' had established was not at once overthrown; and both the episcopalians and the presbyterians of England were keenly interested in the fate of the Scottish church. At the critical general assembly of May 1586, when a programme was accepted which restored presbyteries and greatly limited the functions of bishops, Dr Giles Fletcher was an observer, and he sent an account of the proceedings to his brother Richard, dean of Peterborough, who retailed them to Whitgift,

[18] Ibid., 138, 146, 149, 161, 165, 167, 175, 195, 208, 241, 267, 349, 479, 508, 542; Calderwood, iv, 352, viii, 267–8; *Wodrow Soc. Miscellany*, i, 413–14. These references give evidence of the friendly attitude of Walsingham, Davison and other English politicians to the Scottish presbyterians, of Walsingham's dealings with the exiled ministers in London, and of the policy of the Scottish government.   [19] *Cal. S.P. Scot.*, vii, 233, 236.
[20] The letter (Harl. MSS., 7004, fo. 3) is endorsed 'The receat of his letter I signifiet to her majestie at Nonesuch in Sommer anno 1584'.
[21] [*Blank*] to Whitgift, 10 January 1584/5, Add. MSS., 32,092, fo. 78*v* (copy). This letter, written in Scots and dated from Holyroodhouse, contains only invective against the Scottish presbyterian ministers.

adding some unfavourable, if obscure, comments: 'I have sent your grace these first proceedings of the ecclesiastical general assembly in Scotland lately begun there: but not likely to end in haste for their manifold matters so saltly according to their fyrie humour controverted'.[22] Whitgift, still interested and critical, was not the man to begin open war against Scottish presbyterians. The task had to be undertaken by a cleric who felt less obligation to the civil power and to political considerations and occupied a less responsible position. It was soon alleged by a presbyterian writer that the English and Scottish bishops were conscious of identity of interest and were co-operating,[23] but this propaganda had as yet, so far as the evidence shows, very little foundation in fact. It was, however, prophetic of the course of events in the next few years.

The intense activity of the English presbyterians between 1584 and 1587 had resulted in vigorous repression. In taking the initiative and forcing the puritans to the defensive, the Anglicans had to strike at the Scottish church, whence the rebels derived some of their strength; and for their first overt attack on Scottish presbyterianism they selected no obscure occasion but a sermon preached from the open-air pulpit beside St Paul's Cathedral, the scene of many great public sermons. The day chosen was the first Sunday of Elizabeth's seventh parliament (9 February 1588/9) and the preacher was Richard Bancroft, a London rector and canon already noted for his opposition to puritanism. In making a spirited defence of episcopal government Bancroft used conditions in Scotland as a warning against the 'busy and turbulent humourists' who endeavoured to infect England with the 'corrupt opinions' which had triumphed among the Scots. He was resolved to show that the establishment of the 'presbyterial government' did not, as the 'consistorians' maintained, result in the disappearance of all vice and crime and the establishment of 'a very paradise upon this earth'; and, in order to illustrate the 'fruits of this new government where it was erected', Bancoft drew on two unfavourable accounts of Scottish presbyterianism. The first was *A declaration of the king's majesty's intention and meaning concerning the late acts of parliament* (a manifesto drawn up by Archbishop Adamson in defence of the 'Black acts') which had been published in London in 1585 and subsequently appeared in the 1587 edition of Holinshed's *Chronicles*. This work gave Bancroft material on the association of Scottish presbyterians with the rebellious proceedings of the 'Ruthven raiders' in 1582 and 1584. Bancroft's second source was a letter of Robert Browne, the English separatist, who had seen presbyterianism in action when he visited Scotland in 1584 and had criticised it severely, commenting that the *régime* of pastors, doctors and presbyters produced 'instead of one pope a thousand, and instead of some lord bishops in name a thousand lordly tyrants in deed'. Bancroft welcomed Browne's remark that he had 'seen all manner of wickedness to abound much more in their

[22] NLS, MS. 6.1.13, fos. 33–4; copy in B.M., Add. MSS. 32,092, fo. 88v. Giles Fletcher described the assembly's proceedings to Walsingham also (*Cal. S.P. Scot.*, viii, 407).

[23] John Udall, *Diotrephes* (ed. Arber, 1880), p. 7.

best places in Scotland than in our worse places here in England'. Had the English preacher confined himself to repeating the allegations of the *Declaration* and of Browne's letter, criticism of his sermon could have come only from Scottish ministers and their English friends. But he took it on himself to say that King James had not altered his views since his suppression of presbyterianism in 1584, and implied that he was merely waiting for an opportunity to re-establish episcopacy. This suggestion, it will appear, had serious consequences. By referring to George Buchanan's *De jure regni apud Scotos*, a work composed to justify the Scottish revolution of 1567, Bancroft showed that he was already disposed to lay emphasis on the politics of presbyterianism as the most discreditable and dangerous part of that programme.[24]

Bancroft desired to obtain fuller information about conditions in Scotland in order to justify his views. The necessary agents were ready to his hand. John Copcot, master of Corpus Christi College, Cambridge, had been engaged in combating the puritans' insistence on the necessity and value of the eldership, and in one of his writings he had used *A declaration of the king's majesty's intention and meaning* to show 'what stay to civil government' the eldership had been in Scotland, and how it had been 'injurious to their sovereign's estate and the cause of great troubles'. The Scottish king, he said, had wisely foreseen 'that some went about to establish an ecclesiastical tyranny . . . under pretext of new invented presbyteries'.[25] Copcot, clearly, would be willing to assist Bancroft, and it happened that he was friendly with Robert Naunton, who was at this time attached to the English embassy in Edinburgh. Naunton was not sympathetic to the presbyterians, and in a letter to Copcot, dated 12 November 1589, he described 'the old inveterate grudge conceived by this clergy against Mr Doctor Bancroft for intermeddling with their anarchy here established'.[26] Copcot showed this letter to Bancroft, who realised that he could make use of Naunton to equip himself for the controversy which, as the letter clearly showed, must ensue. When Copcot wrote again to his friend Naunton, on 1 January 1589/90, he enclosed a letter in which Bancroft asked Naunton to endeavour to obtain copies of correspondence between the Scottish ministers and Beza or other continental divines and to send him answers to questions aimed at discovering the details of the presbyterian organisation in Scotland, particulars of the ministers' attitude towards the king, and the political ideas of the kirk. From the way in which the questions are framed, it appears that Bancroft wished to compare the Scottish organisation with the English presbyterian platform, to condemn

[24] Bancroft, *A sermon preached at Paules crosse* (1588), pp. 72–6; Robert Browne, *A new year's guift* (ed. C. Burrage, 1904), pp. 8, 25–6 (the MS. of this work [B.M., Add. MSS., 29,546, fos. 67–72] was used by Bancroft, who underlined the passages which he quoted). Bancroft afterwards explained in a letter to Burghley the line of thought which he had followed in his sermon (NLS, MS., 6.1.13, fos. 46–55).

[25] Lambeth Palace MSS., vol. 374, fos. 135, 228, 229; Dudley Fenner, *Defence of the counterpoyson* (1586), preface and Sig. A. 3.

[26] Add. MSS., 32,092, fo. 106.

it as inefficient, to denounce the Scots as rebellious and seditious, and so, by implication, to discredit the English puritans. He was not fastidious about the means by which his purpose was to be achieved, for he suggested that Naunton should 'insinuate' himself into the ranks of the Scottish presbyterian party 'as one desirous to embrace their devices', in order to have access to papers which the ministers might regard as confidential.[27] Naunton was urged by Bancroft to take precautions to ensure the secrecy of their correspondence, but evidently there was some kind of exposure. Naunton had to leave Scotland shortly after receiving Bancroft's letter,[28] and it seems probable that he therefore deputed John Norton, an English bookseller resident in Edinburgh, to obtain the information required by the Anglican churchman. A letter from Norton to Bancroft was intercepted, and when the bookseller was examined (on 12 February 1589/90) he loyally accepted all responsibility – presumably he had agreed to shield his employer – and declared that he had received from 'his uncle, old Norton' the questions which had in fact been directed to Robert Naunton.[29] A paper containing a series of answers to these questions is extant. It may have been written by Norton and intercepted before reaching Bancroft; but there is reason to believe that either this or another copy of the answers may have come into Bancroft's hands.[30] Bancroft had another instrument in his quest for information – John Gibson, a young Scotsman who had gone from Glasgow university to Cambridge in 1583 and, after graduating in 1585/6, been ordained in England. To him Bancroft signified his 'earnest desire thoroughly to know the order and accustomed fashions concerning the elderships as they are now erected in Scotland', and Gibson sent him a long account, based partly on his own observation and partly on what he had heard from others, of the proceedings of the Scottish church courts. He was able to satisfy Bancroft that 'the success of that government generally in all men concerning reformation in godliness and manners is very small'. This letter from Gibson exists today in the volume of manuscripts which contains the answers to the questions sent by Bancroft to Naunton.[31]

[27] Egerton MSS., 2598, fos. 240–5 (*Cal. S.P. Scot.*, x, 337); cf. R. G. Usher, *The reconstruction of the English church*, i, 56–7.

[28] *Cal. S.P. Scot.*, x, 349, 353.

[29] Calderwood, v, 77. It is possible that there was no connection between Naunton and Norton and that Bancroft had employed the Nortons independently. On the other hand, Calderwood's account may be inaccurate, and Norton's confession may in fact have implicated Naunton.

[30] NLS, MS., 6.1.13, fos. 37–8. Dr H. W. Meikle identified this paper as being a series of answers to Bancroft's questions. The same volume includes (at fos. 33–4) a letter to Whitgift of which there is a copy in the British Museum (Add. MSS., 32,092, fo. 88*v*) and (at fo. 42) a letter from a Scotsman which undoubtedly reached England; it is therefore likely that the papers directed to Bancroft which it contains came into his hands safely. It is noteworthy that Calderwood, who had access to a copy of the questions, did not apparently see any answers to them.

[31] Ibid., fos. 39–41. The identification of Bancroft's informant is conjectural; see Register of presentations to benefices (H.M. Gen. Reg. House), i, 144; ii, 113, 115*v*; Venn, *Alumni Cantab.*, ii, 211; Hew Scott, *Fasti Eccl. Scot.*, i, 353.

Scottish indignation at Bancroft's 'slanderous and infamous' sermon had been growing throughout the year 1589, and on 9 December the presbytery of Edinburgh decided to direct a petition to Queen Elizabeth 'desiring her majesty to take order with Mr D. Bancroft'.[32] Two versions of a letter to Elizabeth were written,[33] and in them the ministers boldly pointed out that they had rendered service to England by supporting the English interest in Scotland, alleging that danger to the 'amity' came from English clerics who were inspired by 'Satan that old serpent' to calumniate the Scottish kirk. This hostility had first been shown when *A declaration of the king's majesty's intention and meaning* was 'received, diligently read, and that in the ears of divers chief personages of the realm [of England] ... printed again at London, and with an odious new preface prefixed thereunto reprinted again ... also insert ... in the Chronicles of ... Holinshed for the perpetual memory thereof'. The petitioners proceeded with their chief complaint: 'Secondly, one Bancroft ... with most impudent mouth took upon him to traduce us, our ministry and whole church openly at Paul's Cross on Sunday the 9 of February last in time of parliament ... where ... he entered upon us, not sparing our very dead, but railing against that famous father Mr. Knox'. Thirdly they complained that 'we, our discipline and whole ministry are most ridiculously flouted, as we hear, in their stage plays, pamphlets and pasquils imprinted day by day', and they concluded this part of the letter with a hint to the queen that she was 'highly provoking our patience' and with a threat of 'a fearful curse within your own bowels'. They went on to request that the *Declaration*, being a forgery by Patrick Adamson, should be deleted from Holinshed; that Bancroft should apologise publicly; that some action should be taken against the authors of the plays and pamphlets; and finally – most astonishing request – that 'it may please you after the example of good Josaphat to proclaim a public fast out-through your realm with preaching and supplication'. The Scottish king had gone overseas to fetch home his bride, and in his absence the audacity of the ministers was unrestrained.

There is no evidence that these immoderate demands ever reached Elizabeth; but the course actually taken by the Scots was sufficiently distasteful to the English government. John Davidson, a minister who had been associated in the preparation of the presbytery's petition, composed a little book, *Bancroft's rashnes in rayling against the Church of Scotland*, which brought out the strength of feeling against the English preacher for his attack on the Scottish kirk and king. In the general assembly of August 1590 James Melville preached a sermon on discipline, making the most extravagant claims for the necessity of the presbyterian courts and for their powers over kings and nobles as well as common men, and he said that his subject was specially apt because 'the belly-god bishops of England by all moyen and money were seeking conformity' between the two churches. This declaration of war was made in the presence of Robert Bowes, the

[32] *Wodrow Soc. Miscellany*, i, 470.
[33] Ibid., 489–96; Calderwood, v, 72–7.

English ambassador. King James, who had returned to Scotland in May, had expressed displeasure with Davidson for writing *Bancroft's rashnes*; but he was unwilling to condemn the book's argument, since his own annoyance at Bancroft's aspersions on his sincerity was genuine enough; and it was in the same general assembly that he made his well-known outburst against the Church of England – 'As for our neighbour kirk in England, it is an evil mass said in English, wanting nothing but the liftings'.[34] On 24 October 1590 Robert Bowes wrote to lord treasurer Burghley, enclosing a copy of Davidson's book and explaining that although the king had endeavoured to confiscate the entire edition some copies had in fact escaped. The matter, he went on, 'hath had sundry consultations and been diversely tossed', for it was 'stomached' in Scotland that Bancroft had charged King James with manifest dissimulation and had used the *Declaration*, which was officially pronounced to be an unauthorised publication by Archbishop Adamson. James and his chancellor were unwilling to make a protest directly to the English government, and on the ambassador, therefore, fell the stigma of taking action, involving as it did a loss of credit with at least the more extreme section of the Scottish ministers.[35]

On receiving this report from Bowes, Burghley sent for Bancroft. The cleric, who had read Davidson's newly published attack on his sermon, guessed why he had been sent for, but, although he was thus prepared, the interview was unpleasant. Burghley pointed to the passages in Davidson's work dealing with Bancroft's remarks about James, told him that the pulpit was 'not a place to deal in much with princes', and appeared to be 'greatly moved'. Bancroft was 'in sort dismayed', and, as time was short and the lord treasurer had many other people to interview, he thought it best to frame an explanation or defence – it is that rather than a recantation – in writing. In a long letter to Burghley, he first explained his motive in making a reference to Scotland, and went on to examine the character of the *Declaration*. He gave illustrations of the violence of the presbyterians and of their seditious attitude towards the king, and praised the 'Black acts' for the check which they had imposed on the ministers. He then explained how calumnies about James had been circulated and how the *Declaration* was set forth to refute them, and he reminded Burghley that neither had the *Declaration* (originally published *cum privilegio regali*) been disavowed nor Adamson censured for publishing it. Bancroft next dealt with the central point, his remarks about King James, protesting that there was a difference between the words which he had spoken in the pulpit and the printed copies of his sermon and urging that no man in his senses would wittingly have offended the Scottish king, since he was Elizabeth's ally. But at the worst, he continued, his words could not bear the construction put on them. He proceeded to carry the war into the enemy's country by referring

[34] *Wodrow Soc. Miscellany*, i, 503–20; Melville, 280–1; Calderwood, v, 100–1, 106, 112.
[35] S.P. Scot. Eliz., xlvi, 48, 58 (*Cal.*, x, 482, 492).

to the violent language used by Knox and, more recently, other Scottish ministers, about the English crown and the English church. 'The consistorian humour is of a strange mixture. They will censure and gall every man, but they must not be touched'. Before leaving this part of his subject, Bancroft returned to his favourite point about presbyterian politics, describing the writings of Knox and Buchanan as 'trumpets of rebellion'. He went on to justify his use of Robert Browne's letter, and concluded by asserting that 'advertisements' which he had received from Scotland since he preached his sermon had tended to confirm him in his critical attitude towards the Scottish ministers.[36]

A copy of Bancroft's letter of explanation was sent to King James, to whom it gave only partial satisfaction. The king regretted that Bancroft had not abandoned Browne as a source of information, and would have preferred that the English preacher should, either at Paul's Cross or some other public place, admit his errors and explain his true meaning. A letter from Burghley to the lord chancellor of Scotland helped to mollify James, who reflected that the differences between Bancroft and the ministers might be debated without involving his honour and that to press his own wishes further might bring contention rather than profit.[37]

Bancroft had laid himself open to attack by the English puritans, who were ever watchful for aspersions on the Scottish church. They now had a surer basis for their attack than they had when Beale criticised Whitgift for negotiating with Adamson. John Penry in his *A briefe discovery of the untruthes and slanders contained in a sermon preached the 8 of Februarie 1588 by D. Bancroft* (1590) mentioned Bancroft's insinuation that the Scottish king 'is a deadly enemy unto the present government established in his kingdom, and watcheth but his time to overthrow it' and his allegation that the Scottish ministers were seditious; these charges, he said, would be answered by the Scots themselves, but he argued that rebellious conduct on the part of the ministers did not prove their form of church government to be false. He also censured Bancroft for giving credit to a letter of Robert Browne, whom he described as 'a known schismatic' and a 'proud ungodly man'.[38] Bancroft had read Penry's book before he wrote his *apologia* to Burghley. After John Davidson had stated the case for the Scottish king and church, a more studied criticism of Bancroft appeared in a puritan petition to the queen, possibly written by Henry Barrowe. The author of this work suggested that Bancroft had turned to Scotland for illustrations of the rebellious tendencies of presbyterianism because he could not find evidence in England, and asserted that he had implied that King James was a 'flat hypocrite'. This writer dismissed the *Declaration*, on which Bancroft had based much of his argument, as 'counterfait by the graceless archbishop of St. Andrews', and expressed his belief that the king was a sincere supporter

[36] NLS, MS., 6.1.13, fos. 46–55.
[37] S.P. Scot. Eliz., xlvi, 69, 71; xlvii, 4 (*Cal.*, x, 505, 517).
[38] Penry, *A briefe discovery*, 42–4.

of the presbyterian polity. He emphasised the most vulnerable point in Bancroft's sermon – the attack on James – by quoting from Davidson's *Bancroft's Rashnes*.[39]

Bancroft apparently attempted to make contact with Archbishop Adamson. It is alleged by the presbyterian historian Calderwood that in 1590 or 1591 Bancroft sent letters secretly to the Scottish prelate, telling him that he had read some of his writings, assuring him of support in any attempt to restore episcopacy, and promising him a welcome if he visited England. It is true that Adamson, although no longer exercising any episcopal functions, was still regarded as dangerous by the presbyterians and was charged in 1591 with having assisted the English anti-puritan controversialist Matthew Sutcliffe in the compilation of one of his works. Calderwood's story, although it may be an unfounded accusation which had formed part of a propaganda campaign against Adamson, is not inherently improbable.[40] But the Scottish archbishop was a dying man, and presbyterianism was in the ascendant, when Scottish episcopacy was offered the English countenance which had been sought in vain from Whitgift seven years earlier. Bancroft, but not Adamson, lived to see the time when the restoration of episcopacy in Scotland would again be practicable.

Bancroft was little affected by the censure which he received for his sermon and by the opposition which he encountered, and he continued the castigation of the Scots in two books, *Daungerous positions and proceedings* and *A survay of the pretended holy discipline*, both published in 1593. His line of argument, indicated in the famous phrase 'English Scottizing for discipline', was that a great deal of English puritan thought could be traced to Scottish sources, and he paid particular attention to the subversive politics of the Scottish Reformation (as illustrated in Knox's *History of the Reformation* and as reasoned in Buchanan's *De jure regni*) and to the association of the presbyterian party with the successive *coups d'état* of 1582–5. He was now equipped with a more adequate knowledge of Scottish affairs than he had displayed in 1589, when, in compiling his sermon, he had drawn on Adamson's *Declaration* and Robert Browne's *A new year's guift*. Of printed books, he had now read the first *Book of discipline*, the 1584 London edition of the Anglo-Genevan service book (*The book of common order*), John Davidson's reply to his sermon (*Bancroft's rashnes*), Penry's *A briefe discovery*, the volume of Robert Bruce's *Sermons* published in 1591 and the 1587 edition of Holinshed's *Chronicles*, which was a useful source for recent Scottish history.[41] Most important among printed books, however, was Vautrollier's edition of Knox's *History*, which Bancroft studied carefully and from which he drew illustrations of his

---

[39] 'A petition directed to her most excellent majestie', Harl MSS., 7581, published probably in 1591 (*Short title calalogue*, 1521). The section dealing with Scotland is on fo. 28 (p. 51) of the MS. and p. 46 of the printed version.

[40] Calderwood, v, 118–23; Melville, 281–2; *Cal. S.P. Scot.*, x, 548.

[41] Bancroft, *Survay*, 48–9, 75, 78, 147, 174, 186, 458–60; *Daungerous positions*, 6.

conception of the politics of the Scottish reformers.[42] In manuscript he had, presumably, the answers to the questions which he had sent to Robert Naunton and the information which he had received from John Gibson, besides other 'advertisements'. He quoted from one of Archbishop Adamson's letters to Whitgift – an indication that the primate may have taken an interest in Bancroft's work and given him some assistance. He referred also to 'James Gibson's conference with the king, penned by himself and delivered abroad in many copies', an account of an interview in the course of which the most audacious of the Scottish ministers had called the king a persecutor who maintained 'the tyranny of bishops, and absolute power'.[43]

The only immediate result of Bancroft's work was to foster an atmosphere of tension in which there flourished the belief of the Scottish presbyterians that the English bishops were conspiring with King James – a belief which had not, so far as we know, much foundation in fact.[44] Bancroft's principal aim had been to discredit the English puritans by stressing the taint of sedition which was attached to their Scottish allies. Whatever his wishes, he could exert no influence in Scotland in the 1590s, for the episcopal cause there was dead and its resurrection not yet possible. But if there was little ground for the Scottish ministers' suspicions, there was ample justification for apprehension about the future, as the first seven years of James's English reign – roughly the period of Bancroft's tenure of the primacy – were to see the complete restoration of Scottish episcopacy as part of Bancroft's scheme for Anglican reconstruction.[45]

[42] *Survay*, 48–9, 228; *Daungerous positions*, 10 ff.
[43] *Daungerous positions*, 5, 27. For James Gibson see Calderwood, iv, 484–8. One cannot fail to comment on the fact that B.M., Add. MSS., 32,092 (which contains a transcript of the Adamson-Whitgift correspondence, letters which passed between Beza and Scottish divines, various papers relating to Scottish ecclesiastical affairs, and a letter from Robert Naunton to John Copcot) is such a volume as might have been compiled for Bancroft's use. With NLS, MS., 6.1.13, it provides the principal material for this subject.
[44] Melville, 679; S. P. Scot. Eliz., lxiii, 85; Peter Heylin, *Aërius redivivus* (1672), 355.
[45] R. G. Usher, op. cit., ii, 154–74.

14

Scottish Presbyterian Exiles in England 1584–8[1]

Reprinted from *Records of the Scottish Church History Society*, xiv, 67–80.

The English presbyterian movement, which, in Fuller's words, had Thomas Cartwright for its 'head' and Walter Travers for its 'neck', was from the outset very closely associated with the parallel movement led by Andrew Melville in Scotland. Melville and Cartwright had been in Geneva together in 1571–2,[2] and in 1575, after Travers had published a complete exposition of the presbyterian programme in his *Explicatio ecclesiasticae disciplinae*, Melville (who himself never produced a comparable work) presented a copy to Alexander Arbuthnot, principal of King's College, Aberdeen.[3] That Melville continued to follow with interest the fortunes of the English presbyterian movement may be inferred from the invitation to Cartwright and Travers, in 1580, to chairs at St Andrews University. The reorganisation of that university, ratified by parliament in November 1579, was aimed at the erection of 'a college of divinity for the profession of learned tongues and theology against the seminaries of Rheims and Rome', and the man chosen to be principal was Andrew Melville, principal of the college at Glasgow. The official invitation to the Englishmen (from the king and the general assembly) was reinforced by a letter from the chancellor, rector, dean and principal of Glasgow, written in October 1580, and also by a personal appeal from Melville in the following March, but Cartwright and Travers did not accept.[4]

Meantime some important links between the two presbyterian parties had been forged at a different level. John Davidson, a young regent in St Andrews University, who had been cited to appear before the council for

[1] Throughout this article, quotations are, with a few exceptions, given in modernised spelling. The documents calendared in the Calendars of State Papers (Scottish, Domestic and Foreign) have been examined in the originals, but it has not been thought necessary to give references to the MS. volumes in the Public Record Office and the British Library.

[2] Charles Borgeaud, *L'academie de Calvin* 1559–1798, 107–10, 113, 119, 316, and 'Cartwright and Melville at the university of Geneva, 1569–74', in *Amer. Hist. Rev.*, v, 284–90; Melville, 41; A. F. Scott Pearson, *Thomas Cartwright*, 47, 48, 53.

[3] Pearson, op. cit., 142.

[4] Fuller, *Church-history*, IX, vii, 52; NLS, Wodrow MSS., fol. vol. 42, No. 3; McCrie, *Andrew Melville*, App. xi.

an attack on the Regent Morton's policy, took refuge in England early in 1575,[5] and became known to the circle of public officials with puritan sympathies which included Francis Walsingham and William Davison. Davison, then English agent at Antwerp, was concerned in 1577 with the appointment of a chaplain for the English Merchant Adventurers there, and informed Laurence Tomson, Walsingham's secretary, of the proposal. Tomson replied that he would try to secure William Charke, a noted puritan, and added: 'I know of another honest Scottish man of your own name, who I think will be very fit for you.' The man appointed, however, was Walter Travers.[6] John Davidson made the acquaintance of other puritans besides the Walsingham-Davison group. He had many conversations with John Field, who acted as a kind of organising secretary to the English puritan party, and the two agreed on the general principle that 'it is no small comfort to brethren of one nation to understand the state of the brethren in other nations'. He also associated with John Stubbs (brother-in-law of Cartwright), William Charke, the other rejected candidate for the Antwerp chaplaincy, and 'many good brethren and sisters'.[7] The connection with Stubbs has its own significance: Stubbs was later known as *scaeva* or the left-handed because he lost his right hand for denouncing the proposed marriage of Elizabeth to the French Duke of Alençon, just as the Scottish presbyterians were to denounce the association of King James with the French Duke of Lennox. Davidson seems to have remained in England until 1579, when he achieved notoriety which resulted in his expulsion from that country: 'One Davison, a Scottishman, in his common preachings and lectures hath uttered certain lewd and disordered speeches to her majesty's discontentation'. As the power of Morton was declining, the preacher seems now to have found it safe to return to Scotland.[8]

The contact which Davidson had made with Field lay behind an attempt made by the general assembly, in 1583, to intervene on behalf of the English presbyterians. In Scotland, the Melvillian party was in favour after the Ruthven Raid had brought into office a faction of ultra-protestants in August 1582. Before the end of the year, some ministers contemplated making a motion at the next general assembly that the government should be petitioned to join in an appeal to Elizabeth 'touching the reformation of some abuses' in the Church of England 'and especially that sincere men may have liberty to preach without deposing by the tyranny of the bishops'. On 1 January 1582/3 John Davidson wrote to Field asking him to consult the English brethren and report whether they thought the proposed petition expedient. Field reported that the English would be grateful to the Scots if they would be so mindful of the interests of

<hr />

[5] *RPC*, ii, 716; Hume of Godscroft, *History of the house of Angus and Douglas*, ii, 242; Calderwood, v, 339, viii, 200–1; *Cal. S.P. Scot.*, iv, Nos. 783, 788.

[6] *Cal. S.P. Dom. Addenda* 1566–79, 442, 528–9, 532; *Cal. S.P. For.* 1577–8, 516.

[7] NLS, MS. 6.1.13, fo. 42.

[8] *Acts of the Privy Council*, xi, 289; *BUK*, i, 388. There is no evidence that Davidson was in Scotland between 1575 and 1579.

the English presbyterians. When the general assembly next met, in April 1583, three ministers were appointed to convey to the king the assembly's wish that he would make it part of the mission of his ambassador to England to ask Elizabeth to 'disburden their brethren of England of the yoke of ceremonies imposed upon them against the liberty of the Word'. James made a gracious reply, but nothing seems to have been done.[9]

The Scottish presbyterians, who during their brief triumph had thus volunteered assistance to their English brethren, were soon in their turn seeking help. The king's escape from the Ruthven Raiders in June 1583 prepared the way for what has been called the 'anti-presbyterian dictatorship' of James Stewart, Earl of Arran, an administration which in May 1584 passed the 'Black Acts', reaffirming episcopal authority and subjecting the church to crown and parliament. The irreconcilables among the ministers had in effect to choose between imprisonment and exile. Their leader, Andrew Melville, had come into collision with the government even before its policy culminated in the 'Black Acts'. Charged with uttering seditious speeches in the pulpit, he was ordered to enter into ward in Blackness Castle on 17 February 1583/4, and fled the same day to Berwick.[10] In May and June he was followed by about a score of his disciples. Some of them were ministers of note, like James Lawson, Walter Balcanquhal and Robert Pont from Edinburgh, James Carmichael (Haddington), Patrick Galloway (Perth) and James Melville, the diarist, Andrew's nephew; other ministers in the party were James Gibson (Pencaitland), David Hume (Coldingham), Andrew Hunter (Carnbie), Andrew Polwarth (Cadder), Thomas Story (Chirnside), Andrew Hay (Renfrew), a James Hamilton and a 'Mr. Strachan' who are hard to identify, and also John Davidson, who was no stranger to England; there were in addition half a dozen younger men who were later to hold appointments in the Scottish church – William Aird, John Caldcleuch, John Cowper, Alexander Forsyth, Archibald Moncreiff and James Robertson.

Melville, so far from choosing England as anything more than a temporary refuge, had thought at first of resuming his academic life on the continent.[11] England was not an obvious haven for presbyterians, as Archbishop Adamson of St Andrews reminded them: the English queen was 'a rare auditrix of preaching' and her clergy were 'burdened with sundry ceremonies and injunctions'.[12] The refugees, however, more favourably disposed to the English sovereign than to their own, thought of Elizabeth (despite her 'injunctions') as 'a notable instrument of God for the advancement of religion' and of her kingdom as 'a receptacle for the troubled and persecuted saints of God'. At the worst they would be able to

[9] NLS, MS. 6.1.13, fo. 42; *BUK*, ii, 613–14.

[10] Warrender Papers (Register House), Vol. B, fo. 62; Spottiswoode, ii, 309; Calderwood, *Vinciciae*, 52; *RPC*, iii, 631–2.

[11] *Cal. S.P. Scot.*, vii, 31.

[12] Calderwood, iv, 90.

live in retirement: 'we may quietly and in peace await upon our books'; but they hoped also to 'travail in our vocation as it should please the Lord to give occasion', in a country where they could make themselves understood in their native tongue[13] Why could not they, like English puritan 'lecturers', evade the vestiarian and liturgical requirements imposed on the beneficed clergy, and 'exercise themselves in the Lord's work safe and free from the impurity and pollution of the Romish and superstitious ceremonies'?[14] They were conscious, too, of the parallel between their own situation and that of the English puritans, for 'the most learned and faithful pastors in both the kingdoms are forced either wholly to keep silence and leave the ministry, or then by flight and exile to save their lives, or else to essay the filthy weariness of stinking prisons'.[15] In short, the Scots, feeling that they had a common cause with the English puritans, expected a welcome from their allies and looked forward to 'consultation with learned men, zealous brethren and whoever has defended the Lord's cause'.[16] One detects a certain lack of proportion in their more favourable view of Elizabeth than of their own king, although both sovereigns were meting out similar treatment to 'the most learned and faithful pastors'.

Preparation for their reception in England came, however, not from churchmen but from those puritan politicians, Walsingham and Davison, by whom, as respectively secretary of state and ambassador to Edinburgh, Anglo-Scottish relations were conducted at that time. Walsingham and Davison had to use a certain discretion within England itself, but elsewhere they gave free rein to their puritan sympathies. It was on Davison's initiative that an 'honest, learned and godly man' had been sought for the Antwerp chaplaincy, and not only was it clear from the names suggested that only puritans were qualified, but the intention was to supersede the Prayer Book by services on the Genevan model, a project which Walsingham discussed with Travers.[17] Davison had made the acquaintance of Scottish presbyterians through John Davidson, and Walsingham was the patron and friend of Thomas Smeton, who was first a colleague of Andrew Melville at Glasgow and then his successor as principal there. Both Walsingham and Davison were acquainted with James Lawson, the Edinburgh minister, before he appeared in England as a refugee.[18] Their ecclesiastical sympathies strongly influenced the attitude of those politicians to Scottish affairs, and made them the supporters of the Scottish presbyterian party whether that party was in or out of favour in Scotland.

The fall of the Ruthven Raiders had so alarmed the English

[13] Warrender Papers, Vol. B, fo. 29; Harleian MSS. 291, fo. 124; Calderwood, iv, 138-9.

[14] Warrender Papers, Vol. B, fo. 44.

[15] J. Melville, Diary, 157, 164, cf. 160. Warrender Papers, Vol. B, fo. 44, shows how an epistle of Beza to the brethren of England was cited with reference to the situation of the Scots under the 'Black Acts'.

[16] Warrender Papers, Vol. B, fo. 29.

[17] Cal. S.P. For., 1577-8, 852; cf. Read, Walsingham, ii, 264-5, and EHR, xxviii, 35, n. 7.

[18] Cal. S.P. Scot., vi, 371-2, 635-6; vii, 54.

government that Walsingham himself had been sent on a mission to Scotland in September 1583, and in the following April, when the Ruthven faction was preparing an attempt to regain power, William Davison was sent to Berwick to be ready to support them. The attempt failed, and Davison, compelled to lie at Berwick and observe the triumph of Arran, was in despondency over the rout of the Scottish presbyterians.[19] In his letters to Walsingham he made no secret of his admiration for the Scottish 'discipline', his disapproval of the 'Black Acts', his detestation of the Scottish bishops and his sympathy with 'the best and most godly learned ministers', who were now threatened with imprisonment or banishment.[20] Other Englishmen might show a proper detachment and consider the ecclesiastical proceedings of the Scottish government to be a purely domestic matter,[21] but Davison wrote as a puritan viewing with dismay the failure of the first Scottish presbyterian experiment.

As Davison did not leave Berwick for Edinburgh until 1 June,[22] he was able to meet not only Andrew Melville, who had been in Berwick since March, but several other ministers who arrived there in May – Galloway, Carmichael, Lawson and Balcanquhal, among others. Davison made it clear to the exiles that his diplomatic mission to Scotland was in the interests of their party, and by befriending Lawson and Balcanquhal on their arrival and arranging that his son, Francis, should receive tuition in Greek from Andrew Melville, he contributed to the hospitable reception of the Scots.[23] If it would not be quite true to say that something like a conspiracy took shape, it does seem clear that plans were made which helped to determine the subsequent movements[24] of the Scots in England.

Andrew Melville took the road to the south about 10 June, perhaps accompanied by Galloway and Carmichael, and on the 20th those three had an interview in London with Walsingham, who gave them the news of Scottish affairs contained in a despatch which Davison had written in Edinburgh five days earlier.[25] Carmichael had another interview with Walsingham on 2 July, and on the 19th Lawson and Balcanquhal (who had arrived in London about 21 June) were received, along with Melville and Carmichael, by the secretary, who again retailed the latest news from Scotland.[26] Meantime Melville had begun to tutor Francis Davison, who, as Carmichael reported to the boy's father, gave 'good proof of his profit

---

[19] *Cal. S.P. Scot.*, vii, 138.

[20] *Cal. S.P. Scot.*, vii, 146, 149, 167.

[21] *Cal. S.P. Scot.*, vii, 148.

[22] *Cal. S.P. Scot.*, vii, 166.

[23] *Cal. S.P. Scot.*, vii, 146, 195, 208.

[24] These movements are calculated partly from James ..elville's account of his own flight to Berwick, which took place 'about the summer solstice', which would be 11 or 12 June according to the calendar then in use (*Diary*, 167, 168, 170).

[25] *Wodrow Soc. Misc.*, i, 413; Calderwood, viii, 260–1; *Cal. S.P. Scot.*, vii, 171. The date is given variously as 19th and 21st June, but it was a Saturday, and the Saturday was the 20th.

[26] Calderwood, viii, 267–8; *Wodrow Soc. Misc.*, i, 414.

in the Greek to Mr. Melville upon the first chapter of Mark'.[27]

While the exiles had thus made it their first business to establish close relations with Walsingham, they lost little time in seeking out their more purely ecclesiastical allies. Before Lawson and Balcanquhal had been in London a fortnight, they had 'talked with the godly and zealous brethren',[28] and some time in July – probably between the 4th and the 19th – Andrew Melville, Lawson and some other Scots visited Oxford and Cambridge and 'conferred with the most godly and learned' there.[29] At Oxford they took part in a conference attended by Edward Gellibrand (the leading puritan in Oxford), Thomas Wilcox and many other English presbyterians, including, no doubt, John Field. One of the matters discussed was a critical one – 'the proceeding of the minister in his duty, without the assistance or tarrying for the magistrate'.[30] This was a subject which had been much in the mind of English puritans in recent months, and on 1 June the question had already been raised 'Whether a minister might cease preaching being forbidden by the magistrate'.[31] The Scots, who were in England for no other reason than because they had defied their own magistrates, must have given stimulating advice.

After their visit to the universities, the Scots returned to London. Some of them lodged in Honey Lane, Cheapside, with one Anthony Martin – possibly the Anthony Martin who signed a petition on behalf of the presbyterian minister Thomas Barber, who was the preacher at St Mary le Bow, on the other side of Cheapside from Honey Lane,[32] and who was, as we shall see, associated with the Scottish exiles. It was at the church of Allhallows in Honey Lane itself that Thomas Wilcox had been lecturer before his imprisonment in 1572,[33] and it may be that the meeting of the Scots with Wilcox at Oxford explains the ease with which they made friends in that part of London.

About the end of 1584 and the beginning of 1585 there was considerable activity among the puritans, including two general conferences in London, one in November (at which a special effort was made to secure a good attendance) and one in February.[34] That the Scottish ministers took part may be deduced from their association with Field. Gellibrand had urged that Field should follow up the Oxford conversations with further discussion with the Scots about 'tarrying for the magistrate', and on 4 March 1584/5 Field admitted that 'there is some meeting of his fellow ministers at his house, as Mr. Barber with others, touching conference in learning, three or four', and that 'he hath resorted to the

[27] Cal. S.P. Scot., vii, 208.
[28] Calderwood, vii, 261; Cal. S.P. Scot., vii, 195.
[29] Melville, 219.
[30] Richard Bancroft, Daungerous Positions and Proceedings, 73–4.
[31] R. G. Usher, The Presbyterian Movement in the reign of Elizabeth (Camden Soc.), 36.
[32] Wodrow Soc. Misc., i, 437, 451; Seconde Parte of a Register (ed. Albert Peel), ii, 220, 262.
[33] DNB on Wilcox; John Stow's Survey of London, ed. C. L. Kingsford (1908), i, 271.
[34] Bancroft, op. cit., 74–5; Usher, op. cit., 40, 42.

Scottish ministers, being three of them, and sometimes they come to his house'.[35] The three Scots who thus took part in discussions with Field and Barber were presumably Andrew Melville, Balcanquhal and John Davidson.

One of the general conferences at which the Scottish ministers were present was the occasion of a number of resolutions which were, in Fuller's words, 'the embryo of the presbyterian discipline, lying yet, as it were, in the womb of episcopacy'.[36] It was decided that no one should accept ordination until he had been 'called' by a particular congregation and his 'call' had been approved by a *classis* (= presbytery). Provision was made for the election of elders and deacons, and for the convocation of classical, provincial and national assemblies. The assistance of the Scots at a very important stage of the evolution of a 'discipline in a discipline, presbytery in episcopacy', was rewarded by a resolution of the general conference that collections should be made for their financial relief.[37]

The event which revealed most fully the close connection between the Scottish ministers and the London puritans was the funeral of James Lawson, minister of Edinburgh, who died at Anthony Martin's house in Honey Lane on 12 October 1584; his funeral, on the following day, was the occasion of a gathering of English and Scottish presbyterians not only more impressive than any other recorded in the sixteenth century, but far more representative of Scots than even the Westminster assembly was to be. The Scottish exiles were represented by their leaders Andrew Melville, James Carmichael, John Davidson and Walter Balcanquhal, and by three young men from St Andrews university who later became ministers in Scotland – John Cowper, Archibald Moncrieff and Alexander Forsyth. An Anglo-Scottish element was present in the persons of one Guthrie, a Scot who kept a school at Hoddesdon, Hertfordshire, and who was related to Lawson's wife; John Morrison, formerly a minister in East Lothian, and now curate of St Botolph's, Aldersgate; and William Lynne, a Glasgow graduate whom Thomas Smeton had sent to England and who later became a student and a fellow at Cambridge. The English puritans were represented by the well-known Walter Travers, now preacher at the Temple; John Field, the party organiser; William Charke, preacher at Lincoln's Inn; Gardener from Whitechapel; Dr Crook of Gray's Inn; Barber of St Mary-le-bow; Stephen Egerton of St Anne's in Blackfriars; Edmonds of Allhallows in Bread Street; 'Hundsone' or 'Indsonn' of St Peter's in

[35] Bancroft, op. cit., 74, *Survay of the pretended holy discipline*, 395; *Seconde parte of a register*, i, 283–4.

[36] Fuller, op. cit., IX, v, 1.

[37] Bancroft, *Daungerous positions*, pp. '45–8' (*sic, rectius* 69–72). Bancroft dates this conference 'about 1583' and was uncertain whether it took place at Cambridge or at London. It seems most reasonable to identify it with one of the London conferences of the winter of 1584–5, when so many Scots were in touch with English presbyterians. R. W. Dale, *A History of English congregationalism*, 152, and Wood, *History of the University of Oxford*, ii, 224–5, however, assign this conference to Oxford, presumably identifying it with the general conference of July 1584 (at which some Scots had been present).

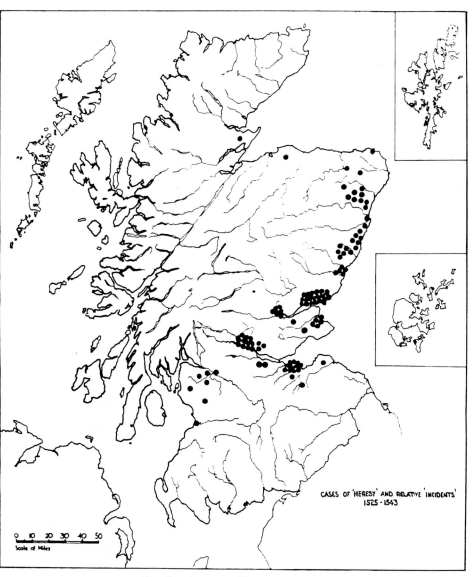

CASES OF 'HERESY' AND RELATIVE 'INCIDENTS'
1525 - 1543

0   10 20 30 40 50
Scale of Miles

22. Map showing cases of heresy, etc., 1525–43

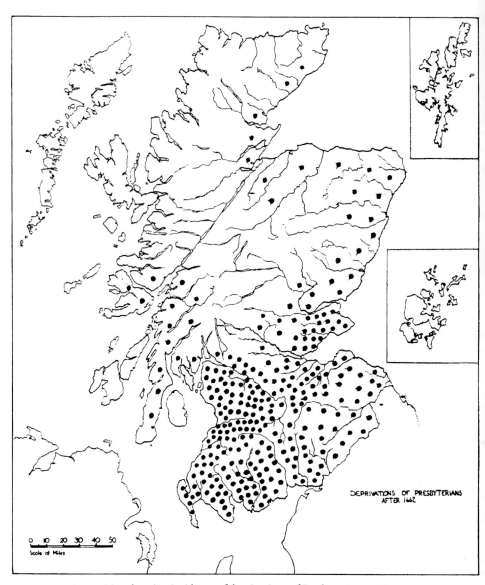

DEPRIVATIONS OF PRESBYTERIANS
AFTER 1662

0 10 20 30 40 50
Scale of Miles

23. Map showing incidence of deprivations of Presbyterians, 1662

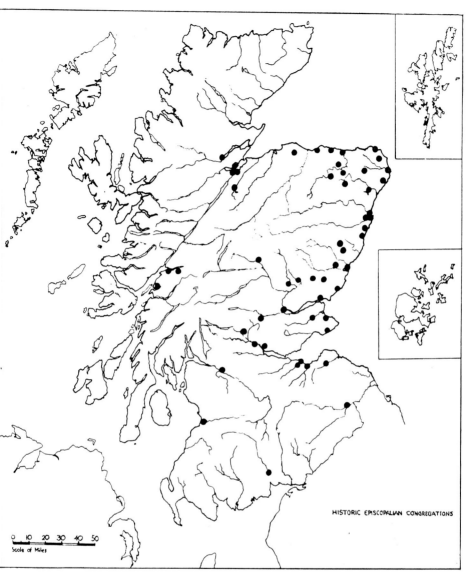

HISTORIC EPISCOPALIAN CONGREGATIONS

0 10 20 30 40 50
Scale of Miles

24. Map showing historic Episcopalian congregations

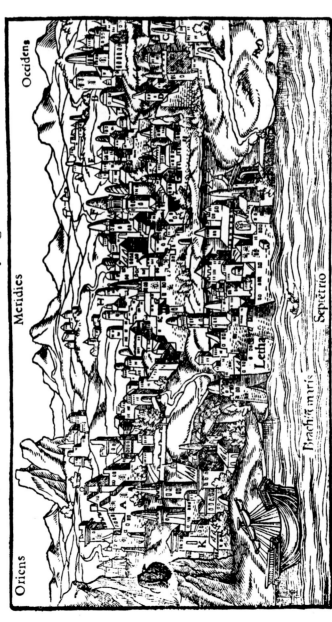

Beschreibung der Königlichen Statt Ædinburg/durch Alexandrum von Ales/Doctorem der Heyligen Geschrifft. Cap. xvij.

Oriens

Meridies

Occidens

Septetrio

Brachiū maris

Letha

Erklärung etlicher Buchstaben so hie verzeichnet seind:

A Königs Pallast.
B Magienschloß.
C S. Guberti Kirch.

D S. Egidij Kirch.
E Zun Barfussern.
F Zu Unser Frawen im Feld.

G Der Königin Collegium.
H Zun Predigern.
K Closter zum Heyligen Creutz.

25. Edinburgh in the sixteenth century through German eyes. Of the nine buildings named, seven are churches: St Cuthbert's, St Giles', Greyfriars, Kirk o' Field, Trinity College, Blackfriars and Holyrood Abbey. The secular structures named are Holyrood Palace and the Castle.

Cheapside; and Lever Wood, recently deprived for non-conformity. The high master of St Paul's school (John Harrison) was there, and the three ministers of the French church in London. Among names difficult of identification, but possibly significant, are those of 'Mr. Bacon, gentleman', 'Mr. Bodley', and 'secretary Walsingham's gentleman'. The total number present was over five hundred, at a time when the average attendance at a London funeral – so at least the Scots believed – was seldom one hundred; there were many women who had been 'careful mothers and sisters' to the deceased, including an alderman's wife who had bestowed twenty grains of unicorn's horn on him.[38] The list of English puritans present at the funeral gives a clue to the personnel of the general conferences held at London in that same winter, when to the leading London puritans there were of course added a number from other parts of the country.

The Scottish community in London was so numerous by this time that it was suggested that it should have its own church, on the analogy of the French, Italian and Dutch churches, and Lawson had tried to enlist Walsingham's support for the project, but the council decided that it would be dangerous to countenance a form of service in the English language differing from that of the Church of England, and therefore refused the Scots a 'peculiar church'.[39] The Scottish government, too, after an attempt at conciliation,[40] began to reflect that the 'air' of England was 'contagious' for presbyterians,[41] and instructed its ambassadors to urge the English government to deal firmly with the exiles.[42] In the autumn of 1584, however, possibly because their English friends made their pulpits available, the Scottish ministers were preaching in London. Balcanquhal preached once or twice before Lawson's death on 7 October, and continued to preach regularly until the following January. John Davidson preached twelve or thirteen sermons in St Olave's, Old Jewry, on Sundays and holy days, beginning on 8 November 1584. He 'so railed against the king of Scots in the pulpit' that he was known at court and among the bishops as a 'thunderer'.[43] The master of Gray, who had come as ambassador from Scotland in October 1584, complained to the queen, trying to play on her dislike of rebellious subjects: 'I beseech your majesty for the weal of your

[38] The account of the funeral is in Calderwood's larger MS. history (British Museum, Additional MSS. 4736, f. 166 *verso*); it is printed in Wodrow Soc., *Miscellany* I, 452, and in Wodrow's *Biographical collections* (New Spalding club), p. 231, but neither printed version is wholly satisfactory. The English preachers can be identified from *The seconde parte of a register* ii, 180 *et seq.*, 262.

[39] Hume of Godscroft, op. cit., ii, 361; *Wodrow Soc. Misc.*, i, 418.

[40] Calderwood, iv, 124-5; *Cal. S.P. Scot.*, vii, 165; B. M. Harleian MSS., 291, fo. 123.

[41] *Cal. S.P. Scot.*, vii, 248.

[42] Ibid., 339, 542; Calderwood, iv, 352. The first attempt to influence the English government against the ministers had been made by Archbishop Adamson in June 1584 (p. 169 *supra*).

[43] *Wodrow Soc. Misc.*, i, 428-9; Calderwood, iv, 247; Peter Heylin, *Aerius Redivivus*, 268; Bancroft, *Daungerous Positions*, 26.

own estate either to remove furth of England the fugitive ministers or then
to ordain some limits to them for avoiding practising within your country,
for . . . their democratical designs be enemy to all princes'.[44] On 5 January
1584/5 both Balcanquhal and Davidson were summoned before the bishop
of London. Balcanquhal obeyed the summons, and the bishop explained
that a command to cease preaching had been issued on the council's
initiative. Balcanquhal's congregation thereupon petitioned the council
in his favour, but without effect. But the Scots were not easily silenced. The
lieutenant of the Tower, who was friendly to the ministers, allowed some
of them to preach and to form a congregation in his church, which was
exempt from episcopal jurisdiction, and Andrew Melville's lectures there
were much frequented.[45]

The contacts between Scottish exiles and English puritans were not
confined to London and the university towns. The earls of Angus and Mar
and the master of Glamis had fled from Scotland after the failure of their
attempt to overthrow Arran in April 1584. They remained in the north of
England until February 1584/5 and then, after a month in Norwich, settled
in London.[46] At Newcastle a congregation on the strictest model was
ministered to by John Davidson (in June and July 1584), Patrick Galloway
and James Melville,[47] and in London Andrew and James Melville acted
together as chaplains to the nobles.[48] Not only did the earl of Angus have
direct communication with 'brethren of the Church of England',[49] but
there is some evidence that the religious exercises of the noblemen made a
favourable impression on English puritans: the Catechism which Galloway
compiled for the use of the lords was subsequently published in England,[50]
and an Englishman, Miles Moss, who ministered to them during the month
they spent at Norwich, retained happy recollections of their piety.[51]

Another indication of the wide ramifications of Anglo-Scottish
contacts is found in the career of John Cowper. He had a connection with
England before he went there in 1584, for his brother William, after
graduating at St Andrews in 1583, had become a teacher in Guthrie's school
at Hoddesdon. John was in London in June 1584 and at the time of
Lawson's funeral, but shortly afterwards he went to Cornwall and spent
about a year there. He took part in the meetings of the 'exercise' of Saltash,
and evidently acted as a kind of chaplain to one of its most prominent lay
members, Anthony Rouse, who was an associate of Drake and Grenville
and later became step-father of John Pym. In December 1585, when it
became safe for presbyterians to return to Scotland, Cowper left Cornwall,

---

[44] *Cal. S.P. Scot.*, vii, 508.
[45] Bancroft, *Daungerous Positions*, 26; Hume of Godscroft, op. cit., ii, 361.
[46] Melville, 165–6, 171–2, 221–2.
[47] Ibid., 171–2, 181–4; *Wodrow Soc. Misc.*, i, 414, 424, 429.
[48] Melville, 221–2.
[49] Hume of Godscroft, op. cit., ii, 377.
[50] Arber, *Transcripts*, ii, 235.
[51] Miles Mosse, *Scotland's Welcome* (1603), 64–5. The dedication of this book is to John,
Earl of Mar, and recalls the association of the author with the Scots nobles.

and, equipped with testimonials from the exercise of Saltash and from Rouse and his first wife, Elizabeth, as well as a passport from Walsingham, went back home, where he soon became a minister in Edinburgh. His brother William joined him there, and became a minister also.[52]

Whatever the activities of the Scottish exiles, and however much they came into conflict with English ecclesiastical authorities, Walsingham thought that they could do no wrong. At an early stage he had commented on the 'cold comfort' they were likely to receive in England and the fact that they found 'fewer favourers' than he thought they deserved. His outlook being determined by his own ecclesiastical preferences, he closed his mind to the possibility that a Scottish administration opposed to presbyterianism could maintain Anglo-Scottish friendship, and persisted in advocating that 'policy' as well as 'Christianity' required English countenance to the presbyterians, who had been 'good instruments for the entertaining of the amity'. He once remarked bitterly to Davison that the treatment of the exiles accorded with 'the course they now hold here in displacing and depriving the best affected ministers. I look for no better fruits from them that use religion for policy and many times abuse it for faction.'[53] After the first interviews of the ministers with Walsingham in June and July 1584, Carmichael undertook to prepare a statement of the case for the exiles, a task in which he was assisted by English politicians and puritan officials.[54] Davison in particular acted as an agent for Carmichael in the collection of materials for the projected *apologia* – the acts of the parliament of May 1584, the second Book of Discipline, the acts of the general assemblies, Knox's History of the Reformation, the first part of Hume of Godscroft's History, and the bishops' injunctions[55] – and was thanked by Carmichael for his 'great fidelity and lawful diligence in the common cause'.[56]

Arran's government came to an end when the exiled lords returned to Scotland and effected a *coup d'etat* at Stirling on 2 November 1585. Andrew Melville, with Balcanquhal and Galloway, went north with the noblemen, and on 6 November these three ministers wrote to the ministers still in England – Carmichael, Davidson, James Melville and 'the rest of the Scottish preachers' – asking them to return.[57] Carmichael communicated this letter to the others (except Andrew Hunter, who had already left for Scotland) and summoned Thomas Story and John Cowper, who were not

---

[52] *Fasti Eccl. Scot.*, i, 53, iii, 460, vii, 345; Calderwood, viii, 261; *Warrender Papers* (SHS), i, 171, 203–6; S. Reed Brett, *John Pym*, p. xix; A. L. Rowse, *Sir Richard Grenville*, 43, 205.
[53] *Cal. S.P. Scot.*, vii, 161, 175, 241; cf. Camden, *Annales* (1717), ii, 409, 420 and Heylin, op. cit., 268.
[54] *Wodrow Soc. Misc.*, i, 413–14; Calderwood, viii, 260–2.
[55] *Cal. S.P. Scot.*, vii, 195, 208; *Wodrow Soc. Misc.*, i, 415. In S.P. Scot. Eliz. xxix are two copies of the second Book of Discipline, accompanied by copies of acts of general assemblies; each is endorsed 'Mr. James Carmichael's book'.
[56] *Cal. S.P. Scot.*, vii, 267.
[57] *Wodrow Soc. Misc.*, i, 437.

in London, to come to the capital in order to arrange for their departure.[58] James Melville soon proceeded to Scotland, being in Linlithgow by 27 December,[59] and most of his fellows appear to have returned home about the same time.[60]

Carmichael, however, had apparently arranged with the Earl of Angus to remain in England 'for advancing of the cause among the brethren here and through this and other countries', and in a letter dated from London on 20 November he told the earl that he intended to 'tarry', in view of 'necessity that the cause presently craves among the good brethren of this country'. It seems that he was still collecting material to discredit the Scottish king and the late government, for he urged that the ecclesiastical and civil records of Scotland should be searched and that 'diligent inquisition' should be made for secret letters which had passed between Mary and her son or any of his subjects, hinting that 'Bothwell's casket served for good uses; there wants not caskets yet'.[61] Little is known of Carmichael's subsequent movements, but letters were directed to him at London on 2 and 16 January 1585/6 and he was in England on 4 March and 9 May 1586.[62] There seems no reason to doubt that he continued to live in England for about two years after the return of the majority of the exiles, and we know that the epistle dedicatory of his *Grammaticae Latinae, de etymologia, liber secundus*, was dated at Cambridge in September 1587.

The other Scot who did not return with the main body of the exiles was John Davidson. During what was his second exile in England he renewed the friendship wth John Stubbs which he had formed earlier, and possibly collaborated with him in preparing a refutation of the English Roman catholic leader, Cardinal Allen. Davidson was certainly commissioned by his fellow exiles to reply to the *Defence of the English catholiques* (1584), in which Allen condemned as seditious the Scottish ministers generally, and especially those who had fled to England.[63] There is no evidence that Davidson returned to Scotland before November 1588, when he refused to resume his former charge at Liberton.[64] In the absence of other evidence of his whereabouts, there is some ground for identifying Davidson with a Scottish preacher of that name who was notorious for his activities in England in 1587 and 1588. Whether Davidson had ever ceased preaching may be doubted, for it is not even certain that he obeyed the summons to Fulham in January 1584/5, and he probably had opportunities for preaching in the Tower in 1585. In August 1587, the activities in London

---

[58] Register House, State Papers, 102A.

[59] Harleian MSS., 291, fos. 188–9.

[60] Cf. *Extracts from records of burgh of Edinburgh*, 1573–89, 455.

[61] Register House, State Papers, 102A.

[62] *Wodrow Soc. Misc.*, i, 438, 440 and n; Additional MSS. 32,092, fo. 80 *verso*; Reg. Ho, Morton Papers, Letters, 9 May 1586.

[63] *DNB* on Stubbs; Calderwood, iv, 38; Allen, *Defence of the English catholiques*, 79, 83, 122, 137 (where several of the ministers exiled in England are named). Stubbs associated with James Carmichael also (H.M.C., *Ancaster MSS.*, 16).

[64] *Fasti*, i, 170.

pulpits of Davidson, Thomas Barber (who has already appeared as an associate of the Scots), Giles Wiggington (whom we shall see linked with Davidson on another occasion), and some other preachers, led to an order from the Court of High Commission that no one in charge of a church in the City should allow any of the ministers named to preach or read lectures, unless a licence from the queen, a university, the archbishop of Canterbury, or the bishop of London, could be produced. Besides the written order, an oral message was sent that Davidson, Wiggington, and another should not preach again in any case.[65] It is conceivable that even this prohibition did not bring John Davidson's preaching to an end, for he may have been the 'Daverson, a Scot', who delivered a sermon in London on 29th June 1588:

'Touching [blank] Daverson a Skott, who preached at Aldermanbury church on St. Peters day in the forenoone, 29° Junii 1588.

'The Manne. he preached with a kerchief on his head, a velvett nightcap upon that, and a felt hat on that: and praied a long praier with all on: in the end, putt off his hat, and laid it by, saieing: Lett us sing a psalme to the praise of god.

'The Matter. he said: There was now a great plague at hande, becawse there is no Love at all in yow toward the gosple. It is a fowle falt that there is no generall fast proclaimed, for the reformation of things. It is no mervail things be amys, for the gosple rules not the Queene, rules not the Counsaill, rules not the clergy, rules not the citizens. The doctors of the universities dare not speak the truth, becawse the spiritt of God is not in them. He said, he was infourmed, that divers of that parishe, were hinderers of the gosple.'

The 'matter' of this sermon agrees with our knowledge of the substance of Davidson's sermons in London in 1584–5, when he had warned the people of 'a great visitation and affliction approaching the Church of England'.[66] It was not only by preaching that Davidson attained notoriety. In 1588 Waldegrave published *A Short Christian Institution made first for the use of a private family, and now communicate by the Author to other flocks and families*, written by 'J.D.'. Some delay in the licensing of the book was known to the author of Martin Marprelate's *Epistle*, and in the course of an attack on the bishops, he wrote:[67]

'They are afraid that anything should be published abord/ whereby the common people should learne that the onely way to saluation/ is by the word preached. There was the last sommer a little catechisme/ made by M. Dauison and printed by Walde-graue: but before he coulde print it/ it must be authorized by the Bb. either Cante. or London/ he went to Cant. to haue it licensed/ his grace committed it

---

[65] *Seconde parte of a register*, ii, 231–2.
[66] Additional MSS. 32,092, f. 100 (endorsed: 'Tuching Daverson a Skott. Buttolfs by Cripelgate'); *Wodrow Soc. Mis.*, i, 429.
[67] *Epistle* (1588), 34; ed. Petheram (1842), 43.

to doctor Neuerbegood (Wood) he read it ouer in halfe a yeare/ the booke is a great one of two sheets of paper. In one place of the booke the meanes of saluation was attributed to the worde preached: and what did he thinke you: he blotted out the word (preached) and would not haue that word printed/ so ascribing the way to work mens saluation to the worde read.'

Cooper noticed this accusation when he replied to Martin in his *Admonition to the People of England*, and gave, in passing, his opinion of Davidson: 'How Dauisons Catechisme was allowed, or how long in perusing, I knovv not: some paultry pamphlet it is, like to that busie and vnlearned Scot, now termed to be the author thereof. D. Wood is better able to iudge of such matters, than either Dauison, or any Martinist, that dare be knovven.'[68] In *Hay any Worke for Cooper*, Martin retorted that although Cooper abused Davidson and Wiggington, their 'good names can take no stain from a bishops chopps'. Davidson's name appears with those of Wiggington and other puritans elsewhere in the same work: 'I see here that they haue quarrelled with thee Walter Trauerse, Iohn Penri, Thomas Sparke, Giles Wiggington, Master Dauison, &c.'[69]

The whole history of the exiles represents a curious anticipation of the alliance which in the next century was to produce the Solemn League and Covenant. The importance of the episode at the time was threefold. Contact with these Scottish ministers, embittered against their own king and the regime which he maintained, and profoundly suspicious of the influence of Mary and her agents, was an element in shaping the attitude of Walsingham and Davison to Scottish affairs and to Mary herself. Secondly, the Scots, who before their exile had been engaged in developing their presbyterian system in defiance of statute law and in the main without official countenance, may well have had a stimulating effect on their English brethren, who at this stage decided to depart from their timid policy of 'tarrying for the magistrate' and to proceed with the development of 'a discipline in a discipline, presbytery in episcopacy'. Finally, John Davidson, who was all along something of a firebrand and who became so engrossed in activities in England that he was in no haste to return home, introduced an interest in Scotland to some of the more extreme elements in English puritanism – an interest which led the pamphleteer Penry and the printer Waldegrave to seek refuge in Scotland in 1589 and make it a base of the production of puritan literature. While the influence of the Scots may thus have been diverse, the personal contacts had been so close and so numerous that they had ample opportunity to exert that influence.

[68] Cooper, *Admonition* (1589), 49.
[69] *Hay any worke for Cooper* (ed. Petheram), 61, 69.

15

Scotland's Conservative North in the Sixteenth and Seventeenth Centuries

Reprinted from *Transactions of the Royal Historical Society*, 5th series, xvi, 65–79.

Some illustrations of the existence of a conservative north are at once apparent on even the most superficial examination of Scottish history in the seventeenth century. No historian has failed to notice, for instance, the fact that the strongest opposition to the National Covenant was concentrated in and around Aberdeen. It was in Aberdeen that the 'doctors', or theological professors of the university, denounced the Covenant and challenged its spokesmen to a debate in July 1638, and it was in Aberdeenshire that the Marquis of Huntly remained an unrepentant royalist during the years of the Covenanters' ascendancy.

The clearest illustration of the division of opinion along geographical lines is to be found in 1662, when episcopal government had been restored in the Scottish church after an intermission of over twenty years and a considerable number of clergy who declined to conform to the new regime were deprived. The deprivations provide a statistical basis for an assessment of the distribution of opinion. At that time the number of parishes, and consequently of ministers, was approximately the same north of the Tay as south of the Tay, but out of the total of 271 deprivations all but twenty-four were in the lands south of the Tay, and over 200 – about three-quarters of the total – were south of the Forth.[1] It is reasonable to infer that, while the south was strongly presbyterian, the country north of the Tay was almost solidly conservative, in the sense that the clergy there welcomed a return to the system of church government which had existed before the outbreak of the revolt against Charles I. After the Revolution it was the turn of the episcopalians to be deprived. In the first general assembly of the new establishment, in 1690, the country north of the Tay was barely represented, and out of the 200 ministers in the synods of Aberdeen and Banff, Moray, Ross and Caithness, only four conformed to presbyterian-

---

[1] The figures for the various synods are given by W. L. Mathieson, *Politics and Religion in Scotland* (Glasgow, 1902), ii, p. 193. Calculations by others have produced almost identical results.

ism. The number of ministers deprived was much higher now than after the Restoration – about half the ministers in the country – and consequently the incidence was wider, but there was no doubt about the firmer adherence to episcopacy north of the Tay. Traces of this pattern still survive. There are at the present day fifty-four historic congregations of the Scottish Episcopal Church which can demonstrate their continued existence from the period before the revolution when the Episcopal Church was the established church, and the location of those congregations indicates the areas where attachment to episcopacy was strong enough to survive through generations of intolerance, prosecution and lack of resources. Of these fifty-four congregations, all but seven are north of the Forth and only fifteen are south of the Tay.

There are clear temptations to detect comparable geographical patterns in other phases of our history, but it is only too easy to advance suggestions which turn out to be at best over-simplified. One classical case is that of the thesis of E. M. Barron to the effect that in Bruce's time all the support for resistance to England came from what he conceived to have been 'Celtic Scotland', by which he meant the whole country except the south-east, but this has been shown to be completely at variance with the facts.[2] Another case relates to the contest between James III and his rebellious subjects, which ended at Sauchieburn in 1488. What precisely the issues were between the two parties it is hard to say, and whether or not the king is to be regarded as an intelligent innovator has been a matter of dispute. Yet it seems not unreasonable to regard the king's supporters, the loyal barons, as in some sense the conservative faction. They were certainly the supporters of lawfully constituted authority, and to that extent represent an element which is usually inherent in conservatism. Was there a significant geographical division? One narrator states that James III advanced against his enemies 'with all the northt of Scottland, that is to say, Rose, Sutherland, Caitnes, Mar and Murray, Buchan and Meirnes, Angus, Gowrie, Fyfe, Stretheirne, Stirlingschyre, Atholl and Argyle, . . . for thair was nane in all their forsaid schyris bot they tuik pairt with him, batht gentillmen and commons, allanerlie except the Lord Gray in Angus and the lorde Drowmond in Strethearne, that was witht the uther pairtie aganis the king'.[3] Another narrator makes the same point with almost equal force: the king's supporters were a group of northern magnates – *viri nobiles et illustres qui ad Boream in Scotia latissime dominantur* – while his opponents, apart from Gray and Drummond, were southerners.[4] The picture thus presented is of a conservative, or loyal, north and, while it requires adjustment, especially in relation to the force actually at Sauchieburn, a recent scholar who is sceptical about almost everything else that happened in James III's reign brings together a lot of evidence in favour of a broadly north-south

[2] G. W. S. Barrow, 'Lothian in the first War of Independence', *SHR*, lv, 151–71.

[3] Robert Lindsay of Pitscottie, *History of Scotland* (STS), i, 204.

[4] Hector Boece, *History of Scotland*, with continuation by Ferrerius (Paris, 1574), pp. 399–400.

division, with the emphasis on royalist northerners like Huntly, Erroll, Marischal, Atholl, Buchan and Crawford.[5]

The division of opinion in 1488 was on purely political issues. If we move forward a hundred years, to the first half of the reign of James VI, there was a division which was partly political and partly ecclesiastical. By the 1570s there had emerged in post-reformation Scotland two factions which stood for two rival policies. On one side was a conservative faction the existence of which has found its way into every account of the period, for books have much to say of those who are called 'the Roman Catholic earls', in the 1580s and 1590s. The term is misleading, for those earls were not characterised so much by religious zeal as by a general conservatism and a distaste for new ways in either religion or politics; they supported the cause of Queen Mary as long as she lived, and they intrigued with the king of Spain. The significant thing is that this faction was associated with the lands north of the Tay: its leaders were at first the earls of Atholl, Caithness and Crawford, and later two earls whose names are better known – Huntly and Errol. Although they were joined in 1590 by one southern magnate, the tenth earl of Angus, whose estates lay south of the Forth and who broke the hitherto consistently pro-English and protestant tradition of his house, the group may be called the northern conservatives.

The ultra-protestant and pro-English party which opposed this conservative *bloc* was as truly a party of the south. Its leaders were Lord Ruthven, created earl of Gowrie in 1581, whose lands lay around Perth, the eighth earl of Angus and the earl of Glencairn, of an Ayrshire family; and with them were associated the earls of Eglinton and Bothwell, Lords Lindsay and Cathcart, Douglas of Lochleven and many lairds from East Lothian. Among the prominent men of this party, the Master of Glamis alone came from north of the Tay and brought a lot of support from the sheriffdom of Angus. It was this southern group which in 1582 engineered the Ruthven Raid, the *coup d'état* which brought an ultra-protestant and pro-English administration into power for a time.

In the post-reformation situation, however, interest centres mainly not on political divisions or on divisions between protestant and papist, but on a division within the reformed church itself, during that period of over a hundred years (1575–1690) when the episcopalian and presbyterian interests were striving for ascendancy within the Scottish ecclesiastical establishment.

The reformation itself had not raised any barrier between north and south. Reforming ideas first came to Scotland from the east, across the North Sea, from Germany, the Low Countries and Denmark, and, entering the realm through the east coast ports, affected first the people of the ports themselves and then the people of the hinterland. The lands north of the Tay were affected at least as much as, perhaps more so than, the lands south of the Tay. 'The greatest fervency appeared in the Mearns

---

[5] Norman MacDougall, *James III*, 236–58.

[Kincardineshire] and Angus, and Kyle and Fife and Lothian' – all east coast areas except Kyle – 'but chiefly the faithful in Dundee exceeded all the rest in zeal and boldness, preferring the true religion to all things temporal'.[6] References, in records and other evidence, to cases of heresy and to various incidents indicative of the existence of heretical opinions do suggest that the reformation was, in its earlier phases, essentially an east coast phenomenon, that the godly town of Dundee did indeed contain a high proportion of Scotland's protestants and that the lands north of the Tay, well into Aberdeenshire, were seriously affected.[7] Indeed, when the Scottish parliament made its earliest attempt to prevent the import of Lutheran books, in 1525, the first known effort to enforce the ban was actually made in Aberdeen.[8]

When the crisis of the reformation came, in 1560, the whole land was so strongly swept by anti-French, if not protestant, sentiment, that a militant opposition to the revolt can hardly be said to have existed. Yet there are some indications even at this stage that there were divergences among the reformers and that the division was following geographical lines. One cause of disagreement was political – the question whether the reformers should repudiate the absent queen, Mary, wife of the king of France, and supersede her by a ruler of their own way of thinking. It is clear that this radical proposal was distasteful to the loyal or conservative north. Thus, in March 1560, the burgh of Aberdeen agreed to support the insurgents only on condition that they did not 'enterprise anything against the authority',[9] and in April the Earl of Huntly, who had withheld his support from the revolt as long as the possibility of deposing Mary was on its programme, consented to sign an undertaking which committed the signatories only to the cause of the reformed religion and opposition to the French.[10] It was, in fact, on this restricted programme that a large measure of unity was mustered to carry through the revolution, and, out of fifty signatories to that undertaking of April 1560, about fifteen belonged to the lands north of the Tay. The numerous lairds who flocked to the parliament of August 1560 (a parliament authorised by the king and queen) likewise included a substantial number from Aberdeenshire and even beyond, but in general 'the farther we move from the east coast and the English frontier the more signs of support for the Reformation dwindle'.[11] The inference that northern support was given in 1560 only on condition that lawfully constituted authority was respected is confirmed if we look forward a few years to what happened in 1567, when Queen Mary actually was deposed:

[6] *Wodrow Soc. Misc.*, i, 54.
[7] The principal evidence is to be found in *RSS*, ii and iii (Edinburgh, 1921, 1936), especially vol. ii, Nos. 1302, 1583, 2420, 2648, 2704, 2733, 2742, 2858, 2923, 2946, 2952, 2962, 2975, 2987–8, 3033, 3612, and vol. iii, Nos. 395, 612, 820. Supplementary evidence comes from Calderwood, i, 83–143 *passim*, and other sources.
[8] *Extracts from Council Register of Aberdeen*, i (Spalding Club, 1844), pp. 110–11.
[9] Ibid., 322.
[10] Knox, i, 314–15.
[11] Donaldson, *All the Queen's Men*, 42.

at the coronation of James VI, only five earls and seven lords were present, and all but one of them were southerners.[12]

The revolution of 1567, however, was not very popular even in the south, and when an attempt was made to reverse it, on Mary's escape from Lochleven in 1568, the army which speedily rallied to her support was a southern army and had a strong Ayrshire contingent. The composition of the party which maintained Mary's cause in succeeding years has been examined: the evidence has an inbuilt distortion in favour of the south, but even so, the many factors which were introduced to cut across the usual dividing lines produced a party with an uncommonly wide geographical spread.[13]

In 1560 there had been another source of disagreement, besides the attitude to the sovereign, and that was the question of the polity and endowment of the reformed church. The first Book of Discipline set forth a somewhat radical plan for an almost complete redistribution of ecclesiastical endowment, and this, it is well known, was distasteful to the nobility and gentry in general, since it was to their interest to preserve the existing ecclesiastical structure, which they had long been exploiting to their great advantage. Ultimately a considerable number of nobles and lairds did agree to append their signatures to the Book of Discipline, though with important reservations, but, of those who did so sign, all belonged to the lands south of the Tay except the Earl Marischal and the provost of Dundee.[14] It might be a fair deduction that, in the north, conservatism as well as self-interest dictated a preference for the traditional ecclesiastical structure.

With the passage of time, clearer indications emerge that there was a divergence between moderate and radical reformers, and an emphatic proof of such divergence can perhaps first be discerned in 1584. At that point, after a period of two or three years during which the presbyterians had been making a good deal of headway, there was a conservative reaction, expressed in the 'Black Acts', which reaffirmed the supremacy of crown and parliament over the church and reiterated the statutory basis of episcopacy. The opposition of the intransigent presbyterians was so strong that about a score of them fled from the country rather than submit; but all of those who fled came from south of the Tay. And, when the ministers were pressed to make formal submission to the regime, the great majority, even in the south, ultimately conformed, while north of the Tay, it seems, not a single minister declined to conform.[15]

Before many years had passed the presbyterians were again in the ascendant and had established complete control of the general assembly. But the assemblies which the presbyterians dominated were assemblies

---

[12] *RPC*, i, 537.
[13] Donaldson, op. cit., 101, 113.
[14] Knox, ii, 324–5.
[15] *Wodrow Soc. Misc.*, i, 432, 436.

with a predominantly southern membership, assemblies indeed in which the conservative north was hardly represented at all. For example, at the general assembly of August 1590, in a total membership of 163, there were only six members from the whole country north and west of Angus and Mearns; there were fifteen from Angus and Mearns and three from Perthshire; but all the remainder, with the exception of one from Argyll, came from south of the Tay.[16] There is no evidence to show whether the northern areas failed to elect commissioners or duly elected commissioners who did not undertake the troublesome and expensive journey to the south.

The implications of this situation – the general conservatism of the northern magnates, as shown by the 'Roman Catholic' earls; the acquiescence of the ministers north of the Tay in the episcopalian regime in 1584; and the inequitable composition of the general assemblies – did not escape the notice of King James, and they of course explain the skilful manoeuvrings by which he broke the presbyterian position. By insisting that assemblies should meet from time to time in more northerly towns, like Dundee, Montrose, Aberdeen or even Perth, he facilitated the attendance of ministers from the north, and their attendance was further encouraged by payments which at least reimbursed them for their travelling expenses. Within a few years some northern ministers were so habituated to attending general assemblies that they came even when assemblies met in Edinburgh or Glasgow.

Already in 1602 a new pattern is discernible, for, although the assembly met at Holyrood, at least 26 out of less than a hundred members came from north of the Tay.[17] The climax came in 1610, when the assembly at Glasgow drew its membership almost equally from north and south: of the 138 clerical members, there were 72 from south of the Tay, 57 from north of the Tay and 9 from Argyll.[18] It was this assembly, in which the north was well represented, which finally agreed to the restoration of an episcopal system of government in the Scottish church. King James's cultivation of the conservative north had produced the desired results. It is a significant commentary on his proceedings that the general assembly of 1638, which was managed by the opposition to Charles I and which denounced episcopacy, contained not more than 70 members from north of the Tay and nearly 170 from the south.

What was true of the general assemblies was true also of the parliaments. King James's innovations in worship and usages, the Five Articles of Perth, were approved by an assembly in 1618 and came to parliament for ratification in 1621. On this occasion it was plainly the northern vote that carried the day for the king. The recorded votes by members from south of the Tay showed a majority of 7 against the king's

---

[16] *BUK*, ii, 762–7.
[17] Ibid., iii, 974–9.
[18] Calderwood, vii, 104–7; *BUK*, iii, 1085–91.

articles; but the representatives of the north were in favour of the articles by a majority of 26 to 8.[19]

It might be difficult to determine what precisely would have constituted an equitable representation of the two parts of the country, but the distribution of the population must certainly be kept in mind. In 1755, when we first have something like census figures, half the population of Scotland lived north of the Tay, and it is safe to assume that much the same distribution prevailed in earlier times. It is equally true, no doubt, that at any time far the greater part of the lands north of the Tay were relatively poor, containing as they do so much mountainous country and infertile soil. But that is far from true of the eastern coastal plain which stretches from the Tay northwards through Angus, Kincardineshire, Aberdeenshire, Banffshire and Moray, and indeed even beyond that into Easter Ross and Caithness. This eastern coastal plain included some of the most fertile, and consequently most wealthy, parts of Scotland, and it contained ports, from Dundee northwards, through which a good deal of Scottish commerce flowed and which were in constant communication with the continent. Examination of the population figures suggests that this eastern coastal plain contained more than a half of the people living in the whole area north of the Tay, and consequently fully a quarter of the people of the country.[20] It has already been mentioned that approximately half of the parishes of Scotland were north of the Tay.

It was obviously not unreasonable to argue that any body claiming to represent the Scottish nation should contain a substantial element from the north. But the presbyterian opposition to King James could never forgive him for bringing in the northerners. Calderwood remarked scoffingly on 'a number of ministers brought from Orkney, Caithness and Sutherland, who had never seen the face of a general assembly',[21] and James Melville, the diarist, described the leader of the party which supported the king's programme in 1597 as 'a drunken Orkney ass'.[22] Indeed, even in our own day some presbyterians have not yet brought themselves to admit the equity of northern representation, and one recent writer has accused King James of packing the assemblies with 'unsophisticated country ministers' from the north.[23]

If the pattern of a conservative north is established, it is necessary to note also the existence of a radical south, and more particularly south-west. The

---

[19] Calderwood, vii, 498–501; Calderwood's evidence is reproduced in *RPC*, xii, 558–559 *n*.

[20] In 1755, when the population of the country was just over $1\frac{1}{4}$ millions, the county figures were: Angus, 69,000, Kincardine, 23,000, Aberdeen, 116,000, Banff, 38,000, Moray, 31,000, Nairn, 6,000. It is true that Aberdeen and Banff were partly highland, but this can be offset by the lowland parts of Perthshire (total 120,000), Inverness-shire (60,000), Ross (48,000) and Caithness (22,000) – as well, indeed, as the whole of Orkney (23,000) and Shetland (15,000).

[21] Calderwood, vii, 97.

[22] Melville, 291.

[23] J. M. Reid, *Kirk and Nation* (London, 1960), 54.

one area, apart from the east coast, where 'fervency' for the reformation was said to be conspicuous, was Kyle, in Ayrshire,[24] and, of the very small number of known cases of heresy away from the east coast, most were in the south-west. The protestant preacher George Wishart, too, who was active mainly up and down the east coast, also received a welcome from 'the gentlemen of Kyle'.[25] When the protestants entered on the militant phase of their reformation, in May 1559, the town council of Ayr lost no time in forbidding the celebration of Mass,[26] and 'the gentlemen of the westland' played a conspicuous part in the struggle against the government.[27] In 1566, when John Knox had to leave Edinburgh after the Riccio murder, he took refuge in Ayrshire, which he described as 'a receptacle for God's servants of old'.[28] Early in the seventeenth century the district of Cunningham, in northern Ayrshire, was characterised as 'the academy of religion, for a sanctified clergy and a godly people'.[29] Such a radical element is not, however, the whole story in the reformation era. At that point two of Ayrshire's three earls – Eglinton and Cassillis – were on the conservative side, and Paisley, in adjacent Renfrewshire, was a place where papists received some encouragement. And in the next generation the position farther south was affected by the accession of a popish Lord Maxwell to a title which had been held at the reformation by a strong protestant.

The radicalism of the south-west is in fact more apparent from the middle of the seventeenth century, by which time Cassillis and Eglinton had moved over from the right wing to the left. It was the south-west which produced the first Whigs – the extreme covenanters who, in the Whiggamore Raid of 1648, marched on Edinburgh to overthrow the government which had concluded the Engagement with Charles I. They did not long retain control, but they held firmly to their principles. It was they who, as remonstrants or protestors, opposed the admission of former royalists to the covenanting army raised to fight for Charles II in 1650, and they refused to acknowledge the authority of general assemblies or other church courts in which they were in a minority. There were, we are told, no protestors among the ministers in the east coast counties north of the Tay, and few in central Scotland or the south-east.[30] It was, of course, the strength of this extremist party in the south-west which explains why that area produced the most strenuous resistance when episcopacy was restored in 1661 and why the incidence of deprivations was so heavy there.

The pattern of the geographical distribution of opinion is well established, and any historian of the period is bound to speculate as to

[24] *Wodrow Soc. Misc.*, loc. cit.
[25] Knox, i, 61.
[26] G. Donaldson, *The Scottish Reformation*, 50.
[27] Knox, i, 126.
[28] Ibid., 48.
[29] William Lithgow, *Totall discourse of the rare adventures* (London, 1632), 495.
[30] Baillie, *Letters and Journals*, iii, 299.

possible explanations. Is the pattern explained by the facts of race or geography, or is it the outcome of more or less fortuitous political or military events?

The 'north' and the 'south' which are contrasted are not to be identified with 'highlands' and 'lowlands', nor has the concept of a 'Celtic fringe' anything to do with it. Contrary to what is often assumed, the division between highlands and lowlands is not a division between north and south, but much more truly a division between east and west, to the extent that almost the entire east coast is lowland and almost the entire west coast is highland. The 'highland line' which divides the two should be thought of as a line which meanders roughly from south to north, rather than one which runs from west to east or even from south-west to north-east. The highlands proper barely come into the subject under discussion, for they played hardly any part in the main stream of Scottish affairs in the sixteenth century and intervened only occasionally in the seventeenth. It can, however, be said that to some extent the pattern of a conservative north and a radical south existed within the highlands as well as within the lowlands, because the most southerly part of the highlands, namely Argyll, tended to follow the pattern of the southern lowlands: Argyll was the most protestant, the most presbyterian, part of the highlands. It would seem, therefore, that racial and linguistic differences cut across, rather than coincided with, the division of opinion on political and ecclesiastical matters, or, at least, that if racial distinctions explain the pattern of opinion they must be racial distinctions other than those between Celt and Saxon.

It is, of course, plain that the opinions which prevailed in any area, or at any rate the opinions which were effective, were in that period mainly the opinions of the magnates. Leadership of nobles and lairds was decisive until the later seventeenth century. And it is a conspicuous fact that a number of families had their traditional, hereditary attachments, to one cause or another. The Douglases, earls of Angus and earls of Morton, were an outstanding example of a family almost consistently faithful to the cause of the English alliance and the reformation, and they and their following dominated areas of the south and south-east. It is even more notable that in the seventeenth century the leading families in Ayrshire were on the radical side: the earls of Cassillis so consistently that when the Cassillis of the time opposed the revival of episcopacy at the Restoration, Lauderdale remarked that he was following 'the laudable example of his forefathers';[31] but Glencairn and Eglinton had similar records, and Eglinton, like Cassillis, was among the 10 nobles who alone opposed the Engagement in 1648.[32] Of those 10, 7 were southerners; and of the 16 peers who sat in the parliament of January 1649, when the Whigs were in control, 12 were southerners. By contrast, no northern families had a record of consistent attachment to a radical cause, whereas the earls of Huntly, who carried most of the north-

[31] *Lauderdale Papers*, ii (Camden Soc., 1885), 200 *n*.
[32] Baillie, op. cit., iii, 35.

east with them, were always conservatives. In 1638 the earl of Sutherland was the only northern peer to be active on the covenanting side, and, whereas 17 peers were members of the revolutionary assembly at Glasgow in that year, none of them came from north of Perthshire (though Sutherland's brother was there). But to allow for leadership in no way helps to solve our problem, for we should still want to know what determined the allegiance of the magnates.

It is true, too, that something was owing to clerical leadership. It has always been acknowledged that the diocese of Aberdeen was fortunate in its post-reformation bishops, and this must have meant that episcopacy commended itself with particular force to the people of that area. Nor can one leave out of account the influence of John Erskine of Dun, who was superintendent of Angus and Mearns from 1562 until his death in 1589. As Erskine had been born in 1509 and had been sympathetic to the reformation almost from its beginnings, his background was that of the early, Lutheran phase. He came down emphatically on the side of episcopacy in 1572, when he pronounced that 'to take away the office of bishop were to take away the order which God hath appointed in His kirk',[33] and, as Erskine dominated the church life of his diocese until his death, it seems unlikely that presbyterian ideas would make much headway there as long as he lived. It was apparently very largely Erskine's doing that the northern ministers were prevailed on to accept the episcopalian regime in 1584, for he himself co-operated readily enough with the archbishop of St Andrews, and an indignant presbyterian wrote, 'as to the North, . . . I fear that Dun hath corrupted all'.[34] No doubt a traditional allegiance, once established among the clergy of an area, would tend to perpetuate itself; but the making of the allegiance of the clergy, if not merely fortuitous, would, like the making of the allegiance of the nobles, require explanation.

The possibility that the conservatism of the north is explained by its remoteness from the seat of government can be at once dismissed in view of the existence also of the radical south-west. The distance from Edinburgh to Wigtown or Stranraer is not substantially different from the distance between Edinburgh and Aberdeen, and Ayrshire is no more remote from the capital than is Angus. Besides, communications were easier up and down the east coast plain or by sea than they were over the southern uplands which separate the capital from Galloway. Geographical isolation, therefore, would clearly operate with at least as much force for the south-west as for the north. It is noteworthy, too, that the division between north and south is at the Firth of Tay, which was not a physical obstacle of any significance; the division is not at the great mountain barrier which used to be called the Mounth and which runs eastwards from the Great Glen until it almost reaches the coast just south of Aberdeen, to constitute a serious

[33] Calderwood, iii, 158.
[34] *Spalding Soc. Misc.* (Aberdeen, 1849), 69–72; *H.M.C. Report*, v, 636; *Wodrow Soc. Misc.*, i, 436.

physical obstacle between north and south. Angus and Kincardineshire, though south of the Mounth, are quite distinctly part of the conservative north. An assessment of the whole position suggests that geography had little do do with the shaping of the pattern of opinion.

One possible solution to the problem may perhaps lie in remoteness of a kind – not remoteness from the Scottish capital, but remoteness from England. English influence, the penetration of southern ideas, must always have been stronger in southern Scotland than farther north. That this may explain the Scottish situation could at once be challenged by a reminder of the conservatism of the north of England: would not even southern Scotland, which lay still farther from London, be still more conservative? The answer is, however, that the contacts which mattered, the contacts which helped to shape Scottish opinion, were not contacts on the frontier between the Scottish borderers and the northern English, but the contacts of lowland Scots generally with southern England.

The view may be hazarded that in one significant phase, at least, Scottish contacts with southern England, or with southern Englishmen, did help to shape Scottish opinion and contribute to the creation of a division between a more radical southern Scotland and a more conservative north. This significant English influence was exerted in the 1540s, and it must be seen in its context of the pattern of the impact of the reformation on Scotland.

Protestantism in Scotland was not, in its early days, a southern phenomenon, but, as was observed, an east coast phenomenon, with no break at the Tay. Yet, as has also been noted, in the second half of the sixteenth century Scottish protestantism was already divided at the Tay. The geographical relation of Scotland to other countries at once suggests a possible explanation. The more conservative protestantism, Lutheranism, which made its influence felt in Scotland in the 1520s and 1530s, came to Scotland by sea, and made its impression on the east coast ports and their hinterland. By contrast, the more radical protestantism which followed came from the south, from Switzerland no doubt, but very largely from, or through, England – the radical England of Edward VI and the early years of Elizabeth. Is it possible that this secondary wave weakened as it proceeded farther north, so that, while it effaced the older and more conservative protestantism in the south, it did not succeed in effacing the Lutheran tradition which had taken root in Angus, Kincardineshire and Aberdeenshire?

Admittedly, English influence within the sixteenth century itself may not be the whole story. We have to remember the earlier English influence which helped to produce and maintain Scottish Lollardy. If we knew more about later Scottish Lollardy the problem might possibly be solved, but the only scrap of evidence is the examination of the so-called 'Lollards of Kyle', in Ayrshire, in 1494.[35] There are indications in England that strongly

---

[35] Knox, op. cit., i, 8–9.

Lollard areas retained a radical tradition throughout the reformation period,[36] and in the Lollardy of Kyle it is easy to see a possible explanation of the radical south-west of the sixteenth and seventeenth centuries. Yet, in the absence of other knowledge of late Scottish Lollardy, it would be hazardous to attach too much importance to that single piece of evidence.

Within the sixteenth century itself, there was, in addition to the penetration of ideas from England into Scotland, a significant amount of personal contact between southern Scots and Englishmen, not least during the English occupation of several strongholds in southern Scotland and on the east coast as far north as the Firth of Tay, between 1547 and 1549. During that occupation hundreds of Scots assisted the English in various ways and hundreds of them actually entered into engagements to serve the English king.[37] The motives of the collaborators were no doubt mixed and various, but it is beyond question that religion was one element, and those Scots who collaborated in a policy which was ecclesiastical as well as political were not doing so without learning a good deal about ecclesiastical developments in England. It is true that the English occupation ended in 1549, by which date the official English reformation had not proceeded very far, but it was already true, as the latest historian of the English reformation has stated, that 'the popular pamphlets attacking the mass – and they became legion in 1547–9 – mostly adopted a Zwinglian standpoint' and that 'new English trends were non-Lutheran and increasingly directed towards Switzerland'.[38] Besides, Scots who had already been brought under English influence at this stage would be aware of the developments in England during the later years of Edward VI, when the foreign influences upon the English reformation 'came not from Wittenberg but from Strassburg, Zurich and Geneva'.[39]

English influence on Scotland in this phase extended as far north as the Firth of Tay, but hardly beyond it. Had the English occupied more strongpoints farther north, very possibly they would have found collaborators there as well, but the fact is that their northernmost point was Broughty Castle, near Dundee, and in consequence their Scottish friends, who can be numbered by the hundred in the southern parts of the country, were very few from the Tay north. The possibility must certainly be considered whether the experience of Scotland at this stage may have done a good deal to promote, or encourage, a division of opinion between north and south.

Plainly, what happened in the 1540s does not completely explain the situation. For one thing, the English collaborators were very few in Ayrshire, the area which had already produced the Lollards of Kyle, and therefore they can hardly have done anything to shape the radicalism of

---

[36] A. G. Dickens, *The English Reformation* (London, 1964), 36.
[37] M. H. Merriman, 'The Assured Scots', *SHR*, xlvii, 10–34; Donaldson, *All the Queen's Men*, 21–5.
[38] A. G. Dickens, op. cit., 201.
[39] Ibid., 231, cf. 286.

that part of the country. For another, if any importance is to be attached to the alignment of factions at the end of James III's reign, then the conservatism of the north had roots which went back to the century before the reformation. Yet it could still remain true that the later divisions within the reformed church owed something to Anglo-Scottish associations in the 1540s.

16

The Emergence of Schism in Seventeenth-century Scotland

This article has been reprinted with only very minor changes from *Studies in Church History*, vol. 9, *Schism, heresy and Religious Protest* (ed. Derek Baker, Cambridge University Press, 1972). It should be noted that additional evidence for the period of the 1620s and 1630s has been furnished by David Stevenson in 'Conventicles and the Kirk, 1619–37', in *Records of the Scottish Church History Society*, xviii, 99–114.

It is perhaps debatable whether the Reformation itself had involved schism, or at any rate whether those who took part in it thought that it did. It is true that in 1555, on the insistence of John Knox when he was in Scotland on a visit from Geneva, some of the reforming party were prevailed on to give up attending 'that idol', the mass,[1] and that before he left Scotland Knox administered the Lord's Supper after the reformed model.[2] It is true, too, that from this time or shortly thereafter Protestants began to gather together for worship, hardly in secret – for the government's policy was not repressive – but at least without official recognition. These 'privy kirks', which existed before there was 'the face of a public kirk' and had their preachers, elders and deacons,[3] were parallel to the congregations which English exiles were organising on the continent in the same years, and parallel, too, to the much more secret congregations which then existed in London. In the 'First Bond' of December 1557 a few notables renounced 'the congregation of Satan' and pledged themselves to work for the erection of a reformed Church, but, as they followed this with a supplication that the 'common prayers' should be read every Sunday in all parishes, it is evident that the aim was to reform the whole Church, not to separate from it.[4]

In England the tradition of the 'privy kirk' survived, or at any rate was soon revived, for the first separatists from the Elizabethan establishment

[1] Knox, i, 120–1.
[2] Ibid., 121.
[3] Ibid., i, 148; ii, 277. *Knox, Works*, iv, 129–40; vi, 78.
[4] Knox, i, 136–8.

were 'zealous Londoners' who 'remembered and followed the precedents of Marian days'.[5] But the Scots, although they may have themselves been schismatic while the Church was still unreformed, were of opinion that separation from a reformed Church – and such they deemed the Church of England to be – was not justified. The English separatists, on their side, failed to understand the Scottish attitude: because they thought the Church of Scotland represented their own ideal and, as they put it to Knox, 'we desire no other order than you hold',[6] they expected sympathy and support. But they got neither. In 1568 some of them went to Scotland, evidently with the encouragement of bishop Grindal, much as in our day Maoists might have been encouraged to go to China. Scotland, it turned out, did not come up to their exacting standards, and they were soon back home, drawing from Grindal the apt comment: 'The Church of Scotland will not be pure enough for our men. They are a wilful company. God grant them humble spirits.'[7] Worse was to come, for Knox formulated his considered opinion in a letter which roundly condemned secession: 'I cannot allow those that obstinately do refuse to hear the message of salvation at such men's mouths as please not us in all things . . . I wish your consciences had a better ground . . . God forbid that we should damn all for false prophets and heretics that agree not with us in our apparel and other opinions, that teacheth the substance of doctrine and salvation in Christ Jesus'.[8] This episode constituted something of a prologue to much that was to follow: but the Scots on the whole were long to adhere to the anti-separatist position which Knox had taken up so emphatically in 1568.

It is hardly surprising that the visit to Edinburgh in 1584 of Robert Brown, the English Separatist, was not a success. As he 'held opinion of separation from all kirks where excommunication was not rigorously used against open offenders not repenting', he had the effrontery (or the courage) to tell some members of the presbytery of Edinburgh that 'the whole discipline of Scotland was amiss and that he and his company were not subject to it'.[9]

John Penry, another English Puritan, spent a good deal of time in Scotland between October 1589 and August 1592. Although he was less radical than Brown, his visit was not a success either. He was at first 'well entertained' by the ministers and appeared at 'public assemblies', but a divergence soon became apparent. One of the books published for him was produced 'without the privity of the ministers',[10] and he clearly had serious differences of opinion with some of them, for some years later, when King James accused John Davidson, one of the more extreme of the ministers, of

[5] M. M. Knappen, *Tudor Puritanism* (Chicago, 1939), 212.
[6] [Peter] Lorimer, [*John Knox and the Church of England*] (London, 1875), 298–300.
[7] Edmund Grindal, *Remains*, ed. William Nicholson (Parker Society, Cambridge, 1843), 295–6.
[8] Lorimer, 298–300.
[9] Calderwood, iv, 1–3.
[10] *Cal. S.P. Scot.*, x, 391.

speaking 'anabaptistically' and having had 'too much acquaintance with Mr Penry', Davidson replied that 'he was no Anabaptist, and agreed not with Mr Penry'.[11] The Scottish ministers seem to have done little to intercede for Penry with King James when the English ambassador, ultimately with success, pressed for his banishment from Scotland,[12] and their attitude to him contrasts with the appeal they supported for the release of Udall and Cartwright and other more orthodox English Presbyterians.[13] But Penry, elusive as ever, successfully evaded banishment for a time, and if he was lurking underground it may be that he found some Scottish friends to shelter him.[14] The king later bracketed Brown and Penry together as 'brainsick and heady preachers',[15] and most of his subjects would probably have concurred.

Long before Penry's visit, the Scottish Presbyterians had found themselves in a situation which might have justified them in going into schism had they been so minded. They were, of course, stronger than their English brethren, and had a weaker executive to contend with, so they had shown little hesitation in disregarding the magistrate. Echoing the familiar English phraseology about 'reformation without tarrying', they pronounced that 'discipline and government . . . hath the command and power given to use it . . . without tarrying for any authority or command of men'.[16] By 1582–3, their presbyteries, organised in pursuance of this policy, were in a fair way to taking over ecclesiastical administration from the bishops in some parts of the country. It was all strictly illegal, and their proceedings were presently to be described as the erection of 'that form lately invented in this land, called the presbytery, wherein a number of ministers of a certain precinct and bounds, accounting themselves all to be equal, without any difference, and gathering unto them certain gentlemen and others of his Majesty's subjects, usurped all the whole ecclesiastical jurisdiction and altered the laws at their own appetite'.[17] The reaction came in the shape of the 'Black Acts' of 1584, which reaffirmed episcopal authority and referred contemptuously to 'the pretended presbyteries'.[18]

This meant, so the Presbyterians said, that 'our whole form of spiritual government, grounded upon the Word of God . . . is altogether cast down'.[19] Some of them fled to England – a curious refuge for Presbyterians, as their adversaries did not fail to point out.[20] Their main reason for flight was fear for their lives and liberties, and they admitted that their bodies as well as their consciences had been brought into 'hazard and

---

[11] Calderwood, v, 698.
[12] *Cal. S.P. Scot.*, x, 454.
[13] Ibid., 574, 587.
[14] Ibid., 499.
[15] James VI, *Basilicon Doron*, ed. J. Craigie, 2 vols. (STS), i, 15.
[16] Calderwood, iv, 229.
[17] Ibid., 259.
[18] *APS*, iii, 312.
[19] Calderwood, iv, 75.
[20] Ibid., 90; cf. pp. 80–81 *supra*.

danger' by the 'Black Acts'.[21] But they shuffled a bit in their explanations, and argued that they were of more use alive than dead to a church which, they said, was 'like to be overthrown':[22] 'albeit it was good for us to have suffered all extremities, and to be dissolved from these bodies of clay and be with Christ, yet was it meet for the kirk that we should preserve ourselves for the comfort thereof'.[23] The really conclusive fact about their outlook is that they came back from England as soon as a political change ensured their physical safety but before the obnoxious legislation had been repealed. This would seem to absolve the exiles from any schismatic intent, but even if it does not, the attitude of the Presbyterians who remained in Scotland was a clear affirmation of a refusal to break the unity of the Church. Thus the ministers of Berwickshire, although they declared themselves opposed to 'the tyrannical supremacy of bishops and archbishops over ministers', nevertheless conformed.[24] Even a minister who told king James to his face that he considered him a persecutor who maintained 'the tyranny of bishops, and absolute power', did not offer to leave his parish.[25] The dissidents had actually given a formal undertaking to refrain from any proceedings which might be deemed schismatic: 'They shall abstain from all faction, privy preachings by [apart from] the common order, in public or private places, or any such quiet conventicles.'[26]

In the later years of the sixteenth century the Presbyterians were in the ascendant, and the ecclesiastical system was largely, though not entirely, shaped according to their proposals. At the beginning of the seventeenth it was evident that the tide was turning against them and that they would again find themselves in opposition. As the king began to tamper with the times and places appointed for meetings of the general assembly, anxiety grew, and when the assembly appointed for Aberdeen in July 1604 was prorogued to July 1605 and then prorogued indefinitely, the Presbyterians felt impelled to make a stand. Therefore nineteen ministers who had gathered at Aberdeen in July 1605 insisted on constituting an assembly and, when charged in the king's name to disperse, appointed another meeting for the following September. These ministers would have been horrified at the idea that they were guilty of schism, but king James, who referred to their assembly as a 'conventicle',[27] put his finger with characteristic precision and prescience on the way in which their action showed the way to schism and anticipated the technique by which later secessions were to take place. An official 'Declaration of the king's proceedings' demanded 'what might let [hinder] as many general assemblies to be convened at any time, in diverse places . . . as there are several numbers of nineteen ministers

[21] Ibid., 104.
[22] Ibid., 104.
[23] Ibid., 103.
[24] Ibid., 604–5.
[25] Ibid., 486.
[26] Ibid., 350.
[27] Ibid., vi, 583; vii, 311.

throughout the country?' and added that if there was nothing to hinder such an outcome, then 'there should be at one instant far more general assemblies in Scotland, one against another, than ever there were popes in one time in our adversary church'.[28] The king put a similar question more directly to the presbyterian leader: 'Whether think ye that where a few number of eight or nine, without any warrant, do meet, wanting the chief members of an assembly, as the moderator and scribe, convening unmannerly without a sermon, . . . can make an assembly or not?'[29]

Within another five years the king had succeeded in prevailing on the Church to accept a modified form of episcopal government. But there was no schism in consequence. Although many ministers, especially in the southern half of the country, were resolutely opposed to bishops – forty-two of them signed a protest against episcopacy presented to parliament in July 1606 – not one resigned his charge.

As yet there had been no question of the imposition of liturgical requirements or of changes in public worship, but when such matters did become an issue feeling was much more profoundly stirred than it ever had been over the presbyterian-episcopalian controversy. The revival of disputes even brought a renewal of the challenge to episcopacy, for John Scrimgeour, minister of Kinghorn, deprived for non-conformity, protested that the archbishop of St Andrews could not depose him, because he had received his admission from the synod of Fife, 'and for anything you do, I will never think myself deposed from it': the archbishop replied that he did not deprive him of his ministry, but only inhibited him from the exercise of it, and affirmed that Scrimgeour could be readmitted without reimposition of hands[30] – one way of anticipating and preventing schism. In the main, however, the argument on polity which arose from the liturgical innovations centred on the location of supreme power in the Church. In 1617, when it was proposed that the king, with the advice of a competent number of the ministry, should be authorised to make laws for the Church, a protest was signed by fifty-six ministers.[31] Then, when the government's liturgical requirements took shape as the Five Articles of Perth and these were passed by an assembly in 1618, the opposition condemned the assembly as 'unlawful',[32] but no one proposed to proceed to schism by calling a rival and 'lawful' meeting.

Yet in the years that followed, there was a tendency towards separatism such as had never existed before since the 'privy kirks' of the 1550s. In 1620 there were 'private meetings of some good Christians in Edinburgh' which the town's ministers called 'privy conventicles'.[33] Now, the term 'conventicle' had a long history in England as descriptive of a gathering of

---

[28] Ibid., vi, 427–8.
[29] Ibid., 573.
[30] Ibid., vii, 423.
[31] Ibid., 256.
[32] Ibid., 339, 428.
[33] Ibid., 449.

dissidents, and in Scotland at the time of the Reformation an indignant Roman Catholic had referred to 'the private conventicles of schismatics and heretics'.[34] At the same time, the word could still be used in 1621 of more innocent 'privy conventicles and meetings' which were designed merely for lobbying parliament.[35] But the participants in the religious 'conventicles' of 1620 were dubbed 'Brownists, Anabaptists, Schismatics, Separatists', and they were accused of bringing in an English preacher called Mr Hubert.[36] The king even charged the conventiclers with assuming the name of 'the Congregation' which had been used by the revolutionaries before 1560.[37] Reports appeared in 1624 of 'divers sects' in Edinburgh, such as 'Brownists, Waderdowpers [or Watterdippers][38] and such like', with their 'private conventicles', and a private conventicle was defined as 'a private meeting of men and women to a private religious exercise in time of public sermon' – not a bad definition of separatism.[39] These varied accusations were on the whole denied.[40] One Edinburgh man, accused in 1624 of keeping a Brownist minister in his house to teach and keep conventicles, denied that the Brownist had ever taught in his house.[41] Perhaps the most significant denial came from another Edinburgh burgess: 'I never separated myself from the kirk and never thinks to do. I know there is no man nor woman but they are sinful, nor any kirk so pure but there are some faults in it. As for myself, I had rather live in the Kirk of Scotland than in any other kirk.'[42] This is the authentic voice of what long continued to be the prevailing Scottish attitude – a willingness to acquiesce in much that a man did not approve of, rather than abandon the Church. This was emphatic enough, and when the archbishop of St Andrews spoke of a 'schism' or 'a great rent in the church' he meant only deep disagreement.[43] However, the protests were so forceful that the obnoxious Five Articles were not strictly enforced, and any possibility there may have been of real schism was extinguished for the time being.

After a spell of leniency, extending through the early years of Charles I, pressure intensified in the 1630s on those who were not disposed to conform, and it built up until it reached its climax with the Prayer Book of 1637. Yet schism or even conventicles seem barely to have been regarded as possibilities. This is clear from the attitude of Samuel Rutherford, one of

[34] Ninian Winzet, *Certane Tractatis* (Maitland Club, Edinburgh, 1835), 44.
[35] Calderwood, vii, 472.
[36] Ibid., 449.
[37] Ibid., 612.
[38] The variants appear in Calderwood, vii, 620 and viii, 123. 'Watterdippers' suggests those who practised baptism by immersion, but Mr David Murison, editor of the *Scottish National Dictionary*, states that 'Waderdowper' is the Dutch 'weder-dooper', literally 'again-baptizer', that is Anabaptist.
[39] Calderwood, vii, 620.
[40] Ibid., vii, 614; viii, 123.
[41] Ibid., vii, 603.
[42] Ibid., 603.
[43] Ibid., 545, 563.

the most extreme and vocal of the recalcitrants. Rutherford was minister of the parish of Anwoth, in Galloway, until July 1636, when he was dismissed by the bishop and banished to Aberdeen. Now, Rutherford was, or at any rate believed he was,[44] the only minister in all Scotland who had not merely been deprived of his living but had been forbidden to preach at all. But, hard feelings apart, he took a very gloomy view of the position and prospects of the Church of Scotland. As far back as 1630 he had come very near to rejecting it as no longer part of Christ's Church. He referred at that time to some English Puritans who had left for New England, and, using his customary erotic imagery, he went on to say that 'Our Blessed Lord Jesus, who cannot get leave to sleep with His spouse in this land, is going to seek an inn where he will be better entertained'. Probably by 'this land' he here meant England, but he goes on to say, in this letter to one of his female correspondents, that in Scotland 'Christ is putting on his clothes, and making him [ready], like an ill-handled stranger, to go to other lands. Pray Him, sister, to lie down again with His beloved.'[45] At a later stage Rutherford took a sympathetic interest in the fortunes of some Scotsmen who were ministers in Ireland and who, when ousted by the bishops, set out for America but were driven back by the weather:[46] he said, 'my soul is grieved for the success' – he means non-success – 'of our brethren's journey to New England'.[47] He told the wife of the provost of Kirkcudbright, 'Try your husband afar off to see if he can be induced to think upon going to America'.[48] This was in 1635, and in 1637 he did not rule out emigration as a solution of his own difficulties: 'If I saw a call for New England, I would follow it'.[49]

Yet even Rutherford never quite came to the point either of emigration – which in the circumstances would have implied a separatist attitude – or of schism within Scotland itself. In 1632 he wrote: 'It is our Lord's wisdom that His Kirk should ever hang by a thread: and yet the thread breaketh not.'[50] His attitude seems to be summed up in his own picturesque phraseology to the effect that although – as he never wearies of saying – the Church of Scotland is a harlot, heading for the brothel of Rome,[51] and although at one point he even calls her 'this apostate kirk', which 'hath played the harlot with many lovers',[52] yet the harlot was still his mother: 'We have cause to weep for our harlot-mother; her Husband is sending her to Rome's brothel-house . . . Yet . . . this Church shall sing the Bridegroom's welcome home again to His own house',[53] again, 'there is no

[44] [Samuel] Rutherford, [Letters,] ed. A. A. Bonnar, 2 vols. (Edinburgh, 1863), i, 249.
[45] Ibid., 63–4.
[46] Ibid., 170, 228, 232.
[47] Ibid., 194.
[48] Ibid., 145.
[49] Ibid., 376.
[50] Ibid., 93.
[51] Ibid., i, 242, 261, 265, 370, 446; ii, 50.
[52] Ibid., i, 392.
[53] Ibid., ii, 50.

question but our mother-church hath a Father, and that she shall not die without an heir'.[54] There is more about 'our mother-church' in the same vein, but less tastefully put.[55]

One of Rutherford's contemporaries was Robert Baillie, a much more moderate man, and one more disposed to conform. In January 1637, when the Prayer Book was imminent, he wrote, 'I am resolved, what I can digest as any ways tolerable with peace of conscience, not only in due time to receive myself, but to dispose others also, so far as I can in word and writ, to receive quietly the same'.[56] When he wrote, 'I look for the most pitiful schism that ever poor kirk has felt', he probably meant no more than controversy,[57] but he seems to have feared that others might be less accommodating than he was, because in that same month of January he was asking for 'some good treatises of Brownism', by which he apparently meant works refuting 'separation', for, as he explained, 'I fear to have too much use of such pieces'.[58]

The National Covenant, the great manifesto of the opposition, opened up the possibility of a real division, and in April 1638, a few weeks after it had been signed, there were rival communion services in Glasgow, one, in the cathedral nave, where the communicants knelt, and the other, in the crypt, where they sat. Baillie saw this as 'a proclamation of red war among the clergy of that town'.[59] Had the Covenant not been followed so soon by the collapse of the king's system, there might well have been schism, and had the Covenanters then been crushed men such as Rutherford might well have gone to America like Scottish Pilgrim Fathers.

Later in 1638, when the Glasgow assembly abjured episcopacy and cast out the liturgical innovations, the Presbyterians were again in the saddle and it was the turn of the Episcopalians to be under pressure. But they had no more taste for schism than the Presbyterians had had under similar circumstances. It is true that nine bishops fled to England, much as Presbyterians had done in 1584. But the reason was – and again there is a parallel to the presbyterian exiles of 1584 – that at home the bishops were not safe from rude handling, if no worse, and one bishop who did not escape actually suffered a fourteen months' imprisonment. But it is more significant that five bishops carried their conformity so far as to abjure episcopacy, and four of them, apparently quite happily, returned to the office of a parish minister.[60]

---

[54] Ibid., 82.   [55] Ibid., 112.

[56] [Robert] Baillie, [Letters and Journals,] ed. David Laing, 3 vols. (Bannatyne Club, Edinburgh, 1841–2), i, 2.

[57] Ibid., 5.

[58] Ibid., 12.

[59] Ibid., 63.

[60] James Fairlie, bishop of Argyll, became minister of Lasswade; John Abernethy, bishop of Caithness, became minister of Jedburgh; Alexander Lindsay, bishop of Dunkeld, became minister of St Madoes; Neil Campbell, bishop of the Isles, became minister at Campbeltown. George Graham, bishop of Orkney, abjured episcopacy but retired from active life.

But the National Covenant was itself to prove a source of discord. With the passage of time, it was political rather than ecclesiastical issues which proved divisive, but there are indications of other factors. At a time of close collaboration between Scottish Presbyterians and English Parliamentarians, some Scots became acquainted as never before with the ideas of English Separatists. Orthodox Presbyterians of course detested them. Robert Baillie condemned Brownism as 'democratic anarchy',[61] he lamented the growth in England of Brownists, Separatists, Anabaptists, Antinomians and Independents,[62] and he put in hand a refutation of some of their tenets in a work to be called *The Mystery of Brownism*.[63] This never saw the light of day under that title, but no doubt it provided the matter for his *Dissuasive for the Errors of the Time* (1645), which he expected to bring 'a shower of Independents about my ears'.[64] Rutherford, as it happened, was in print on the subject before Baillie. In 1640 he had written: 'As for separation from a worship for some errors of a church, the independency of single congregations, a church of visible saints, and other tenets of Brownists, they are contrary to God's word. I have a treatise at the press in London against these conceits.'[65] This was *A peaceable and temperate plea for Paul's presbytery in Scotland*, published at London in 1642. Rutherford's condemnation of 'separation from a worship for some errors of a church' reflects the classical Scottish view. However, while he saw a simple issue between Presbyterianism and Separation, Baillie was more perceptive, for he detected a danger that Presbyterianism itself might slide towards Independency if too much power should be vested in congregations, and for that reason he opposed any proposal that congregations should elect their ministers: this was 'too near the main foundation of Brownism – the divine right of the church, that is the parish, to elect, admit, depose, excommunicate their ministers and elders, of which right neither prince nor presbytery nor assembly can deprive them'.[66] That was written in December 1639, and it must remain uncertain whether Brownist influence had anything to do with the agitation which actually led to the abolition of patronage ten years later. At any rate, the Brownism which Baillie so detested in England did show signs of spreading to Scotland, as an unexpected and to most Scots unwelcome by-product of the association which produced the Solemn League and Covenant. As early as 1643 Baillie remarked that 'rigid Brownism', had appeared in the south-west of Scotland and 'avowed Brownism' in Aberdeen.[67] There is not much other evidence at this stage, but already in 1641 a somewhat cryptic act of the general assembly had instructed ministers to avoid 'all meetings which are

---

[61] Baillie, ii, 115, 194.
[62] Ibid., i, 293, 311; ii, 27, 111, 117, 320.
[63] Ibid., 71, 76.
[64] Ibid., 327.
[65] Rutherford, ii, 304.
[66] Baillie, i, 241.
[67] Ibid., ii, 54.

apt to breed error, scandal, schism',[68] and in August 1647 the assembly found it necessary to pass an act against 'vagers [wanderers] from their own ministers',[69] which must mean that there were separatists of a kind, in the sense of people who repudiated the concept of the strict adherence of all the inhabitants of a parish to their parish church.

It may be, therefore, that the rigidity of the presbyterian system was shaking somewhat loose when the political divisions arose which led to the first real schism in post-reformation Scotland. In 1648 the royalist majority in the Scottish parliament approved the Engagement whereby the Scots undertook to invade England on behalf of Charles I, and the majority in the general assembly opposed it. After the failure of the expedition to England the extremists gained control, and several ministers who had supported the Engagement were deposed – eleven in the synod of Perth and Stirling and eighteen in Angus and Mearns.[70] Yet royalist opinion grew after the execution of Charles I, and when it was proposed that the Scots should commit themselves to support Charles II, after he had agreed to take the covenants, the mind of the assembly had changed. The majority now supported 'Resolutions' to the effect that all who were willing to fight for king and country should be permitted to do so, irrespective of their past records, but a minority supported a 'Remonstrance' (17 October 1650) against the admission of 'Malignants' or former Royalists to the army and against the agreement with a king whom they suspected of insincerity.

When the Resolutions were formally approved by the general assembly in July 1651, between twenty and thirty ministers[71] protested against the lawfulness of the meeting. Thus the minority, from being known as Remonstrants, became known as Protestors.[71] The assembly deposed three of the leaders of the protesting party and suspended another.[73] In October the leading Protestors summoned their brethren from 'sundry parts of the country' to an 'extra judicial meeting' at Edinburgh. They spent much time in prayer, fasting and confessing their sins, but they also challenged the general assembly's authority. They repudiated the commission appointed by the 1651 assembly and resolved to restore that appointed by its predecessor, in which their views had prevailed and which they therefore recognised as 'lawful'. Sixty-six ministers are said to have been present at that meeting in October 1651, and when the next assembly, in 1652, was in turn rejected, the rejection was signed by sixty-seven.[74] The intention of the dissidents to

---

[68] *Acts of the General Assembly of the Church of Scotland* (Church Law Society, Edinburgh, 1843), 47.

[69] Baillie, iii, 15.

[70] Ibid., 91, 97; [W. Law] Mathieson, [*Politics and Religion in Scotland,*] 2 vols. (Glasgow, 1902), ii, 112–13.

[71] Figures vary from 21 to 28 [Archibald] Johnston [of Wariston, *Diary*] 1650–54 (SHS), 93.

[72] Ibid., 146n; compare Mathieson, ii, 165–6.

[73] Rutherford, ii, 357, 375.

[74] Mathieson, ii, 165–6; Johnston, *1650–54*, 181.

protest against yet another assembly, in 1653, was forestalled by the action of Cromwellian troops in dissolving it.

The political wranglings which had thus split the assembly had repercussions at other levels. When Baillie wrote in July 1652 of 'a clear beginning of a schism',[75] he was thinking especially of recent happenings at presbyterial level. The Remonstrants had for a time had their own army – the 'holy army' as it was called[76] – and the ministers in it described themselves as 'the presbytery of the western army':[77] this would seem to have been the first appearance of anything like a schismatic presbytery, a presbytery claiming independence of the officially authorised church judicatures, but it was a special case in that it was a non-territorial presbytery. However, in June 1652 the presbytery of Dumbarton was so openly split that a section of it proposed to ordain a minister without the concurrence of the rest of the members,[78] and in July the majority of the presbytery of Glasgow, led by Patrick Gillespie, who had been deposed by the previous assembly, voted against sending commissioners to the current assembly.[79] Six months later, ministers who had seceded from the presbytery of Glasgow claimed to constitute a rival presbytery, and Baillie observed that Gillespie had 'his separate presbytery'.[80] In the presbytery of Stirling, three ministers formed a schismatic presbytery; three or four more, who stood by the decisions of the general assembly, formed the legal presbytery; and three more were 'neutral and abstained from both'.[81] This goes some way to justify King James's taunt in 1605 that if authority should be disregarded there might be more assemblies at one time 'than ever there were popes at one time in our adversary kirk'. The presbyteries of Lanark and Linlithgow also divided, though the former subsequently reunited.[82]

Divisions spread from the presbyteries upwards to the synods as well as down to the congregations. 'The brethren of the protesting judgement in the synod of Perth' desired that the synod would declare that certain of the acts of the assemblies of 1651 and 1652, censuring those who would not acknowledge those assemblies, should be of no force within the bounds of the synod, and that the synod would declare two ministers capable of voting in presbytery and synod despite their deposition by the 'pretended assembly'.[83] The synod of Glasgow divided in April 1653,[84] and when an 'anti-synod met synodically very frequent at Glasgow' and appointed a committee for purging the synod and presbyteries of ministers not in

[75] Baillie, iii, 191.

[76] J. Nicoll, *Diary of public transactions and other occurrences*, ed. D. Laing (Bannatyne Club, 1836), 39.

[77] Baillie, iii, 122.

[78] Ibid., 186.

[79] Ibid., 194.

[80] Ibid., 203, 211.

[81] Ibid., 257.

[82] *Consultations of the Ministers of Edinburgh*, ed. William Stephen (SHS), ii, 3.

[83] Rutherford, ii, 405.

[84] Baillie, iii, 215.

agreement with it, the 'other part of the synod' retaliated, for it was determined to have its purging committee 'as well as they'.[85]

The attitude of the Protestors, reduced to the simplest terms, was that they would not accept majority rule. Already in 1655 Baillie observed that 'our brethren regard little either presbyteries or synods when opposed to their desires'.[86] But worse was to come, when they 'proceeded further to declare the body of our presbyteries, synods and congregations to consist of a plurality of corrupt members' and therefore 'refused openly submission to the sentences of any of our kirk judicatories';[87] and 'when they are censured, they deny subordination, avowing themselves to be right and their censurers wrong'.[88] They were quite candid about it: one minister opposed the resumption of meetings of the general assembly because his party would find itself in a minority: as the Church, he said, was 'in a troubled state, and the plurality thereof corrupt, we conceive it [an assembly] ought not to be granted without security to the godly'.[89] By a process of reasoning which has puzzled later historians as it puzzled contemporaries, the Protestors managed to pay lip-service to Presbyterianism and did not formally renounce its principles, however much they ignored them in practice. One writer has remarked that 'though devoted to Presbytery in the abstract, they allowed themselves great latitude as members of a Presbyterian Church' and that 'they revolted against a system of ecclesiastical government which they still asserted to be divine'.[90] Much the same point had been made by Baillie two and a half centuries earlier – 'they seem to be for the thing in general, but not for submission to our judicatures'.[91]

Contemporaries were in no doubt that it all amounted to schism, and when the ministers of Edinburgh in 1657 deplored 'what scandal there is given to the whole Church by their schism'[92] they were using the word as we should use it. They had reflected earlier on the whole problem of schism and on the differences, as they thought, between the Scottish situation and the English. In England, they reasoned, there might have been a case for separation, because there had been persecution and there had been errors in 'the worship and ordinances of God', but they firmly believed that there was no case for separation in 'a church so constituted and reformed in all the ordinances of Christ as the Church of Scotland'.[93] If there was anything more in this pronouncemnt than national conceit, it suggests a belief that separatism could be more easily justified by differences about worship than by differences about polity. This would, of course, be related to earlier statements about the greater cause for separation in England than in

[85] Ibid., 254.   [86] Ibid., 284.
[87] Ibid., 305.   [88] Ibid., 379.
[89] Consultations of the Ministers of Edinburgh, i, 351.
[90] Mathieson, ii, 170.
[91] Baillie, iii, 300.
[92] Consultations of the Ministers of Edinburgh, i, 274.
[93] Ibid., 42.

Scotland, though such statements are nevertheless somewhat ironical. It must be recalled that in 1618, although there had been those who characterised as 'unlawful' the general assembly which had passed the Five Articles, no schism had then followed. Now schisms did follow, though the differences which were splitting the Scottish Church were political rather than ecclesiastical and, besides, most of the later secessions in Scotland arose from disputes not about worship but about 'Church-State' relations. However, the Edinburgh ministers were on perfectly sound ground when they reaffirmed that the essence of Presbyterianism was subordination to presbyteries, from which, in the event of grievance, appeal must be made to the synod and thence to the general assembly,[94] and when they denounced the proceedings of the Protestors as 'destructive of the visible kirk' and 'destructive of the government of the kirk'.[95]

This was a serious charge, but, if it was justified even in relation to what was happening in presbyteries and synods, it is evident that at parish level there were those who formally renounced all pretence of presbyterian principles and turned to something more like Independency. This, no less than the schisms in presbyteries and synods, was a novelty, and it did not arise, any more than they did, from the differences about worship which some had always held to provide some ground for separation. Possibly it would be fair to conclude that political divisions went deeper than ecclesiastical divisions, but this might be to ignore three other factors which caused schism to deepen and spread. For one thing, schism at con-gregational level was facilitated, if not indeed for the first time made possible, by the abolition of patronage in 1649 – a step which, as Baillie had foreseen ten years before, might open the way to Brownism. Secondly, there was the readiness of the Cromwellian administration to support the extremist minority of Protestors or schismatics. As Baillie put it: 'When a very few of the Remonstrators or Independent party will call a man, he gets a kirk and the stipend, but when the presbytery, and well near the whole congregation, calls and admits, he must preach in the fields, or in a barn, without stipend.'[96] In the parish of Douglas, in 1656, the Protestors incited some of the elders to put up a rival nominee for the parish and bring him to the church; when refused entry, he preached on a hill-side to a small number of the members, and they, by appealing to the army, got support to declare him minister of the parish.[97] At Lenzie, when the presbytery admitted James Ramsay, the 'dissenting brethren' procured an order from the English forbidding the presbytery to give any ordination without their approval.[98]

A third factor which intensified the drift to separatism was the influence of English Independency. The earliest hint of a link between the Protestor

[94] Ibid., 90–1.
[95] Ibid., 269.
[96] Baillie, iii, 244.
[97] Ibid., 248.
[98] Ibid., 215–17.

standpoint and Independency is to be found in January 1651: the Remonstrants' 'holy army', besides having its own presbytery, also contained 'a seed of hyper-Brownism'.[99] It was not purely a matter of English influence: once patronage was abolished, the transition from the Protestor position to Independency was not a difficult one at congregational level, and some were quite conscious of its logic: it was their principles as Protestors that had led them to separate from the Church of Scotland and deny its constitution.[100] The trend towards something like a 'gathered congregation' can be seen in Glasgow in 1653: 'they are moving to celebrate a Communion here . . . They will exclude such multitudes for one cause or for another that the end will be the setting up of a new refined congregation of their own adherents.'[101] But even earlier, in 1652, the minister of Stonehouse in Lanarkshire was said to be 'embodying in a church so fast as he can, and celebrating the Communion to his proselytes'.[102] This minister was subsequently translated from Stonehouse to East Kilbride, where he formed another Independent congregation. When he was accidentally killed in 1656, Johnston of Wariston – who persisted in reconciling the Protestor standpoint with theoretical adherence to Presbyterianism – was exultant: 'God has blasted the only two gathered congregations in Scotland.'[103] There were, however, other instances. Some people in Fenwick, in Ayrshire, had declared in favour of 'separation', and the dissidents in Lenzie proclaimed themselves Sectaries.[104] The main centre of separatism seems, however, to have been in Aberdeen, where Baillie had noted 'avowed Brownism' as early as 1643. In 1652, when Wariston said that colonel Lockhart had 'gathered a congregation', apparently in Edinburgh, he added that there was danger of the same thing happening in Aberdeen,[105] and it is evident that provost Jaffray had a separate congregation there.[106] Wariston himself received a letter from Jaffray and three others, in name of a larger number, 'wherein they declare their judgment against the constitution and government of this kirk'.[107] When, in 1653, the ministers of Edinburgh had commented on 'the way of separation from this church, to which the inclination of some is working, and into which several already have involved themselves', they made special mention of 'some of our Christian brethren and friends in Aberdeen'.[108] In 1654 it was noted that 'almost all in both Colleges [of Aberdeen], from Remonstrators, have avowedly gone over to Independency and Separation'.[109]

---

[99] Ibid., 127.   [100] *Consultations of the Ministers of Edinburgh*, i, 269–70.
[101] Baillie, iii, 200.   [102] Ibid., 187.
[103] [Archibald] Johnston [of Wariston, *Diary*,] *1655–1660* (SHS), 35.
[104] Baillie, iii, 193, 215–17.
[105] Johnston, *1655–60*, 169.
[106] Ibid., 171.
[107] Ibid., 173, compare xlvi.
[108] *Consultations of the Ministers of Edinburgh*, i, 38.
[109] Baillie, iii, 242, compare 364–5.

One characteristic of some leading separatists is specially worth noting. Provost Jaffray, the Independent leader in Aberdeen, had been a prisoner in England and had learned English ways. Lockhart, who founded the separatist congregation in Edinburgh, was an agent of the Cromwellian government. And Johnston of Wariston has a significant remark about another of the collaborators with the English, Sir John Swinton, who said that he repented of 'leaving ordinances and engaging to the Englishes',[110] by which he seems to have meant that his understanding with the Cromwellian administration had involved abandoning the worship of the Church of Scotland. It is plain that there was a strong English flavour about the whole separatist movement, at any rate among its leaders, though no doubt they found ready followers among disgruntled Protestors. The direct influence of chaplains to the occupying forces and of itinerant English preachers must not be left out of account.

It would appear, further, that the presbyterian schism led in some places not only to separation but to Quakerism, which also filtered into Scotland from England in the 1650s. Its history can be traced from 1653, when meetings were held at East Kilbride and Glassford in Lanarkshire and at Kirkintilloch, which lies between Glasgow and Stirling – in other words, in areas where the presbyterian schism had made its mark. Moreover, provost Jaffray of Aberdeen, who had formed his separatist congregation in 1652, passed over to Quakerism ten years later.[111]

While schism in several forms had thus unquestionably emerged in Scotland in the 1650s, it did not have a continuous history thereafter, at least if we discount the persistence of the numerically insignificant Quaker testimony. Episcopacy was of course restored in 1661, but the objectors were no more ready to form a rival church now than they had been in the early years of the century, for, now as then, no changes of any substance were made in the forms of public worship,[112] and it was such changes, rather than episcopacy, which had caused men like Rutherford to come so close to a schismatic point of view in Charles I's reign. The appetite for schism would seem still to have been very limited, and adherence to the national Church showed far more vitality than might have been expected after the experience of the 1650s. There were men who were firmly presbyterian in their principles and were ready to refuse to give an undertaking to do nothing to overturn episcopacy, but they saw the presbyterian-episcopalian issue as one within a single church and were

[110] Johnston, 1655–60, 304.

[111] There is a brief account of early Quakerism in Scotland by W. H. Marwick, *Short History of Friends in Scotland* (Edinburgh, 1948), 1–3. Dr Nuttall has drawn my attention to additional material in the Swarthmore MSS. in the Library of the Society of Friends at Friends House, Euston Road, NW1, a calendar of which he compiled in 1951 under the title *Early Quaker Letters*. There is information about baptist churches in Scotland both in this collection and in the Clarke MSS. (Worcester College, Oxford), 27, fo. 133. See W. T. Whitley, *A Baptist Bibliography*, 2 vols. (London, 1916–22).

[112] *Studies in the History of Worship in Scotland*, ed. D. Forrester and D. Murray (1984), 56–62.

prepared to continue their work within the episcopalian establishment just as their fathers and grandfathers had done. When one of them said that, although he was a Presbyterian, 'I will not separate from the Church of God',[113] he was expressing Samuel Rutherford's belief that the harlot-mother was still a mother. Even when a large number of presbyterian ministers assembled together in the late 1670s, they made it clear that their meeting was for consultation only: they were neither constituting a general assembly nor providing for presbyterian ordinations, which would have *ipso facto* created a schismatic church.[114] It would seem to need some explaining why even Protestors, who had been ready enough to separate from the Presbyterian Church of the 1650s, were much less ready to separate from the Episcopalian Church of the 1660s and 1670s. It was not until about 1680 that some of them – and even then only a very small number – repudiated not only the establishment but also government by 'plurality of votes' and made provision for their own ordinations.[115]

It is hard to believe that the idea of adherence to the national Church took a new lease of life, and some other explanation must be sought. It is probably to be found in the government's attitude and measures. In the 1650s there had been no penalties for separation – indeed, the government of that period instead rather encouraged the separatists. After the Restoration, on the contrary, the firm measures of the government gave little scope for conventicles, let alone a schismatic church, and a realistic outlook must take account of this. The bold words used nearly a century earlier about discipline and government having the command and power given to use them without tarrying for any authority or command of man seem to have been forgotten. It is a singular commentary on much that had happened before, and perhaps an indication of a certain hollowness in a lot of the rationalising that had been going on, that when schism first became serious again it was the result not of any reconsideration of attitudes to the Church but of a change in the law, when all repressive measures were suddenly removed by James VII in 1687. Although the Presbyterians detested toleration, few of them were prepared to refuse it when it was offered to them. And since that date – 1687 – there has never been a time when there have not been congregations and organisations outside the Scottish establishment.

[113] Robert Wodrow, *History of the Sufferings of the Church of Scotland*, 2 vols. (Edinburgh, 1721), i, 189.

[114] Ibid., 436 and Appendix lxix.

[115] Ibid., ii, 133, 222, Appendix xlvi and cxxi.

17

Church and Community

The reorganisation of local government in 1974–5 eliminated from the administrative scene the burghs of Scotland, some of which had a history beginning in the 1120s, and went a long way to efface the ancient parishes as well. Some parishes, like burghs, go back to the 1120s, and by 1200 there is definite evidence of the existence of so many hundreds of parish churches as to create a strong presumption that most if not all of Scotland's 1100 or so medieval parishes had already taken shape and it had become true that there was no scrap of land in the country that was not within a defined parish. The unit was sometimes a very small one. In the sixteenth century, with perhaps 700,000 people in Scotland, there was an overall average of less than 700 men, women and children, or about 150 households, to a parish. But, as ever, overall averages are apt to be misleading. Most Scottish burghs (unlike English towns) contained only a single parish – Edinburgh with perhaps 10,000 people, Dundee, Perth and New Aberdeen with perhaps 3000–4000, and smaller burghs in the 1000–2000 range. Consequently, most rural parishes, by contrast, must have had far fewer than 700 inhabitants. Even when we first have population figures which can be taken seriously, in the middle of the eighteenth century, there were still a good many rural parishes with less than 500 people, fewer than 100 households.

This meant a close-knit community. What gave it cohesion? The ties of kinship – for there was heredity and intermarriage – the tie of neighbourliness, joint action in some agricultural operations like ploughing, and a degree of economic homogeneity closely associated with the rhythm of the seasons. True, not all of the parishioners were tenant-farmers; there would, for example, be a miller and a smith. But interest must have been focussed predominantly on the state of the crops, not only because even the miller and the smith, even the cottars, all had some land and some animals, but also because the produce actually grown on the land of the parish constituted the daily bread of the people and its abundance or scarcity might mean the difference between life and death. There were no shops selling foodstuffs brought in from elsewhere and there was not the transport – or the money – to make up for local shortages. There was hardly a road system, though there were well recognised tracks proceeding from burgh to burgh and from one to another of the many bridges, in the construction and maintenance of which the church took an active interest.

A parish traversed by such a track, or situated on the coast, saw a certain amount of movement of goods and humans, but parishes without one of those advantages knew only the limited mobility which was at once the cause and the consequence of the self-sufficiency of the rural units.

Clearly, social and economic cohesion there was in plenty. But institutional cohesion was limited. Where there was only a single landlord in a parish, he gave a measure of cohesion, to the extent at least that every householder paid his rent to the same individual, whose residence and estate were a source of employment, who held a court where tenants' disputes were settled, who gave them protection in troubled times and whom they followed in battle. But how often there was only a single landlord it is impossible to say. In the eighteenth century it was very rare for there to be only a single landowner in a parish,[1] and there is no reason to think that the pattern had been very different earlier, so one can hardly regard tenurial links as providing complete cohesion or a landlord as necessarily providing a focus for unity. It can hardly be doubted that the main agency for giving institutional cohesion to a rural parish must have been ecclesiastical. The community, accustomed to meeting on Sundays and holydays for worship, was very conscious of its unity and its identity with a homogeneous territorial unit. The inhabitants of the parish may or may not have all paid their rents to the same landlord, but they all paid their teinds to the same ecclesiastical institution and they all paid their offerings to the same parish priest.[2]

In medieval times the distinction between ecclesiastical institutions and secular institutions, even between what are loosely (and often thoughtlessly) called 'church' and 'state', was in realistic and practical terms a distinction between the two groups of people whom the king always greeted separately when he addressed his subjects – the clergy and the laity. In general the clergy, endowed with spiritual authority which, if taken seriously, was nothing short of terrifying, enjoyed important privileges at law in respect of their office, without regard to their personal merits, and at diocesan and provincial level laymen were, in theory at least, wholly excluded from any voice in the direction of church affairs. On the other hand, the direction of secular government, 'the state', was, formally at least, mainly a matter for the laity, and 'spiritual men', as they were called, claimed exemption from the processes of the civil and criminal law to which the rest of the community was subject. Thus, when 'the church' claimed 'independence from the state', in the jargon of historians, the claim was in effect a demand for the exclusion of the laity from any authority in the church. To the extent that 'the church' was in this context essentially a professional organisation striving for the maintenance and extension of rights and privileges, including a right to disobey and defy the law of the

---

[1] *Directory of Land Ownership in Scotland* (SRS).

[2] There is a most valuable account of 'Parish Life in Scotland 1500–1560', with full documentation from a wide range of sources, by Denis McKay in *Essays on the Scottish Reformation*, ed. David McRoberts, 85–115.

land, there is a parallel in Trades Unions. In the Middle Ages a criminal could escape penalties if he could prove himself a 'clerk'; now a man labelled a Trade Unionist or a 'picket' is not subject to the law applying to less privileged citizens. On 8 October 1984 an M.P. (and a barrister) was reported as saying: 'There should be no situation in British law where any Trade Unionist can be placed in a position where he is threatened with imprisonment and the sooner the establishment understand that the better' (The Scotsman). Medieval clergy, like trade unionists, could bring pressure to bear by giving their services only on their own terms – for instance, by withholding rites until the appropriate dues were paid – and could ultimately have recourse to a general strike, in the shape of an interdict, which suspended all church services. What this meant was vividly recalled a few years ago when there was a strike of grave-diggers in England and the dead lay unburied. It was a very one-sided business, because, although no layman had any voice in decision-making in the church, the clergy, through representation in parliament and courts and the holding of political office, had considerable influence in 'the state'.

The rivalry, competition, almost conflict, which those generalisations suggest did not entirely prevail at local level, where there was enough involvement of the laity in church affairs to take some of the sting out of the hostility between cleric and layman. In parishes where the right to nominate the priest was in the hands of a lay patron, the idea of the propriety of a lay voice in such an appointment was kept alive. The patron had originally been a local landowner who gave of his substance to build and endow the church, and sometimes the patronage continued to lie with a local landlord (who may have taken the people's wishes into account). But in most cases patronage had passed to a religious house, a bishop, a canon or chapter far distant from the parish, and there was no provision at all for the expression of lay or local wishes. However, even such apparently faceless absentees did not necessarily ignore the congregation: in 1497, when the abbot and convent of Holyrood named a new chaplain for the chapel of St Nicholas in North Leith – a quasi-parochial appointment – the chaplain held a meeting with the inhabitants, whom he asked to ratify his appointment and receive him as their chaplain, and nineteen of them are named as doing so.[3] Even where the laity were not associated, formally or informally, with the choice of the priest, they shared in the appointment of other officers of the parish church. The parish clerk, who assisted the priest in the services, could be chosen, or at least approved, by a vote in which not only male tenants but also females had the franchise. True, the patron sometimes nominated the clerk for mere approval by the people, the office was apt to remain in a single family (not infrequently the patron's family), there seems never to have been more than one candidate, there was of course no secret ballot and at the end of the day the bishop could conceivably refuse to admit the clerk-designate. But, even so, a number of lists are extant which show that there were polls of up to 150 persons, which

[3] Protocol Book of James Young (SRS), 851.

surely could represent all the households in the parish. Besides the parish clerk, some representation of the parishioners was provided by the kirkmaisters (the equivalent of English churchwardens). The rule about the maintenance of the church fabric was that while the 'parson' was responsible for the choir, the parishioners were responsible for the nave. The 'parson', however, was usually an impersonal institution which regarded the parish church as a source of revenue and was not likely to incur heavy expenditure on the choir, which might be neglected, but so far as the nave was concerned the duty of the parishioners was discharged by kirkmaisters. How they were appointed and how they operated is not clear, but they did have a right to compel parishioners to pay their share in meeting the bills for church repair, which was another communal duty to draw the parish together.

The church for which they were responsible, purely as a structure of stone and lime, dominated the scene in contrast to the humble dwellings of the parishioners, scattered here and there in small groups, always of a single storey and often of a single apartment. The one building which could challenge or surpass the church in prominence was a castle or tower-house if there happened to be one nearby. In a number of parishes that focal point, the residence as it was of the leading proprietor, who might be the patron and in later times chief heritor, was visibly associated with the church and suggested a somewhat monolithic structure in local society. Borthwick is a good example of a church, still partly of fifteenth-century date, in close proximity to the great fifteenth-century tower. There were more instances of this in earlier times, because there are well-known cases where church and village alike were deliberately removed from the laird's doorstep – Tyninghame, Scone and Lecropt are examples. In Aberdour the medieval church of St Fillan was adjacent to the castle and, abandoned for a new church in 1790, was restored and brought back into use in 1926. But the church, wherever situated, was the only public building in the parish and, despite periodical legislation to preserve its sanctity, it was constantly used for a wide range of secular purposes, from the fairly respectable holding of courts (not only church courts, which themselves dealt with a great variety of cases[4]) and transaction of other legal business, down to less reputable games, dancing and worse: to reconcile a church polluted *sanguinis vel seminis effusione* was a routine episcopal function.[5] In the absence of any other public building, the parish church fulfilled functions which today belong to broadcasting, the theatre, the newspaper, the local government offices, council chamber, law courts and social centre. Sunday mass was the great occasion for public announcements; and the place for the display of public notices – for those who could read – was of course the church door. In a very mild and respectable way the parish church continued to serve as a many-purpose building right down to the era of the village hall. It long remained the practice to hold there a *soirée*, when tea and buns would be

[4] pp. 43–4 *supra*.
[5] Patrick, *Statutes*, 76, 283; *Formulare*, i, 20, ii, 123.

passed round in the interval of a kind of semi-sacred concert. There was nowhere else to do that sort of thing. The church building also served as time-keeper for the parish. Indeed, until the days of wireless, country folk (who usually had no public clocks to glance at as their urban cousins had) continued to set their own clocks and watches when the church bell began to sound its invitation to worship on Sunday morning. People within earshot of a medieval religious house were more fully served when, several times each day, bells rang for the round of 'offices'. But the church was the time-giver with even more primitive methods, for every church, with its east-west orientation, was a sun-dial, from which everyone in view of it could follow the passing hours on a sunny day.

The urban parish, like the rural parish, had economic and social cohesion. The weather and the state of the crops were important in the outlook there too, partly because most burgesses were themselves part-time smallholders, with their own crops and animals, but also because even in a burgh a good crop or a bad crop in the vicinity might make the difference between plenty and scarcity. But some burgesses were concerned with commerce and the fortunes of shipping ventures, so the direction and strength of the wind would be a topic of conversation and sometimes of anxiety, the price of wool in the Low Countries and conditions in French vineyards would be of interest. Here and there men would discuss the movements of the royal court, the meetings of parliament and council, the visits of great men and their retinues, all of which might mean business for both merchants and craftsmen. But a burgh owed greater cohesion than a rural parish did to secular institutions, for town council, burgh officers, burgh court and the gilds all helped to bond together the people of the burgh, where society was organised to some extent on the basis of incorporations. And those incorporations or gilds, while they had important functions in connection with the organisation of the craft, such as the trial of apprentices and their admission as master craftsmen, had also charitable and religious purposes and for that reason each craft had its own chapel or its own altar in the church. The various gilds were also associated with the pageants, plays and processions which took place on certain holydays. The crafts financed the chaplains who served their altars and exercised over their behaviour a formidable measure of control which represented an assertion of lay authority far exceeding any influence that parishioners in town or country could exert on their parish priest.

The massive fabric of the burgh church, which was far and away the most conspicuous feature of the town, concerned the burgesses individually and collectively. Most of the dwelling-houses were still of modest height, there were no industrial premises or office blocks such as leave their marks on the landscape and the skyline today, there were no factory chimneys. The only other public building besides the church was the tolbooth or town house and that was such a modest structure in comparison that it could look like a mere appendage to the church. In Edinburgh, thanks largely to contours which defy the worst that modern architects can do, the tower of St Giles is still visible from far and near, but it was even more conspicuous in the little medieval town. The same is largely true in Haddington, Linlithgow, Perth and Stirling, though the expansion of the town has tended to efface the old uniqueness of the church building. More of the medieval pattern is to be seen in a place like Kirkwall, which remains relatively small and is still, after 800 years, dominated by the cathedral.

In the small and compact town which was medieval Edinburgh, extending only from the site of the foot of the castle esplanade to the Netherbow, no one lived more than a quarter of a mile from the centrally placed church. Like almost every other medieval burgh, Edinburgh contained other churches as well, notably two or three friars' churches, but even in Edinburgh there was only one parish church. The Canongate, a separate burgh, had its own parish church (then the nave of Holyrood Abbey) and other areas adjoining the burgh but outside the walls also had their own parish churches: St Cuthbert's, Restalrig (of which South Leith was a dependency), Corstorphine, Liberton, Duddingston. But in the burgh proper everyone contributed to the upkeep of the church of St Giles and its clergy, and every inhabitant had the right to avail himself of its services. A burgh church, to an even greater extent than a country church, was a time-keeper. Not infrequently there was a clock in the church, and even if there was no clock-face on the outside of the tower, the clock gave the time by which bells marked the hours and their quarters. They still do, and continue to be audible over considerable distances, not only (very sweetly) in a small town like Dunblane but even (more harshly) in Edinburgh. I remember how one used to hear the bell of St Giles marking the quarters as one listened to tedious lectures – or delivered tedious lectures – in the Old College on the other side of the valley now spanned by the South Bridge. When the sacristan of a burgh church or his post-reformation successor was designated 'keeper of the knok (clock) and kirk'[6] the priority was right. As the church served the community in so many ways, secular as well as spiritual, it was appropriate that the town council took substantial responsibility for the care of the building, towards the erection and adornment of which the burgesses had given lavishly of their substance. There is a good deal of evidence in burghs of the activities of kirkmaisters, chosen by the townspeople. Anyone who wants to find out how much money was being spent on the church of St Giles in the sixteenth century must look at the town records, especially the accounts of the dean of gild, which detail expenditure on the structure and its furnishings, including the purchase of oil to lubricate the mechanism of the all-important 'knok'.

The reformation introduced concepts which could have revolutionised the relations between the local community and its church. Carried to their logical conclusion they would not only have abolished clerical privileges

[6] *RSS*, vi, 1365, 1860.

but would have gone a long way to eliminate the distinction between clergy and laity altogether and vest authority in the community or congregation, of whom the minister was merely the chosen delegate. In worship, the effect was to make all services corporate actions in which congregational participation was essential. The Eucharist was no longer to be something done by a priest alone at an altar but an action involving the Communion of the people, gathered round a table with the minister, and baptism, marriage and penance, formerly rites often conducted in private, became actions in which the congregation was immediately concerned. The change extended to organisation as well, for authority was to be derived from the people and not vested in a priesthood claiming supernatural sanctions.

It was originally intended that the people of a parish should elect elders and deacons every year, so that office went round, and also that the congregation should choose its minister (and even, with the superintendent's consent, depose him). These intentions surely represented the acme of democratic and anti-clerical principles. They may have made comparatively little change in practice in community activity in a town, for men already accustomed to acting corporately in the council or the gilds began to serve as elders and deacons in the new kirk sessions. Indeed, it may seem odd that in burghs, where there were already organisations expressing the institutional cohesion of the community, it was thought necessary to set up kirk sessions at all. However – leaving aside the fact that the sessions were intended to offer more free choice of members and more frequent change of personnel than the town council had done – sessions had first been established in some burghs before the reformed church attained official recognition, and, even after it did, the town council was likely to include some men unsympathetic to protestantism; besides, it was as logical to select elders from among the community as to select ministers, and there was a clear concept of a kind of godly élite. In a rural parish it must have been far more of a novelty for members of the community to hold office and to take part in the regular deliberations of an organisation like the session. In the appointment of ministers congregational choice did not in general operate, for patronage was long maintained both in law and practice, but patrons were now nearly always lay, and, especially if they were resident landowners, seem sometimes to have taken the people's wishes into account. In towns, however, the council regularly came to have a hand in selecting the minister and in making financial provision for him. The town councils also maintained their traditional interest in the fabric of the burgh church, but responsibility for rural church construction and maintenance, as well as the manse, the stipend of minister and schoolmaster, the school and schoolhouse, fell to the 'heritors' or owners of land rather than to the whole body of parishioners. There was some justice in this, but it was socially divisive and reduced the interest of the community at large in church maintenance. That apart, the effect of the reformation was to increase the contribution which the parish church made to the cohesion of the community, with a greater involvement of the people in the church and its affairs, but the rural parish still had less cohesion of a kind which involved the general body of parishioners than a town had.

The grand design of the reformers to bring about the involvement of the entire community in both worship and organisation was only very partially fulfilled. The same men tended to hold office as elders year after year and elections might have fallen into desuetude even if there had not been a major change in the concept of the eldership. According to the second Book of Discipline, which came about twenty years after the first, the eldership was to cease to be a lay office and was to be a 'spiritual office as is the ministry'. Elders were to be set apart for life and thus acquire a kind of clerical 'character' among the 'ecclesiastical persons' who alone were now to vote in church assemblies. Some saw ministers and elders as alike constituting a single order of presbyters and differentiated only between preaching presbyters and ruling presbyters. This involved the elimination of the democratic vision of the reformers and a return to the medieval distinction between clergy and laity, with the elders on the clerical side of the divide. If the concept of a corporate priesthood survived, it did so only in a very attenuated form, for it was no longer vested in the whole congregation. It is true that, while doctrinaire theologians emphasised that there were no longer 'lay elders',[7] in the popular mind the elder was apt to be thought of as a layman, and it is also true that there has never been agreement among presbyterians as to the precise nature of the eldership.[8] On the whole, however, what may be called the 'clerical' view of the elder has increasingly prevailed in the Church of Scotland. A writer in 1885 remarked that 'in the Church of Scotland elders and presbyters mean the same thing';[9] Cox's authoritative *Practice and Procedure in the Church of Scotland* (1945) is firm that 'all are elders – ministers being, teaching and preaching, as well as ruling, elders, and the others ruling elders only'. The form of service in the Book of Common Order of 1979 for the 'Ordination and Admission of Elders' puts it beyond doubt that an elder is ordained and receives *character* which remains with him for life: he cannot be ordained a second time and if already ordained can only be 'admitted' in a second congregation, exactly as a minister, once ordained, can be inducted to successive charges. It is evident that, whatever the elder was, he ceased to be an elected lay representative of the community.

The significance of the church as a contributor to the institutional cohesion of the community did continue, and survived changes in the economic and social character of the parish as the rural landscape changed, especially in the late eighteenth century and the nineteenth. The Scottish countryside became very largely a countryside of villages and less one of scattered 'ferm touns' as it had been previously. But one of the most

---

[7] John Corbet (1603–41), quoted in David Reid, *The Party-coloured Mind*, 66.
[8] J. H. S. Burleigh in *Relations between Anglican and Presbyterian Churches* (1957), App. IV; T. F. Torrance, *The Eldership in the Reformed Church* (1984).
[9] Andrew Edgar, *Old Church Life in Scotland*.

conspicuous features of the village was quite often an impressive parish church. Two examples which immediately spring to mind are Killin and Kenmore, at opposite ends of Loch Tay, and there are many more, like Carrington and Aberlady. Sometimes the village seems to have clustered round an old church, sometimes a new church was erected for the village, but in either event the village may actually have increased the significance of the parish church building as a focal point. Often one finds the school alongside as well – and sometimes also the public-house, so that in the familiar expression there was visible evidence of education, salvation and damnation. On the other hand, there were places, in the country as well as in the growing towns, where new communities were poorly served by the existing parishes and their churches, and failure to adjust the ecclesiastical system to economic and social realities had much to do with the agitation which preceded the Disruption.

While it had started as a purely ecclesiastical unit, the post-reformation parish (which, it must be remembered, could be created, united, suppressed or disjoined only by act of parliament) became an important unit of secular organisation, as one function after another passed from the church to secular authorities but continued to be based on the territorial parish. This is conspicuous in education. The programme from the Reformation onwards was for parish schools; schools were based on the parish, parish authorities were responsible for their maintenance. Even when control passed to the school boards, in 1872, the parish was usually still the unit, and with all the later changes a good many schools continue to be something like parish schools, in practice if not in law or in name. The same development is noticeable in poor relief. When poor relief ceased to be a function largely of the church, in 1845, the parish remained the unit, not only under the Parochial Boards, but even when Parish Councils took their place between 1895 and 1929. And 'to be on the parish' was the usual way of expressing that a pauper was in receipt of poor relief, even after Parish Councils had disappeared. With the changes made in the nineteenth century the parish remained a community, with perhaps stronger institutional cohesion than ever before (though probably weaker social and economic cohesion). But the institutional cohesion now came much more from secular organisations than from the parish church, which, owing to the oligarchical nature of the eldership and the growing importance of dissenting congregations, was differentiated from the entire lay community in a way it had not been in earlier times.

While the identification of church and community with administrative units is clear enough at the level of parish and burgh, it is not so clear at all other levels, perhaps if only because individuals felt more involvement in their immediate surroundings and less constant awareness of the significance of large units like sheriffdoms and dioceses. Besides, sheriffdoms and dioceses, although they were as deeply rooted in a long history as were burghs and parishes, never coincided with each other and seldom coincided with the areas which had given their names to ancient earldoms and which, for historical and geographical reasons, commanded a measure of attachment and conscious loyalty. Sometimes, as in Fife, it was the sheriffdom which most approximated to such a unit, more often it was the diocese; sometimes it was the sheriffdom which seemed to have highly artificial boundaries, sometimes it was the diocese. The people who lived in the diocese of Moray may have had a sense of community, inherited from the ancient province of Moray; the people who lived in the diocese of Galloway may likewise have had a sense of community, though their diocese did not wholly coincide with the ancient lordship of Galloway. The diocese of Argyll was probably too far-flung to represent a community, and it did not include the offshore islands of Argyll, which were in the diocese of The Isles. The fact that people lived in the diocese of St Andrews, which straggled from the Tweed up to the Dee, can hardly have meant very much; the same would be true of Brechin, another straggling diocese, and perhaps even of Glasgow, unless there were lingering memories of the ancient kingdom of Strathclyde. Fife and Lothian, which had a kind of provincial identity in a secular sense, were each in the main a part of the diocese of St Andrews, but its parishes were intermingled with scattered parishes of other dioceses. Laymen were very likely more conscious of the sheriffdom in which lay the land on which they laboured and of the sheriff court in which they might be regular 'suitors' or occasional litigants, than of the diocese in which their church lay, for they had no involvement in diocesan activities, seldom saw the bishop and were not likely to be regular litigants in the diocesan court. The parish priest, who knew the bishop as his 'ordinary' and sometimes had a link with the cathedral through the relationship of his own benefice with a cathedral canonry, would no doubt be more aware of the diocese. Even the parish clergy, however, had no more share than the laity in choosing a bishop, who, after early times, was imposed from outside by pope or king. When the reformers proposed that their superintendents should be elected by the clergy and people of the diocese they put their finger on a weakness, but their revision of diocesan boundaries did little to align them with those of historic areas.

In addition to the communities based upon or associated with territorial units, there were other communities. There was the link of blood and also the related complex of personal ties, constituting a great family and its 'following', which extended far beyond the bonds of kinship. Such communities, based on the extended family and on the 'following', may possibly have found some ecclesiastical expression in the collegiate churches. Some of these were in burghs and tied in with the burgh communities already mentioned. But the majority were endowed by landed proprietors to provide, *inter alia*, for prayers and masses for the salvation of the founders and their families, and in their clergy these churches were apt to be something like a preserve of the founding family and its clients. There was, in short, a strong proprietory element which reflected an assertion by the laity of control over the clergy similar to that over chaplainries in burghs. The initial emphasis can hardly have been other than individual or at most familial, but one wonders if the many people associated with those proprietors saw their collegiate churches as being related to the extended family or even to the wider community of the 'following'. There were, after all, churches which bore the names of families – though admittedly they were the names of places as well: Crichton, Seton, Bothwell, Methven, Hamilton. If there is anything in this notion, the concept may have extended even to churches which did not actually bear the name of the family which had founded it: did Humes, for instance, feel some attachment to the collegiate church of Dunglass, or Cunninghams to the collegiate church of Kilmaurs, or Sinclairs to the collegiate church of Roslin?

In the whole Highland area there was only one collegiate church, and it was a Campbell foundation at Kilmun on the Firth of Clyde, a place as nearly out of the Highlands as it was possible to be – a fact eloquent of the vast difference between Lowland and Highland society and between Lowland and Highland culture. But the West Highland grave-slabs, those remarkable examples of monumental sculpture, with their emphasis on pedigree and family connections, may reflect something of the same outlook as was reflected contemporaneously in the collegiate churches, by offering a kind of demonstration of the ties of kinship and the hallowing of those ties by ecclesiastical blessing.

The largest unit, the largest community of all, was the kingdom or the nation. Nowhere is the influence of secular institutions, and the readiness of the church to accommodate itself to them, more evident than in the recognition of the church of the kingdom as a unit even when it did not have status as an ecclesiastical institution. The church of the kingdom, the national church one might almost call it, was a distinct entity in practice and in secular law even when it had no real place in ecclesiastical law. Attention has often been drawn to the fact that, ecclesiastically speaking, there was no such thing as the Church of England: there were only the two provinces, of Canterbury and York. Yet from very early times men were thinking and speaking and writing about the Church of England – *Ecclesia Anglicana*. Of course the creation of Canterbury and York long antedated the existence of the kingdom of England, but later on an ecclesiastical province under its archbishop was frequently created to coincide with a kingdom. Thus, Denmark obtained its archbishopric in 1104, at Lund, in Skåne, now the southmost part of Sweden but until the seventeenth century part of Denmark. Norway followed, with Nidaros (Trondheim) in 1152, and Sweden with Uppsala in 1164. The only reason for the appearance of those archbishoprics was the purely secular reason of the existence of the kingdoms of Denmark, Norway and Sweden. The process continued until the fourteenth century: Bohemia got an archbishop in 1344, Portugal in 1394.[10]

[10] I. P. Shaw, *Nationality and the Western Church before the Reformation* (1959), especially p. 4.

In Scotland there was no archbishop until so late as 1472. But from the end of the twelfth century, if not earlier, Scotland did form a distinct and recognisable province, and was referred to by the pope himself as *Ecclesia Scoticana*, the Scottish Church, the Church of the kingdom of Scotland, the Church of the subjects of the king of Scots. The only reason for the existence of such a church was the political reason of the existence of a Scottish kingdom. In Scotland, as elsewhere, the association of church with kingdom emerged with particular clarity when the pope imposed an interdict, for the interdict applied to the kingdom, not to a province – an acknowledgment of the identity of church and nation which perhaps aided their cohesion.

It is true that, although there was an *Ecclesia Scoticana*, ecclesiastical and secular frontiers did not entirely coincide. The bishopric of Galloway remained subject to York and formed no part of the Scottish province. But that is a small exception to the general picture, odd though it was, for the Galwegians certainly regarded themselves as within the Scottish kingdom and were treated in all respects as subjects of the Scottish king, and the bishop of Galloway, whatever his ecclesiastical allegiance, attended the Scottish parliament in the same way as any other Scottish bishop. A more important qualification to the identity of ecclesiastical and secular frontiers is the position of the religious orders. Only some of them had an organisation within Scotland: many straddled national boundaries and looked to headquarters overseas – the important Cistercians, for instance. Not only so, but the possessions of religious houses spilled over the Border: some thirty Scottish parishes were appropriated to English monasteries and a few Scottish monasteries owned property in England.

However, as the medieval centuries went on the tendency to identify ecclesiastical and political boundaries became stronger. Galloway did pass gradually into the Scottish province in the fifteenth century and was formally subordinated to St Andrews when the archbishopric was created in 1472: the diocese of The Isles, which for some time had lain partly in Scotland and partly in England, fell apart, with the emergence of an English diocese in Man and a Scottish diocese in the Hebrides, the latter subordinated to St Andrews; and, almost immediately after the Scottish king had acquired the rights in Orkney formerly enjoyed by the kings of Norway and the earls of Orkney, Orkney too was absorbed into the Scottish ecclesiastical province. Besides, there was a growing tendency as time went on for religious orders to develop their own separate organ-isations, coinciding with the political frontier. A Scottish province of the Dominican friars was created in 1481 and a Scottish 'circaria' of the Premonstratensian canons regular appeared about the same time. In the case of the Cistercians, while a separate province did not develop, the Father Abbot of Cîteaux appointed a Scottish abbot or monk as his commissary with powers over the Scottish houses of the order. Under the pressure of Anglo-Scottish hostility and the allegiance of England and Scotland to different popes during the period of the Schism, Scottish parishes which had been appropriated to English religious houses in the main recovered their independence or were attached to Scottish institutions instead. All in all, one can see the growing importance of national identity in church life.

The identification of the church, in territory and personnel, with the secular realm, very likely did something to facilitate the extension of lay authority over it. The Scottish kings had, from the earliest period for which we have evidence, sought a voice in the selection of bishops and it is a familiar story how, after a period when the pope arrogated to himself sweeping powers over appointments to all high offices in the church, the crown had such success in extending its control that before the reformation its right to nominate was formally acknowledged. Crown authority extended farther than that. It was on the mandate of King James IV and not on that of any ecclesiastical institution that new service books 'efter our awin Scottis use' were prescribed and other books forbidden. Parliament, too, again and again passed acts not only for the curbing of papal powers in appointments but also for the reform of clerical morals, the care of church buildings and similar matters. In one way or another the three estates of the realm, which were the only institutional means by which the nation possessed anything resembling representation, expressed the will of the community in ecclesiastical affairs.

The identification of the church with national boundaries in the later Middle Ages, and the increase of lay power in the church, helped to set the stage for the reformation. The changes which were then made in some ways greatly simplified the situation, at least in lands which rejected the papacy, because the only relationship now was between the national church and the national government. In theory, if not always in practice, there was only one church in the nation. Church and nation were co-terminous. The entire nation belonged officially and legally to one and the same church and owed allegiance to the nation's sovereign and to no foreign prince, prelate, state or potentate.

This identity of church and nation had two consequences. Firstly, if church and state were but two aspects of one and the same society or community, if they were identical in composition and personnel, it was perfectly logical that the same authority could govern both of them. If king or parliament or council was governor of the nation, it was not easy to deny that king or parliament or council was governor likewise of the church, which consisted of the same subjects. To put it differently, if the three estates in parliament represented the entire nation in directing its secular affairs, it was perfectly logical that the nation, or the Christian community now equated with the nation, should exercise its direction of ecclesiastical affairs through the same meeting of estates.

Secondly, it followed equally from the identity of church and nation that the government was a Christian government. If the nation was composed entirely of people who were members of the same Christian church, then the governor of the nation could be expected to maintain

Christian moral standards. That is, the state would punish not only crimes but also sins like adultery and blasphemy, and there are old acts of parliament against moral lapses of various kinds. It was no idle form of words when the Prayer Book petitioned that the government would 'truly and indifferently minister justice to the punishment of wickedness and vice and to the maintenance of true religion and virtue'. And very similar words were used in the Book of Common Order: God was petitioned so to govern the heart of the king 'that he may in such sort execute his office that thy religion may be purely maintained, manners reformed and sin punished, according to the precise rule of thy holy word'.

The anti-clericalism of the reformation reinforced those other factors. Laymen in one way or another began to have a considerable influence in ecclesiastical affairs, while the clergy lost most of their influence in secular affairs, partly because wider education was creating greater numbers of professional laymen and partly because some protestants explicitly repudiated participation by churchmen in civil affairs. There is no doubt that in general the reformers thought of power in the church being vested not in churchmen but in representatives of the whole Christian community, who, ideally, would be identical with the nation. The reformers, by going so far towards effacing the medieval distinction between clergy and laity and by introducing the concept of a single authority over ecclesiastical and secular affairs, should have made any conflict between 'church' and 'state' inconceivable.

When the Scottish reformers turned their attention to applying their concepts at national level they found themselves in a quandary. A political and ecclesiastical revolution had been carried through in defiance of the crown, and the country was controlled by a revolutionary party with no clear legal basis for its power and with support by no means coextensive with the nation. In the circumstances, there was no possibility of accepting the authority over the church of crown-and-parliament or of the three estates representing the whole community of the realm, at any rate as they normally operated under crown headship. The first Book of Discipline spoke, in wonderfully vague terms, of a 'great council of the church' or a 'council of the whole church' but was silent about either its composition or its relationship to the three estates. It would seem that for a time the successful revolutionaries were feeling their way and having recourse to various devices, each in its own way demonstrating the subordination of ecclesiastical affairs to the laity. It was 'commissioners of the burghs, with some of the nobility and barons' – that is, a selection of the successful lay insurgents – who arranged in July 1560 for the appointment of ministers. Then it was the 'lords of secret council' – that is the leading lay magnates among the insurgents, who for the time had executive power – who nominated the superintendents and authorised them to act. In December 1560 some decisions were taken by a gathering of three dozen lay commissioners of churches and towns – mostly of middle-class rank – along with half a dozen ministers, but they reported to a convention of estates in January, and this may have been more or less the kind of machinery the Book of Discipline had envisaged.

After these experiments, and to some extent embodying the various elements which they represented, what took shape was a general assembly comprising the three estates in much the same way as a parliament did – nobles attending in their personal capacity, lesser landowners elected by shires, burgesses sent up by town councils and superintendents accompanied by such ministers as they chose (cf. pp. 113–19 *supra*). This body was, however (except on one occasion), presided over by a cleric, at first always one of the superintendents or commissioners. This device could be justified as long as Mary reigned, but thereafter it was challenged on the ground that under a protestant prince the three estates in parliament should now be accepted as the appropriate organ to express the voice of the community in church affairs.

The second Book of Discipline, which proposed to exclude lay people from any voice at congregational level and terminate the annual election of elders, made short work of the idea that the laity at large, mustered as the estates of the realm, should legislate for the church as a whole. This negation of the ideals of the reformers took a long time to prevail, in official as well as popular attitudes, for commissioners to the assembly, even when selected by presbyteries, were still apt to be called 'barons'; and in the seventeen peers, nine knights and 25 lairds who masqueraded as 'elders' in the Glasgow assembly of 1638 it was difficult to discern 'ecclesiastical persons'. Indeed, it could be argued that the concept of the exclusion of the laity did not finally triumph until 1929, when burgh commissioners, chosen by town councils, finally disappeared from the assembly. It is only right to add that over the generations the assembly has become a good deal more broadly based socially than it was in 1638.

But the estates of the realm, and in later times representatives of the entire adult population, though excluded from the assembly, continued to meet in parliament, and the principle of establishment should have implied that ultimate authority in ecclesiastical affairs, as in secular, lay there. The classic argument has always been that if a church claims to serve the whole nation and if it is a church on whose services everyone in the nation has a claim, then everyone in the nation should have a voice in determining its government, worship and perhaps even doctrine. This, however, could not be squared with the second Book of Discipline.

Andrew Melville's concept of 'Two Kingdoms' was at best a paradox and is certainly not helpful, if relevant at all, in any discussion of the relations between church and community. There were not two different nations, there were not two different societies – or at best there were two societies which substantially overlapped – and there were not two communities. No doubt Melville might have argued that the two kingdoms did consist of the same persons but were distinct because they had different heads. But can one conceive of one community which has two heads? The concept of the 'Two Kingdoms' was ultimately untenable. When

Melville told King James, 'There are two kings and two kingdoms in Scotland, and in Christ's kingdom, the Church, you, the head of the state, are neither a king nor a lord, but only a member', that sounded fair enough: but the fallacy was that no one would dare to apply the converse and assert that Christ, the King of the Church, was in the civil kingdom not a head, nor a lord, but only a member. Christ, manifestly, was head of the state as well as of the Church, and the ministers, as interpreters of the will of God, could instruct the king and the civil authority generally how to do their duty. When the king remarked to Robert Pont, a milder man than Melville, 'I think I have sovereign judgment in all things within this realm', Pont retorted, 'There is a judgment above yours, and that is God's, *put in the hands of the ministry*, for we shall judge the angels, saith the Apostle'.[11] There is another succinct expression of the same concept: 'Far otherwise does the king sit in the synods among the pastors than he doth in the throne of the kingdom among the estates: here to make laws for subjects and command, but there to receive laws from God and obey'.[12] Whatever fine phrases might be used, what it all would have meant in practice was the control of affairs, directly in the Church, indirectly in the secular sphere, by the majority in the general assembly. In short, Melville's two kingdoms dissolved on examination into a single kingdom, and one in which the community had little say. Ministers preached politics but denied the civil power any jurisdiction over what they said in the pulpit. The king was responsible to the church courts, the ministers were not to be responsible to the civil courts. It threatened to be a one-sided business, even more one-sided than the medieval relationship of clergy and laity had been, and shows how very difficult it is to achieve real ecclesiastical independence without ecclesiastical superiority.

The frequent assertion that 'Christ is the sole King and Head of the Church' settles nothing. The kingship of Christ over his Church is acknowledged by all. What is at issue is not the kingship of Christ but the agencies on earth through which that heavenly kingship is exercised. The notion, dear to many presbyterians, that in some way Christ is Head of their church while other churches have to make do with mere human heads, is only irritating. The real rivalry is not between Christ and other agencies, but between the various earthly agencies, which, under Christ, direct church affairs. Besides, preoccupation with the Kingship of Christ over His Church may be actually dangerous. Such a preoccupation, and the Two Kingdom theory from which it stems, are apt to lead to a view of the state as purely secular. The One Kingdom theory, on the other hand, sanctifies the state as well as the church, seeing them as both alike subject to the Kingship of Christ. The Two Kingdom theory and the preoccupation with the kingship of Christ over the church may obscure His kingship over the whole life of the nation and over all human activities; the concept

[11] Calderwood, v, 131.
[12] Ibid., iv, 165.

behind the One Kingdom theory is the integration of church and community under divine kingship.

In practice, it proved impossible to separate the Two Kingdoms; it
proved impossible to separate 'Church' and 'State'. On the place of parliament and its right to legislate in the ecclesiastical sphere, the presbyterian
attitude was ambivalent. While ministers could prate of ecclesiastical
independence and an 'intrinsic power' of the church, they did not take the
logical step of denying parliament the right to legislate for the church or
declaring that ecclesiastical legislation was *ultra vires*. The fact was that the
ecclesiastical system could not be shaped by the church unilaterally and
on the three occasions when the presbyterian system was legally established – 1592, 1639 and 1690 – it was established not by a general assembly
but by parliament. The classical presbyterian attitude was illogical. The
logic of Melville's teaching would have been to deny the right of parliament, the body representative of the community, to legislate on church
affairs. But parliamentary action was acceptable when its statutes were in
favour of a presbyterian system and validity was conceded to such statutes,
while when parliament ventured to legislate in favour of episcopacy its
authority was repudiated. Here again the clerical attitude was extraordinarily like that of the Trades Unions today, which pick and choose among
the laws and decide which to disregard. Parliamentary power was disputed
when patronage was restored and toleration granted to episcopalians in
1712, and again it was disputed, more sweepingly, in the debates preceding
the Disruption, when so much was heard of the church's 'intrinsic power'.
The attitude of the contenders for 'ecclesiastical independence' contained
a good deal of opportunism. Not only was parliament's authority rejected
when it was disagreeable, but even majority decisions in the general
assembly could be rejected by a minority showing similar opportunism.[13]
In the peculiar circumstances of 1690, when the presbyterians found themselves in the ascendant as a result of parliamentary action but were well
aware that the majority of the ministers in parishes were episcopalian, the
one thing they would not accept was a fully representative general assembly,
in which they would have been outvoted: the executive of a Trades Union
today may refuse to hold a ballot of its members from similar motives.
To take another parallel episode, in the late 1640s the general assembly
found itself able to dictate policy to the government and tried to consolidate
its position by an Act of Classes, which, by excluding from office any who
did not accept the party line, was extraordinarily like the 'closed shop'.

The establishment party in the 1830s argued that the church's position
was founded on statute and must therefore be subordinate to the courts of
the land and the law as administered by those courts, and they were clearly
right to the extent that the church's position did depend on statute law,
which only parliament could alter. The opposition party, however, passed
the Veto Act, which was tantamount to a repeal or at least amendment

[13] Pp. 214–15 *supra*.

by the assembly of the parliamentary legislation upholding the rights of patrons.

The simple fact is that all along a simple conflict between 'church' and 'state' makes nonsense. The conflicts surely must at best have been between the people who made decisions in the church and the people who made decisions in the state. It makes sense to speak about a conflict between the parliament and the assembly, between the council and the assembly, perhaps even between the council and the ministers; it certainly makes sense to speak about a conflict between the king and the assembly, just as there can be a conflict between the king and the parliament. But a conflict between the king and the general assembly was no more a conflict between church and state than a conflict between king and parliament was. Parliament and assembly did at times consist very largely of the same personnel, and certainly the same individuals could sit and vote in both; were they entitled to have their say in ecclesiastical affairs as members of one but not as members of the other? If you ask, who composed the church, the answer is, the people of the country; and if you ask, who composed the state, you get the same answer. It is all very well to speak about wearing two hats, and possibly an individual might take one view wearing his parliamentary hat and another view wearing his assembly hat. But what logic is there in a system which permits the same individual, wearing an elder's hat, to have a voice in church affairs, and, wearing an M.P.'s hat, to have no such voice? Does the conflict between 'church' and 'state' resolve itself into a conflict between two hats? There can be few fields in which there has been so much sloppy thinking.

Until the 1920s the position of the Church of Scotland continued to conform more or less to the classic pattern of an established church: its constitution and form of government were defined and authorised by a statute of 1690, ratified by an act which formed part of the Treaty of Union in 1707. The Lord President had remarked in 1874: 'We are dealing with a presbytery, an established judicature of the country as much recognised by law as the Court of Session itself. . . . It is just as much the creation of law as that of any other court in the kingdom' (quoted by W. G. Black, *Parochial Ecclesiastical Law* [1891], 177). In terms of legislation, the sovereign at his or her accession took an oath to maintain the government of the Church of Scotland, referring to a statute which defines that government as by 'kirk sessions, presbyteries, provincial synods and general assemblies'; the crown had never abandoned its claim to be able to name time and place for the assembly's meetings; parliament had never abandoned its claim to legislate on Scottish church affairs; the church drew endowments, payable from land and legally enforceable; and the duty of maintaining church buildings still lay not with the members of the church but with the heritors. In 1921 and succeeding years the position was radically altered, in order to reach an accommodation with the United Free Church: parliament acknowledged the right of the Church, 'subject to no civil authority, to legislate and adjudicate finally in all matters of doctrine, worship, government and discipline in the Church'; the crown's claim to be able to name time and place for the assembly's meetings was abandoned; the heritors were relieved of their obligations, but the endowments were retained in a modified form, in the shape of a 'standard charge' on land. The sovereign's oath, however, was not abolished, and it was asked how the church could be free as long as the sovereign was pledged to maintain it as it had been in 1707.

The settlement has been criticised as not only inconsistent but also inequitable. The Church still receives financial support from people to whom it denies any voice in its affairs. In addition to the income from the standard charge, the church also receives the benefit of having the cost of the education of its ministers borne by the universities, which means in effect by the state, or rather the population at large, whereas other churches have to shoulder the burden of maintaining their own colleges. The Church boasted of its independence, but it did not reject financial assistance from the government in the way that the Episcopal Church did in the nineteenth century when it repudiated the *Regium Donum*. To this extent church and nation, church and community, are still associated and no separation of 'church' and 'state' has been achieved. On the other hand, there is no longer a 'Church'. There are several churches, even the largest of them a minority in the whole community, whereas the state can be taken to represent the whole community, or at any rate the voting majority of the whole community.

When in 1921 parliament was thus, or so it was thought, finally excluded from legislating for the Church of Scotland, the latter did nothing to compensate by widening the representative character of the general assembly, which actually was steadily becoming rather more of a clerical oligarchy as the 'high' view of the eldership increasingly prevailed.

The only lay person who retains any authority in the Church of Scotland would appear to be Her Majesty the Queen, who in terms of the Act of Security and her Accession Oath would have the duty to intervene if the general assembly proposed to revive the office of bishop or even, some think, if it proposed to abolish synods. There is very little doubt that if the general assembly decided by a majority to restore the office of bishop, the minority would, with an opportunism worthy of their seventeenth-century predecessors, appeal to the Queen and forget about their vaunted 'independence of the state'. But whether Her Majesty would act in a personal capacity or through the normal machinery of the constitution no one seems to have determined.

Index

Abel, archdeacon of St Andrews, 26;
bishop, 33
Abercorn, bishopric, 12, 13
Abercromby, William, prior of Scone, 75
Aberdeen, assembly at (1605), 207–8
bishopric and diocese, 18, 22–3, 29, 35, 37
burgh, 194, 217
Aberdour (Fife), 223
Aberlady, 228
Abernethy, 2–3, 12–15, 22
Acheson, John, 115–16
Adamson, Archbishop Patrick, 96, 165–70,
173–7, 180
Ainslie, William, vicar, 75
Aird, William, 180
Aitchison, James, 160
Albany, John, Duke of, Governor, 37, 139
Alexander I, 7, 11, 16, 29
Alexander, Sir William, 146
Allan, John, curate and minister, 78
Anderson, Archibald, 150
Duncan, in Church of England, 154n
Edmund, chief justice, 162
John, vicar of Cleish, 87
Angus, Archibald Douglas, Earl of, 186,
188, 193
William Douglas, Earl of, 193
Anti-clericalism, 225–6, 233
Antwerp, 179
Arbuthnot, Alexander, 178
Archbishops, 15–17, 68, 230–1
Archdeacons, 42
Archibald, Margaret, 55
'Ardepscop', 15–17
Argyll, bishopric and diocese, 28–9, 229
Archibald Campbell, Earl of, 113, 118,
140
Arran, James Stewart, Earl of, 165, 169, 180
Atholl, John Stewart, Earl of, 193
Auchinleck, John, friar and reader, 84
Ayr, reformation in, 198

Bacon, Mr, 185
Baillie, Robert, 146, 211–17
Balcanquhal, Walter, 180–6
Balliol, Edward, 34
John, Lord of Galloway, 27–8
John, King of Scots, 28, 36
Balnaves, Henry, of Halhill, 113, 119
Bancroft, Richard, 170–7
Bannatyne, Richard, 91–2
Barber, Thomas, 183–4, 189
Barbour, John, 143

Barchane, David, vicar, 75
Baron, John, minister, 56
Barron, James and John, 114–17
Barrowe, Henry, 175–6
Barton, Isobel, 162
Beale, Robert, 168
Bellenden, Sir John, justice-clerk, 113, 119
Bennet, James, bishop of St Andrews, 35
Bernelm, Bishop, 16
Beaton, Archibald, 47
Beza, Theodore, 121–36
Bible, in English, 140, 145
Birnie, church, 21
Birsay, church, 3–4
Bishop, office of, 68–9, 94–6, 105–6,
111–12, 122–31
Bishoprics, spirituality and temporality of,
36–8
Bishops, movables of, 32–6
Bisset, Habakkuk, 147
Black, David, 151
John, friar, 84
'Black Acts', 180, 206–7
Blantyre, priory, 83
Blind Harry, 144
Blinseill, Robert, minister, 75–6
Blyth, Richard, 117
Blythman, Andrew, 86
Bodley, Mr, 185
Bogbinder, Hans, 64
Boncle, Michael, minister, 85
Boniface, bishop, 14
Book of Common Order, 94, 146, 176
Book of Common Prayer, 145, 181
Book of Discipline, First, 66–70, 93–4, 97,
119, 146, 176, 195, 233
Second, 227, 234–5
Books of Assumption of Thirds, 99–100,
109
Boord, Andrew, 150
Borthwick, church, 223
Sir John, 46
Bothwell, collegiate church, 230
Adam, bishop of Orkney, 45, 78, 94, 113,
119, 149
Francis, 85n
James Hepburn, Earl of, 105
Bowes, Robert, 173–4
Boyd, Archbishop James, 96
Brechin, bishopric and diocese, 18–20, 23,
229
tower, 2–3
Brice, bishop of Moray, 21

239